BACKSTAGE & BEYOND

VOLUME 1

45 YEARS OF CLASSIC ROCK CHATS & RANTS

JIM SULLIVAN

TROUSER PRESS BOOKS

First Printing July 2023
LS261

ISBN 979-8-9856589-8-9
Published by Trouser Press Books
Brooklyn, New York

www.trouserpressbooks.com
books@trouserpress.com

Cover images (from top): **Ray Davies and JS:** photographer unknown, **Nico and JS:** photograph by Susan Wilson, **JS and Iggy Pop:** photograph by Roza Yarchun (sub-Roza), **Jerry Lee Lewis:** photograph by Johnboy Franklin, **Alice Cooper**: photograph by Hunter Desportes, used under the CC Attribution 2.0 Generic license.
Back cover: photograph by Roza Yarchun (sub-Roza)

PRAISE FOR *BACKSTAGE & BEYOND*

"The marquee names first draw you in, but it's what's behind the storefront that's really the main attraction here. Sullivan fashions a kind of extended narrative from interviews, performance reviews and his own thoughts and rethoughts on the music and the musicians who make it. His informed commentary and the professional and personal revelations he elicits from his subjects place *Backstage & Beyond* several leagues above the average rock read. At this late date, that's saying something.

—writer and broadcaster **Gene Sculatti** (*The Catalog of Cool, For the Records*)

"When I was a cocky young whippernsapper of a musician, songwriter, record store employee and student of English literature out in Los Angeles, I tended to appreciate the critics as much as the artists themselves. As far as I was concerned, James Boswell was as important as Samuel Johnson and at various times I felt the same for Lester Bangs and Lou Reed. This book reads like a *Norton's Anthology*, a collection, a distillation of what mattered as only the best critics with the most heart can do. Maybe Jim Sullivan will never write a song as good as 'Accidentally Like a Martyr' or 'Space Oddity' but he contributes his own mark on the community by shaping, categorizing, adding and subtracting focus to the ones he (and most of us) consider the greats. That's an art form all in itself. Cantankerous shrink, besotted instigator, fly both on the wall and in the ointment, Jim delivers the goods." —**Steve Wynn**

"Sullivan's evocative writing makes you feel like you're right there with him, drinking till dawn with your favorite rock stars, back in the days when no one could get no satisfaction! Every story feels so real, your head will be splitting by morning. Loved it!"

—singer-songwriter **Jen Trynin**

"In our parallel, constantly morphing and competitive worlds of rock journalism and rock MAKING, Sully is a Jimmy Page in a vast sea of timid, punter music writers. Jim has always asked and continues to ask the questions we all WISH we had the *cojones* to ask our music gods and goddesses and manages to do just that with a deep knowledge and sensitivity to what matters most — which is, of course, the music. His work and decades long legend speak for themselves as you shall read right here.."

—**Johnny Hickman** (Cracker)

"Jim Sullivan is a personable and sensitive writer who does his work and research way before he does an interview, so you never feel intrusion. That to me is very comforting in some uncomfortable memories. Very admirable. Genuinely interested, and that's a talent! His questions are pertinent and important to the reader and his subject, yet down to earth and knowledgeable. He has the kind of personality that makes you feel like you're talking to your best friend. That's just not done by most interviewers. I respect Jim Sullivan and would read anything he writes about! At least it's the truth."

—artist and record producer **Genya Ravan**

"Reading these portraits, I can't help but be wistful for the bands and artists that are no longer with us, for the artists I never got to see live, and for when music criticism mattered. Sullivan brings us back to the era where the artists mattered more than anything, but the writer and the writing was just as important.

—music industry veteran **Adam Lewis** (Planetary Group)

"A buncha fuckin' lies! I never said I killed Elvis! And, if I did, I wuz drunk!"

—the ghost of Jerry Lee Lewis

DEDICATION

To my wife, Roza, without whom ... well, let's just say her encouragement and urging me to get all the gears in sync and the writing process rolling was instrumental in putting this book together. It could not have been done without her input and insight. Together since 2003, married since 2007, I love you *truly*, *madly* and *deeply*.

ACKNOWLEDGMENTS

Thanks to Ira Robbins, editor and publisher, for meeting with me in the summer of 2022 and adding fuel to the fire Roza had lit, and then doing a bang-up job of editing. And to photographers Michael Grecco, Ebet Roberts, Ron Pownall, Doug Quintal, Susan Wilson, Roza Yarchun (sub-Roza), Linda D. Robbins, Lisa Tanner, Tony Levin, Sven Mandel, Bryan Ledgard, Jim Neill, Rocco S. Coviello, Johnboy Franklin, Paul Robicheau, Leo Gozbekian and Al Cocorochio. Thanks also to David Bieber and the David Bieber Archives (Chuck White and Joe Packard) for photo and memorabilia research.

Thanks especially to people in the way-back years, when I was pretty much an absolute beginner at this writing game: Christine Palmer, arts editor at the *Bangor Daily News*; the late David Wright and Ryan Wright at *Sweet Potato* magazine; the late Ernie Santosuosso, Steve Morse, Cindy Smith, John Koch and, later, Scott Powers and Michael Larkin at the *Boston Globe*. To Michael Howell, a former *Boston Phoenix* music critic — a longtime friend and occasional colleague. And, for getting me in through the backstage doors — no passes, just his vouching for me — in Maine concert halls early on, promoter Andrew Govatsos, who later became an ace radio promo man for Warner Bros. in Boston.

Thanks also to the innumerable publicists throughout the ages who helped set things up, and, of course, all the artists, most of whom seemed to enjoy the time we spent, especially Bryan Ferry, David Bowie, Iggy Pop, Richard Thompson, Warren Zevon, Peter Wolf, Joe Perry, Alice Cooper, Ian Hunter and those loving/battling Davies brothers, Ray and Dave.

To the late Jerry Lee Lewis for, shall we say, his candor or attempts thereof, and the late Roy Orbison, whose warmth and genuineness carried over from the stage to dressing room. And even to the irascible late Ginger Baker, who clearly did not enjoy the time but gave me an excruciating half-hour that led to one of the most entertaining and unintentionally humorous — to readers, at least — interviews of my life.

To the high school teacher who got me into writing, Mary Helen Georgitis, and, at the college level, professors who encouraged me: the late Brooks Hamilton at the University of Maine as an undergrad and the late Jon Klarfeld at Boston University as a grad student.

And finally, family-wise, a deep bow to the late Maxine and Kent for life itself (and a splendid later-in-life connection) and my late parents, Paula and Frank, for the love, upbringing and encouragement.

CONTENTS

PREFACE
(OR, HOW I CAME TO FEEL THE NOIZE ... AND THEN WRITE ABOUT IT)

IN 1975, RAY DAVIES WROTE A SONG called "No More Looking Back" for the Kinks' *Schoolboys in Disgrace* album. It's a wistful tune, mostly about the singer spotting an ex-girlfriend every time he turns around. He sees her in every bar and in every cafe. Her memory haunts him. In the chorus, he has to remind himself that the past is the past. She's gone. It's not easy, but all we've got is what's in front of us in the here and now.

And it's so true. We've got today and, hopefully, what may lie ahead. I'm a firm believer in the idea that you've got to live in the moment — you can't change yesterday or predict tomorrow, so, as the Grass Roots put it, "Let's Live for Today." La-la-la-la. And yet this book is unquestionably a look back at various moments in time. Moments that mattered and time to take stock of those moments. It's an anthology of sorts, a personal greatest hits of music writing, remade and remodeled for the 21st century.

Tom Waits co-wrote and sang "I Don't Wanna Grow Up." In "Rock 'n' Roll High School," Joey Ramone declared his lack of interest in history. (The Ramones covered Waits' and his wife Kathleen Brennan's song as well.) I was right with 'em. Waits is still with us, croaking and emoting, but all the original Ramones are deceased: Joey in 2001, Dee Dee in 2002, Johnny 2004 and Tommy in 2014.

I'm not as young as I used to be. As Mick Jagger put it, "Time waits for no one, and it won't wait for me." I've been doing this — writing about pop and rock music and all their subgenres — for four-plus decades. The stars and not-the-stars. Bands I've loved, bands I haven't. It's time to collect the better pieces.

It's inevitable, as we realize that we're closer to the end than the beginning, to look back and see where we've been. And hope it's been fruitful.

Well, it has. Here's how it began.

If you like what you read here — or, for that matter, *don't* like what you read here — credit or blame Slade: Noddy Holder, Dave Hill, Jim Lea and Don Powell. The mid-'70s kings of foot-stomping English glam rock, the fellas who gave us loads of great rock songs with weird spellings and one of their homeland's most popular Christmas songs ever, "Merry Xmas Everybody." That was after my time with them. They started me on this sprawl of a career path about a half-century ago.

Why Slade?

For that, blame rock magazines of the day, like *Rock Scene*, *Circus* and *Creem,* for turning me on to them. Slade was a tarted-up four-on-the-floor bunch of former skinheads from Wolverhampton who thought they could conquer the wide expanse that was America in 1975. They sorta miscalculated.

I got back in touch with guitarist Dave Hill after all those years and asked him about it. "There's always afterthoughts of what went with us and reasons we didn't crack it big. I remember Elton John watched us play Australia and said, 'I cannot understand why you have not been big in the States.'

"My answer is not simple. We were a great band with great songs at the wrong time. Other [British] bands [playing] in the States learned from us and made it later. Still, on a good note, we made some good friends there and had some great shows. Not all was lost."

I was one of those good friends. Temporary, of course, but very good for a night. (I'd repeat this sort of exchange many times over my career.) They played "Gudbuy t' Jane," "Cum on Feel the Noize" and "Mama Weer All Crazee Now" as part of a half-hour opening set on a ZZ Top tour, September 26, 1975 at the Bangor Auditorium, smack dab in the center of the state of Maine, the closest city to my college town of Orono, or the last outpost of civilization in the state, as I used to (and still) call it.

The guys in Slade became my first rock interview, and I couldn't have asked for a better entry to the world I'd inhabit — from the outer circle, mind you, the writer's perch — for all these years. It was the warm welcome they gave me, an unscheduled post-show backstage visitor, an interviewer who was not yet a writer per se, just someone en route to that end, a college DJ toting a reel-to-reel tape deck with the idea to do an hour-long special program on the band, interspersing music with interviews.

Not that they really knew this (or cared) when they said hello and offered that embrace. I think they were just happy to have a Yank who knew who they were. Or not only knew who they were but was a real fan of the band. That four-man welcoming committee set me on course for a life reviewing hundreds upon hundreds of concerts and doing hundreds upon hundreds of interviews with rockers of all stripes, moving from the penthouse to the pavement (as Heaven 17 put it).

It didn't hurt that I shared the name of a famous English session guitarist, of whom I'd yet to hear. So, although I was of average height and build, they greeted me with a chorus of "'Big' Jim Sullivan!" Well, okay then, thanks dudes. Sure.

Would I like a beer? Why, certainly. And, in fact, another. So, a whole lotta backstage yak ensued. It was a tad bawdy, but not particularly decadent. Just lads being lads. It was to Slade's immense bonhomie that I was treated as one of those lads. A younger outsider — by roughly ten years — but an outsider who knew the band, the songs, the attitude.

I remember asking Noddy if he still got excited every night. He said he very much did: "My jeans are as stiff as a board!" And that loud burp in the middle of a vamp during John Sebastian's "Darlin' Be Home Soon" on *Slade Alive!*, was that planned? It was not! It happened, they left it in. My Slade special aired on WMEB-FM sometime later that fall, and was heard, I'm sure, by a handful of students as well as many moose and squirrels.

I learned two things that night: (1) that I was pretty comfortable talking to rock stars (Slade weren't "stars" in the U.S., but certainly were in England and in my Anglophilic head) and (2) if you were able to get on someone's wavelength, knew something more than skin-deep about them and didn't plunge into cliché-land, they would likely engage with you with a level of respect for what you do. I hesitate to invoke that trope of "Stars! They're just like us," but in a way it's true. I have rarely encountered musicians who courted adulation or wanted only softball suckup interview questions.

I have always operated on that premise. You may recall Lester Bangs' famous line about musicians not being your friends. Mostly true, just as most people you talk with

Top left:
Ray Davies and the author
Top right:
Bryan Ferry and the author
Left:
Ian Hunter and the author
Bottom:
David Bowie and the author

Photographers: (Davies) unknown, (Ferry) Leo Gotzbekian, (Hunter) Roza Yarchun, (Bowie) unknown

don't become close friends. And for some artists, you're just a necessary, if sometimes bothersome, part of their job — self-promotion. But some you really do connect with, becoming "friends" of a sort. At least for a time. Some relationships last, others don't. We all have strengths and weaknesses, and one strength I think I developed and maintained over the years of writing is being able to strike a knowledgeable, inquisitive but conversational tone. Some of these interviews have been therapeutic — for them and for me.

I have served as both critic and feature writer, the line sometimes agreeably blurring. There's a tendency among some chest-puffing rock critics to take a position of I AM RIGHT after penning some pro or con take about an artist. In the early '80s, I sat in with a group of well-known rock crits who argued these things voraciously; I remember one prominent member of the group was appalled by Magazine's "Permafrost" because the character in the song said, "I will drug you and fuck you on the permafrost." Sure, that was creepy. Wrong. Evil. But it was the character in the song, not songwriter/singer Howard Devoto. Like some of the bogeymen Stephen King has conjured up since time immemorial. In this circle, everyone deferred to Bigfoot. He was right because ... well, because of who he was. I disagreed, but I kept my mouth shut. (I was a new kid on that block and, really, where would arguing have gotten me?)

I've never claimed my subjective opinions to be absolute truth; at best, I've tried to offer well-argued pieces that explore the strengths or weaknesses of an artist, generally ignoring the "audience loved 'em" fan base factor. Chances are pretty good that if someone paid good money to see a band, they're going to like what they see. Except that time a semi-wasted Johnny Thunders played a Cambridge club one night in the early '80s. Some people hooted and hollered at him for the sloppiness and junkiedom, while others hoped he'd die onstage in front of them. (I guess, in a way, that group *did* like what they paid for, though he did not die that night.)

While I believe what I've written to be "right" — that is, true to my beliefs and interpretations — there's no absolutism in this job. Criticism is subjective by definition. I've usually enjoyed a good verbal tussle with someone on the opposite side. I've been surprised how many on the inside (critics) and how many on the outside (readers) don't grasp that concept. Opinion. Hopefully, informed opinion. Opinion backed up with rational and descriptive thought. The English critic Paul Morley wrote a brilliant essay about that once.

I did have a great vantage point, being that I interviewed and reviewed many of these artists multiple times. While some of these chapters are, indeed, snapshots in prose, rooted to one time and place, more are like EPs — extended plays lending a sense of deeper perspective.

For me, the writing part came shortly after the DJ part, and both jockeyed for prime position at the University of Maine for three years. I was the main rock writer for the student paper, *The Maine Campus*, taking a job that Stephen King (yes, him again) held in the late '60s, penning the crazy-ass music and pop culture column *King's Garbage Truck*. Over at Maine's largest paper, *The Bangor Daily News*, arts and features editor Christine Palmer liked what she saw in my writing and made me a regular freelance feature writer and weekly columnist. Column name: *Rock Garden*. (Coulda been worse, and I did choose it.) I got paid (!) and also got college credit for it. The "A" she gave me in my last semester just pushed me over the 3.0 line. I also started writing for a new Portland, Maine-based music magazine called *Sweet Potato* — more opportunity, more access and more opportunities to take metaphorical leaps off bridges. That is, I could be a little more free-from than the newspaper columns and features.

The best part about the job? The constant change. Writing about one artist and then moving on to another. Sure, there have been certain routines — and I'm sure I certainly over-use certain words — but as repetitive as striking the keyboard might be (and I began doing it in the pre-Internet age), every story had its own rhythm, its own shape. There was pleasure in being out there, taking it all in, seeing the show, sometimes engaging with the artist one-on-one later. The fun factor came into play most every day.

I won't say there wasn't some nervousness now and again in talking with the famous rock set, but not that much. What helped was to establish that I knew what I was talking about, conveyed some depth of knowledge in the queries and used humor when appropriate. Granted, it wasn't investigative journalism, and I didn't ask too many "hard" questions. (Of course, "hard" is in the ear of the beholder, and it doesn't take a lot to put thin-skinned artists on the defensive. For instance, if you'd tried asking a Judas Priest guitarist about their singer's sexual preferences — so blatant on album covers and in song content — you'd get a "fuck off" or a quick hangup. This was before Rob Halford went public about being gay and the hard rock world said,

"Yeah, cool, whatever" or "We kinda knew and don't care.")

Bob Geldof and I were talking before a club tour in 1990. "I came through immigration," he said. "I gave them my passport, and they looked at me, and then the picture — put the Irish passport into the computer to see if I was a terrorist — and just as I was going away, the guy said, 'Mr. Geldof, can you sign this picture of me beside your statue in Madame Tussaud's?' 'Yeah, sure.' Then he goes, 'I loved you in *The Wall*.' 'Thanks very much.' I move on, and another guy says, 'Hey, Bob, *Live Aid*, fuckin' great!' And there's this woman who stopped me, clutching my book, saying, 'Oh, my God, this is the best book I ever read!' 'Thanks very much.' I go through customs and not one person mentioned a fucking song!"

I laughed, and said, "Geldof: The Unheard Musician. Or, a superstar without portfolio." Another musician might have been insulted. Not Geldof.

"That's a very good expression," he said, with a rueful laugh. Geldof was well aware of his ironic position, one where fame and acclaim haven't crossed over to his prime field of endeavor: pop music. He's not got the hits. "The cult of personality had reached outrageous proportions, which, at best, was limiting," he said, "and at worst was foolish and sickening."

Actually, I did have to ask two people if they had ever killed anyone. One account you'll read about in the first chapter: Jerry Lee Lewis. The other time wasn't with a rock person, but with a man very much associated with a tragic event in rock festival history. I was having lunch in Boston's Back Bay with the *Altamont*-infamous Hells Angel Sonny Barger. He'd written a memoir and was on a book tour. I was doing a story. After two doses of liquid courage, I asked if he'd ever killed anyone. He had throat cancer and spoke in a gravelly voice-box monotone. He fixed me with a (benevolent?) glare and croaked: "There's no statute of limitations on murder."

Somewhere in the process of writing this, we decided to split the book into two volumes. Call it Fear of the Doorstop Syndrome. My original idea was to borrow the technique Kurt Vonnegut employed in *Slaughterhouse-Five,* where he had his protagonist, Billy Pilgrim, jumping from one life experience to another, zipping between past and present. In a single volume, you might be reading about what Roy Orbison was doing in 1958 and then what Joe Strummer thought in 1979. The better idea was to make it two slightly more compact packages, broken up, somewhat imperfectly, into those who began or thrived in the classic rock area (this book, Volume 1) and those who came to life in the punk/post-punk/new wave era (Volume 2).

None of these chapters are intended as definitive biographical portraits of the artists — there are plenty of available bios about and memoirs from many of the people you'll encounter here. Yes, there's some backstory, but it's mainly those extended moments with people I interviewed and reviewed at various junctures of their artistic pursuits and personal lives. Maybe spent some hang time with. The concerns an artist expressed then could have mutated over time. Lost the importance they once had. Or gained. Or changed. Twelve of the artists featured in this book have died. Twenty-one are in the Rock and Roll Hall of Fame.

I realize many of my generation think we hit the sweet spot when it comes to rock and roll. I certainly do. I was a wide-eyed kid during the early days of Beatlemania. I listened to "She Loves You" and "I Wanna Hold Your Hand" repeatedly through my dad's mono speaker in the corner of the living room. My first concert was Johnny Cash, the Statler Brothers and the Tennessee Three at the Bangor Auditorium, November 13, 1969. I was a fan of Top 40 when Top 40 was good; I was a young teen as psychedelia took hold, a bit older when glam rock and hard rock/metal crashed into the picture. I couldn't get enough of Black Sabbath's *Masters of Reality* and Blue Öyster Cult's *Tyranny and Mutation.*

I was right on time for punk and post-punk. The guys in the latter groups were my peers, my age group, making this kind of noise. Many had the we're-not-rock-stars! manifesto embedded in their DNA, at least initially. I was never happier than when singing along to the Ramones' "Glad to See You Go" or "We're a Happy Family." When Buzzcocks' "Ever Fallen in Love ..." came out, Hillery, the woman I moved from Maine to Boston with — my intended wife-to-be — and I sang that song loudly and, yes, joyfully to each other in the car along with the 'cocks as we were, indeed, breaking up.

Between freelance and staff, I was at the *Boston Globe* for 26 years, many of them during a heyday for rock journalism in daily papers. Many of my features, I found out later, had been widely circulated via the *Globe*'s wire service and picked up by dailies from Chicago to Greensboro, North Carolina. And beyond. One early-'80s story reached France in *Le Monde.* I was on vacation once, visiting family in Sarasota, picked up the *Sarasota Herald-Tribune* and started reading a rock story. It read well, looked good, the prose seemed familiar. Checked byline: Me. Oh, OK then.

Space was certainly bountiful in the *Globe*: ads were plentiful and print acreage was generous. I had an editor who didn't for a moment question my pitch to do a 1,500-word piece on Robert Wyatt. Who? I'm sure most readers wondered. If it was, indeed, read by dozens, *man*, those people dug it.

Freelance gigs along the way have included *USA Today, The Boston Phoenix, The Boston Herald, Trouser Press, Record, Creem, Music-Sound Output, Where* magazine, *The Cape Cod Times, The Bangor Daily News, Sweet Potato, City Limits, The Christian Science Monitor, New Musical Express, Rock's Back Pages, The Guardian, The Hard Noise, Music Aficionado, Best Classic Bands,* WBUR's *ARTery, Rock and Roll Globe,* Northeastern University's *Experience, The LA Weekly, Time Out Boston, Newsweek, Playgirl* and *The Forward.* I'm sure I've forgotten a few.

There was an advantage to being a generalist. I don't mean "generalist" in the sense that my coverage was so broad I liked or accepted everything. Far from it. (I did a year-end wrap-up piece for the *Boston Globe,* where I operated under the published motto: "Vicious, but fair," nicking that from an old Streetwalkers album title. I could be a tad judgmental.)

And by generalist, I don't mean that I knew everything about everything going on. All of us have gaps in our knowledge or expertise, whatever the specialty. I was a hard rock and prog kid, but I learned about rockabilly, reggae, folk, R&B, soul, country music, early rap and more. A daily newspaper rock critic and feature writer is not limited to a single type of music, so I was forced (willingly, I must say) to explore genres outside my immediate comfort zone. More people should do that kind of thing.

Aside from covering acts you thought or knew would be huge and those that already were, there were the discoveries in clubland, where you spotted something and it all clicked. You got in on the ground floor. Some of those acts "made it," but many didn't, and that's OK. To have given us one song, one album, something that made our lives better for a brief while, that's all we ask.

My hope is that the recollections contained here do some of that. Trigger some memories, bring you back to where you wanted to be — backstage and beyond, as it were. And if you weren't around then, I hope this transports you back to several golden ages of rock and roll.

—Jim Sullivan
March 2023

"I have a right to fuck anything I want to.
I'm Jerry Lee Lewis, your motherfucker of them all!"

Jerry Lee Lewis

Carl Perkins (second from left), drummer Tom Hambridge (center) and Jerry Lee Lewis (right) backstage at Sullivan Stadium in Foxboro MA 1986

PHOTOGRAPH BY AL COCOROCHIO

JERRY LEE LEWIS

I FIRST MET JERRY LEE LEWIS IN 1982. He was playing the Club Casino in Hampton Beach, New Hampshire, and I was reviewing/writing a feature for the *Boston Globe.* It was a great set, brimming with full-tilt rockers yet strewn with pensive country pearls. Near the end, he played one of those reflective country songs, "39 and Holding," adding, "45 and holding? 46 and holding? I'm just thankful to be alive. You're here today and gone tomorrow."

It wasn't shtick.

Lewis, at 45, had just come back from another brush with death: two operations for a perforated ulcer. Longtime road manager J.W. Whitten told me that doctors gave him a less-than-50-percent chance of surviving the first one and just five percent for the second. "Five holes in his stomach, one the size of a teacup," J.W. said.

What did that mean to a post-op Jerry Lee?

"I changed," he tells me backstage after the show. "I think a lot more. I've settled down a lot. I'm more positive on what I wanna do. I'm thinking about it before I jump." Jerry Lee is sitting quietly, tightly clutching the hand of his fifth wife, Shawn Michelle Williams: young, blonde, pretty and silent.

Nick Tosches, in his great biography *Hellfire: The Jerry Lee Lewis Story*, quoted Lewis as stating that he was dragging his audience to hell with him. I ask if he is still dragging them there?

"No, I wouldn't say that," Jerry Lee says. "I hope not." He pauses. "That's a hard question to answer. It's up to the individual; everybody knows right from wrong." He pauses again. "I don't think I'm draggin' anybody to hell." Another pause. "I don't know. I'll leave that open."

Three years later, Jerry Lee Lewis threatened to kill me. I don't flatter myself to think I'm unique in this regard — although there may be a couple of ex-wives/ghosts who might say, "Yeah, well at least he didn't follow through ..." You never know.

We were backstage again after a concert at the long-defunct Channel Club in Boston. Jerry Lee was on fire. He had just ripped the joint up and he was feeling *good.* Sippin' whisky.

"I thought [that] was the best damn show you ever seen in your whole life," Jerry Lee said. "If you give me a bad write-up, you dead." Which I'm pretty certain was a joke-threat. He seemed pretty jocular and I'm sure I smiled. He *was* nicknamed "Killer," but he also called me (and other male pals) "Killer," which I took as a badge of camaraderie. And, fact is, there was a period — 1982 to 1987 — where we had some sort of odd, almost endearing, rocker-writer bond. I can't explain why we hit it off or why he trusted me, but he did, and we did. I was in my mid-late-twenties and grew up in central Maine; he was in his early fifties and hailed from Ferriday, Louisiana. Generations, locales, religious beliefs, accents and upbringing miles apart, but we somehow connected. All for the love of rock and roll. Maybe.

Jerry Lee fingered his left hand with the right. Those were his money-makers, mind you. Precious. His critical digits. It seems that, three weeks earlier, he had broken his left hand punching out an Eldorado. Moved it four inches, he said, not without pride. He was angry because J.W. wouldn't let him drive.

Was he drunk?

"We was *all* drunk!" exclaimed Jerry Lee.

His body was thin, his muscles taut, his eyes piercing. He was getting old, sure, but "at least I don't look as ugly as the Everly Brothers." He punctuated his comments with karate stabs and scattered barbs, plunging into redneck humor and employing frequent profanity. Raving about ...

- Getting arrested after shooting a gun off outside Elvis Presley's Graceland mansion: "I shot the hell out of that! If I could have made it in ... I run out of bullets."

- *Class of '55*, the reunion album recorded with Sun vets Johnny Cash, Roy Orbison and Carl Perkins: "Worst album I ever heard, 'cept for my parts. Johnny Cash is the worst singer in the world. Roy Orbison is the ugliest sonofabitch I ever seen. Carl Perkins is a one-hit wonder." And of the missing member? "Elvis Presley — they laid him out in blue suede hip boots."
- His charter membership in the Rock and Roll Hall of Fame: "Bullshit. The Rock and Roll Hall of Fame means ... no royalty checks. I was indicted, I mean inducted, into the Rock and Roll Hall of Fame by threat. I told Chuck Berry I'd kill him. I killed Elvis Presley anyway — got rid of him, finally. It took a long time. I got him! I got rid of Ricky Nelson. Everybody around me dies."
- Booze: "I drank enough whisky to lift any ship off the ground. Drank enough beer for a whole damn town."

And yet, amid this juggernaut of crude wit, braggadocio and (good-natured?) peer disembowelment, Jerry Lee Lewis turned serious and said, "Son, if you and I don't go to heaven, what have we gained? We have missed it all. Everything."

This comment was delivered almost as an aside, more like the reflective Jerry Lee Lewis I'd talked to previously. Generally speaking, he has been a sinner looking for salvation.

Rock and roll's prototypical bad boy, Jerry Lee wrecked cars, hotel rooms, pianos and marriages. At 22, he married his cousin, Myra Gale, age 13. "It's my third wife, but this time it's the real thing," he told the Associated Press at the time, neglecting to mention that he was still legally married to the second one. Two of his sons died in accidents; two of his wives met untimely deaths. He blasted holes through the door of his own office (Memphis, 1975) and shot his own bass player in the chest (Norman Owens, 1976). He's fought the law, the IRS and, at least in 1985, he won. ("Stay off my ass! I beat 'em bad!").

Skip forward two years. We're hanging out backstage after a gig at the Bottom Line in New York. A fair amount of whisky has been consumed, by both of us. Jerry Lee says he wants me to co-write his memoir. Hell, yeah! Head swimming with hard liquor and flooded with ego, I think maybe that's a swell idea ... 'til I wake up the next day with a hangover and realize what I might be in for. There'd be a lot of mythologizing and mistruths and, moreover, a hell of a lot of time spent in the company of the Killer.

Don't get me wrong, he could be a funny bastard and quite a raconteur. It's just, well, not everybody who spends time in his orbit comes out the better for it. Neither of us ever mentioned the book again.

OK, we're backstage at the Channel again, 1985. Jerry Lee is on a roll and in love — make that deeply in lust — with his own myth. Which is only right. The man ain't lacking for ego and the myth ain't lacking for color. The myth, of course, is tattered, torn and at least partially true, full of all the right rock and roll stuff: ups and downs, sin and salvation, heroes and villains, drugs and drink, sex and love, guns and glory, Million Dollar Quartets and more wives than some folks have had girlfriends. He's even got that sumbitch of a cousin, preacher Jimmy Swaggart, and a better one in Mickey Gilley.

He once shook — and still shakes — the rafters with the most frenetic of rock and roll songs, "Whole Lotta Shakin' Goin' On." He plays the keyboard with his hands and feet. Kick out the jams, motherfucker! He sings the most soulful "Georgia on My Mind." And he's always sung "Sweet Little Sixteen" like he means it, man: ain't nothing in the world he wants more than sweet little sixteen. Still. Forever. Always.

With Jerry Lee, there's more contradictions and convolutions than you can shake a stick at. Tonight, the bottle of whisky stays on the side table, but something's coursing through Jerry Lee's veins. He's *primed.* He's *pumped.* He says he's had 73 number-one hits (actually, while he's had a handful of country chart-toppers, he's never had a number-one pop hit; "Great Balls of Fire" reached number-two in 1957) and three of them with a bullet.

Yeah, I ask, setting him up, wiseass style, what kind of bullet?

"Hollow point," he says.

Tonight, Jerry Lee's mind is a jukebox. He's scatting from one old song to another, rendering bawdy snippets of rock classics. He's also bantering with Kerrie McCarver Lewis, 23, who became wife number-six 18 months ago, on April 24, 1984. Tonight, she's a surprise guest. Over the past half-year — along with the expected accounts of Jerry Lee's hospitalization and near-death (a regular occurrence) — the wire services have reported severe marital strife. And now it seems Kerrie has filed for divorce.

"It's true. We're getting a divorce," says Jerry Lee. No one is unhappy about this. Kerrie and Jerry Lee sing "The Hallelujah Chorus" in unison. "Finally got it through to her," he says. "When you gotta go, you gotta go. It happens. You burn out."

"Burn out *bad*," says Kerrie. "We couldn't make it."

Why?

"'Cause I don't eat her!" hoots Jerry Lee. "Think about it now. I've thought about it: a man [dick] is clean, some of them, but I'm not sticking my tongue in!" Kerrie winks at me and sasses him.

"I'm gonna pinch your head off," he shoots back, "shit in it and screw it back on."

"Then," snaps Kerrie, smiling, "I'd be full of shit."

"My life is like a damn good country song," he growls later. (That's pretty much the title of a Tom T. Hall song "My Life Would Make a Damn Good Country Song" Jerry Lee recorded in 2003.) To her: "And, honey, you'd make a good casket."

"I would, wouldn't I?" smirks Kerrie. "I'd be a pretty casket."

"You're gonna miss those 12 inches of my love," he says, after she taunts him again. "Nobody tells Jerry Lee Lewis what to do. Now, you told me for a long time, but you don't tell me no more, baby. I swear to God that's the truth."

The next year. Same place. Jerry Lee has finished up another concert and is sitting in the dressing room, chewing the fat with a few fellow old-timers, talking mostly about friends who'd died. Seems like most of 'em had. Kerrie isn't with him. The mention of her name brings a curt look.

"She slowly got those demons," Jerry Lee says. "She kept saying she was good for me. The only thing she's good for is she was gonna kill me. You won't see her 'round no more. It's a shame, too. I shouldn't have married the girl. If I get married again, I'm gonna do the askin'. I like to do the askin' sometime ... Ain't nobody in my life now." (Evidently, they kissed and made up later. They didn't get divorced until 2005.)

Flashback to that summer. Kerrie and Jerry Lee are in love, cruising through the New Hampshire night in a limousine, headed to a nearby airport to fly south. The conversation is pleasant until the topic turns to Jerry Lee's previous wife, Shawn Michelle Stephens. Then the air gets thick.

Shawn and Jerry Lee married June 7, 1983. A little more than two months later, she was found dead at Lewis's Nesbit, Mississippi, ranch. An autopsy done in Memphis attributed her death to an overdose of methadone. A grand jury found no reason to suspect foul play on Jerry Lee's – or anyone else's – part. But an exhaustive *Rolling Stone* story by Pulitzer Prize-winner Richard Ben Cramer raised a number of disturbing issues. Cramer implied that, at the very least, Lewis was not blameless in his wife's death and that, quite possibly, he'd killed her and tried to cover it up. Cramer painted a strong circumstantial case: broken glass on the floor, a sack of blood-stained clothes in the master bedroom, blood and bruises on Shawn's body, which was neatly laid out on a bed in another room. Cramer suggested inept and/or corrupt police work. Cramer reported that Shawn's mother had received a phone call from her the day before her death. Her mother claimed Shawn intended to leave Lewis.

I knew I was going to have to ask Jerry Lee about this. The friends I'd driven from Boston to New Hampshire with for the show knew this, too, and followed the limo in our car, y'know, just in case I was forced to make a hasty exit.

"I loved Shawn very much," says Jerry Lee, softly, addressing the issue for the first time in any depth since Cramer's story. "She was a good girl, a fine person. She just made a mistake. I think she thought she was taking a handful of aspirins or something and she took some methadone pills that were prescribed for me two years ago that I didn't even fool with. They were just setting on my cabinet. She didn't know what they were. And they killed her. It made me mad, real mad. I got very angry."

At what?

"I don't know. I was angry with her at first. Then, I could see it really wasn't her fault." So, Jerry Lee tells his story of Shawn's death. "She never intended to kill herself. The furthest thing from her mind. That's why when we went on the bed and went to sleep, I couldn't imagine that she had took anything that could kill her. And she didn't know it, either. She didn't die until 30 minutes before we woke up."

Before *we* woke up?

"Before *I* woke up. Excuse me. Before *I* woke up — wishing that it could have been a 'we.' I didn't know she was dead. She was still warm and everything. I kept trying to wake her up. And then I got to thinking about it and I still wouldn't accept her being dead. She lived all through the night. I know a couple of times I checked Shawn through the night, to see if she was breathing. I just felt her heart beating and everything and it was perfect.

"My life is an open book. I have nothing to hide. I know it's a very suspicious-looking situation. I can see to where it would be, and I don't blame anybody looking at it suspiciously, but believe me, Jerry Lee Lewis would never harm a hair on nobody's head, much less take someone's life. That I could never do."

"That's the truth," Kerrie says softly.

"I'd die for someone," says Jerry Lee, "but I would never hurt nobody." The mood is serious. "I believe everybody's got to die and face God someday," he says. "And I believe that I'll go to heaven when I die. We don't know what God's gonna do. We know there's a Supreme Being. We've never met the Supreme Being, but we believe there is a God. He holds the key. I believe sometimes we punish ourselves. But I believe God lets us live with reason. I believe there's something more to be lived for, I would imagine. I want to live as old as I can, go as long as I can.

"And God knows this. I think this is our main purpose in life: to live as long as we can and do as much as we can to help people, to give as much of our talent as we can in the best way we know how to give it. Sure, we foul up sometimes down through life. And we make our mistakes, but God's always there to forgive us. I don't mean I've tamed myself down or anything like that. I just mean I respect God."

What would Jerry Lee Lewis like his fans to know?

"Tell 'em I'm a sober man, straight as an arrow right now and we're gonna continue to be that way. I'm a very happily married man and I got a good wife. And I thank God for it ... I'm used to drinking, and not doing it kind of takes some getting used to. But before I kill myself, I will get used to it. I think God has warned me enough on the booze and the pills. I just have to use my own brain to take care of myself now."

Spring 1986: You drinking again, Killer?

"I never did stop."

What kind of woman are you looking for next?

"Hey, hey, hey. I'm looking around for a hot one — about 13 ... my cousin ... I have a right to fuck anything I want to. I'm Jerry Lee Lewis, your motherfucker of them all!"

The last time I saw the Killer was in the spring of 1997, at the Hot Tin Roof club on Martha's Vineyard. It'd been a decade since our kinda special relationship. I wanted to see the show and was there to review it, but I thought it best not to try and rekindle anything personal. Would he remember me? If so, where would we pick up? If not, it would just be awkward. I'd had my time with him.

He started off with Chuck Berry's "Roll Over Beethoven" and soon God-blessed the crowd of about 400. His set was weighted toward rock and roll — "Great Balls of Fire" and "Jailhouse Rock" — more than country but his version of Hank Williams'

"You Win Again" was a tearjerker. It was a rollicking show, but there was a moment of tension. He spotted someone near the front who he thought was mocking him. "I'm trying to do the best I can for you," Jerry Lee said. "I know when people are making fun of me. I am what I am, not what you want me to be."

There was no more mocking. You really don't want to fuck with the Killer.

Rick Bragg wrote the authorized biography in 2014, *Jerry Lee Lewis: His Own Story.* And he was one of the go-to guys when NPR wrote an appreciation on October 28, 2022.

"Most of us are amateur sinners, at best, when compared to Jerry Lee," Bragg said. "But then there are times when he is evangelical." Bragg went on to say that, in his old age, Lewis tried to set things right and was able to find redemption. He gave Hank Williams credit for getting the white working man off his knees long enough to enjoy some music. "But it was Jerry Lee that put 'em to dancing, And I thought that was the prettiest thing he said. And how can that be a sin?"

Bragg's book is certainly a deep dive — and it doesn't flinch from the bad stuff — but he gave Lewis a pass for Shawn Michelle's death. I e-mailed Bragg in May 2022 and asked him about it. (A story I wrote for the *Boston Globe* was listed in his index.) "He was very ill when we did the thing. I was, too — cancer," Bragg replied. "The truth of it all, the darkest of it, I just don't know."

On March 9, 2021, Jerry Lee renewed his marriage vows with his seventh wife, Judith Coghlan Lewis, on their ninth anniversary. The officiant was Rev. Donnie Swaggart, son of televangelist Jimmy Swaggart. At the conclusion of the ceremony, he said, "Killer, you may kiss your bride."

At 71, she was the first wife even close to Lewis's age. Prior to falling in love and marrying him, she worked for several years as his caretaker at his home in Nesbit, Mississippi, just south of Memphis. Judith was previously married to Jerry Lee's cousin Rusty, whose older sister is Myra Gale Brown, the girl who married Lewis when she was 13. You can't make this stuff up.

On October 28, 2022, the Last Man Standing — the last member of the Million Dollar Quartet, that one-time thing with Elvis, Roy and Carl — stood no more. Pneumonia finally got him at 87. He's buried in the town where he grew up, Ferriday, Louisiana.

I can't say I didn't think a few times about how Jerry Lee debated himself about the afterlife — whether he'd end up in heaven or hell — and, as an agnostic bordering on atheist, I don't think it matters. But it sure mattered to him. If there is a God — if *I* was that God — I don't know what the hell I'd do. Cousin Jimmy Swaggart gave Jerry Lee his send-off. *The Memphis Commercial Appeal* reported that Swaggart called him "one of the greatest entertainers who ever lived" and told funny stories of their childhood but grew emotional speaking of Lewis's death: "I lost the brother I never had. I stand here today because of the mercy and grace of God, and I know my cousin is with the Lord in the portals of glory. How do you know he was saved? How do you know? He always had a heart for God, always. Even in his lowest times, he had a heart for God." ◆

"What inspired me was great natural people like Little Richard and Jerry Lee Lewis. I just wanted to try and be as good as them."

Ian Hunter

Ian Hunter at the City Winery, New York, April 2010

PHOTOGRAPH BY MICKEYDB

IAN HUNTER
& MOTT THE HOOPLE

MAKE NO MISTAKE, Ian Hunter is in it for the long haul. It's 2018, and he's talking about the Rant Band, the backing group he's had since 2001, the current lineup for six years.

"We did about 80 gigs last year," Hunter says. "We went all over Europe, and we did a bit in the U.S. We get on great. It's two or three very responsible people involved, people who run their own businesses, stuff like that. And I get to just sit in the band. They just ferry me about and I get up and do what I do, because basically I'm stuck at a mic and it's good if people can see some kind of movement going somewhere."

Yeesh, he's being modest. We're talking as he's readying a date at City Winery in Boston with his young(ish) backing band. There are eight of these Winerys scattered around the country, and the (mostly) sit-down clubs work for him and the fans. He's 78 and has done a fair number of gigs in various cities over the past few years. "We do a lot of Winerys, and they're usually fine."

Part of me thinks, "No, I'm a rocker, I want to stand and dance!" The other part goes, "I don't have that kind of stamina. I don't mind a nice, close seat." Evidently, I'm not alone. "I find with my [fans], half of them wanna stand up and the other half wanna sit down," Hunter says. "Usually, my lot will be a little older, so they don't mind sitting down, and they don't mind having a meal, and they've got a few bob which other people don't have. All in all, it works fine."

Given all this, I ask: Why are you so busy? Do you still like touring?

"I don't know," he says. "That's what I do. What am I going to do? Sit in the kitchen going 'Oh, my God?' That don't work for me."

Me: "I remember asking Lemmy that question back in the '90s. Saying something about his kind of hard rock being a young man's game, so did he envision an end point? He said, incredulously, 'What else would I do, host a fucking talk show?'"

Hunter: "Yeah, it's between that and a lack of relevance. You want to keep your end up."

Hunter has kept his end up for more than half a century. For six years, starting in 1969, he was lead singer and main songwriter of Mott the Hoople, the band most people got to know through the David Bowie-penned "All the Young Dudes."

There have been countless ups, downs and turnarounds for him in that time. "The rollercoaster — I think it's great!" says Hunter. "It's terribly boring being successful all the time; it's even more boring being a failure all the time. I'll never change. I just write songs. Sometimes they're good, sometimes they're bad. I'm just me, and that's the way I live me life."

There's no one in the biz savvier than Hunter about its vagaries, at least no one so willing to share those thoughts in public, in print and in song. In 1974, he published one of the best on-the-road books, *Diary of a Rock'n'Roll Star,* about Mott's five-week tour of America in late 1972. Among the insights: "It may look flashy, but it's over and you are finished before you know it. If you aren't already broken by one thing it will be another ... The rock business is a dirty business, full stop."

Would he ever consider writing a sequel? "No, not really. It don't pay well. Comparatively speaking. Well, it probably does now, but back then, no, it was just a waste of a lot of lyrics." (For a new edition in 2018, Hunter added diary entries from a 2015 Japan tour that he'd written for *Mojo* and Johnny Depp supplied an introduction.)

Hunter has written loads of songs about life on the road, the nature of rock and roll itself, about being in a band, what fans mean to touring musicians: "The Ballad of Mott the Hoople," "Saturday Gigs," "Marionette," "The Golden Age of Rock 'n' Roll" and "All the Way From Memphis." In "Ballad," Hunter calls rock and roll "a loser's game" that "mesmerizes." In "All the Way From Memphis," he acknowledges that fame can make "your heart grow cold." And he offers the admonition that rock and rollers can never grow old.

"All the Way From Memphis," a rollicking piano-pounder, is one of those life-on-the-rock-road songs that actually makes you feel like you're on the trip, not an outsider peering in. "What inspired me in the first place was great natural people like Little Richard and Jerry Lee Lewis," says Hunter. "I just wanted to try and be as good as them. I never will be, but that's always been my goal in life. Along the way, I started writing songs, which those guys weren't so great at."

As far back as 1973, when Mott was at the peak of its creative powers and popularity, one of England's top hard-rocking bands, Hunter (who first became a rock star at 34) considered the aging process. We all kind of thought about that at some point in our lives, didn't we? Rock and roll was exclusively for the young, and the young was us. Of course, the perception of "old" shifted with time and mattered less.

In 1988, I asked what it's like growing older in a young man's game? Hunter was 49 at the time.

A pause. "It's better. Less body and more head. It's not at all what I thought it would be. I like it a lot better; I'm more balanced; I'm a lot more confident. There was a lot of desperation involved the first time around, which is not a bad thing, but it used to mess my stomach up a lot. I'm confident. I think I know I'm good after all these years. I never really thought I was up to much for years and years. But now, looking back, I did some good stuff. I feel at peace with myself that way."

Still, "I don't know a [song]writer that doesn't doubt himself constantly. Every time you sit down and confront a keyboard or a fretboard with the view to writing, you're pretty vulnerable. It can be lonely."

We talked about the writing process. "I've got notebooks all over the place, and I still use a lot of cassettes. My memory stinks and it always did. I lost a lot of stuff. I blew it so many times. There was a song called 'All the Good Ones Are Taken' that we did two different versions of on a record because we couldn't remember the original groove. Now, if I'd had a cassette when I wrote the song, I'd have remembered what the groove was. We found it many years later. But at the time, we were doing a video of it and I knew it wasn't right. Just 'cause I didn't have a cassette [recorder with me].

"'Just Another Night' was another one. We were in there with the E Street Band, and the keyboard player [Roy Bittan] played it and [I sang] "Just another night on the other side ..." just like Bruce. I was really worried that I'm gonna get slagged off for this because it was *too* Bruce. And [guitarist Mick] Ronson pipes up and says, 'Why don't you do it like you wrote it?' I had no idea how I wrote it. [I said] 'You might have told me that two days ago when we were putting the backing track down!' But he didn't tell me then. We made a deal. He got half the writing. He had the [album] title as well — he got it off a toilet wall. And it was a title I wanted so we traded, *You're Never Alone With a Schizophrenic*."

Thirty years later, we were talking again and returned to the age thing, It was kind of the hook that kept on giving. He was still doing what he was doing and, for that matter, so was I, in my early sixties, both of us recognizing time and life are finite. I'd written a lot of non-music stories over the years — branched out as a journalist, if you will — but this was still where my heart and soul were.

So, what about rocking (or writing) deep into the arc of life?

"It don't bother me. You go to anybody my age, or ten years younger, you're gonna see the same thing. It's a little catch phrase. He's over 70?! Well, there you go. Now, if I stood on the end of a pier, doing "Chirpy Chirpy Cheep Cheep" [a bubblegum hit from 1970] I think I'd feel slightly guilty, but my stuff sort of stands up so we don't have a problem with it." Coincidentally, I'd been listening to Blue Suede's "Hooked on a Feeling" on YouTube recently and it ran into "Chirpy Chirpy Cheep Cheep." I told him I liked it, that it took me back to my AM radio youth. "That's YouTube for you, right there. You're gonna get this for the next three months now."

All the Young Dudes was one of those "mirror stars" LPs for me as a teen. Y'know, singing into a can of Right Guard spray, playing a tennis racquet guitar. "One of the Boys" was my fantasy fight/gang song. I hated fights but loved a good fictional clash. Another relatable point: that line in the title track, "Don't wanna stay alive when you're 25." I had my dark moments as a teen and I remember singing along with my crappy bedroom stereo system, "Don't wanna stay alive when you're 1-5."

Hunter did the reverse in 1981, changing the age from 25 to 35. "Have to move with the times," he said later, smiling.

Speaking of the song Bowie gave them and saved Mott's career, he admitted, "I never really did know what it was all about. They told me I was bringing gays out of the closet all over place. I spent the following six months escaping [that]. Then I stopped and talked to a few people and found out that gays were just like me, only different."

Mott formed in 1969 and released four pretty strong albums to middling success. Their music was often raucous, and Hunter, while keeping his English accent intact, had a very Dylanesque delivery. The rock press, always on the lookout for a new Dylan at that time, thought they might have found one. Or an ersatz one.

"What am I going to say?" asks Hunter with a laugh when we spoke during the band's brief 2019 reunion tour. "He's the man. Did I use him to find myself, my own voice? Yeah. Everybody uses somebody. I didn't know what the hell he was talking about but, boy, it just felt right. The sound of his voice, how you getting away with that? And he was confident, too. He knew."

In late 1981, I was backstage with Hunter at the Metro, talking about the Clash, particularly Mick Jones, who had played on and co-produced (with Mick Ronson) his fifth solo album, *Short Back 'n' Sides*. As Jones once famously said, "If it hadn't been for Mott, there would be no us."

"It's a mutual admiration society," Hunter says. "I'm not really a believer in what they say politically — I find them rather naïve as a band — but I kind of like the noises Mick makes, if you will. He's a very clever man — very religious about rock and roll, which is admirable."

Is Hunter?

"Am I?" he asks, appearing slightly startled behind his trademark sunglasses. "That's a good question. Really is. Never got asked that before. I have to smile at it. If I don't smile at it, I get annoyed with it. But I basically am it, and I'll never be able to get away from it." Back in the pre-*Dudes* days, he says, "We played rock and roll and played our asses off. We didn't know what we were doing, and it was great. But we were on the wrong label [Island in the UK]. We were more like a showoff band and they had all 'natural talent' people like Free and Traffic."

Just as it looked like 1971's *Brain Capers* would be it, lights out, Bowie entered the picture, giving the band he loved "All the Young Dudes," without which we wouldn't be reading this today. Legend has it that Bowie supplied the song in order to keep the band from breaking up. Almost. Not quite.

"We *had* broken up," Hunter explains. "[Bassist] Pete Watts rang him for a gig 'cause David was putting a band together. Pete said, 'I'm available,' and David said, "*You're* in Mott the Hoople." Pete said, 'We split up.' David went all funny and said, 'You *can't!*'

"David offered us 'Suffragette City,' which we thought was a good song, but we didn't think it was for us. Then he came back with 'Dudes.' He was really on our case for about a nine-month period there. We learned so much. David was extremely generous with his time. He was great, he really was. He was great with a lot of people, very unselfish."

Mott rode the glam-rock train with "Dudes" and built on it with two subsequent studio albums, *Mott* (the last with original guitarist Mick Ralphs, who went on to co-found Bad Company) and *The Hoople* (with his replacement, Ariel Bender, a.k.a. Luther Grosvenor, late of Spooky Tooth) and *Live* (also with Bender).

A reunion of the original members, save ailing drummer Dale "Buffin" Griffin (Martin Chambers of the Pretenders subbed for him), played the UK and Europe for brief stretches in 2009 and 2013. For the 2019 reunion band, dubbed "Mott the Hoople '74," Hunter was joined by Grosvenor and keyboardist Morgan Fisher, who also played on *The Hoople*. They played several European dates and figured that was it, but Hunter says promoter Ron Delsener persuaded him to do New York and the tour expanded from there.

"I thought I owed Morgan and Luther because they never got a shot on the first two get-togethers. They both turned up at those reunions and were real sports about it. They could have been upset, but they weren't. There were a few people who joined and left Mott, but those two, to me, have the same heart of the band as the original vibe did. So, it was important that they got their other 15 minutes. And I always thought that if I got a little window there, I'd do something."

The first window was three European festivals. Hunter doesn't particularly like festivals ("People go there for a good time, not to see anybody. It's more a celebratory sort of situation"), but the reconstituted Mott did them, had a blast and then added a handful of gigs in the UK.

"It worked out great between the Rant Band and Luther and Morgan, and they are now friends," says Hunter.

New Jersey guitarist, mandolinist, saxophonist and bandleader James Mastro, who was in the Bongos way back when, joined the Rant Band in 2001. "Ian is one of the least nostalgic people I know, and I tend to be the same way," he says. "You're only as good as your last song, guitar solo or show. That said, I must admit I went into [the Mott reunion] with a bit of trepidation, not wanting it to feel like an oldies act. Those worries were quickly dashed, as I think we all were carried away by how powerful, valid and vibrant it still felt."

Asked how simpatico they were, Mastro says, "Morgan and Luther have only gained chops over the years, so I feel like I'm in a master class working with them. They've done everything they can to make us feel a part of 'the band'; it is by no means an us-and-them situation. The two hours onstage have usually been preceded by a lot of laughing and hanging out together."

I asked Hunter how he got back into the mindset, the head, of himself in 1974. "I don't do that. It's a whole different ballgame. Luther comes in and Luther's still crazy, as he always was — he's not aged a bit. Morgan does his sartorial stuff and we just fall into it. It's the old getting-on-the-bike-again syndrome. And the Rant Band, they've been with me 17 years. They know this stuff backwards."

At the Boston show, a pair of tunes about rock and roll itself pretty much bracketed the set. Hunter sang several verses of Don McLean's "American Pie," but when he got to "the day the music died" line, he posed the question, "Or did it?" The band then slammed into a rollicking "The Golden Age of Rock 'n' Roll," with Hunter singing, "You gotta stay young, you can never grow old." During the frenetic first encore song, "All the Way From Memphis," he repeated that sentiment, almost word for word.

No doubt Hunter believed that — or believed that was the world's *perception* — when he was younger. Here, in 2019, sipping champagne between songs, he was trim, fit and didn't look very different from his sunglassed and golden-tressed young self. He was 79. A very limber and agile 79. Another line from a veteran band comes to mind: Jethro Tull's "You're never too old to rock if you're too young to die."

The 100-minute show hit all the marks: Mott's distinctive version of Lou Reed's "Sweet Jane," Bender's absolutely nutso guitar intro to the hard-rocking pre- "Dudes" nugget, "Walking With a Mountain." And, before we leave the songs-about-rock thing, I must note the concert highlight, "Marionette." The twisting, turning song encompasses soft piano interludes and soaring electric guitar riffs as Hunter weaves the cynical/realistic tale of a young, defiant rocker (him) being ground down by the music biz. He realizes that, in the end, "I'm just like all the others ... I'm just a marionette."

We'd discussed "Marionette" before the gig. "It's a good song, yeah," Hunter says. "As you get bigger, which we were in the process of doing at that time, you come up against the other side of the business. Any corporation's going to dive in and ruin anything, and that's what [the song] was about. It was getting to be a job. Mick Ralphs had left and I was [counted] on to write all the stuff. The band didn't like doing interviews, so I was doing them as well. And then the gigs and records: it was too much. I felt like a puppet. That was the beginning of the end for me. I never liked the premiership. To this day, I don't know how people survive that. It takes a special kind of balls to put up with the business on the top end."

He and the band followed "Marionette" with a jam-packed medley, beginning with "Jerkin' Crocus" but hitting full stride with "One of the Boys" and "Rock and Roll Queen." It moved into menacing territory with "Crash Street Kidds" (a gang of angry youths on the march) and then "Violence." As recorded for the *Mott* album, the song featured a droog-like creature right out of *A Clockwork Orange* singing "Violence! violence! It's the only thing that'll make you see sense." Onstage, Hunter stepped out of that character to revamp it as "Violence! violence! It doesn't make any sense." And he stripped both "Jerkin' Crocus" and "All the Way From Memphis" of their small, but potentially offensive, racial references. (I honestly don't believe either song had an iota of racist intent, but 21st century perceptions of linguistics being what they are ...)

Hunter's solo career has not been without its hits. And misses. Hits such as "Once Bitten, Twice Shy" from his first solo album, 1975's *Ian Hunter* (please try to forget the fucking Great White cover) and "Cleveland Rocks," which became the theme song for *The Drew Carey Show.* You can also try and forget Barry Manilow had a Top 10 hit with "Ships," a ballad from Hunter's second disc, *You're Never Alone With a Schizophrenic.*

"I sat with 'Ships' for six years," exclaims Hunter. "I had the verse; I had the bridge. When you have a good verse and a good bridge you really don't want to mess it up with an average hook. I waited and waited and I was [talking to] a drummer one night in the bar, he just happened to say something and 'That's it! Fuck, that's it!'"

Misses? I'll turn it over to Hunter in 1989, finding himself on the comeback trail once again. "I'm having a great time being a loser!" Hunter says with a hearty self-deprecating laugh after a November Hunter-Ronson Band gig at the Channel. Ronson, the onetime Bowie sideman who was also in late-period Mott, is Hunter's best mate. [Ronson died of liver cancer in 1993. He was 46.]

While he's been critical about his place in the rock world through the decade, this time Ian's having fun. The new Hunter-Ronson record, *YUI Orta* (Three Stooges by way of Van Halen), isn't an out-of-the-box success, but he has confidence in its quality and staying power. It towers over most of his '80s albums. "I kept on writing these appalling records," Hunter said candidly of his recent past. "That's why I like this one so much."

Addressing the modest venues he's currently playing, he says, "It's difficult being people like us. We're small, but we've got lots of things to play. Half the people think you're God, and the others think, 'Who are they?' Mick and I both have the same problem. It's quite schizophrenic, it's quite comical. I've never been able to come to terms with it. It's difficult being halfway up."

Flashback to 1981: Hunter was talking to me about how he'd been at a low ebb a few years earlier. "I was feeling sorry for myself. It was about the time all the new wave bands were saying chaps like me should leave. I should have been put out to grass or something." Some may have said that, but in truth Hunter was one of the few older rockers *not* dismissed by the punks. He produced Generation X's second album, worked with Mick Jones and got namechecked as an influence by others. But UK rock critics could be a vicious bunch, and he was yesterday's papers.

"It was funny," Hunter recalls, "because the press in England at that time slagged us off. They thought I wouldn't be cool with the punks. And the punks said, 'No, he's all right,' so the press did a U-turn. It was brilliant to watch. Wait a minute. You said I was shit last week! How does this work? You live and learn, you know."

When David Bowie died in 2016, Hunter was moved to write about his old pal and benefactor in "Dandy," a song on his *Fingers Crossed* album. "David was an incredible artist with an insatiable curiosity for everything," Hunter says. "I like the line 'and then we took the last bus home.'"

Was it something he needed to get off his chest?

"Not really. I mean if you're a songwriter, you're like a detective. You see these detectives who put all these bits of paper up on the wall. It's to do with the case, and they're trying to solve the case and they keep looking at these bits of paper. It's the same sort of thing. I have loads of paper, lyrics and all that and you keep staring at them and something happens and you write. It can be anything. A couple of days after David passed, I was working on [another song] and out came this circa '72 *Ziggy* stuff. And I thought that's really cool from a fan's point of view — it really wasn't from my point of view — and it came."

Postscript, 2018: Hunter and I are backstage after his show at City Winery in Boston. He graciously offers my wife and me champagne. He's wearing a Jerry Lee Lewis T-shirt, so I tell him some of my Jerry Lee stories — bits of the preceding chapter — and he tells me his.

Jerry Lee was his hero, hands down, but he never ever wanted to meet him. He had opportunities to do so but passed because, well, "he's an asshole." At one show Hunter recalled seeing, an orchestra played first and then the Killer was due to follow an intermission.

It was closing in on closing time, 11 o'clock. No Jerry Lee. It's quarter to and Lewis finally takes the stage in a bright red suit, spends five minutes preening and combing his hair and adjusting himself at the piano and then, with 10 minutes left, bangs out three great rockers, "Whole Lotta Shakin' Goin' On," "Great Balls of Fire" and (I forget the third). Ian thought, "It was fantastic! So memorable!" His youthful goal was to be able to play like him.

That night in Boston, Hunter sang a rare gem and one of my favorite Mott album tracks, "I Wish I Was Your Mother," with Mastro on mandolin (and the rest of the Rant Band doing what they do). Hunter told me about a point of view he frequently takes in song, that of people who are a bit broken or outsiders or incomplete. That's what he did when he wrote this wistful sweet-sad song about wanting to have a close family and observing his wife Trudi's. It's a pained plea for a better childhood — at least in dreams, but even then, as the song goes, "Is there a happy ending? I don't think so."

This beautiful song meant a lot to me as a kid, being an only child and adopted. I had great parents, but there were the usual conflicts and times where I had this wish, too, and Hunter's song captured the pathos perfectly. A family not my own, a better family.

"'I Wish I Was Your Mother' can still make me cry," says Mastro, "and 'Memphis' can still make me feel like I just discovered rock and roll."

Hunter and the Rant Band didn't play "Trudi's Song," an ode to his wife of (now) 50 years. "It's a quiet little song some people would like," Hunter says, "but a lot of people might get bored. I don't mind doing ballads in my set, but there's a lot of them and they slow the set down."

We got to talking about starting out, him playing music and me writing about it. I told him my quasi-embarrassing/ultimately funny anecdote about being a young writer interviewing Rockpile, asking Nick Lowe and Dave Edmunds if their original motivation had to do with achieving some sort of artistic or musical goal. They looked at me blankly and incredulously and ... Ian beat me to the punchline: It was all about getting girls. Girls liked boys with guitars. Guys picked up and played guitars to get girls. End of story.

Or, really, the beginning. ◆

“I have this unquenchable enthusiasm. I probably drive people around me mad with my enthusiasm.”

David Bowie

David Bowie performing in Foxboro, MA in September 1983

PHOTOGRAPH BY MICHAEL GRECCO (GRECCO.COM/DAYSOFPUNK.COM)

DAVID BOWIE

I AM ON THE PHONE WITH DAVID BOWIE in the summer of 1990 when I pose a question you'd think he would expect, so I am a bit surprised when he pauses and says, "Hmm ..." before formulating a response. But then, when he does answer, it is quite a discourse.

The question: "Your career has often been called chameleon-like for all the musical changes and image shifts you've undergone. Do you agree with that assessment? Do you see yourself as a chameleon?"

The answer: "I think a painter who fell into that category was Picabia," says Bowie, citing the French artist who began as a post-Impressionist and later embraced Cubism, Futurism, Dada and Surrealism. "He had a very hard time being taken seriously as an artist because he changed so rapidly and continually throughout his career. If you aren't seen as a craftsman who will stick to your so-called guns, I think you unfortunately start falling into the realm of 'dilettante.' I got plagued with that for a while, and I think I probably always will.

"But I can't change my focus. My focus is very short-lived. I'll fool around with a side of art or a side of music or whatever and then my attention is not there anymore. I don't wish to take it any further. I've done what I want to do with it and then I move on. That just happens to be the kind of artist I am. I'm not sure whether that means chameleon. It just means there are so many aspects of music that are interesting to me, it really is fun playing in there, like a big playground."

Bowie goes on to quote his friend and sometime collaborator Brian Eno: "'You know what the great thing is about music? It's like being a jet pilot and you can crash your plane and walk away from it.' Which I thought was a marvelous observation. You can really afford to make mistakes in music that you don't make in real life. That kind of makes it exciting."

Bowie is on a roll. He is also in an affable, expansive mood. He is greatly enjoying his *Sound + Vision* greatest-hits stadium tour, which he terms one of the most social tours he's ever been involved in.

But back to the chameleon thing.

Bowie has fully earned the description, even if only for the many visual guises he's presented. He's looked like a hippie, a carrot-top with lightning bolts painted on his face, a sleek soul singer, a stylish new waver and many other things over time. But then he gave us a pretty good hint about that in 1971 with "Changes," singing, "So I turned myself to face me / But I've never caught a glimpse / Of how the others must see the faker / I'm much too fast to take that test."

On his 1973 breakthrough, *The Rise and Fall of Ziggy Stardust and the Spiders From Mars*, he exclaimed, "I could play the wild mutation as a rock and roll star!" *Play*: as in act or act out, become someone who isn't quite him. That concept runs contrary to what many rockers have implied through their music, or at least what we often take away: that they are almost always the protagonists of their own songs, that this isn't a fabrication, it's real life. Or a credible simulation thereof.

In "playing" the doomed hedonist-egotist rock star Ziggy, Bowie invited fans to question his own sexuality; he made rock and roll with dancing wordplay that pulsed with eroticism and danger. It was highly charged, quirky, conceptual — very English and totally unlike anything else that entered the mainstream.

An adventurous, colorful and androgynous image moved Bowie to the forefront of glam rock, which found far greater commercial success in England than it did in America. The success of *Ziggy* led RCA to reissue — and fans (I was one) to discover — two of his previous albums, *Space Oddity* and *The Man Who Sold the World*, not to mention the immediate predecessor of *Ziggy, Hunky Dory*. Even in his pre-star days, Bowie was delivering a dizzying mix of material: sassy pop ("Queen Bitch"), churning, heavy boogie ("The Width of a Circle") and perhaps Bowie's best "obscure" song, "Memory of a Free Festival," in which he sounded spaced-out and sad, singing about the failure of communal idealism.

As Bowie puts it, he caught a wave with glam. "I think you're very aware of that. It must be kind of what it must be like for surfers, when they can't do a thing wrong. I suppose, like every new rock era, the bands that so-called 'spearhead' the era feel that they're wiping the slate clean and starting off with 'this is what's gonna happen now.' And we had the same kind of derisive feelings about everything that had happened before us. Which," he adds with a laugh, "you get now from new bands about us guys, and it's perfectly understandable. You really have to feel as if you have an answer, or a message, that meteoric kind of feeling, that euphoria that you just discovered something brand new."

Bowie popularized the idea of rock fiction — of adopting a character and convincing us it was him. I was an impressionable teen when *Ziggy Stardust* came out and bought that as the *real* Bowie. After *Aladdin Sane* and the Orwellian futurist of *Diamond Dogs,* I was a bit let down when I realized each was just a phase. Then came the self-described "plastic soul" singer of *Young Americans.* And that only got us through the mid-'70s.

Not that he didn't seek it, but success forced Bowie to deal with fame. He railed at its downside in the spiraling, haunting hit of the same title in 1975 and was still discussing it 15 years later: "The fact is, when you start off writing, you are the observer, but then you get to this ridiculous situation where you're the observed. You feel nullified. You feel as though it's all been taken away from you, the power of writing sort of evaporates. It's terribly important to keep putting yourself in touch, one way or another."

Bowie played so many characters, took many guises, over time. That's how it went in those years: New album, new image, new Bowie. How calculated was it all? Is it still?

"Believe me, it's very hard for me to say this," says Bowie, almost pleadingly, "but there's very little that I do as an artist that's actually calculated. I do change an awful lot, and I have been through such a lot it's *made* me change. I think I've got a very keen sense of survival — I would agree to that. But I think it's personal survival; I don't think it's as an artist. And the personal survival has formulated and dictated the way I was going to write and exactly what I was going to be."

So maybe we should give him a break — lay the chameleon label to rest, or at least modify it. Because it implies that Bowie has few original ideas, that he's a creature whose method of survival is simply to adapt to a changing environment. To an extent, that's true — he has not always been a pioneer, more a popularizer of new styles.

Marc Bolan and T. Rex ruled glam-rock before Bowie hit it big with *Ziggy*, and Kraftwerk was making austere electronic rock before Bowie's celebrated "Berlin" period of 1977–'80, when he collaborated with Eno.

But Bowie's stylistic choices — with the notable exception of his work of the mid-to-late-'80s, the "*Let's Dance* so-called celebration" period, in his words — have never been tailored to suit the mainstream. With the German period, during which he made *Low*, *"Heroes"* and *Lodger*, Bowie risked losing his audience, and did, in fact, leave behind fans puzzled by the oblique lyrics, challenging song structures, instrumentals and synthesizer-based tracks. Critics raved, however, and fans enamored of the boundary-breaking sounds of punk and new wave saw him as a kindred spirit, one of the few old-guard rockers who, by delving into a new, difficult and somewhat dissonant form of music, proved he was not just coasting.

"I actually think that was luck of the draw," says Bowie modestly. "If I hadn't chosen to go to Berlin, I probably wouldn't have been caught up in the techno-rock scene that was happening in Germany, which far overshadowed what was happening in England with punk. The Germans knew they had something no one else was touching. All of that rubbed off onto me and Brian. I guess we didn't exactly bypass the punk thing — it's as though we took the other fork in the road, which, inevitably, was the other of the two things that were going to happen to music. If I'd stayed in America, I can't imagine what would have happened. I probably would have sunk into that obsolete thing that happens once you become tied to L.A."

Before they relocated to Germany, Bowie had been living in Los Angeles and palling around with Iggy Pop. Both were ruining themselves. "Musically, I was pretty damn happy," says Bowie, who had rung up his first number-one U.S. single with "Fame," and recorded a brilliantly unsettling album in *Station to Station* — later revealed to be a pretty coked-up trip — and was working his way toward mainstream acceptance in a big way. "But during the early-'70s period up until the middle portion there, I had a massive drugs problem." He might have made music with Iggy, but cocaine was his real partner.

"For me, my accidents are mainly emotional and spiritual. I guess, like a lot of us, it was my most serious accident. It took me away from people. If we'd stuck around L.A., one or both of us wouldn't have been alive today. I just know it. It was sort of a brave thing to do, going to Berlin, 'cause we didn't know what the hell we were getting into. But it felt like such an exotic thing to do, to go and live in this place where we'd heard about the new art movements and the things happening in music and the Wall and the paranoia. And we liked that you could get around and not be pulled into cliques and very unhealthy situations."

The Bowie I met in person twice and spoke to on the phone several times was always warm, witty, gracious, analytical and self-deprecating. I know others will tell gnarlier tales about earlier periods in his life and career; Angela Bowie, his former wife and manager, evidently had a tempestuous time with him.

In 1993, I had dinner with Angie, who with Patrick Carr, had written *Backstage Passes: Life on the Wild Side With David Bowie.* She was his wife of 10 years, and pretty certain she was the architect of his success. They'd been divorced for 12 and, until recently, she was under a gag order not to say or write anything about the man she once loved. Bowie, she writes, was not too keen on personal hygiene, wasn't much of a lover, had a high degree of self-loathing, was an oft-ruthless human being, had a monstrous cocaine addiction and dabbled in Satanism.

Near the end of the book, she calls him "a friend-abusing, sense-mangling, money-bleeding, full-fledged Vampire of Velocity. Like coke addicts long before and after him, he'd learned to travel far and fast, to keep his mind spinning in tight little circles even when standing perfectly still, to arrange an existence almost entirely devoid of daylight, to assume a worldview of utter paranoia (in his case, no great stretch), and to start slowly sucking the life out of everybody close to him."

Angie dished a lot of dirt. Was she, I asked, a tad vengeful?

"Vengeful? No, not at all. Did you feel that way?"

Uh, yeah, in places. Certainly, there's anger and bitterness.

"I don't think there's any bitterness. If something is nasty, how can that be bitter? Being throttled isn't particularly pleasant. Talking about it is not being bitter, it's telling the truth. It's got nothing to do with being bitter."

What might David Bowie and/or the people close to him think about *Backstage Passes*?

"I have no idea and I could care less. It's totally irrelevant to me."

If he had a publicity purpose the times we spoke — promoting an album or a tour — Bowie never tried to steer the conversation that way. We got to those things, but he was happy to go with the flow and engage in a genuine thought process. He was not someone to toss off glib by-the-book responses.

Even though Bowie's late-'70s music was hot and hip in new wave circles — his videos were daring, his rock, which he calls "the most mature music I'd written," was artful and agitated — the mass audience was not buying it, with the exception of, say, *"Heroes."* His superstar status was on the wane. Bowie had captured mainstream hearts; now he, seemingly, was turning his back on them. In *Bowie: An Illustrated Record,* English journalists Roy Carr and Charles Shaar Murray report that Bowie's record company, RCA, was aghast at his prolonged commercial dive.

The reversal began in 1980 with *Scary Monsters (and Super Creeps)*, which contained the quirky and delightful "Space Oddity" sequel "Ashes to Ashes." In 1983 came the big breakthrough of *Let's Dance*, featuring the title cut, "China Girl" and "Modern Love." Not an adventurous record, but a satisfying dance-pop collection. The follow-up records, however — *Tonight* and *Never Let Me Down* — plus tracks on the soundtracks of *Labyrinth* and *Absolute Beginners* — stalled. Bowie seemed to have shed the role of innovator. Pushing no envelopes, he seemed to be making slighter versions of "Let's Dance."

"I don't think I was actually treading water," Bowie says of that period, "but what I was doing was reevaluating why I wanted to write anymore, and it slowed me down to a certain extent. I thought I didn't need to, and that's what happens when you really feel as though things are going well for you. The whole cliché about the angst of being a writer — it is in there somewhere."

What brought Bowie around again was collaboration, especially a hookup with guitarist Reeves Gabrels and the rhythm section of Hunt and Tony Sales, who all joined Bowie in Tin Machine at the end of the '80s. The group released studio albums in 1989 and 1991. With the exception of the Traveling Wilburys — which was kind of an all-star studio gimmick — I can't think of another famous artist who abandoned a solo career to form a band, to try and subsume his ego into a group format.

"The Rolling Stones, it ain't," said Bowie of Tin Machine. "I think it aligns itself far more to what would be termed the underbelly of music ... decidedly underground. I don't think there's anybody in this band who's planning on playing to teenagers."

At one point, I thought I'd take a side trip into Bowie's acting career. Take a scan of his film credits — the alien-with-a-message in *The Man Who Fell to Earth,* the lead vampire in *The Hunger*, a POW in *Merry Christmas, Mr. Lawrence*, the evil king in

Labyrinth and Pontius Pilate in *The Last Temptation of Christ*, to name a few — and you'd probably assume that Bowie had really been pursuing a second career as an actor.

"That's very generous of you to call it a 'career,'" says Bowie, chuckling at the term. "I get a little embarrassed about that whole area, although it's great fun. I've ended up with a few cushy parts by some quite fabulous directors. I just look at it like that: If I'm lucky enough to be offered a cameo by some great director, I'm over the moon. I don't think I have the commitment to be an actor. You have to really want it, and you have to be prepared to study hard. There's such a lot of good actors out there, I was intimidated.

"I saw a rock star who I won't name on television saying, 'Well, you've gotta understand when you see people like me up in a movie acting, we're learning our craft as we're working.' And I'm thinking, 'Why the hell did you accept the part when there's a hundred actors who could do the part better?'"

Some of Bowie's movies have been hits, others bombs, but he did reap commercial rewards and loads of critical praise for his performance on Broadway in *The Elephant Man,* a role he handled without the sort of "deformity" makeup John Hurt employed in the David Lynch film. The *New York Times* reported, "It was not unnatural to think [that Bowie] had been cast simply for the use of his name. Dismiss that thought now ... As John Merrick, the Elephant Man, he is splendid."

Opines Bowie, the show now a memory: "That was probably the most boring thing I ever did in my life. I did six months, eight times a week. I mean, oh God, that's hard work!"

The trouble, Bowie says, is repetition: "After the first couple of months, the rest of it seemed like I didn't know how to reinvent it every night."

In 1990, Bowie claimed his *Sound + Vision* tour would be the final one for which he'd trot out old favorites — a last gasp for Ziggy and all the other characters. He also said (wrongly, as it turned out, sort of like previous "retirement" announcements) that it would be the swan song for David Bowie as a solo artist.

"Knowing that I won't be doing these songs again, it's quite exciting," said Bowie. "They can be imbued with quite a lot of integrity. I really thought quite hard and long," he said, about retiring the songs. "It just seemed to me to be an important time in my life, being 43 now — that I honestly didn't want to feel like at 45 and 46 that if I was still working as a writer and performer that I didn't want to rely on what I had done in the past to keep an audience with me. It's kind of a soft option to say, 'Well, I've got this new album out, but — eh, only some of it's good — so I can always pad out the rest of the show with the old songs, and then I've got a guaranteed audience.' I think that's probably what will happen to a lot of guys who are approaching my age or who are already my age. They want to carry on performing and writing, but it'll be harder and harder to get away from their old stuff."

So, you can subtitle *Sound + Vision* the "Soft Option" tour. Still, it seemed odd that someone so keen to take artistic risks would go on the road to flog his back catalog. Bowie played 17 of the 18 tracks included on the *Changesbowie* compilation at the tour's official kickoff in Montreal in early March. The song selection wasn't even Bowie's doing: he'd set up an international 900-number line and allowed fans to vote for their favorites. The notion seemed odd enough when it was announced — does the ultimate in-control artist have no opinion about what he should play in concert? — and even made it seem Bowie was trying to cash in on the lucrative pay-per-call racket. Did he really need cash that badly?

No, as it turned out. Bowie didn't say anything about it at the time, but later acknowledged that "every single cent is going to Save the Children. Nobody's making a penny. That particular charity is the charity I do most if I do the charity thing."

So, it's not a crass moneymaker, but the 900 number did make for a conservative set list — especially in contrast to 1987's *Glass Spider* tour, where Bowie pulled out such obscure gems as "Sons of the Silent Age," "All the Madmen" and "Big Brother."

For this tour, fan requests make up about 80 percent of the show, while he's reserved a couple of selections for himself, such as "Station to Station" and "Stay," "just because I can," he says with a laugh. "My own personal choices would be stuff like 'Joe the Lion' and 'Red Sails,' very obscure things. But it's not my choice of songs. The people have come along to hear 'Changes' and 'Rebel Rebel,' that kind of song."

Bowie acknowledges the considerable distance he feels from some of his creations. "It is hard to relate to stuff I did 20 years ago, when I was in my young twenties. You write from a different perspective, and a lot of things have changed for me, an awful lot has changed. I feel fairly diffident at the moment about things like 'Rebel Rebel' and 'Suffragette City,' although I know my audience are terribly enthusiastic about those two particular songs. For me, I can't help but remember who I wrote them for

— the whole *Ziggy Stardust* thing and that period and what it represented. And they are, for me, imbued with that era; it's very hard for me to intellectually shake off that era when I'm performing them. It's hard to see them through new eyes."

So, it is perhaps ironic that the man who titled an album *The Man Who Sold the World* is now the man who will sell *to* the world. One last time.

But what saves him is his cheek — his candid admission that this one isn't so much about the art as about the commerce — and his what-the-hell willingness to come out and celebrate a shared past. Then there's Bowie's enthusiasm for what lies ahead. "For me," he says, as a songwriter, "it's a return to the Berlin period. I don't think we know what we're making yet. And that's what makes it exciting."

Earthling, his best album since *Scary Monsters,* came out in 1997. That August, before an international arena tour to support it, Bowie and Gabrels visited Fort Apache Studios in Cambridge for a WBCN-FM-sponsored (and simulcast) concert and Q&A session with contest winners. Bowie had already done something similar that morning in Atlanta.

Speaking of his common musical ground with Gabrels (who much later joined the Cure), Bowie said, "We both vacillate between melodic pomposity and quirky abhorrent sounds that are really ugly. Somewhere in there we find little jewels."

Here, outside Boston, it was the re-return of the Thin White Duke — all acoustic, warm, genial and at ease with his surroundings, which included candles and big bouquets of flowers.

WBCN gave away 52 pairs of passes to the people who sent in the most interesting questions. Program director Oedipus said the station received more than a thousand entries. Winners asked such things as:

- Do you have a pet? (A: He once owned a German Shepherd.)
- What books are you currently reading? (A: Life of Picasso and a biography of Dada artist Marcel Duchamp.)
- If you could visit any moment in history, what would it be? (A: 1907-1913, Paris and London, because it was the most exciting time for music and art — and before World War I.)
- If an asteroid was certain to hit the earth in a week, wiping out civilization, how would you spend the time? ("Apologizing," he said, after a pause. "Just in case...")

Bowie, who subsequently said that he admires how Ray Davies weaves together his music and stories, proved a master at it himself. Asked why he spends so much time in America, Bowie blustered, "Do you have a problem with that?!" — before praising an American pop landscape full of rebels: James Dean, the beatniks, "the dear-departed Allen Ginsberg." He discussed Buddhism and history; he praised Neil Young's dignity and grace.

The lucky fans and another 50-plus VIPs who joined them were treated to a C&W version of "Scary Monsters" (Bowie as Johnny Cash?), "Seven Years in Tibet," a snippet of "The Supermen," "Dead Man Walking," "The Jean Genie" and the Tin Machine song "I Can't Read."

Gabrels was an amiable foil throughout the hour-long set, during which Bowie discussed mysteries large and small, from the genesis of the songs to the role of art. He said he drew "Heroes" from the "hokey" situation of a couple that met at the Berlin wall every day.

What made art art? Did it have to have intention?

"I'm not sure any kind of artwork has to have intentions behind it," he said, explaining his frequent use of science fiction allegories and modern man's distance from traditional religion.

Asked about Ziggy Stardust, he said the character was partially based upon a real person, Vince Taylor, who once performed a rock show as Christ and ended up a maintenance man for Swiss Airways.

"We," he said, post-set of himself and Gabrels, "are enjoying the hell out of it."

We spoke on the phone later in 1997. Bowie was still promoting *Earthling*.

We started with some backstory.

"I'm not without luggage," said Bowie with a chuckle, admitting the obvious. A few of the bags he's carried: legend, star, pioneer, provocateur. Also, chameleon and stylistic thief. He's had to groan over more than a few things he's said and done over a quarter-century in the public eye.

But, he added, perhaps some of that luggage "makes travel easier. Plus, I just have this — I don't know — unquenchable enthusiasm. I probably drive people around me mad with my enthusiasm."

Bowie, who had turned 50 a month earlier and celebrated with a star-studded concert at Madison Square Garden in New York, was in a reflective mood. Last year, an English interviewer tossed a self-analytical question at Bowie and he took the bait. Bowie described himself as "a populist and a postmodern Buddhist surfing my way through the chaos of the 20th century."

"Pretentious, moi?" offered Bowie, with a hearty self-deprecating laugh.

"I'm not sure what to do with these things," he said, sighing, of that quote in particular and his proclivity in general for making pronouncements and expounding philosophically. "I like dreaming them up, but they come back at me. Some people get them as what they are [poking fun at myself], and other people think that's kind of what I really think. I'm not sure which side to go on because I half believe it's true, that's the trouble."

Bowie said a London friend — "a girl who's very much a clubber" — brought him a stack of vinyl: early jungle music. "I was just so impressed. It just sounded like the whole dichotomy of the music was a parallel of how society exists. There was the hard throbbing pulse underneath — regular and very directed — and there was this incredible chaotic freneticism on top with the speeded-up snare drum that seemed to break beats continuously and didn't seem to follow any regular pattern. It really felt like a real social manifesto laid out in music, and I was totally seduced by it."

That became the blueprint for *Earthling*. Following a 1995 festival tour of Europe, Bowie and Gabrels went to work. "We wrote all the material to support the dynamic of this band. The intention was to capture the spirit and intensity of what we were as a working band, and the music was written specifically as a platform for that expression."

A mathematician might look at Bowie as a musical equivalent of fractal mathematics, where chaos is created through something called "amplification via interaction," in which the outcome of a system is fed back to the system itself.

In 1995 and 1996, Bowie toured on a bill with Nine Inch Nails — winning some fans, alienating many others — promoting a rather harsh album, *Outside*. That album, about murder-as-art, was billed as the first of a trilogy. Yet he followed it with *Earthling*, which Bowie calls "an interruption."

"Typical me. My attention wandered. This album was waiting to be made at the end of the last festival tour we did ... But the next in the trilogy is called *Contamination* and hopefully that will surface at the end of the summer. [It never did.] It'll be quite startling, I think. I guess it won't be accessible, really, although I might keep it shorter. I think maybe 76 minutes [the length of *Outside*] was an awful long time, today's attention spans being what they are and all that.

"I do feel that that's what I'm good at doing. Maybe I have this strange set of antennae that allow me to actually understand why — to a certain extent, maybe intuitively — why culture works and what the messages are and what we are sending out and receiving. That may be my contribution. I'm not a futurist. I'm very thoroughly sure-footed in the contemporaneous."

Bowie observed. Bowie borrowed. He took from the outré and avant-garde and reconfigured, shaping and squeezing it toward the mainstream.

I posed this parodic fantasy to Bowie: There he is, this thin, handsome older man in a long leather coat, lurking outside a club, maybe incognito, notebook and tape recorder in hand, waiting to get inside in order to assimilate, process and steal the sounds of the hippest music. Inside, the creators of the music hear of his presence and cower and cringe, afraid of the Pillager.

Bowie laughed heartily. This parody came to fruition, he said. "I've been featured in a long-running cartoon in Britain as being just that, a rather disengaged culture vulture. A bit of a mad pilot that kind of flies from avant-garde trees, making this nest out of glittering jewels that belong to other beings. Well, I guess that's me. The thing is, I agree with all that, and I don't see anything wrong in that. Yes, that's what I do. I'm a contagious, infectious enthusiast. It's what I like doing."

Still, Bowie had a history, and depression was part of it. He swore he didn't get depressed any longer. He went through that when he turned 40.

"In terms of adjusting to who or what I was, I mean, I hit every cliché in the book. Should I be with younger people or should I let go of the youthful feelings? Am I now supposed to settle back into something? Should I change my life entirely? I did in fact, in a way, change my life. I just treat the rest of whatever life I've got as the adventure it used to be, so I'm not just kind of by myself, just left on the sands of this awful, nostalgic, rather poignant, sad old life.

"I'm actually glad to be alive," he said, alluding to his time in drug hell, dealing with paranoia and doubt. The happiness, he suggests, may have to do with "surviving all that stuff and finding that actually getting older ain't such a bad thing, that really, I would be left with an appetite for life and finding at 50 I really do have one. It's the last thing that I imagined at 25. I thought I'd be all burned out, or at least really bored or boring. Both probably. I find that life is more stimulating to me than it was at 25, when I was just racked with ambition."

A line from *Earthling*: "And I've gone through the cracks in my past / Like a dead man walking."

He's like his pal Neil Young, whom he helped out in 1996 at a benefit for Young's charitable Bridge Foundation concerts. He merrily goes his own way, follows his nose, explores genres that right-thinking people wouldn't attempt. Most rockers slow down or mellow out as they age.

Why hasn't Bowie?

"I think I've had the advantage of not believing in myself as a 'rock' person. Therefore, I don't think that I imbued those qualities that were so much part of the rock character, which was agelessly young, being the permanent social rebel in that stereotypical fashion." Think back to that early lyric of his: He could play the wild mutation as a rock and roll star.

"I had these dreams of rock music being the great art form of the late 20th century. To me, it still is the greatest art form of the 20th century. It has surpassed, in its communicative powers, the visual arts, theater, opera — maybe cinema is the only competition it has. I didn't feel myself as being such an integral part of [rock] in that way, but somebody who utilized the rock platform as a way of expressing themselves as an artist. So, maybe, I was not weighed down with the thinking 'Hey, I'm a rock god.'"

Bowie said that one of the most miserable points of his life was when he was most popular in the United States, the post-*Let's Dance* era, when he confronted the "strange irony that I was out there playing to a Phil Collins audience and coming home and listening to Sonic Youth and Glenn Branca."

Here, of course, is a situation Bowie may now encounter: His long-term audience may find itself uncomfortable with the jarring tempo shifts of jungle and take a pass.

"I couldn't agree more. I've set myself some real problems."

And, conversely, a younger audience may not care about someone so, well, old.

"Exactly, exactly. I appreciate both sides of that argument."

So, how do you deal with it?

"I don't know, I really don't. I don't have any answers for that whatsoever. All I know is that I don't want to play anything other than the stuff that's really interesting me and exciting me at the time. I've always gambled on that. The most successful I've been is when I've just gone with my gut instinct about what I should be doing as an artist. And the audience will wax and wane, and I just have to count on the fact that someone will like what I'm doing ... I don't want to be an audience-pleaser in that way. I don't want to say, 'Well, I'm going out this year: I wonder what kind of songs they'd like me to do?'"

As the end neared — not that we knew it, he wasn't doing interviews — Bowie stepped even further away from rock. *Blackstar*, his final LP, came out on his 69th birthday in January 2016, more than three years after *The Next Day*. Who knew he'd been working on it? It was one of the best-kept secrets in music, and as connected to skronky free jazz as to rock.

Two days later, David Bowie was dead. Liver cancer. He'd battled it for 18 months. Who outside of his wife Iman and his innermost circle even knew he was that ill? Sure, we'd heard about his retirement from touring. There was a New York picture circulating that showed him unwell, and there were rumors about illness. (Later, we learned he'd ended cancer treatments in October of 2015.)

The man always had a flair for the dramatic and theatrical, but Jesus, new album/birthday/death! We were told it was all coincidence, not orchestration and I believe that. But how Bowiesque! I have to believe he knew the end was near and that people would be reading the tea leaves of his music, as ever, and especially the videos.

Once the shock had subsided slightly, I thought back to a line Bowie boldly sang on the title track of *The Next Day*: "Here I am, not quite dying!" Great! I thought. No new music for ten years ... and then this fabulous comeback. Even if the declaration of life might have been shaded cheekily, maybe even a hint. Not *quite* dying. Anyway, that's what I thought then.

The video for "Blackstar" was posted shortly before the album's release: a spooky, meandering, jazz-inflected 10-minute song, with a mournful Bowie, bandages with black buttons over his eyes, singing about being "in the center of it all ... on the day of execution." Was this Major Tom, back again, dying? Or was it something more personal?

The next video was "Lazarus." I watched it the day before he died. It was chilling. Bowie in a hospital bed, same bandages, groping, elevating, leaving us. Bowie singing, "Look up here, man, I'm in danger, I've got nothing left to lose." At the beginning we see glimpses of a dark figure — angel of death? — poking out of an armoire. At the end, he gets up from his desk and his bed and jerkily backs into the armoire, as if being pulled in. Bowie's hand reaches out to close the door. Did I have a premonition about Bowie's imminent death? No, not exactly. It could have been a character — Major Tom again? — and we knew Bowie loved his characters.

In retrospect, we see Bowie's music and video addressing his own mortality, intentionally or not. The cover of the *Blackstar* CD is white with a black star in the center. On the inside, it's all black, a photo of a pensive Bowie during a sunset, above him a circular sunburst image. He's half in light, half in dark, between two worlds.

Prior to all this, I'd talked to Tony Visconti, Bowie's frequent producer (including collaborating with him on *Blackstar*), about his longtime friend's future post-*Blackstar*. No tour, certainly, but he floated the possibility that Bowie might do a one-off concert, simulcast in theaters around the country.

In January 2016 my wife Roza and I were looking for a cool gig to attend during the usual winter doldrums in clubland around Boston. One that struck our fancy was a small-scale celebration of *The Rise and Fall of Ziggy Stardust and the Spiders From Mars* at the intimate Lizard Lounge in Cambridge. A lo-fi trio of Lake Street Dive drummer-singer Mike Calabrese, guitarist-singer Taylor Ashton from Fish and Bird and saxophonist Chris Miller from the Revelers was going to play the album's songs sequentially. It had been booked weeks in advance.

Of course, it turned into something else when Bowie died two days before the gig.

Calabrese said he hoped the gig would prove "cathartic." The musicians did their best to keep the sorrow away from the songs, but sorrow suffused the show, even as lines like "She wants my money, not my honey / She's a funky-thigh collector, laying on electric dreams" tripped off their tongues.

For two days, I'd been my semi-detached professional self, had written appreciations for Bowie and talked about him on the radio. But I lost it during "Five Years," tears welling up, and then again when they came to "Starman" and launched into the chorus, "There's a starman, waiting in the sky ..."

At the end of *The Wizard of Oz*, Dorothy is bidding her Oz pals goodbye and tearily says to the Scarecrow, "I think I'll miss you most of all."

I think right now I'm Dorothy and David's the scarecrow. ◆

“The wild part of that wild life only lasts a couple of years. After that, it’s just self-crucifixion.”

Iggy Pop

Iggy Pop at the Orpheum Theater in Boston, April 11, 2016

PHOTOGRAPH BY DOUG QUINTAL

IGGY POP

"A LOT OF CRAZED PEOPLE now seem to be professionally crazed. You've got guys doing commercializations of my prior lifestyle. You hear these songs that codify and ritualize intoxication and quick-sex behavior, usually by guys who are living more like young businessmen."

It's 1990. Iggy Pop and I are conversing in what you might think a very un-Iggy-esque setting: his room at the Four Seasons Hotel in Boston. Y'know, *not* a fleabag. A composed Iggy — who seems more like Jim Osterberg (his real and offstage name) right now — is dressed casually, in a bright multicolored T-shirt and faded black jeans. He's not a street-walkin' cheetah with a heart full of napalm at the moment. He's wearing glasses. He's in a ruminative mode.

"I learned all the survival skills from David Bowie," Iggy says. "Lust for Life" — the song and the album — came from 1977 recording sessions in Germany which Bowie co-produced. He also wrote the song, providing encouragement and motivation, probably for the both of them. And for us: "No more beatin' my brains / With the liquor and drugs!"

Iggy counted Bowie among his close pals. He popularized several of Iggy's songs, most notably (in 1983) "China Girl," which kept him in pocket change during the lean years. Bowie attempted to rescue Iggy at several points in his career, first in 1973 when he co-produced (or weirdly under-produced) *Raw Power,* then again in 1976 when they began a series of collaborations.

Of this second rescue, Iggy says, "The main thing was that we both escaped from L.A. He was on top of the heap of L.A., and it was ruining him; I was on the bottom of it, the other end of the circle from him. We were so far apart we were together. If he walked out his door, they wanted to bend over and kiss his butt. He was absolutely the flashiest dude in Hollywood. And I was the most reviled street-scum in Hollywood of no fixed address. I was Top Cat with body odor. It was like, 'Oh no, here he comes, excuse me, I'm headin' out the door.'

"The wild part of that wild life — it only lasts a couple of years," Iggy goes on. "After that, it's just self-crucifixion, where you're not even wild anymore, you're just so whacked-out you can't get out the door anyway. I remember some dodgy bits, and it's scary and weird. I keep thinking that's why I'm in a good mood, basically 'cause I go, 'Wow!' I'm not without my wounds, you know, I got plenty of wounds and everything, but I am alive. So, it's kind of cool, you know."

I discovered Iggy Pop as a junior in high school, 1973. *Raw Power* first, then a rush to the cut-out bins for *The Stooges*. (*Funhouse* was unavailable at the time.) He was Iggy Stooge then. I knew of him because of the rock press, *Creem* and *Rock Scene* mostly. There was no FM rock radio of note near where I grew up — not that they'd have played the Stooges anyway.

I took to the Stooges right away, full blast on the crappy stereo in my bedroom. As a high school baseball player growing up in central Maine, I used to pump myself up for games with *Raw Power*, especially "Search and Destroy." The ultimate adrenaline rush. My friends and teammates didn't get it — they liked Chicago (the band) and whatever Top 40 stuff crossed their path. But that was OK, too: I was secure in my choices and my taste. Ferocious Iggy and the Stooges worked for me. I hit about .290 that year and played good D at first and third. Thanks, Ig!

I moved to Boston in 1978. Since that time, I've seen Iggy maybe a dozen times over the years with various bands, twice with a reconstituted Stooges.

Two classic Iggy onstage moments:

He's playing the Paradise Theater in Boston, December 8, 1980. (That's a significant date.) I'm reviewing for the *Boston Globe* and my notebook is full of scrawled praise, starred items, exclamation marks and the notation that Iggy took little Iggy out of his pants for a ride at one point. Don't think I'd seen any rocker do that before (although Lux Interior of the Cramps would grace us with little Lux several years later).

I go back to some friends' Beacon Hill flat to decompress post-show, planning to write at home later that night. The radio is on. WBCN DJ Oedipus breaks into the music to announce that John Lennon has been shot in New York. Shocked and stunned, I call my *Globe* colleague Steve Morse, and we both rush to the newsroom to bang out a Lennon tribute. No words about that Iggy show (or little Iggy's appearance) ever see the light of day.

Nearly a year later, Iggy is responsible for one of the most memorable encores — or maybe parting shots — I've ever seen. It's August 1981, at the Metro in Boston. Iggy and band had done a ferocious but short set — an hour, if that. Iggy was, once again, at the top of his game. He's riding high, in the midst of his successful post-Stooges comeback, touring behind *Party*.

Iggy leaves the stage. The crowd is going wild, screaming for the (let's face it, obligatory) encore. Iggy milks it for five minutes, all of us punters looking at each like "WTF? How much more applause do you need?" It's hard to keep clapping that long, especially when it's just a gambit. Then, he comes back onstage. All of us, collectively: "Whew. More Iggy. Let's keep rocking."

Wrong. Iggy strides to the mic, looks out at us and politely says, "Thank you, but fuck you, good night." I gotta say I was kinda pissed off at the time but I also gotta say, it was pretty punk rock. And I never forgot it.

This is also punk rock, though I suppose in hindsight it could be filtered through a different — some may call it "woke" — lens. I dunno. I'll just lay it out.

It was my first interview with him, a phoner in 1979. After about a half-hour, I'm doing the polite-ish thing, saying, "Hey, this has been great" — and it was, truly — "and I appreciate your time ..." Iggy says, "Hey, I'll talk to you as long as you want. I'm downstairs, but upstairs in my hotel room, there's this girl I've been fucking, and I just want her to leave." Ok, then. We continue talking. (I do not know if Iggy's stay-away strategy worked.)

Flashback to a memorable scene, one I was not present for, chronicled by the late Danny Sugerman in his book *Wonderland Avenue*. Somewhere in the early '70s, in the wee hours of the night, the aftermath of a big, debauched L.A. party, and Sugerman — the Doors' attaché and biographer — had to hose down one of his guests. That guest was Iggy, who was passed out, lying in a pile of garbage in his kitchen.

"I sprayed as much of the garbage up around Iggy as I could," Sugerman wrote. "Then, using him as a sort of rotating stop block and mop, I got the shovel out of the service pantry and piled everything into the sink where the garbage disposal was. I hosed him down and poured the rest of the Ajax out and wiped up the floor, holding him by the ankles. I can still see those blue specks dissolving in that platinum hair of his. I was almost done mopping up when he began to come to."

Sugerman hailed a cab, handed the driver $100, told him to drive as far north he could with the money and dump the lump of Pop out, wherever that was.

Two days later, Pop returned at 5 a.m., banging on the door — my image is of Fred Flintstone, locked out and yelling "*Wilma!*" — screaming, "I don't think it's funny; I'm not laughing, let me in."

That's pretty punk rock, too.

Nearly two decades after that little incident — and I'm sure it *was* little in the grand scheme of Pop-ish misbehavior — I ask Iggy about it at the Four Seasons.

"I don't remember any of that," he says. "I don't know if any of that's true or not, and it really doesn't matter. The main point is somebody else is talking about me.

"If I look at the things I did, the actual things I did, on one hand I think, 'Boy that really screwed up my career.' On the other hand, I have a feeling of great pride. Like, once I did an interview in a guy's office and, during the interview, I wanted to pee, but I didn't want to leave the room, so I peed in his wastebasket. You've met these kinds of guys; they need somebody to pee in their wastebasket sometimes."

He's looking a tad professorial — it might be the spectacles — as he leans back on his couch. Those specs have caused him some trouble. You know, public image vs. private Iggy.

"Outside, in the real world, I have to face that a lot," says Iggy, about matching his madman persona in the off-hours. "They expect me to be that way. I even had a thing last night. I was eating dinner with some people, and I was wearing my glasses and some guy who had a few comes up to me — 'What's with the glasses?!' — and I got mad. I nearly choked the guy."

Nearly. He didn't follow through.

Iggy was 43 when we talked. He'd stopped doing drugs and drinking to excess. He was traveling with his wife, Suchi Asano.

Iggy's had a patchwork career. Some albums clicked; others fell by the wayside. He certainly rode the proto-punk cred during the punk/new wave era. Early Iggy was him going against whatever grain there was to go against, beginning with a fist in the face of the hippie movement. Consider "TV Eye," "No Fun" and "I Wanna Be Your Dog" or the long, slow dirge that was "We Will Fall." There was *Raw Power*, of course. There was his synthesizer-based "Germanic" period — *The Idiot* and *Lust for Life* — when his textured collaborations with Bowie scored in my little world but missed the mainstream. Then a more listener-friendly trilogy for Arista: *New Values*, *Soldier* and *Party*.

"I think they were all running contrary to the fashion of the times," Iggy says of his records. "Then again, I thought all the albums were pretty good."

By his own account, it's been a wonderful, if strange, life.

"I've been spit at, I've been slugged, I've been egged," he wrote in his autobiography, *I Need More*. "I've been hit with paper clips, money, cameras, brassieres, underwear, old rags and with expensive garments and belts and things. I've been hit with, well, a slingshot. Yeah, you just get used to it after a while."

Action of that sort is documented on *Metallic KO*, a live album of the last Iggy and the Stooges concert (until a 21st century reincarnation), in Detroit, February 1974. (Actually, some of it was recorded in 1973.) Pop had been on a local radio station and challenged a biker gang called the Scorpions to come to the show and do their worst. They took him up on it, pelting him with bottles and eggs. As you can hear on the record, Pop rises to the challenge. "You missed me!" he taunts after an egg splats audibly. He and the Stooges stagger through an endless, profane "Louie Louie," upping the annoyance ante.

Iggy knows damage, much of it self-inflicted. He's shot himself full of heroin and speed, snorted mounds of cocaine, dropped acid, drunk himself into uncounted stupors, repeatedly cut his chest with broken glass and smeared it with peanut butter. He acknowledges the self-abuse was fueled, at least in part, by the drug abuse. In the late '60s, the Stooges were making a big, squalling noise, ranting about boredom and ennui. But having fun, too, and getting a music career started. Things took a big dive in 1970, Iggy says, after he discovered heroin.

Part of the problem of being Iggy Stooge was that fans wanted to party with the star; hence, they supplied the drugs. To some extent, the situation persists even now.

"Somebody will always give you something," he says.

The late Stiv Bators of the Dead Boys copped his style (terrifically, I must say) but Iggy remains one of rock and roll's most preeminent performers, a cobra always ready to strike. When we spoke in 1990, he was promoting *Brick by Brick*, an album (once again) positioned to crash the mainstream. Hot-handed Don Was, who produced breakthroughs for Bonnie Raitt and the B-52s, was at the helm for this one, too. Iggy thinks this is the album that might click, might kick him up a level. It has songs from the Iggy you know, like "Pussy Power" and "Butt Town," and one co-written with Slash called "My Baby Wants to Rock & Roll." Also: A lovely (!) pop duet on "Candy" with B-52s singer Kate Pierson. On "Neon Forest," Pop pictures himself sliding "like a lizard on my belly and back" and marvels that he hasn't "fallen through any cracks."

So, right now, Iggy has reasons to be cheerful: "I got a good record. I might as well laugh."

One of the album's subtexts is Pop's anger at rock and roll's many pretenders. In "Main Street Eyes," as opposed to "huge mainstream stars," he proudly declares himself to be "really what we are." In "I Won't Crap Out," he prophesizes that singers he calls "material" will "fade into dust" and compares them to "forgotten merchants of disgust."

"You hear these power ballads," says Pop. "I can't bear them. They dress up in these clothes where the image is 'We're tough, we're bad,' and then do a song where they basically suck up to radio. If the clothes really match the music, they should wear a little nursery-school outfit. Or maybe a leisure suit. I also get ticked off when it's these political pronouncements, and I don't get anything personal from the singer, 'cause they aren't going to tell me what's personal 'cause they're probably ashamed of what they're doing with their time or they're just too lazy to write about themselves. Yeah, war is bad. I agree. Now what?"

For Iggy, the answer is to keep writing personal songs, to rail against the complacency he sees around him. To assemble a band for a tour. To keep on keeping on.

"The rewards you get," he says, "feeling, like, wow, I'm gonna get up this morning and it's gonna be a hard day, and we're not in a totally secure situation here, but at least I feel like I'm living and I'm doing something that has some of me in it, learning from situations when you're in your forties, the same as I was when I was 18 ... I'm not gonna be the person who goes through their life like a lot of people do, I think, feeling like, 'They don't know me at work, I have to put on a mask, they don't know that my personality isn't used in my job.' I've always tried to fight against that. You know, in the House of Iggy, here's the way we do things."

At the end of 2010, I revisited the House of Iggy at Boston's House of Blues. This was a temporary thing, Iggy and the Stooges howling and ranting and raving like it was 1969 or 1973, or whatever raw and visceral era you'd care to reference. Iggy Pop, drummer Scott Asheton, bassist Mike (Minutemen/fIREHOSE) Watt, guitarist James Williamson and saxophone player Steve Mackay uncorked a set of proto-punk classics. (Williamson was the guitarist on *Raw Power* but did not join the re-formed Stooges until guitarist Ron Asheton's death in 2009.)

We talked before the gig.

Who'd have thought there would be a Stooges in 2010? I mean, who would have thought you would make it this far on the planet?

"I always assumed I would. I wasn't sitting around preparing for death, though a lot of people thought ..."

You did some fairly public, well-documented damage.

"[Americans] are still one of the most easily scandalized people on Earth. Who better than me could carry the scarlet letter? It's fine, and eventually what happened was I waited long enough and didn't die, and it's now become a plus. In the mid-'90s, large corporate groups wanted a little adventure in their lives and there I was. Everything changed at that point. When I had Don Was, an awfully nice guy, as a producer in the '80s, he was trying to help broker what finally happened, that society and I have kind of met halfway.

"That's what's happened. One item in his scheme was to get me to play *Farm Aid*, so I did *Farm Aid*, and I did an interview for CNN. I crossed over into American society that day. [The interviewer] only had one thing to ask me. He stared at me and said, 'So, are you gonna roll in broken glass today?' I politely didn't answer him. I wasn't gonna punk out on him, or say a mea culpa either, so there was some of that 'Everybody's done fine and we're all happy now.'"

I saw you play the main stage outdoors at South by Southwest *in the early '90s, and it seemed like a watershed moment: Iggy Pop singing these primal, decadent songs for kids, parents, everyone in the street.*

"It's a beautiful thing. I have the changing organization of the music business to thank for that. The advent of the music conference and of the festivals, especially in Europe, the advent of the Internet, the demise of the sort of record companies focused on a huge profit very quickly, and that are foolishly focused on the record business when it's always been a branch of show business anyway, which is a branch of corporate structure, which is a branch of banking. That's how it works. All that had gone down, and I hadn't bitten anybody lately. I have songs about that, people can enjoy works of art without completely fearing or loathing me. That's how I do it."

Whenever I've seen you, you've been so on. Amazing stamina. Still.

"There are some nights where the setup suggests that the show will be better if you use 75 percent. That doesn't happen too often. Generally, it's 100 percent-plus thing. It's just the way I do it; I wouldn't know any other way to go about it. It gets a little less physical with some of the songs. You want to portray the song correctly and try not to rip off people who came out to see you and paid some money."

And then the gig ...

"Does anybody wanna take a trip with me?" asked a shirtless, sweaty and giddy Iggy. Well, of course we did! "It's a 'Death Trip'!" he exclaimed, revealing the title of the hard, bluesy downward spiral of a song about to be played. Still OK!

His introduction got to the nub of what Pop and his four mates mined for 75 harsh but celebratory minutes at the House of Blues. That theme became crystal-clear during the last encore, "No Fun," in which a declaration of ennui never sounded so exuberant. There's nothing quite like creating joy from anger.

Cynics might have called Iggy and the Stooges circa 2010 a market-savvy re-creation: pre-punk nostalgia for grown-up punks and their kids. Well, sure, OK. But such cynicism would not have held up through the four-song opening salvo of "Raw Power," "Search and Destroy," "Gimme Danger" and "Your Pretty Face Is Going to Hell." It was explosion after explosion. On "I Wanna Be Your Dog," as Williamson played wah-wah guitar licks, Pop got on all fours and put the microphone cable in his mouth like a leash.

Skinny and muscular, with torso bulges and muscles where they maybe shouldn't be, Iggy was in constant motion. He was playful at times, inviting fans onstage to dance during "Shake Appeal" and saluting the folks in the plush seats with, "Hello, people in the balcony. You're comfortable and I can't smell you."

He didn't cut his chest with glass, smear himself with peanut butter or take little Iggy out for a ride. But he mimed shooting dope during "Penetration" and dove from the stage several times. He maintained focus while conjuring up the most chaotic and beautiful mess you could ever want. ◆

"As you get older ... why would you want to listen to what an 18-year-old is getting off on?"

Lou Reed

Lou Reed performing in Boston, 1980

PHOTOGRAPH BY MICHAEL GRECCO (GRECCO.COM/DAYSOFPUNK.COM)

LOU REED

I WAS AT SISTER RAY ENTERPRISES, Lou Reed's Manhattan office; the singer at his desk, me sitting across from him, tape recorder on. Reed was dressed, as usual, in a plain black T-shirt and faded blue jeans. It was 1996, the year the Velvet Underground was going into the Rock and Roll Hall of Fame, and he was musing about rock star mannequins at the Hall in Cleveland. Mick Jagger and David Bowie were there. I asked if he'd like to join the menagerie.

"Absolutely," he said. "Before I'm gone I'd like to see myself stuffed and on display. So I'm able to bitch and moan about the look."

There was some laughter. Along with everything else — and there were many, many sides to him — Reed was a funny sonofabitch. When I asked what was most misunderstood about him, he said, "I don't think people realize the sense of humor that's running through these things [songs]. To say my sense of humor is dry is in itself a dry joke. I think I'm very funny. I find most things very funny." Reed says his friends understand his upbeat moods. "People have always been happy that I've been happy. Maybe the attitude is, 'If Lou Reed can get it together, then who can't?'"

I first interviewed Reed by phone in 1980. It was the dawn of the Reagan era, and the fear was out there that the Cold War would become a nuclear conflagration. That we'd all be ashes. Soon. Reed talked about *U.S. News and World Report*'s recent "How Ready to Fight?" issue (he termed it "their annual end of the world issue") and likened the times' anxieties to the Bay of Pigs incident.

"Those of us who were in school" — in 1961, Reed was at Syracuse University, studying film and drama and being mentored by poet Delmore Schwartz — "were all ready to hop in cars and drive to the mountains and hide. Wasn't everything going to end then?

"If you sat down and seriously thought about things, you'd drive yourself nuts. This is New York, where a few weeks ago a guy got shot with a bow and arrow and there's a guy running around with a meat cleaver down on the subway. What can you say about that?"

I wasn't sure. But he answered his own question: "I think it at least shows some innovation on physical assaults on the citizenry — going back to more primitive weapons. Now, I would find it perhaps scary if they found out that somebody were laser-beaming people to death in the subway. A guy like that would be hard to catch."

He laughs. "Just little ashes, little bags through the subway, like 14 people in a little pooper scooper. Think about it. People say, 'You ought to put that on tape,' and I say, 'I do. I make records.'"

Back at Sister Ray, as we were talking, a punk-pop song came on the radio that was playing in the background. Fine, fine music from a (college) rock and roll station — and it was all right. Reed turned it up. It was "All Kindsa Girls," by the Real Kids, a Boston band that had a bit of Velvets in them. He lit up. Loved its primal energy. Asked me about 'em. I told him they were led by John Felice, who'd been an early member of the Velvet Underground-loving Modern Lovers alongside Jonathan Richman.

And then he talked about bipolarity, about depression. He said he tried to look at it like the hands on the face of a clock. The minute hand may be on six, he said, but inevitably it will come back to 12. Sounds simplistic, maybe, but I got it: Life is cyclical, not linear. I thought of a line in his "Pale Blue Eyes," "Down for you is up." I've used Lou's clock trick at times in my life.

Reed's drug and alcohol days were behind him. During a break from the interview, he asked if I wanted something to drink from the small fridge. Sure. He said he had nothing alcoholic, but there was Kaliber non-alcoholic beer. I politely said, "Oh, great, thanks." Reed's response was, and I'm paraphrasing, no, it's not "great," but it's what I have to drink. So, I had a Kaliber. He was right. It was not great.

Reed and I talked about his new album, *Magic and Loss,* in early 1992. "I keep getting told, 'This is too depressing,'" Reed said of the response to the record. "'It's depressing, it's depressing, it's about death, and it's depressing.' I must say, if you look at it that way, *Hamlet*'s synopsis would seem pretty down, too. *Macbeth* would seem pretty awful. I think of *Magic and Loss* as about love and friendship, and it's a very up thing. It is very emotional, also. These are not bad things. And I don't see why a contemporary work of music can't contain all these things. But when they do contain these things, you're thought of as being too cerebral, or too down.

"I remember reading this book by Saul Bellow where he was quoting Walt Whitman and he said, 'Until Americans and American poetry can deal with death, this is a country that has not grown up.' There might be something to be said about that."

I spent a fair amount of time with Reed and his music over the decades, first as a fan, then as a rock critic and feature writer. We did maybe a half-dozen interviews.

Lou and I, we got on pretty well. Once, we had a phone interview scheduled at the same time as a televised New York-New England football game. Remember in "Coney Island Baby," Reed told us he "wanted to play football for the coach." On the Velvets' *Live 1969,* he told a Texas audience it was wrong the Cowboys beat up so unmercifully on their opponent. We were both watching the NFL game (him in New York, me in Newton, Massachusetts) and Lou, a New York Jets fan (shock!), rang up and suggested we do the yak at half-time. I'd been thinking the same thing but would never have broached it. But we did. He called promptly when the first-half clock went to 0:00, and we concluded 20 minutes later when the game resumed.

But Reed did not always play nice with rock writers. Most famously, he battled Lester Bangs in a number of tendentious confrontations; in one 1975 *Creem* story, Bangs calls him "a completely depraved pervert and pathetic death dwarf and everything else you want to think he is. On top of that he's a liar, a wasted talent, an artist continuing in flux, and a huckster selling pounds of his own flesh."

When I asked Reed about that, he said he didn't care at all for the aggressive and accusatory type of article and interview. How about the portrait painted in *Rolling Stone* by Mikal Gilmore, who wrote that "Reed has created a body of music that comes as close to disclosing the parameters of human loss and recovery as we're likely to find"? Reed found it "very dark and foreboding. A poet that's going to burn out quietly at 5:30 in the morning with no one there to care. A very romantic notion that bears no relationship to the truth."

As an interviewee, Reed could be loquacious and witty; he could also be taciturn and desultory, I'm told. He could approach catatonia, though this only happened once in my presence. He was at the Rat club in Boston to promote a concert movie which would be screened after he chatted it up briefly. It seemed ridiculous. He mumbled laconically for a minute before being escorted upstairs to the offices with me and a few other inner-circle folks tagging along. He spent the "interview" time basically staring off into space, saying next to nothing.

When he went on the offensive, look out. In 1978, Reed took Robert Christgau (and by proxy the whole rock critic profession) to the whipping post on his rock and (acerbic) comedy live double LP, *Take No Prisoners*.

There were two earlier live albums that decade, both recorded at the same 1973 gig: *Rock n Roll Animal* (1974) and the 1975 sequel, called (imaginatively) *Lou Reed Live*. Some call them seminal; others think they're too hard-rock-y, Reed trying to wedge his music into the heyday of Alice Cooper (whose band his two guitarists, Steve Hunter and Dick Wagner, would soon join).

Reed had dissed those discs in the past, semi-joking, "It took me so long to tune, I was restricted to just shaving my skull, taking diet pills and just standing around wondering when the next train's coming up," but had come to consider them a "really good live album."

I especially liked the second disc, which features two songs I love from *Berlin*: "Oh Jim" and "Sad Song," 18 minutes in all. On the vinyl version, at the very end of "Sad Song," if you turn up the volume, a voice from the crowd yells, "Lou Reed sucks!" When I commended Reed on leaving that critique in, he said he'd never heard it before, knew nothing about it and, more than 20 years after the fact, got all pissed off at RCA (again). I felt like maybe I had done a public service.

First with the Velvets and then as a solo artist, Reed consistently wrote what he called "adult rock and roll." Sure, "Real Good Time Together" was about having just that, and he also wrote "Beginning to See the Light" and "Crazy Feeling." But many of the trips he took were darker and deeper. "Perfect Day," one of his signature songs, given new life in the movie *Trainspotting*, is the most bittersweet of uplifting tunes, where that perfect day — and no doubt it was, it's so resplendent — is cut with nuanced pain and doubt. It closes with a thought about her keeping him hanging on and a Biblical warning about reaping what you sow.

His songs often cut to the core. They could be brutal, vivid. The title track of *Street Hassle*, playing off the "Waltzing Matilda" riff, remains one of the most harrowing songs of his (or anyone's) catalog, a litany of casual violence and diffidence in three parts, featuring an uncredited spoken-word segment by Bruce Springsteen.

Reed said most of what he writes is "not totally autobiographical, more an amalgam of people." He wanted his songs, even the ones he delivered as protagonist, to be regarded as third-person narratives. "They're very personal," he explained, "done with a great deal of distance. I try to keep myself invisible."

But not everything he wrote harbored deep meanings. After all, in the title track of 1976's *Rock and Roll Heart*, he called himself dumb. "Sure," he said, responding to that reference and his own dumb-fun discography. "And 'I Love You, Suzanne.' I like that kind of stuff. My record collection is filled with it ... I had a song called 'Banging on My Drum' where that was the entire lyric. I can't play drums; I can't even keep the simplest beat on the drums. Cannot do it. I thought banging on my drum would be such fun. Air drums." (Some critics suggested the song was a metaphor for masturbation. Lou adamantly said no. It was just and only what he said it was.)

In 1992, Reed and I talked about good times and mature rock and roll. "I'm saying you can *have* a real good time. Just on a different level. Where is the rock equivalent of *A Streetcar Named Desire*? Is that such a far-fetched idea? Is that completely impossible? Why have any resistance to that? That's like having your cake and eating it. As you get older, be able to have that level of writing *plus* the fun of rock. Why would you want to listen to what an 18-year-old is getting off on?

"I like to have a broad palette. You don't want to just eat guacamole all day. Of course, I have that side to me. I'm just trying to combine my love for that stuff with love for other stuff and trying to bring it all together, so that I could listen to it. I do this stuff for myself in the first place; I'm the audience I'm aiming for, and I don't think I'm particularly different from the other people that are out there. There's nothing that special to me.

"I can only hope there are enough grown-up people out there that want to hear something meaningful along with all this other stuff out there. There's certainly room for a lot of different kinds of things, and I hope there's room enough for my little thing." He believed that his lyrics worked as poetry — "The bulk of them are meant to stand alone. That was the *raison d'être*. The fact that there's some rock going to it, that's great."

In 1989, Reed released *New York*, a striking comeback, his grittiest effort in nearly a decade and his best album since 1978's *Street Hassle*. Rather than a celebration of his town, it was a reckoning: the evils of crack, the corruption of patriotism, the selfishness of America, the horror of Vietnam, the Louis Farrakhan-generated rift between Jesse Jackson and the Jewish community. Also, poverty, drug addiction, racism, police brutality and child abuse. The album's single, "Dirty Blvd.," is an apt summation of the album's sound and vision, a scabrous swipe at the Big Apple. Reed saw the Statue of Liberty's utopian message now mocking poor immigrants. Those foreign stragglers? Kill 'em and dump 'em on that dirty boulevard.

New York is 58 minutes long, a record Reed intended to be heard as a movie is viewed: in one sitting. It's a concept album about the underbelly of New York and America; it's about characters caught in a trap; it's a tough, terse record boasting a thick, yet sparse, rhythmic two-guitar sound. Reed's voice is low and guttural, shot full of lacerating wit and brutal truths.

"They're the kind of topics that, unfortunately, are always going to be with us," Reed said. "All you have to do is look outside. It's not that way every day, but it's always in the back of your mind. You're always watching. I'm not making disposable records. I'm trying to make one you can play five years from now."

In the second half of the 1980s, Reed began what might be perceived as a public image makeover. He was a friend and supporter of Václav Havel, the playwright, poet and president of Czechoslovakia whose progressive movement was called "the Velvet Revolution." Havel credited the Velvet Underground as an inspiration in his country's revolt against communism.

Reed played at *Farm Aid* and was shocked that critics were shocked at his munificence, as if he were incapable of charitable impulses. Or that he wasn't, deep down, an asshole. Reed's musical tools may have been rudimentary and his voice limited in range, but he was expressive and, as he long insisted, his writing went in many different directions, from despairing all the way to upbeat. "I love lots of stupid stuff," he said. "There's a streak in me that's never progressed beyond [age] 11."

Reed's image rehab even got him a once-unimaginable invitation in January 1993. "I was at the White House for the inauguration of Clinton and Gore. I go to the vice president's house and there's Gore and his wife Tipper and these really nice kids that they have. They came over to me and said, 'Oh, we really love your records.' And then I meet Tipper, and she's shaking hands with me and looks at me and, in all sincerity, says, 'Lou Reed, How can we communicate with our children better?' Meaning generic children. I thought of saying back to her, 'Get rid of the Parents [Music Resource] Council, Tipper,'" a reference to the music-warning-label organization Tipper Gore helped found in the 1980s.

"And then I thought, this is a pointless conversation. She doesn't mean the question; I'm not here to give her a fucking answer; I don't want to get into a conversation that is completely pointless. What am I gonna say? Grab her by the hand and say, 'Tipper, Tipper, Tipper: Listen to the sound of my voice ...' You can't do it — you're in line shaking hands."

So, what did he say? "Something like, 'We would have to sit down and discuss something like that for a while over a bottle of Scotch and maybe some crack.'"

Aside from the biting humor and the harrowing portraits of life in the tangled city and in the hidden shadows, Reed was capable of letting go with simple, exultant rock ("Rock & Roll") and uplifting, hummable pop songs (most pronounced on the *Coney Island Baby* LP), presenting images that challenge the perception of a semi-wasted artist writing depressing songs about burned-out characters (maybe himself).

"What are you gonna do?" Reed asks with a laugh. "I always like that stuff, don't you? I don't know anybody who doesn't, except my jazz friends, and I think they really would if they thought about it."

Reed's posture has always been that of an outsider looking in, or, most often, etching chapters in the lives of fellow outsiders. The characters who inhabit Reed's songs are often losers or tarnished heroes confronting their demons.

I remember first hearing "Heroin" and thinking it (then and now) was the ultimate voyage into the abyss, a chilling masterpiece. I didn't hear it as a kid, when it came out on *The Velvet Underground & Nico* in 1967. I was 11. Even if I had heard it, I would have had no idea what to make of it.

Later, I did. Not from personal experience, but, yeah, I knew people who shot up and whose lives it destroyed or claimed. I wrote this about a 1980 show:

> Reed employed a precise, tension-fraught build. As the band interwove the pulsating rhythms and raced toward a frantic peak, Reed let go: "When that heroin is in my blood and that blood is in my head ... thank God I'm not aware." Reed presents the drug's siren-like allure and then drives home the horror with images of impending death. The attraction and the repulsion are captured eloquently.

Back with the Velvets, Reed's tense, nervous rhythms and unflinching portrayals of lives lived on the edge countered the hippie dream of the late '60s. Viewed as an anomaly or an annoyance back then, Reed found a wider audience after the dream crashed and burned. When punk rock burst into the open in the mid-'70s, Reed was perfectly positioned as its godfather. (Or at least one of them, along with Iggy Pop.) He understood the currency of nihilism and negative thought, of three chords and a take-no-prisoners attitude, of the joy in confrontation.

The Velvets never had what could be called a hit. Reed had to become a solo artist to reach the mainstream, at the end of 1972, with "Walk on the Wild Side," the laid-back and racy shock hit single from *Transformer.* His trans friends like Candy, who never lost her head, even when she was giving head? The "colored girls" singing "doo-doo-doo-doo-doo-doo-doo" over and over? In a Top 40 hit?! And this from a David Bowie-produced album, where Reed pushed the question of (his) sexuality. Who was gay, straight, bi? Who wasn't just a little bit confused?

Then *Berlin,* which Reed called his "massive disappointment" from a commercial standpoint. The haunting, stark concept album portrays two unsympathetic characters — a couple caught up in a web of drugs, sex, sado-masochism, betrayal and, finally, the woman's suicide, accepted with a so-what she-deserved-it shrug by her lover. It is not pretty, but it is grimly compelling and musically beautiful. Reed always liked playing *Berlin* songs in concert. "I thought the people who liked me for real would love to see that particular thing done live," Reed told me. "I wasn't kidding. It's one of my favorite albums. [*Berlin*] gives you a dose of realism, if I may dare use that word." In 2008, he recorded a live album of *Berlin* at St. Ann's Warehouse in Brooklyn.

The Velvet Underground began playing in 1964 and came to notoriety as part of Andy Warhol's Exploding Plastic Inevitable, part of the Factory scene of musicians, actors, artists and models. *The Velvet Underground & Nico* was named the thirteenth-greatest album of all time by *Rolling Stone*. Warhol "managed" the band, but Reed fired him. Reed also fired John Cale, his primary collaborator in the Velvets, and left the band in Doug Yule's hands for a final album, *Squeeze*.

In 1989, Reed got back together with Cale to create a tribute to Warhol, who died in 1987. Since then, Warhol has been the subject — some would say victim — of at least a half-dozen books: biographies, picture books and, of course, *The Warhol Diaries*, the artist's own gossip-drenched account of club-hopping and name-dropping.

Despite their differences, Reed was profoundly influenced by Warhol. He wanted to counter the way Warhol had been portrayed. Acting on Cale's suggestion, the duo spent two weeks writing furiously and came up with *Songs for Drella*. The 15-song set was performed four times at the Brooklyn Academy of Music in New York late in 1990; the two later recorded the work for a studio album.

"It's an antidote to the books that were coming," Reed said. "Painting him as such a piece of fluff, or as such a negative person, not giving him his due. We just wanted to show him in a positive light, as we really felt towards him." *Songs for Drella* is bittersweet, caustic, terse, wry, barbed — and yet affectionate, rich in both detail and emotion. Done in the spare, piercing style of the Velvet Underground, it is a complex, conceptual effort.

"It's emotionally honest, which is something I've tried to be on all my records," said Reed. "I mean, if there's a thing that is negative towards me I don't take it out. If it works in the context of the project and if it's true in the context of the project, I leave it in."

Indeed, Reed, who wrote the bulk of the lyrics, doesn't flinch when it comes to portraying himself in an unflattering light here. A hospitalized Warhol is dismayed because Reed won't visit him. Warhol complains, in "A Dream," a sequence spoken by Cale, about not being invited to Reed's wedding. He complains that he did a black-and-white album cover for Cale who then went and changed it to color, diminishing its value. Sighs Warhol, not for the first time on *Drella*: "You can't tell anybody anything."

"You'll find out a lot about John and I and Andy from this thing," said Reed. "All these relationships running through it. It's interesting because there's a lot of conflicting feelings.

"I was very turned on by him. I just thought he was one of the most amazing, intelligent, creative, catalytic people I've ever had the pleasure of coming into contact with, and that's why John and I were joined in this venture — out of our mutual respect for Warhol. What a great opportunity he afforded us. If you wanted to take advantage of the opportunities he gave you, you certainly could."

The portrait Reed and Cale etch here is not always that favorable. Their Warhol is not the glib, blithe trendy of the 1970s. Reed and Cale genuinely respected the man. What they do is invoke Warhol's ideas about art, such as his fondness for repetition. (A Velvet Underground tenet as well.) They also address Warhol's fears and self-doubts. In fact, perhaps the work's greatest achievement is that it humanizes a man many viewed, for better or worse, as just a shallow celebrity.

Here, we hear of his quirks and habits, his passion for work, his trauma when, in 1968, he was shot and nearly killed by Valerie Solanis. Reed and Cale use music that swings from snarling, machine-gun punk to swirling, classically inspired balladry. Some of it is historical; some of it is impressionistic; some of it is frighteningly fierce. In "It Wasn't Me," Reed takes Warhol's voice to target those who bought into a debauchery they thought he extolled. Reed spits out the verse, rejecting the role some saw him in. The closing line — Reed's simple, plaintive "Hello it's me, goodnight, Andy, goodbye, Andy" — is sincere and moving.

The next album Reed released, in 1992, was *Magic and Loss*. "It's not a negative album," Reed insisted. "It's not a bad trip or anything like that. It's like, how do you deal with these situations? And it's also, I might add, like a real celebration of friendship and the spirit of your friends. I object when people say this is a death album, that it's really down. It's about friendship and loss and how you deal with it, which I find particularly appropriate to these times, although that's not why I wrote it. That's in retrospect. Everyone who hears this record — well, not everyone, but everyone I come in touch with — suddenly tells me their story, their mother, their father, their sister, their friend down the block ... I made every effort to be realistic but also to give you what I call a positive viewpoint about the whole thing: that the record might be helpful.

"The people I'm describing were like giants in stature." The people in question are songwriter Doc Pomus, a close friend of Reed's, and a woman he has only identified as

Rita, possibly a Warhol associate from the '60s. "I learned a tremendous amount from them, and they live on through me. And that incredible humor that runs through the most appalling circumstances; that was an astonishing thing to witness and be a part of, and I want to communicate that to listeners."

As his friends were dying, he wasn't thinking about wresting art out of illness. "No, not at all, [but] I know from personal experience that everything I encounter is fair game. The turnaround came when I actually started writing, and when I saw what was coming out. That's when I realized what was going on. Then I had to make a decision: Did I really want to do this? I thought this could be misconstrued by a lot of people. This is not the kind of thing people want to hear about in the first place, in the United States, in particular."

In its sense of tragedy and narrative structure, *Magic and Loss* recalls *Berlin.* "It's a direct descendant," said Reed. "I just think, you've got somebody who's listening, who may be at home, alone, putting on headphones, or whatever, and you're telling them a story. It's illustrated with music, with the best lyrics I could write. It's an hour's worth of music about a subject where you've got a beginning, middle and an end. I feel I can go up against a novel or a stage play or a movie easily.

"They all have funny things," Reed noted of *New York*, *Songs for Drella* and *Magic and Loss*, picking out "Harry's Circumcision: Reverie Gone Astray" from *Magic and Loss* as an example. It's about a botched suicide, based on a real-life attempt by Reed's college roommate Lincoln Swados. In the song, Harry slits his throat. "But he lives to tell about it." And it hurts him to laugh.

"Right!" said Reed. "I guess that's what people mean when they say I have a dark sense of humor. Maybe they mean things like that."

Give Reed an open field in an interview and he'd make a mad dash to talk about tools of the trade — amps, pickups, guitars. During the interview in his office, a call came in: a friend had located an ancient amplifier Reed wanted. His spirits soared. The sound of his music was as important to Reed as the shape of his ideas. "We used a lot of technology to make a very, very well-recorded raw album," he said about *New York.* "And that's all I'm willing to do. The kind of a sound that's based around wood and tubes and power — thickness. The sound of *New York* is a vintage hot rod.

"If something doesn't sound right, it hurts me. Literally. So, I have trouble listening to pianos sometimes, which may sound odd coming from someone in the Velvet

Underground, which was doing dissonance and everything, but dissonance is one thing, and being out of tune is another. I like being in tune."

VU didn't come up much in my conversations with Reed, partly, no doubt, because Reed felt he'd said his piece. And those were different times. Reed didn't even own an original copy of *The Velvet Underground & Nico.*

As respected and influential as Reed and the Velvets have become to generations of punk and post-punk rockers, Reed's sales figures have never come close to matching his critical acclaim, and radio airplay was hard to come by. It mattered to him. "I've gone through this all my life," he says, "going back to the Velvet Underground. That's the way it is, and I find it difficult, to tell you the truth."

Was the Velvets' legacy ever a burden? "Not really. What could be a cooler thing to be a member of? It's like playing for the New York Jets when Namath was there."

There are those who consider the Velvet Underground the heyday and Reed's solo work as anticlimactic. How does Reed respond to that? "I just remind them that every lyric that was ever sung by the Velvet Underground was written by me."

PBS did a feature on Reed for its *American Masters* series in 1998, putting him in the company of Martha Graham, James Baldwin and Lena Horne. I had to ask: Are you an American master? "That's not for me to say. I'll leave that to others."

Was there a part of him that thought PBS attention marked a change in the way popular culture is perceived?

"Maybe."

The ultimate tribute, of course, is the many offspring of the Velvets: bands like Luna, the Feelies, Bizarros, Dream Syndicate, Television, R.E.M, Strokes, Spacemen 3, Modern Lovers, Violent Femmes, Yo La Tengo and, of course, Brian Eno, credited with a famous quote that if only 30,000 people bought the Velvets' records, all 30,000 went on to start bands.

Of his recognition in the punk and post-punk world, Reed said, "If it is true, it's very flattering. Some bands, I hear the Velvet thing, something from a certain period, and I say, 'That's really great. It seems such an obvious way to get a two-guitar, bass-drum thing going. Two incredibly — or even one — really cool guitar parts and it's not R & B. But it's also not white bread.'"

The Velvet Underground, with guitarist Sterling Morrison and drummer Mo Tucker, reunited for a European tour in 1993, but Reed and Cale suffered a falling-out that derailed plans for an American continuation. (Morrison died in 1995. Nico died in 1988.)

"We said we would do it till it wasn't any fun," Reed said of the reunion. "There were some people [in America] that were silly enough to say, 'He's doing it for the money, and we'll wait for you to come here.' I said, 'I'm telling you; it's not being done for money, it's being done for fun.' At a certain point, it didn't become fun — we all disagreed [on issues] — and we all said, 'We don't have to do it.' So, we agreed to disagree and went our separate ways."

In 1997, Rhino did a wonderful re-release (*Fully Loaded Edition*) of the Velvets' 1970 album *Loaded*. Reed's last album with the group contains two of the best-known VU songs, "Sweet Jane" and "Rock & Roll." The Rhino version added a second disc of demo and alternate versions of songs, plus tracks released only on the expensive *Peel Slowly and See* boxed set.

Reed's reaction? "I haven't thought about it. There's been no reason for me to think about it. It's a long time ago. I don't even know what these tracks are that are re-released. All the Velvets' records are a little bit different, so I don't really rank them. It would never occur to me to rank them." Also, Reed left the group just before *Loaded* was released. "There was this terrible, terrible management problem going on. That's why I have such a problem with it."

"Sure, there's an amazing collection of songs on there," he allows. But it was a period in which Reed went through some personal trouble, perhaps a breakdown of sorts. "Seriously," he says, testily, "I don't want to talk about it, and it's precisely because of these kinds of questions. I don't mind talking about the music, but the personal stuff ..."

Everyone loves the Velvets now, but he thought they had been unfairly ripped in the past. "To me, there's a degree of vindication involved," Reed says. "Going back to Year One, being vilified ... Just being given credit for what it really was, as opposed to what people accused it of being." At the time, he continues, his work was considered "a very negative thing — the lyric matter and all the rest of it."

Although he has never been known as a people-pleaser, Reed says, of the songs he plays live, "I always want to satisfy the faithful because I know when I go to see people, I like to hear them do stuff I know also." But the last time I'd seen him, he'd omitted two longtime staples, "Rock & Roll" and "Heroin."

"It's interesting what people think are staples," muses Reed. "One man's staple is another man's spit. You never know. I enjoy playing them all. But it'd be fun to do a tour where I did a bunch of [obscurities]. I'd like to do 'The Bells' — things I don't think anyone wants to hear about. It's one of my favorite lyrics." At any rate, he says, "It's just rock and roll."

Late in life, Reed found happiness with performance artist and musician Laurie Anderson, who he married in 2008. One of their bonds: She was also a gearhead.

"Laurie can run a [mixing] board; I couldn't," says Reed. "There's other things I'm into. She's into effects and keyboards and all that; I'm into guitars and — not really extreme effects, but reverb and all that. We do talk gear. What we do more than that is play together. Melodic and heartfelt."

The last time I saw Reed play live, he was accompanying Anderson for a music and spoken word show at Boston's Institute of Contemporary Art in 2009. It was pretty much her show; he was the sideman. Reed, then 67, sat on a chair stage left and played electric guitar and synthesizer, complementing Anderson's violin and voice. With vocoder and synthesizer, they veered between a cacophonous storm and disquieting ambience, like the creaking of a ship's masts. If music had a color, this would be dark gray. There was no banter between them, little chat with the crowd. No hits. (Meaning no "O Superman" for her or any of many choices for him.) They wove 13 or so stories and songs together. One piece bled into another. Noise gave way to calm and then it reversed itself. There was no applause until the work was completed.

The two shared the spotlight effortlessly, often overlapping vocals and instrumental leads. In "Fenway," Anderson spoke of "an old married couple that always hated each other." When they got divorced in their nineties, people asked "Why not earlier?" They answered: "Well, we wanted to wait until the children died."

The couple certainly had a complementary sense of humor.

Reed's thoughts about Anderson were woven through *Set the Twilight Reeling*, his 17th solo album. There's an impossibly infectious, upbeat song called "HookyWooky." It's all fireworks and romance, until it isn't: Suddenly, the singer is threatening to push all of her ex-boyfriends off the roof. Good old Lou. But "Adventurer" praises Anderson's spirit, and it would seem her muse floats throughout the album. It's almost *Songs for Laurie.*

"This is dedicated to Laurie, but not necessarily about her," said Reed. "I have seen the theme of the album as being about change, growth and how good that is. It's all transformation. I was actually thinking of calling it *Transformer Squared,* and then I regained control of myself."

Late in his career, Reed told me, "I think the singing is improving and the guitar playing with it, and the ability to differentiate between tones, and trying to craft a lyric. I wouldn't want to come off as glib or trendy or secondhand, but I'm out there trying to chisel something out of that rock of words available to us. Some of what I like is using words common to all of us and that is the challenge to me: to be able to use them so it can go directly to your heart. Hope that doesn't sound pretentious."

I happened to buy a CD of *The Velvet Underground Live 1969* at a Newbury Comics record store in Boston a couple of weeks before Reed's death on October 27, 2013. I've had it on vinyl for years, but the uncontrollable urge hit, and I wanted to pop the CD in the car deck immediately. So, it was coincidentally there right before he died and then, not coincidentally, for a long while after.

Reed once described *Magic and Loss* to me as "painful writing." This chapter, too, was painful writing. Necessary, painful writing. Reflections on an artist who was part of my life for over 40 years, someone high in my pantheon.

The last song I heard before learning of his death was the ten-minute-plus "Ocean," its swelling chords and gentle brushes; Reed gently singing about those waves lapping the shore. Eternally. Flowing over rocks that have been there forever. ◆

“I’ve been in a bad mood since I’ve been in New York. More or less: there have been days of exception.”

Nico

Nico and the author backstage, 1982

PHOTOGRAPH BY SUSAN WILSON

NICO

NICO AND I ARE SITTING in the second-floor cocktail lounge of a Howard Johnson's in Cambridge, Massachusetts. It's June 1979, and she's drinking an afternoon breakfast of Bloody Marys and beer. It's a dreary, overcast day; raining off and on and threatening to do so again, but we're sheltered in here. The friendly bartender brings a dish of cheddar cheese goldfish and turns on the TV for the benefit of the half-dozen or so businessmen at the bar. We can all be happy in our private asylums.

Nico has just woken up. She and her young boyfriend/acoustic guitarist Lutz Graf-Ulbrich spent the night here after performing at the Paradise Theater in Boston; too exhausted to take the late train back to New York, they'll travel today. Nico looks better than she did last night, but she's uneasy about her appearance. Upon noticing the photographer I've brought along, she says, "I have to really look at myself to see if I'm right."

Nico, who was born Christa Päffgen in 1938, doesn't do many interviews, and I didn't really expect her to do this one. I'd called before last night's concert and asked if we could meet briefly after the show. Hesitatingly, she consented. When I went backstage, however, I met a closed dressing room door and word that Nico was doing an interview and didn't want to be disturbed. Perplexed, I waited. When she emerged 20 minutes later, I introduced myself, reminding her that we'd arranged an interview. An expression of alarm spread over her face. "*You're* Jim ... I thought ... *he* was!" she said, gesturing to her unknown interviewer. "Then who is *he!?*" She sounded at once both perturbed and horrified. I couldn't help her.

So, we're meeting today. "I woke up three times," she says, "and the last one was the best — I remained in a good mood. Sometimes you wake up and it's really terrible ... as if ... the whole thing would collapse."

The hour or so I spent with Nico was not the deep dive interview I might have plotted out had this been later in my career. And probably better for it. I didn't have a notebook with bullet-pointed topics — modeling, being one of Andy Warhol's superstars at the Factory, her days as the Velvet Underground's sort of co-lead singer, her volatile relationship with Lou Reed. Nor did I ask her about heroin. I mean, I knew, but I didn't *know*. It probably scared me to think about bringing it up. This was more an open-ended conversation, trying to follow where she was going after I tossed out a thought.

She speaks as she sings — in a deep mournful voice that is simultaneously expressive yet detached. She brings a sense of tragedy to many of her ideas, from the serious and profound to the innocuous.

"I'm so happy that you remember me," she told the audience at the start of the previous night's concert, seated at her harmonium, an odd keyboard-and-pedal-pushing instrument that produces wheezing sounds not unlike a bagpipe.

Nico was not at her best. She made a lot of mistakes: forgetting lyrics, notes and passages, stopping songs in mid-stream to start them over. "I don't know where the notes are," she said, after aborting one song.

"I thought I was a total failure," she says, but I can't bring myself to agree. In some odd way, her mistakes reinforced her vulnerability; it made me warm to her. Her music walks the borderline between sensuality and gloominess and somehow, when she broke down and joked (however sadly) that she'd forgotten this or that, it was not disappointing — it was endearing.

She created a fascinating atmosphere in the club. After the applause abated, the club fell silent — no glasses clinked, no one chatted — the crowd unwilling to shatter the fragile aura she'd constructed. She left the audience mesmerized, discomfited and a bit awed. And, maybe, a little afraid for her.

Nico has not released an album since *The End* in 1974. I ask her what she's been doing since.

"You want me to tell you what I do every day?" she replies. "I've been hesitating, I guess," she says. "I was under contract to some terrible guy who wanted a percentage of my next record, although I had nothing to do with him anymore, besides *The End*. I had to wait until that was over."

And is it over now? "Yes, I'm going to do this record, *Drama of Exiles*, and I have to do it quick ... or else something might happen, because I've waited four-and-a-half years to do it."

I wait for her to expound, for some clarification. But she's stopped talking. Her mind has drifted elsewhere.

Will it be coming out soon?

"I have to make it first. It's a very slow procedure. A woman from Elektra who's an A&R person ... I'm seeing her this week. Elektra wants to re-sign me — that's great. I have one record out with them, *The Marble Index*. It has been re-released nine years later." She smiles.

I ask if she'll be working with her former Velvet Underground bandmate John Cale again and the sadness returns. "It depends if he wants to, because he's a little angry at me. I didn't show up at the Carnegie Hall benefit concert because, first of all I wasn't on the poster, and I was supposed to sing only one song which I thought was too little, and then I was really sick, too. He was very angry; he still is. Says I'm not reliable ... so I have a bad reputation now."

After almost a year in Berlin, Nico has been living in New York for a little over two months. "I hate New York," she says, but amends that a moment later. "I don't love it, but I don't hate it either." She doesn't resolve the contradiction; I'm not sure she knows she made one. Silence.

What kind of mood are you in these days? Do you see yourself as basically a happy person? (This may be the dumbest question in my rock writer career, but there you go.)

"My mood has been ... grouchy," she answers, spending over a minute searching for the right adjective. "I've been in a bad mood since I've been in New York. More or less. There have been days of exception." I look at her encouragingly, as she pauses. She smiles ever so slightly and says she's enjoying the cheddar cheese goldfish crackers.

Did she enjoy working with Eno on *The End*?

"He came in and by the time I realized that he was there he was already out again. He did things so quickly. He is so well-disciplined; he gets up every morning at seven even if he went to bed at five. Brian is very stoic; he doesn't allow himself any pleasure."

She becomes more animated. "We have the same ideas about life. We are both infatuated with war. It's much more exciting when there's war going on — at least it's not boring." She laughs a bit and I look at her, puzzled.

Finally, I come out with, "But how can you justify ..." She cuts me off. "I lived through the war when I was little. I know some of it ... by the time the war was over I was already seven. My father was killed in 1943 by the Nazis." (Her father, Wilhelm Päffgen, was recruited into the Wehrmacht and killed in 1942. Her mother, Grete, worked in a munitions factory.)

I'm reminded of "Deutschland Über Alles," the 19th century German unification song that became the Nazi anthem, a song she has recorded and still sings. It was her encore in Boston, where she introduced it by saying, "Whether you like it or not, I'm going to do another German song. That doesn't mean I'm a fascist."

"It's such a pretty song," she tells me. "It's something, I don't know — a secret, I guess. Like nostalgia. Something you never knew because your grandparents and your parents were against that very deeply."

Does she think people understand her intent?

"I think so ... or else they wouldn't clap. That's all they want to hear in New York. There are so many Jewish people around, and they like it very much. I have no reason to like the Nazis at all. I know it's 'Deutschland Over All' but I think it's ridiculous to sing those lyrics."

She recalls one instance of hostility. "In Berlin, they went insane. They wanted to nail me to a cross. Isn't that insane? I mean they maintained the Reichstag instead of blowing it up. They made a museum out of it. It doesn't make any sense being hostile against that song."

Does she ever have the urge to write in a more optimistic manner? (Second stupidest question.)

She doesn't exactly answer, but says, "That's how you get when you are writing and you have lived through the war — always writing about gloomy things. There's a sort of happiness about sad things."

She says she wants to get young punk musicians to play on *Drama of Exiles*. She wanted Sid Vicious to play with her. "But he can't play for me now." (Sid had died a few months earlier.)

She wore a Sid badge during the show. Did she know him? "No, but I've met his kind. Jim Morrison was very much like that — very self-destructive. He was coughing blood, that's why he couldn't sing anymore. But he was a great singer, no?"

I nod.

I suppose this is where I could note — though it wasn't part of our talk — that the famous men she took to her bed included Morrison, Reed, Bob Dylan, Iggy Pop and Alain Delon.

Nico is applying makeup for the picture-taking. "I find it very tiresome to be famous," she says.

What part?

"The part where you get drunk and you can't get up the next morning," she laughs with a mixture of amusement and sadness.

After the pictures are taken, it's time to go. I help her with her gear and say goodbye. I wonder if I got to know her and conclude that, no, I didn't. I only caught glimpses, scratched a surface that seems to be impenetrable. I think of Bruce Springsteen and "Candy's Room": "There's a sadness hidden in that pretty face, a sadness all her own, from which no man can keep Candy safe."

And then it's back out into the rain and Boston traffic.

Three years later, the second and final time I saw her, she played a Harvard Square club called Jonathan Swift's, backed by a four-piece rock band. When we spoke between sets, I reminded her of our last encounter.

"It was horrible," she said. "I was really ready to kill myself."

She's better now. Though still heavy and draped in black, she's dropped 40 pounds and her famed high cheekbones are visible again. "Age doesn't mean anything," she said. "People just aren't strong enough to stay in shape."

Drama of Exile, the album she'd talked about trying to make for five years, was finally released in 1981, and that brought her up. Which makes me think of the Velvets' "Pale Blue Eyes" and its "Down for you is up" line. But even if everything was still shaded gray or black, it was a much more confident set. The band put a piercing rock and roll kick into "One More Chance," "Saeta" and three from the Velvets catalog: "All Tomorrow's Parties" and "Femme Fatale" (both of which she sang with the group) and "Waiting for the Man."

Still, the hypnotic rockers drew into an extended, downward spiral. "Focusing on running down the drain / And those tears carved inside your brain," Nico sang in "Sixty Forty." Her vocals lagged a bit behind the band's pulse.

Near the end, the band exited and Nico played three songs along with her harmonium, from which she wrenched funereal tones. "Can you dare to be insane?" she boomed as waves of chords rolled out.

She closed the night with "The End." How could she not? Less menacing than her old flame's version, more somber. (No one did somber like Nico.) Maybe it had become as much her signature song as "Femme Fatale."

Backstage, a fan gave her a copy of one of her albums to sign. She did so, writing: "Do or die, Nico."

She died, in July 1998, on vacation. She was on the Spanish island of Ibiza and fell from a bicycle, suffering a brain hemorrhage in the process. It was about a decade after her final concert, in West Berlin. She had a bad headache and was heading into town for cannabis she hoped would alleviate it. Nico was 49.

In late 2022, I was able to track down Lutz Graf-Ulbrich and ask, via e-mail, about his time with Nico.

"I saw Nico for the first time in Paris in March '72," he says. "We had the same manager, Assaad Debs. He was managing my krautrock band, Agitation Free. When I saw Nico performing it blew my mind. Never before had I seen such a performance; it was pure magic, and I was stunned. Her voice, the harmonium, her attitude, her beauty. Everything was so unique. It was fantastic. I fell in love with her right away. We later met a couple of times, and [then], at a come-together at Assaad's parents' house, she asked me to come with her in another room and we had a short chat. I was flattered that she had chosen me, but it took quite some time until we really lived together.

"In autumn 1974 we both played at a festival. I was living in France and performing solo. We had a good time together and she invited me to the hotel. That is when it all started. Next day she invited me to go to Paris with her and to stay at her apartment, where she was living with [film director] Philippe Garrel. From then on, we met from time to time, but I still did not live with her, as I had gone back to Berlin. But we met there when she played with Cale and Eno and later in 1975 in France again when we played at a festival in Arles together with Ash Ra Tempel and Can."

So, you were both accompanying her on guitar and becoming her boyfriend?

"Exactly. I was still playing with Ash Ra Tempel and living in Berlin [and with] Nico in Paris. But that changed in 1976 when I decided to quit Ash Ra Tempel to live and play with Nico. We toured and lived in Paris and Berlin, in Amsterdam and Ibiza and traveled around quite a lot."

How long did the musical/romantic relationship last?

"It ended in summer 1979 when we had a physical fight in our room at the Chelsea Hotel, where we had stayed for five months. I left New York and went back to Germany."

Did you maintain contact with her?

"Yeah, back in Germany I produced my first solo album and invited Nico to sing 'Reich der Träume.' She came to Berlin and stayed a while and we became good friends until her end. We met once a year from then on."

From what I know about her history and what she told me, she battled heroin addiction. Where was she in that fight when you were with her?

"She just started it at that time. She offered me heroin, [and] I refused to take it [for] quite a while. But when you love somebody you want to join them, which I did and became a junkie for one-and-a-half years. She loved heroin and did not want to stop taking it. It made her calm down, as she was complaining [about having] too many thoughts all the time."

What did her music mean to you?

"I loved her songs and the way she was performing. It was so unique. She really had created her own style, and that is a huge achievement. There is no other Nico around. With me as guitar player, she could sing songs like 'Femme Fatale' or 'All Tomorrow's Parties' or 'I'll Keep It With Mine.' We even played 'You're Lost Little Girl' by the Doors, but unfortunately there is no recording. I do not listen to music much, and whenever I hear Nico's music it is so heavy it is quite exhausting. It goes so deep, like no other artist."

Did you get the sense of shared sadness we as an audience got from her?

"Yes and no, I think she could be quite funny onstage even [if] her songs are sad. But all the concerts I played with her were great, even when she broke down or was too drunk to perform. It was always dramatic, always powerful and strong."

Was there any sense of uplift for you?

"I think that was the other way around. I am a quite positive thinking and acting person, but to live with Nico was pretty exhausting." ◆

“The ‘rocking’ Eno is not as successful an entity as you’d think. It turns out history has made it look like the rock records were the hobby.”

Brian Eno

Brian Eno relaxing in his New York hotel room, August 1974

PHOTOGRAPH BY LINDA D. ROBBINS

BRIAN ENO

IN 2010, THE NEW YORK BAND MGMT RELEASED an ode to Brian Eno called, well, "Brian Eno." In it, Andrew VanWyngarden sang, "Dipping swords in metaphors, yeah/But what does he know?/We're always one step behind him/He's Brian Eno, Brian Eno."

What does he know? A few answers will be forthcoming but, trust me, it's a sliver of the answer. Eno knows lots.

The name he was given at birth, on May 15, 1948, in Woodbridge, Suffolk, England, was Brian Peter George St. John le Baptiste de la Salle Eno.

Pretty much everyone just calls him Eno, even *New York Times* crossword puzzlers. (*Especially* those crossword puzzlers.) They may not know who he is exactly, but they sure love cryptic clues like "One backward musician?" In 2020, *Times* crossword columnist Deb Amlen reported that his surname had appeared in the paper's puzzle 290 times.

There have been so many Enos over the years, so many variations and offshoots, it can make your head spin. As a musician (not that he calls himself that), producer or whatever role he's playing, Eno has had a hand in the music world pie for more than five decades. I am tempted to write "pop music" or "avant-garde music," but, really, the word is simply music, and Eno's music encompasses a wide range, from the most dissonant to the most calming. There's his work with early Devo and Ultravox to superstar mid-career bands like U2 and Coldplay, the electronics he added to Peter Gabriel's

Full Moon album in 2023. Add to that his videos, his environmental installations, his lectures, his books ...

But first there was Roxy Music.

Eno was the band's self-professed non-musician. He handled "treatments" (running instruments through tape recorders and synthesizers) and tweaked the sound. It's commonly thought he supplied the weirdness, and I'm sure he was a main factor, but Roxy was (and remained) primarily Bryan Ferry's vehicle.

Onstage, Eno was a flamboyant presence, a visual foil/equal to Ferry. (Not that I saw him with Roxy, just clips online. Few American audiences did: Eno did one U.S. tour with the band in 1972 and played his last show in York, England on July 2, 1973.) So, he was long gone by my first time seeing Roxy, on the *Country Life* tour in 1975. And, as Eno stepped back from the stage many years ago, I have never seen him perform live music at any point in any context.

But we've talked. Oh, how we've talked. Eno takes the art of conversation seriously. He's expansive, analytical, witty.

Let's start with those first two albums, the ones Eno is on. *Roxy Music* and *For Your Pleasure* were (a very pleasant, very jarring) shock to my system in the 1970s. As were Eno's first two solo albums, *Here Come the Warm Jets* and *Taking Tiger Mountain (by Strategy).* They were albums that, should you put them on your dorm room turntable, would send fans of more conventional rock on their way. Trust me. Drop the needle on the whooping and wailing mindfuck "Driving Me Backwards" and you'd drive most everyone out frontwards.

Eno's early work was strange and vaguely subversive, dissonant in many places, parts of songs cobbled together. It was beyond Roxy's retro-futurism. There was no genre I could peg it to. Hell, no known universe. Where did all these diverse, sometimes contrary, ideas about music — sound and vision — come from anyway?

"I didn't sit and scratch my head about it," Eno told me in 1990, speaking of those early sound collages (or maybe collisions). "Or anything else I've done. At the time, I wondered why nobody thought of doing it before — it's so obvious. I've nearly always had that feeling. Generally, it hasn't happened, but it all seemed terribly obvious to me."

Eno set the course for much of what would become post-punk and post-modernist music: The first rule is there are no rules. Anything goes: whimsy, dissonance, horror, sarcasm, haunting subtexts. Snakelike guitars, clacking typewriter rhythms, gliding soundscapes. Gleeful, engaging, everything-but-the-kitchen-sink stuff. Generally, when musicians are credited on albums, their instruments are listed. Eno was once memorably credited "Eno [played] Eno." As in, something/anything.

In a special Roxy Music edition of *Uncut* magazine in 2022, Peter Watts wrote about Eno "stretching himself and discovering the full range of his talents," celebrating a different genre and "perfecting a sound, perverting the arrangement and then moving swiftly on." That pretty much nails it. As Eno himself said in 1973 to Geoff Brown, "I'm interested in things being absurd, and there was something really exciting in Roxy at the time. We were juxtaposing things that didn't go naturally together." That philosophy clearly carried over to *Here Come the Warm Jets* and *Taking Tiger Mountain (by Strategy)* and, to a somewhat lesser extent, *Before and After Science* and *Another Green World* — Eno's first four "rock" albums.

To glam-rockers and art-rockers of that '70s era, he was the sound sculptor and self-styled satyr who gave Roxy Music its space-age flavor and polysexual aura. To the post-punk generation of the early '80s, he was the influential artist who'd discarded pop's rules and created a new proto-new-wave musical language.

He could spin an elliptical tongue-twister as well as Bob Dylan, although Eno's lyrics were crafted more to exploit phonetics and alliteration than to have any linear meaning or poetic waxing. "Third Uncle," for instance, pulses and throbs maniacally, a hurtling blur of flatly joyous declarations-cum-nonsense. Eno sings about what is "there": "Shoes, boots, Turks, fools, lockers, schools," etc. and ends verses with "Then there was you." Finally, he sets it all afire.

Consider "King's Lead Hat": "King's lead hat put the poker in the fire / It will come, it will come, it will surely come." Means nothing right? But "King's Lead Hat" is an anagram for Talking Heads, the song a coded tribute. He met them in 1977, at a Ramones / Talking Heads gig, and went on to produce or co-produce three of their albums: *More Songs About Buildings and Food* (1978), *Fear of Music* (1979) and *Remain in Light* (1980). In 1981, he helped usher David Byrne (and, by extension, Talking Heads) into world music and found sound with the Eno/Byrne collaboration *My Life in the Bush of Ghosts.*

"It was quite controversial at the time," muses Eno. "I remember the *Village Voice* accusing us of being cultural imperialists for using other people's work within our own. As if we had stolen from these poor natives and were going to make a bundle out of it. Funny enough, they did that on the same page where they reviewed a black punk rock group from the South Bronx who they were complimenting for having stolen the currency of white punk. I thought, 'This is real inverted snobbery.'"

He collaborated with David Bowie for three killer avant-garde/pop albums in the 1970s, *Low*, *"Heroes"* and *Scary Monsters*. He recorded four instrumental albums with Robert Fripp. He scored a hit with the English band James's *Laid* album in 1992. In 1997, I thought his collaboration on the same group's *Whiplash* might be Eno's last foray into the field.

"He just sets up an environment that is really creative, open, not critical," James singer Tim Booth told me. "He's very experimental, very playful. He's got a great sense of humor and he's also quite a grumpy old man. We tease him a lot. His highs and his lows are quite extreme. He's a very easy guy to love and to loathe." Booth said he would work with Eno again in a heartbeat.

Eno will take some credit for kicking open doors for many a new wave and post-punk band.

"It's thrilling," he told me the first time we spoke, on the phone from his London studio in 1990, "because it vindicates the position I took back then. Everyone said, 'Well, it's nice, but you can't sell this kind of music. Where do you find it in the shop?' There was every argument advanced why this wouldn't be any kind of success."

By then, the wild days were mostly in the rear-view mirror. He was certainly more interested in talking about the present and the future than the past. Yes, he was still doing rock (or at least rock-ish) albums — songs with vocals (*Nerve Net* and a rather mellifluous 1990 collaboration with John Cale called *Wrong Way Up*) — but his emphasis was primarily elsewhere, creating ambient music himself and producing rock or post-rock for others.

The ambient journey started early. Eno reckons his best-selling album is 1975's *Discreet Music*, a soothing instrumental release that inadvertently ushered in an era of new age music.

Discreet Music, which includes Pachelbel's Canon in D Major as its second side, was a startling break from what people knew from Eno, that barbed, topsy-turvy rocker and tongue-twisting wordsmith. It was a calming album from an artist associated with chaotic storms. It has sold, guesses Eno, 200,000 copies. "I don't know, actually."

After that, he launched a series of electronic ambient records, music which he once defined "as ignorable as it is listenable." The first, *Music for Airports*, did actually play at LaGuardia Airport in New York at one point. I've listened to it for years to wind down or mellow out.

One of his related projects from that era was Jon Hassell's *Fourth World Vol. 1: Possible Musics* (1980), which he and Eno co-produced. I had coffee with the brilliant but somewhat obscure trumpeter in the *Boston Globe* cafeteria in 1982. Hassell compared his association with Eno to chemotherapy in that it was beneficial but came with Eno's celebrity, which was inadvertently painful to an accomplished musician. He said the "cancer" it cured was "obscurity, and the side effect [was] always being linked with him." Hassell, who died in 2021, said he still considered Eno a friend, but added, "I'm not going to devote 30 years of musical study and come in and act like I'm on equal terms with a guy who's been to art school, picked up a guitar and has an interesting conceptual attitude."

Eno likes some of the offshoots he inspired — "the backgrounds, the beautiful post-ambient landscapes" — but loathes "the absolutely pathetic tunes. You know, you'd hear a song begin, be drawn into this lovely space that a new piece of music made, and then a melody comes in and it's just a mind-numbingly stupid melody."

New age is a no-go for Eno. "The reason most new age music is hard to listen to," he says, "is that it's extremely cheerful, pleasant. The things I like always have more complex emotions than that; there's always undertones, hints of bitterness.

"It's a little bit like you get dumped on Mars and what do you decide to do? You decide to switch on *The Jay Leno Show*. 'Here we are in this fabulous new world, let's watch TV.'"

On Land was also a good seller, he says, as was *Music for Airports*. So, the most commercially successful Eno — aside from the U2-producing Eno — is the ambient Eno, not the rocking Eno?

"The 'rocking' Eno," he says with a laugh, "is not as successful an entity as you would think. It's much more visible because its audience is identifiable, but in terms of sales it's not way ahead. Everyone thinks, of course, that's the stuff he made the money from — the other stuff he released because he is a bit of a fruitcake and likes putting out funny records. That's sort of what I thought at the time, too, but it turns out history has decided things were a little different and has made it look like the rock records were the hobby." Eno conveys this information with a tone of mild bemusement.

Still, Eno stands by everything he's done. The throbbing, squalling "Baby's on Fire" is one of rock's best twisted jokes and features Robert Fripp's long, skronky guitar solo. Eno's take on the Kinks' "You Really Got Me" on *801 Live* transforms Ray Davies' unbridled glee into creepy possessiveness. ("What?!" Davies exclaimed when I told him about it in 1981. "Eno's done that song? I must hear it.")

Eno's version of "The End" with Nico on the live Ayers-Cale-Nico-Eno album *June 1, 1974* makes Jim Morrison sound like a kid at play. You want dour? We got dour. And then there's the flip side of dour. Eno gets a kick from the fact that his seven-year-old daughter goes around singing a verse from "Miss Shapiro," a Phil Manzanera-Eno collaboration on the Roxy guitarist's solo debut, *Diamond Head,* and *801 Live.* It's so *Eno* — clever wordplay and alliteration, sense and nonsense, a reference to a long-running English soap opera (*The Archers*), an observation that life is cyclical, not linear, and that everything gets bollixed up at Christmas. What's not to love?

"There's nothing worse than this sort of simple sense that you get so much in songs," Eno tells me during one of the three talks we had in the 1990s. "The stupid same old story as being told with no humor and no sense of subterfuge or mischief."

Having let go of lyrics and anything halfway conventional, Eno came back to "pop" in 1990 with *Wrong Way Up.* What brought him back?

Eno pauses. And then lets fly.

"One of the things that's awful when you start to become well-known," he explains over the phone from California, "is the weight of expectation that builds up behind you, and it's like momentum that keeps pushing you in the same direction. And that momentum crystallizes around people's theories of what you're doing — 'He stands for this.' That sort of fossilizes [into evolving] from something that was probably soft-shelled and whimsical and exploratory into an ideological position about who you are and what you do. It forces you to take harder positions than you want. I've tried to avoid that trap of feeling what people expect of me. 'Oh God, I'm supposed to be so innovative' is the most paralyzing feeling of all, to think you should do important things.

"I'm equally pleased by whether it succeeds or whether it fails. If it really fails, it's almost a better outcome because then I have carte blanche. It will have diffused all those expectations: Nobody's interested anymore, and I can do what I want."

But wait, there's more. His collaborator, John Cale, helped him feel more comfortable as a singer. And the real kick in the creative pants came from working with U2.

"The payoff for me has been starting to enjoy again something I hadn't been able to enjoy in years: watching music evolve from a group of people. It really started me thinking about starting to work that way and working like that. And, of course, with them I also occasionally helped out a bit on writing songs. So, I think that was starting to ease me back into songwriting and singing as well."

His theory on successful pop music?

"Any pop song that keeps engaging you does so because there's almost a mismatch between the emotions. Sometimes, you'll have a very happy feeling over a very aggressive beat. For example, Donna Summer's 'I Feel Love.' I've always loved that song because of the beautiful, sweet, gliding quality of the voice and the absolutely manic, robotic beat underneath. They're so incongruous. And I'm sure it's the incongruity that thrills everyone. What's disappointing in music is when no new impressions arise on future listenings. The other thing I find disappointing is when the emotion is simple or singular."

Calling from his current home in St. Petersburg, Russia, in 1997, Eno says he has a theory. Actually, Eno has lots of theories — he probably leads the rock and roll league in that category — but this particular notion has been buzzing around his brain for the past 18 months, and it's taken hold. It is, in part, why Eno has more or less withdrawn from the pop process, why, to use but one example, he passed up the opportunity to co-produce U2's *Pop* album. "It probably would have been a good idea professionally." He helped U2 climb to the top of the pop mountain in 1987 with *The Joshua Tree*. "But I felt I didn't have any contribution to make. I'm not one of those people who can just turn on the juice. I have to want to make it work and really care about it to get to the level of commitment necessary. And, um, I didn't really care that much. Not just about that record but any record."

Why?

On one level Eno suggests it's because pop music has lost its place at the "center of the cultural conversation." Throughout its history, "pop music has been a primary source of conversation, the main way young people communicated, expressed shared values. If in 1977 you met someone wearing a Clash badge and you wore one, too, you could make assumptions about each other. However, pop has fragmented into so many subgenres and subcultures that it's become too successful. There's so many records out there, there are 50,000 conversations. It doesn't have the same kind of focus. That isn't the end of the world. Art forms don't have to be at the center of everyone's attention to do something useful, but I think the conversation has shifted, and I would like to be where it is."

So, the door is now open to what?

Eno laughs slightly. The new primary form of conversation, he says, is, well, conversation.

It's the Internet and the increasing number of faxes and phone calls people are making. (Keep in mind, this was nearly half a decade before the onset — and then onslaught — of social media.) The Internet, Eno says, is "much-hyped and very clumsy but bloody great conversation — the idea that you can take part in a potentially enormous conversation regardless of any fact about yourself other than you own a computer, which is not really a big entry-level qualification."

What is the artist's role in this?

There are many multimedia possibilities. "A new art form," he offers, "that builds in all the art forms we already know. There's no reason it shouldn't involve music or pictures."

And it did. Oh, did it.

Eno could have gone on, but he had a new (plain old) 17-track CD, *The Drop*, to discuss. It was no chart-topping heat-seeker (not that any of his albums were), but a brooding instrumental album tilted more toward the ambient than the rock side of the spectrum. It's a quirky, dark-tinged, snaking effort — soundscapes that hint at the dirt and worms that lurk underneath the pretty foliage.

In a promotional booklet, Eno described the album as "what you might expect from sketchily describing modern jazz to a person who'd never heard it and then forgot most of what you said and tried to play it anyway."

"I found myself playing things that had these strange, angular, somewhat sour melodies which didn't quite go right," Eno tells me. "They kept turning funny corners. There's an obscure landscape in terms of the sonic area it's in, and the melodies take you through a very peculiar walk through that landscape."

To which the veteran Eno aficionado might smile and ask, "So, what else is new?

The man never shot straight." Have Eno cover Little Willie John's "Fever" and he'll turn that unbridled passion into a disturbing obsession.

Eno's interests are not limited to recording. He has done sound and video installations in museums across the world, including one at the Institute of Contemporary Art in Boston in 1983. He's written and lectured about the importance of the confluence, and acceptance, of high art and low art — I saw him do that at Boston's Museum of Fine Art in October 1990. He expounded on songwriting: "Writing lyrics was to set in action the game of interpretation for the listener. It's making a kind of detective story with the lyrics." He also stressed the importance of lyrics being "phonetically active." He argued against too-literal interpretations of rock lyrics and songs. He advocated the use of randomness, what he calls "oblique strategies."

In 1995, he published a diary in England in which he termed himself "a mammal, an Anglo-Saxon, an uncle, a celebrity, a masturbator."

Certain albums, Eno suggests, arise out of particular circumstances: where one lives, where the world is at, internal feelings. It's a conflation of variables. Of taking a look back or trying to dissect why something worked or didn't work, Eno says, "It's impossible. And not only is it impossible, but trying to do it is mind-destroying ... It's awful to bring to life something that doesn't exist anymore."

One example of Eno's unorthodox yet successful approach: for "The Royal, The Choke," a song on *Nerve Net* (1992), Eno says he used an English bell-ringing pattern where the bells ring 1-2-3-4-5-6 and then 2-1-3-4-6-5 (and so on). "It's a permutation pattern that runs through the piece with no musical logic to it. It has completely mathematical logic and it makes you think there's something going on there.

"I don't want to release things I've heard before. When I make a solo album like this one, I want to at least have the illusion, whether it's true or not ... I want to feel this is kind of a new place to be in music. That's my job. I love being a pioneer of some kind. I like breaking ground. And I'm not particularly keen on carefully plowing and tending it. That's also an important job; I certainly don't want to underrate the value of people who get it right as opposed to people who get it first.

"I think a lot of traditional music forms have to do with plowing the same land and constantly improving the yield of it, finding the richness of it. And I have every respect for that. But my taste and inclination — and talent, I suppose — is in proposing, really:

proposing a possible music at some time. And with this one I think I have something on the cusp between — well, I don't know all the things it's on the cusp between — but certainly jazz, dance music, film soundtracks. It also has an anti-Hollywood quality that I like a lot. Anti-finish, anti-gloss."

Nerve Net doesn't, though, have many lyrics. While Eno is one of rock's most clever, oblique lyricists — someone who favors sparkling syntax, dry wit and allusive alliteration over a cogent narrative — he feels lyrics often take on too much importance, especially for critics.

"It's very easy to write about words. They're already in the same language as the one you are using. It's very hard to write about music without writing about it boringly in terms of notes — like, he uses D minor 7th to an X sharp major. Nobody wants to read that because it tells you nothing. But writing about the lyrics doesn't tell you much, either. The result is that most musical criticism isn't about music.

"The problem with writing songs, and I see everybody grappling with it in different ways, is nobody knows what to put in the middle. That's to say, you have a whole technology, a whole art form based around creating the edges, if you like, the background, the support system, all the things we call music. But there's been hardly any advances about what you then do in the middle. What do you sing about? And what it always turns out to be about is relationships! It always turns out to be about the 19th century in vision. Music, the ability to make music, has moved on leagues, hundreds of miles, but songwriting, by and large, has not."

Rest assured, when Eno does put words to music, he's not playing by the old rules. "Ali Click," a spooky throbber on *Nerve Net* that may concern the clash of two characters named Jolly Roger and Silly Sally, features deadpan tongue-twisters. "Silly Sally is a pally with her crackers in the alley / She's a smacker and a whacker with a dally in the slacker." Jolly Roger, it turns out, is "a sucker for a shocker." Eno calls it "an English rap song — I nicked the bass part from [bassist] Jimmy Ali, who used to work with Isaac Hayes, so it's a tribute to him."

At that multimedia installation at the ICA in 1983, Eno talked about simplifying his art, working more from a subtractive than an additive basis. Now, he says, he's blending the two.

"One of the nice things about working in a recording studio is that you can paint and sculpt. Sculpting in the traditional sense is basically taking something away and leaving a form; painting is putting things on and creating a form. Most recording, until the whole dub and remix thing caught on, was about adding. But now there's a whole new feeling with doing both things at the same time, and I'm keen on this."

Eno says he was recently approached to remix a song called "Heartbeat" by the Grid. Eno had never met the band but was up for the challenge after they asked him for something "a bit Brian Eno-ish, a bit strange."

"I said to them in my letter these mixes range from the fairly ugly to the totally repulsive. And they actually sound great! They have a totally different mood from the original. They might hear it and say, 'This is too far out for us.' Sorry. I did say it is too weird. I don't mind.

"A lot of the job of being a producer or a collaborator is to make people enthusiastic about their own ideas. Because if an idea is new to you, you don't know, you can't evaluate it. It could be just a sort of weird conceit; it could be a phase you're going through. And if you meet people who say to you, 'Hey, it's a bit weird' or 'I really liked that record you did five years ago,' you start to think, 'Bloody hell, I wonder if I'm completely off the rail.' And then it's a tremendous relief when someone whose opinion you respect says, 'This is so exciting.' You think, 'Oh, thank God, maybe it's all right.' I'm sure everyone thinks that. Most people think artists have this amazing self-confidence and arrogance and are completely self-validating and don't care what anyone thinks. And there are some artists like that. But not very many."

There was a time in England when people scrawled musical declarations on fences, like this or that band "rules." One frequent scrawl of the '70s: "Eno Is God." Replacing, one supposes, former deity Eric Clapton.

"Of course, one can't deny being flattered," reflects Eno. "But it's slightly dangerous, this feeling you don't want to be attached to. I've seen people who've had a bit of that adulation, and they've really taken it to heart and believed it, and it's really paralyzing. You just have to remind yourself that, for someone of 17 or 19, at this moment in time you fill a space in their life. This is what they would like to imagine artists are like." ◆

"I used to hate interviews with a passion. Now I think it's great. It's quite inexpensive therapy."

Bryan Ferry

Bryan Ferry onstage with Roxy Music in New York, February 1975

PHOTOGRAPH BY LINDA D. ROBBINS

BRYAN FERRY
& ROXY MUSIC

IT WAS A SPRING DAY IN 1993 IN BOSTON. Bryan Ferry had spent the previous afternoon, a splendid sunny Sunday, strolling Boston Common, remarking on how fine the city looked and how happy the people seemed to be. Ferry was glad to be here.

In the mid-'70s, Boston was one of the first American cities to take to his band, Roxy Music. And they were the only band I'd hitchhike from Bangor, Maine to Boston to see on a snowstormy Thursday in early February 1975 — the day my ticket finally arrived in the mail. (I made it to the show. Caught the flu.)

Ferry, still lean and dapper at 47, took his walk incognito, dressed in shorts and a tennis shirt which, he says, "might have thrown people off the scent. They'd expect to see me in a tuxedo or something." He went unrecognized. No doubletakes, no autographs, no photos.

Is anonymity a good thing or a bad thing? "Good and bad," Ferry says after a moment's thought. "Actually, one person did recognize me: the manager of the Four Seasons Hotel. But he's English."

If Ferry can go unrecognized in America, at home he is a magazine cover superstar, a position he's held for two decades, ever since the wildly inventive Roxy Music stormed the glam-rock and art-rock scene of the early '70s, creating unique retro/futuristic collage-type rock and roll.

In Roxy Music, the handsome vibrato-and-falsetto-inclined high baritone, a former art student, wrote lyrics that blurred the line between sincerity and irony. Long since exploited by the post-punk generation, irony was in short supply back then. Roxy mixed melody and noise, synthesizer squalls and saxophone stutters, bracing electric guitar riffs and thunderous percussive passages. Ferry's most expressive love song of that early era, "In Every Dream Home a Heartache," was an eerie, quasi-comic paean to an inflatable doll. "I blew up your body ... But you blew my mind!" Ferry sang at the climax as the instruments whooshed in for a cacophonous, swirling climax and coda. Later, in his and Roxy's world, the love songs would become much less twisted. The object of affection was most definitely female and human.

As Roxy Music went through its ups and downs, creatively and commercially (three distinct phases, as Ferry sees it), he pursued a concurrent solo career. That became a full-time pursuit — well, *sort of* full time — when he disbanded Roxy in 1983. Until an all-covers LP of mostly R&B songs called *Taxi* was released last month, Ferry had been absent from the scene for five years: a pop eternity.

"Of course, five years is a very long time to most people," Ferry agrees, now settled in a conference room at his record company's branch office. "I think a lot of people follow what they see on MTV. I don't know how important a part of their lives [radio or music] is. There does seem to be a craze for early-'70s music now; the circle seems to have gone around in some way.

"I don't feel I'm out on a limb, particularly, except I know the album I just did is very subtle. Although I've always liked dance music in theory, it just seems so machined now. Records are just too similar to each other. But I don't know. I could talk all day and go around in circles. I just don't know. I'm not sure what the audience is right now."

To some, Ferry might be seen as a remote, cool character. Certainly, he's expressed more than his share of melancholy and old-world romantic yearning; certainly, he's also sent up those same emotions. They recall the tuxedos he used to wear onstage and on the cover of his second solo album, *Another Time, Another Place*, portraying him as an upscale lounge lizard or a country squire.

"That's quite a long way away," Ferry says. He generally spends his working week in London, in the studio, and then heads out of town to spend time with his wife and four sons. "All you need is one photograph with a tweed jacket in a country setting and they've got you," he says with a laugh and a sigh. "It's extraordinary how an image can build up alongside of you, like a shadow or a ghost of yourself. People have a perception; they always seem surprised that I'm like I am."

Which is?

"Well, it's embarrassing [to say], but warm and more humorous. There are too many pictures where I'm tight-lipped and looking rather cross. I never used to enjoy being on that side of the camera. And I used to hate interviews with a passion. Now, I think it's great. It's quite inexpensive therapy."

Ferry claims not to feel the confidence people assume he possesses. He marvels at his ex-Roxy partner Brian Eno's gift of public gab. His parting comment this afternoon is, "You've got to be paranoid and messed up to be a singer." It's delivered with a laugh, but you know there's a kernel of truth in there as well.

Basically, Ferry looks at making music as "an interesting job — if you want to call it a job. It's a career. I like all the other aspects of it, writing — well, writing is very difficult — recording and doing the artwork. I try to make it as interesting as possible."

Like many of his peers, Ferry tries to balance career and family. He admits that for all the joys his home life offers ("I'm sure it brings something; I'm sure it helps you as a person") it has made the job harder. "It's affected the writing. It sounds silly to you, maybe, but just the weekend thing: that's when I used to write most lyrics [with Roxy]. I probably wouldn't work in the studio on weekends, but the record would still be going through my head and I'd write on a Saturday night. Now I escape completely."

Lyrics have been a problem for Ferry in recent years. He has a nearly completed album, *Horoscope*, which was supposed to have been out a long time ago. After his solo 1988 tour, Ferry re-entered the studio full of zeal. "The muse came very fast," he says about writing the music. "The usual thing that happened to me was with the lyrics: concrete wall, a block. Instrumentally, they were fantastic. But I just couldn't get songs to sound how I wanted."

That block led to *Taxi.* Ferry is no stranger to the world of cover versions, of doing unique, stylized remakes of songs both classic and obscure. When it comes to his knowledge of soul and R&B, particularly, he is no dilettante. The songs on his first three solo albums were all covers, including remakes of five Roxy Music songs (!) on 1976's *Let's Stick Together.* His later versions of Neil Young's "Like a Hurricane" and John Lennon's "Jealous Guy" are definitive.

He decided to record a couple of R&B covers to give *Horoscope* a potential hook or hit single. But he didn't stop there. "As soon as I started looking at these old songs, I said, 'This is something I haven't done for 10 years, since 'Jealous Guy.' And it's a very long time since I'd done a whole album of stuff. So, I thought I'd keep it fairly pure, not mix it up with *Horoscope*. It was certainly pleasant. I was pleased to find myself as the singer again." He included renditions of "Will You Still Love Me Tomorrow," "I Put a Spell on You" and "Amazing Grace," among others.

Ferry fans, who are invariably Roxy fans (pretty much the reverse is true as well), keep asking if he might consider reassembling the Roxy Music machine for one last go-round.

"When people ask me, I say, I'd be open more to the idea than I was two years ago, simply because as time goes by you start getting a bit nostalgic and curious about what it would sound like. But then I say, 'Which band do you want? The first one, which is the first two records, which was very exciting?'"

I'm in the office with M. Howell, a friend, Roxy fan and critic for the *Boston Phoenix*. Both of us simultaneously smile and shoot up our hands, raising a single digit.

"Yeah," Ferry laughs. "Erm. Or, there's the middle period, where we were trying to become more musical, with [violinist] Eddie Jobson in the band, and I'd stopped doing keyboards onstage and became the singer. That period stopped with *Siren* [in 1975]. Then I went and did another solo tour, an album, *In Your Mind*, then *The Bride Stripped Bare*, which was quite a turning point, which led to *Manifesto* and then up to the end, *Avalon*. During the final period, the records kept getting more sophisticated, in a way. A more atmospheric sound, softer on the drums. I got into a blacker thing, which personally I like better, but unfortunately it meant I stopped being as zany and, perhaps, quirky."

Ferry suggests that *Horoscope* has its somber and turbulent sides and feels that it falls somewhere between the off-the-deep-end experimentation of 1972's *For Your Pleasure* and the smooth-gliding *Avalon*, his two favorite Roxy LPs. During the writing, his mother died and his management collapsed. He says the turmoil he felt is reflected in the music.

But *Horoscope* won't show up until next spring. [In fact, it never showed up at all, but the sessions resulted in 1994's *Mamouna*.] Now he's got *Taxi*, and it has done well, selling 200,000-plus copies and getting play on alternative radio. Ferry, who recently appeared on *The Tonight Show*, is hoping to mount a U.S. tour in the fall.

Speaking of his fans as family, he says, "I'm not a very good father, especially since the last tour, when I saw my audience again. It sounds corny, I know — you'll probably howl with laughter — but it meant an awful lot to me. It was a part of my family that I'd developed over my career, and it made me keen again."

In 2001, Roxy Music was back, raising the question: why?

Ferry, guitarist Phil Manzanera and saxophonist Andy Mackay got on the phone from London during a pre-tour rehearsal break.

"The time seems right," offers Manzanera. "It happens to be the 30th anniversary, so that's a neat little thing. I sort of always felt there was a bit of unfinished business to be done."

"We'd been in touch," adds Mackay. "Phil was best man at my second marriage. We talk. We talked about it in the early '90s, and it didn't happen. Then this coherent offer was made with a certain number of dates and a set [financial] guarantee. So, we knew we could do the technical side of it. It's quite expensive to put a band together, to look good, sound good, have that all in place."

"There seems to be a lot of goodwill about, as far as I can make out," muses Ferry. "I'd just done quite a long [solo] tour in the last year, and as the tour developed, I was adding more and more Roxy tunes to the repertoire. I enjoyed singing them very much. And I felt really huge waves of appreciation from the audience. Coupled with the fact that I've always been asked [to reunite Roxy] — people almost pleading for just one gig. And this time it just made sense to do it."

Much like the Velvet Underground, Roxy Music is a band whose acclaim and influence far exceeds its record sales. Co-founder Eno, of course, put a stamp on many a group — directly as a producer and indirectly in his own music through the jarring juxtaposition of sound and words. Those first two albums with their art-school-inspired cut-and-paste collages.

But the band also inspired England's new romantic movement in the early '80s, which spawned Duran Duran, Spandau Ballet, ABC and Visage, among others. Roxy provided a partial blueprint for the Cars. They brought a sense of irony and style to the pop realm. And with the tuxedo-clad Ferry emerging during an Allman Brothers Band period of rock (in America anyway), they demonstrated that rock and roll need not be a blue-jeans-and-T-shirt affair.

Fans still remember. In England, definitely. "You go to get the milk in the morning, and there's a guy delivering it to you who says, 'When are you getting back together with Roxy?'" says Manzanera, who played with Eno in 801, recorded jazz in Quiet Sun, has a career as a producer of Spanish-language rock and roll and has played as a sideman to Joe Cocker and Bob Dylan.

How's the vibe?

After 12 days together, Ferry says, "There seems to be nothing but a good feeling toward the music. So far I've encountered no negatives."

He says the 1983 breakup wasn't contentious. "Every band has its flare-ups. We would go through frosty silences from time to time. But, no, there was never a case of 'musical differences' or any of that. I think at the end of the *Avalon* tour I just wanted to try different things and did that."

Roxy's music, from the early chaotic retro/futuristic glam days to the more sophisticated and soulful later era, stands the test of time. Virgin released a compilation, *The Best of Roxy*, after issuing remastered CDs of the band's catalog last year. And the UK label Pilot has put out a new live double-CD, *Concerto*, recorded in Denver in 1979.

A while ago, Ferry says, he was driving with a couple of his children. The song "Out of the Blue" was playing quietly on the sound system. "They said, 'That was really good, that one, you should put that one out next!'" recalls an amused Ferry. The kids didn't know that was a key tune on Roxy Music's 1975 LP, *Country Life*; they thought it was a recent demo.

"That was reassuring," says Ferry, who told the kids, "Yeah, maybe I'll do that." That "reassurance" could be read two ways, I guess: genuine (as in this would-be new song stands up to a great old song) or not (as in the kids didn't know his stuff. Then again, parents — *ecch!* — so square.).

A revelation dawns: A generation or two of rock fans who've heard Roxy's albums and heard the band praised as pioneers have never seen them live. "But they do listen to the music," says Mackay, whose early inspiration came from the treated sax sounds of King Curtis.

They were assembling potential set lists when we talked. Asked which period he is closest to and most wants to play in concert, Ferry says, "Obviously, the early period. The two early albums [*Roxy Music* and *For Your Pleasure*] are very close to my heart, so I want to draw heavily from those. On the other hand, *Avalon* was the most successful album, so I think I owe it to the audience to represent that period as well. Those three albums. And the middle period, there's always 'Love Is the Drug' and those songs from *Siren*.

"I [have] about 40 songs on a wish list that I want us to run through, and we'll see which ones we're going to finalize from that. It'll be a mixture from all of them, so all are represented. The hits will be catered [to]. The most fun for me will be doing the obscure ones, like 'In Every Dream Home a Heartache.'"

And how does it feel for a respected crooner of a certain age to sing to a polyethylene partner?

"Just like falling off a log," Ferry says with a soft laugh. He cherishes that music, which he terms "interesting and dark."

"You have to be careful not to take yourself too seriously," says Mackay, who echoes Ferry's take on the early days. "It's kind of tricky."

Ferry admits a measure of regret about Roxy Music's shift after those first two albums, with Eno off to pursue a solo career. It was not so much the ego clash reported back then, he says, but restlessness on Eno's part to keep going further out on limbs (as evidenced by his first two solo albums).

Stranded retained some of the band's experimental essence — the mix of whimsy and poignancy, spoof and sincerity — but Roxy was clearly headed toward smoother seas and a somewhat more conventional image with a singer perceived as suave and debonair, a romantic roué. Semi-hits from that era: "Oh Yeah" (*Flesh + Blood*, 1980), "Dance Away" and "Angel Eyes" (*Manifesto*, 1979).

"I think we did tend to straighten out," Ferry says of Roxy's evolution. "Possibly too much, when I look back now. But at the time, we felt, 'We've done that; let's try doing this.'"

That first Roxy show? The one I hitchhiked from Bangor to Boston for in 1975? The one where Ferry took the stage in swashbuckling gaucho garb? That was synched to promote their fourth album, *Country Life*, a transition of sorts between the early wild art-rock and the more sophisticated, less disruptive music to come. (Eno was not on the third album, *Stranded*, but his influence was.)

If you were in a record shop, perusing the racks, how could you not stop and be startled — in the best way possible — by the cover? Roxy had utilized a sexy woman on their previous albums, but they took it to the max on this one, with two gorgeous (stern) women, nearly nude.

Photographer Eric Boman posed statuesque German models Constanze Karoli and Eveline Grunwald, wearing the sheerest of undergarments, in front of lush green foliage. (There's a Can connection: Karoli was the sister of Can guitarist Michael Karoli; Grunwald was his girlfriend.) That cover lasted for a while, sometimes covered in opaque green shrink wrap; later the record company, Atco, issued a version that excised the ladies, blandly leaving what had been the back cover: more foliage. What a wussy move, but probably done so the rack jobbers could get the album into department stores.

Country Life may be my least favorite of the first four Roxys, which still puts it in the A-strata. It starts with the seductive, bracing "The Thrill of It All" and ends with one of Ferry's grandest, most resplendent songs, "Prairie Rose," a shimmering ode to a Texas woman which, over the years, everyone believed to be Jerry Hall. One of those classic rock myths; the two had yet to meet. The concert I saw kicked off with this song and, in fact, included everything from the album save "Triptych."

There are whiffs of decadence here — "Casanova" flirts with heroin "... or is it cocaine?" — but it's the most straightforwardly romantic Ferry had ever been. "Out of the Blue" is a zinger with a sizzling violin solo from newcomer Eddie Jobson, but the version on *Viva!*, a live album released the following year, is even better.

Roxy Music 2001 would be fleshed out by players from Ferry's last solo tour, two other musicians, a backup singer and original Roxy drummer Paul Thompson, who signed on late in the game.

Any fears about lack of chemistry?

"No," says Ferry. "I'm pretty confident that it's all going to sound great, because we have the main elements in place in Andy, Phil and now Paul, and I found I could still sing the songs as convincingly as I've ever done."

Is there a future for them as a recording band?

"There's a slim chance," he replies. "We really haven't thought of it yet. We just thought we'd do this tour, and if we're still on cordial terms at the end, we'll take it from there and see what happens."

On the Boston stop, July 17th, about a third of the way through a set at the Fleet-

Boston Pavilion, Roxy Music played the elegiac "A Song for Europe," which, like many a Roxy song, is about love lost. As the majestic music swelled, Ferry, dressed in a black sharkskin suit, sang, "There is nothing to share but yesterday."

And that is what Roxy Music, after 18 years, shared on the first date of its first U.S. tour since reuniting. But *what* yesterdays: the irony and gleeful chaos of its early period; the sleek sheen, percussive accents and romance of its middle and later periods; and, moreover, the engaging elegance of one of England's best-ever rock bands.

It recalled something Ray Davies once told me: "The Kinks are the only band where you can leave a show and be over the moon with enjoyment and yet walk away disappointed." As with the Kinks, Roxy Music has a catalog so rich, and gives a concert so (comparatively) short, there's a lot of history you miss hearing.

For the most part, the band picked songs wisely. Eight of the 18 selections came from its first three albums, A-level, groundbreaking affairs all. The concert kicked off with three gems: "Remake/Remodel," "Street Life" and "Ladytron," in which Ferry crooned, "I'll use you and I'll confuse you and then I'll lose you. Still, you won't suspect me." The cad!

Of course, what was once radical in terms of structure, arrangement and attitude has been somewhat tempered by time. (New wave, no wave, post-punk, etc.) The pleasure, however, has not diminished. When Manzanera and Mackay leapt into the swirl of sound in the chaotic, dreamy "Ladytron" or the extended, bluesy version of "My Only Love," heaven was in reach. This was heady rock without pointless solos, ensemble rock with a point.

Ferry is one of rock's most commanding vocalists, but a fair part of the enjoyment came during the instrumental mesh, when he would step back (or move to the piano) and the gears of the band would lock in. Instruments once foreign to the rock mix (sax, oboe, violin) were deployed. There was a dexterous weave during both "Avalon" and "Dance Away" and a lovely duet between Mackay and violinist Lucy Wilkins on the instrumental "Tara."

The four original members were augmented by six other players, including guitarist Chris Spedding and keyboard player Colin Good. Sarah Brown handled soaring and soulful backing vocals; her orgasmic emoting during "My Only Love" was most notable. Violinist Wilkins doubled on percussion, joining Julia Thornton. Four sexy female dancers were employed judiciously, onstage during the smoldering "Both Ends

Burning" and back for the encores of "Do the Strand" and "For Your Pleasure," dressed as Vegas showgirls.

The finale was perfect: spooky yet comforting. "In the morning, the things that you worried about last night will seem lighter," sang Ferry. "You watch me walk away."

Then he did, followed by Mackay and Manzanera. One by one, to rapturous applause, the others left the stage, until finally only Good was left, his spare, eerie synth parts spiraling into the summer night.

I checked in again with Ferry the following year on the phone from Newcastle. I posed a question: What's the best kind of music?

"All the best music is sad," he mused, as his latest solo album, *Frantic*, hit the shops.

For the first song on the album, Ferry had returned to a favorite source, Bob Dylan. He drenches "It's All Over Now, Baby Blue" in sadness and loss and tinged with spite. Four songs later, he's in Dylan land again with "Don't Think Twice, It's All Right."

Ferry goes back a long way with Dylan. "Hard Rain's A-Gonna Fall' was the first song on his debut solo album. "I did it in a kind of provocative way," Ferry says. "It was a good way to kick off a solo career, with a bit of a bang. Now [my covers are] chosen for the beauty of the songs. You're looking for fresh material and you think, 'Here's a song I've loved for 30 years,' and the Dylan songs, especially the early period, had such wonderful lyrics and a great feeling about them."

One thing that's changed about Ferry's approach to covers is that he once treated them with a certain irreverence and irony amid the respect. He is now more likely to hew closer to the original sound, to toy and tinker less.

Frantic is half covers, half originals, many of them co-written with such folks as ex-Eurythmic David A. Stewart and Brian Eno. Whatever tension that might have existed once between the onetime bandmates has dissipated over time.

"When people are together for too intense a time, they start bristling, especially if they're controlling types, like I am," Ferry says. "I think it's good that he went and did his thing and I went and did my thing."

They co-wrote "I Thought," which closes the album. Ferry calls it a "thrill to work with people you have a history with and feel inspired by. Brian is very intelligent and very amusing. We both laugh at each other all the time, and we complement each other very well."

What Ferry found on the road with Roxy in 2001 was great love and warmth from the audience. "I think one of the benefits of getting older is that the audience becomes more and more affectionate," he says.

And no doubt some of that affection may be due to his close call on December 29, 2000, when a suicidal man attacked the pilot of a London-to-Nairobi flight Ferry was on. That sent the plane into a 10,000-foot dive. Crew members came to the rescue. "I believe in fate, and I think that meant that my number wasn't up yet. Hopefully not for a while."

For his 2002 solo tour, Ferry would employ most of the previous year's company (minus the Roxy men). He expects to play five songs from *Frantic,* Roxy material and songs from other solo albums. Some will be elegant and graceful, others chaotic and dissonant.

"I embrace variety. I like the current show because it has a lot of dynamics in it. We do about 20 minutes that's acoustic. One of the girls plays harp and doubles on percussion; the violin player doubles on synthesizer. It's essentially a kind of rock band, but the skills are there to do very quiet things. And I enjoy singing that kind of music, whereas in the early days I didn't have that kind of confidence."

Asked to assess his personal evolution, Ferry says, "I think I'm more comfortable with myself now. It's interesting rediscovering the touring process and the performance part of my life in the last couple of years. It's been really exciting because I'd stopped touring for such a long time." He favored working in the studio. "It's been good for my recording too, because I'm a bit less precious than I'd become in the '80s and '90s."

One reason Ferry stayed off the road for so long was to help raise his four sons. After dating American supermodel Jerry Hall (who upgraded, if that's the word, to Mick Jagger and then downgraded, that's definitely the word, to Rupert Murdoch) Ferry married model Lucy Helmore (she's on the cover of *Avalon*) and started a family. Recently, the London tabloids reported that Ferry was involved with Katie Turner, 21, one of his backup singers.

I gotta ask ...

"There's not much to say, except [my wife and I are] separated, and we've been separated for a lot longer than the papers realize." (Perhaps another reason to record "It's All Over Now, Baby Blue"?) Ferry doesn't call the split amicable but says he and his wife are on "reasonable terms, and it's all up in the air." What's been written, he adds, "is not accurate. I don't really talk about it other than to confirm that we are separated." [They divorced in March 2003. Helmore remarried in 2006, battled drug abuse, alcoholism and depression and, on July 23, 2018, shot and killed herself. She was 58.]

Ferry married PR executive Amanda Sheppard, 38 years his junior, in 2012. They divorced two years later.

In June of 2007, Ferry was in New York doing interviews to promote *Dylanesque*. Sure, he'd covered a lot of Dylan in the past, but this was full-blown, all-out Dylan in your face.

I took the Acela train down from Boston and met Ferry at the Carlyle Hotel. He looked slightly disheveled in a *GQ* kind of way: faded blue jeans, a light blue shirt and a loose green tie, his elegantly mussed black hair dangling across his angular face. At 61, Ferry was affable and cordial, but at times his body posture suggested exhaustion, sitting practically prone in an easy chair. If he seemed a bit wan, he was still game.

Over the years, Ferry's solo work has been tilted heavily toward covers. "It's no secret that I write very slowly, and I don't really write that many songs. I have other things to do. Rather than thinking, 'Oh there's something wrong with me,' I've just been enjoying the other things that I do — solo shows and also some Roxy shows. We did Roxy in 2001, a big tour, and a few smaller tours since then. Last year, we did European festivals, three weeks in July and August, and after the tour is when I went into the studio to do the Dylan thing. Roxy Music did some recording earlier in the year, and then it was down to me to go and write the lyrics to some of the songs. I thought, 'This is going to be a very long-haul project,' and I didn't want to wait two years before I put anything out. Simple as that. And the Dylan thing was a project that's been in the back of my mind for a long time."

Despite all the Dylan covers he's done down the years, "Dylanesque" is not a word that comes to mind when you think of Ferry. I mean, vocally. But time and again throughout his career, like so many other artists, Ferry has gone to the Dylan well.

"I've always liked his voice. I like the way he changes songs. I know some people don't care for [his voice], but I just think the songs are so strong they can be done in many different ways, whether it's the Byrds or Hendrix."

Ferry says Dylan is the only artist he'd ever consider devoting an entire album to. *Dylanesque* is an eleven-song tribute to an artist Ferry has never met and hadn't even seen in concert until last year. At that show, Bob did what Bob does nowadays: he stood at the piano, faced side-stage, sang gruffly and said nothing. I'd been spoiled by seeing Dylan's Rolling Thunder Revue in 1975, so the taciturn non-hit-singing, non-guitar-playing Bob was not my favorite. Most songs were bluesy shuffles; in one review I called him bar-band Bob.

"My teenage sons took me," Ferry says. "Otherwise, I probably wouldn't have made the effort. He wasn't playing guitar. He didn't even come to the front of the stage. The audience don't mind; he gets away with it. He's great."

The songs on *Dylanesque* aren't, for the most part, surprising choices. Ferry brings his expressive baritone and reined-in art-rock sensibility to the familiar and poetic "Just Like Tom Thumb's Blues," "Simple Twist of Fate," "Knockin' on Heaven's Door" and "All Along the Watchtower."

"For me," Ferry says, "the great freedom of the solo career is that I have been able to go in different directions and stretch myself — like doing '30s songs with an orchestra. The Dylan thing, it seems very natural to me. These songs are very poetic, very accessible to me." The bulk of the tracks were written between 1964 and 1975, though Ferry does include "Make You Feel My Love" from 1997's *Time Out of Mind.*

With hundreds of Dylan tunes to choose from, Ferry managed to select eleven. The album clocks in at about 42 minutes. "I think that's the proper length of a record. [CDs routinely ran to 60 minutes or more then]. Rhett Davies, my producer, and I just think of it that way. And I didn't really think about what I *didn't* want to do. Certain songs have an appeal. 'Positively 4th Street' stood out. I like the lyrics; I like the tune ... There was no pain in terms of flogging away at it. Either it works or it doesn't work. I like to think there are a few different moods in the songs. Different keys and eight or ten ballads."

With the ill-advised war in Iraq outside raging, I wondered if the Vietnam-era anthem "The Times They Are A-Changing" might have renewed resonance.

"I think you could say it's appropriate now because there's another war going on that's just as unpopular. But that isn't really why I did it. There are many inspired lines in it: it's a song that works outside of the period it was written in."

Ferry used to inject an element of camp or irony into his covers. These renditions seem more straightforward.

"I didn't analyze how I was going to do it other than the fact that I've been enjoying playing with most of the same musicians on tour and I didn't want to overproduce the thing. 'Baby, Let Me Follow You Down' is just straightforward rock with the band enjoying the song. Same with 'Simple Twist of Fate.' There's something naturalistic about it I liked."

He addresses the furor that erupted in England earlier this year when the tabloid press distorted remarks he'd made to the German newspaper *Welt am Sonntag* about Nazi-era German art. "You're not allowed to talk about art anymore," says Ferry, decrying cancel culture more than a decade before cancel culture was a thing. "I was just talking about art and style to a very intelligent guy. We talked for about 45 minutes in January. Some of what I said got picked and distorted, taken out of context, and you name it. I was very upset about it. The one good thing was that my Jewish friends came to my defense. I have a very strong connection, almost an homage, to Black American culture and Jewish culture, especially all the great moviemakers when they first came to Hollywood, the great writers, directors and actors. And musicians also, who wrote a lot of the songs I've covered.

"What was distressing was how all these tabloids jumped on it without checking with me. First, the word 'Nazi' was never used. The interviewer sent me the tape the next day. It was unbelievable, very sad. It did cause a lot of trouble. It's the age we're in. You talk about certain things and other people interpret them. It makes you think of Big Brother, freedom of speech denied."

I posed a question that might be anathema to working musicians of a certain age, but generally elicits a good response. It did here: "You're at a point in your life where it would be perfectly okay for you to say, 'I've done my bit, I'm going to retire.' Have you thought about that?"

"Quite the opposite, really. I like to work, and there's a momentum as well to what I'm doing. Ever since I got divorced — I suppose I lost half my fortune five years ago, can't remember now, something like that. More than I could afford. That was a very big strong motivation to go out and work."

Asked what the best part of the job was, Ferry replies, "the applause probably. I think that I missed it for quite a few years. I don't know what it was: it coincided with the Roxy break-up in '82 and when I got married. There's a link to how bands break up and people get married and having another life. So, the last two years I've really started again. It's been good."

In 2022, Ferry got the old gang back together for a 50th anniversary tour of the U.S. (first) and the UK.

I reviewed the Boston show, September 17, 2022, at the new venue connected to Fenway Park, the MGM Music Hall at Fenway.

> Roxy Music — or, if you will, lead singer and chief songwriter Bryan Ferry — has always been, in part, about looking back to youth, about a certain embrace of wistful ennui even in the throes of in-the-moment pleasure. It was there when Roxy was a young brash retro/futurist glam band in 1972, and it was there in Boston with Roxy at full strength with the originals — Ferry, guitarist Phil Manzanera, saxophonist Andy Mackay and drummer Paul Thompson — all in their seventies. Ferry is about to turn 77.
>
> "When we were young" and "When you were young" are key lines in the final stanza of "If There Is Something," a centerpiece song off their first album, played mid-set last week. Ferry is looking back to the open-eyed enthusiasm and optimism of youth even as they seemed to have passed by him and the woman he's singing about. (He was 26 when it was first released.) When they played it at Fenway, it brought little shivers down my spine, that ineffable mix of melancholia with just a glint of triumph at recapturing what once was.
>
> It was there in the sadly graceful sway of "Oh Yeah," about that song Ferry and his lover used to groove to with "the rhythm of rhyming guitars" in his car "on the way to the movie show." The song begins with the two of them; at the end, Ferry's in the car, on the way to another movie show, but alone, the act bringing those memories of young lost love back to him.
>
> In "Same Old Scene," Ferry sang, "Nothing lasts forever," and both he and the backing trio of singers to his right, Phebe Edwards, Fonzi Thornton and Senab Adekunle, sang the rejoinder "Of that, I'm sure." Ferry shot a smile their way during that bit.
>
> And then, not to belabor the point, there was the opening line of "Jealous Guy," "I was dreaming of the past ..." Yes, it's a John Lennon

ballad, but Roxy de-Yoko-fied back in 1981 on a European tour and subsequent live EP. It's been a frequent set-closer for Ferry, solo and with the group. The song's ending is like a wave, a fond farewell to the faithful, those who, even with their doubts, paid big money and showed up. The song winds down with Ferry, as did Lennon, whistling.

Those who did not show up had their reasons, and Facebook was full of them. (1) The tickets were too expensive (2) too nostalgic/living in the past (3) Ferry's expected diminished vocal prowess (4) the anticipated setlist. You can damn or praise setlist.fm for that advance knowledge.

Roxy Music's stint as a recording band was darn near Beatleesque: eight studio albums in ten years. They disbanded in 1983, after *Avalon*. And they were on hiatus from 1976 to 1979. So, the oldest material is 50 years old and the newest nearly 40.

I spoke to Steve Wynn of the Dream Syndicate, a good friend and huge Roxy fan, the night after the show. He *could* have gone to the New York show but passed, having seen them first in 1975, then the *Manifesto* tour in 1979 and finally the (terrific!) 2001 reunion. But he couldn't quite pull the trigger on this one, primarily because of worries about Ferry's voice; he'd rather live with the memories.

So, how *was* Ferry's voice?

Well, there was no falsetto employed and, in general, he seemed to take everything down a register. He didn't try for some of the highs, he was happy to have his backing vocalists soar where he couldn't. At times, this was a tad irksome and other times not an issue, but, ultimately, not unexpected. I'm pretty sure most people who bought tickets didn't expect the Ferry of yore.

This year's Roxy featured 13 musicians. Manzanera's got an extra guitarist to work with (Tom Vanstiphout); Mackay's got an extra saxophonist (Jorja Chalmers, who doubles on keys); Thompson has an extra percussionist (Nathan "Tugg" Curran). Ferry played occasional piano centerstage, but the keyboard chores are mostly handled by Christian Gulino (also the music director) and Chloe Beth Smith. Roxy has had roughly a million bassists over the years, but this year it's Neil Jason.

They played 100 minutes, coming out of the gate fast and furious with "Remake/Remodel," the greatest and most gleeful introductory song I think a band has ever had: campy, mysterious, zipping all over the place, the players introduced through brief, whimsical musical statements.

The structure of the show? I was looking back at Tim De Lisle's *Daily Mail* Ferry review from 2018 and had to smile: "His setlists are largely predictable, with a cross-section of his career — sparkly start, melancholy middle — teeing up the same old stompy finale. So why are his shows so satisfying? It's partly that, like your favourite restaurant, he varies the menu just enough."

Yep. I should state that I am more of a fan of the "sparkly" and the "stompy" and those songs — the ones on which Manzanera and Mackay excel — get my blood pumping. "Out of the Blue," "Ladytron" (slashing power chords from Manzanera!), "If There Is Something," "In Every Dream Home a Heartache," "Editions of You," "Do the Strand." (Even if the latter two were a tad sluggish.)

And, while I view them as lesser delights, I enjoyed the smoother songs of conflicted romance (a subject that Ferry called "inexhaustible" with a laugh in 2016) like "While My Heart Is Still Beating," "Dance Away," "The Main Thing" and "More Than This." The more mannered, less quirky, dance-and-romance-oriented, post-Brian Eno period, if you will.

This, let's face it, is where the bulk of Roxy's American audience, especially the female part, came aboard. "Love Is the Drug" was the entryway in 1975.

Oh, you may be wondering, was Eno there? Yes, he was! On the large video screen behind them, at least twice during clips of back-in-the-day videos. Roxy used, but didn't overuse, the video element during the show.

What was ultimately disappointing was the omission of "For Your Pleasure," the best walk-off song you can imagine and what Roxy did in 2001, with musicians leaving the stage one by one.

The takeaway for me? Very glad I went. These are like old friends and if they're old, so am I. (Maybe five to ten years younger, but still.) I loved it when Manzanera and Mackay got cranking; if Phil's a guitar hero, Andy's a sax hero. Thompson was aces on the kit.

The song that keeps swirling in my head after all these years is "In Every Dream Home a Heartache," that paean to a sex doll that floats in Ferry's pool "deluxe and delightful." The setup is sublime and the idea that Ferry could transpose his world-weary romantic yearnings to this doll — in his seventies, mind you — still tickles me pink. I love the idea that Ferry believes "my role is to serve you" and yet considers her a "disposable darling." After all the exposition, the band kicks in full-bore and the music goes absolutely mental, a crazy quilt of strands and shards, explosions and implosions, with Ferry wailing, "Oh those heartaches ... dream home heartaches!"

Yes, this is not a relationship that will not last. Which is pretty much the case with all the romantic entanglements in Roxy songs. ◆

ROBERT FRIPP
& KING CRIMSON

I HAD MY FIRST LIVE ENCOUNTER with the small mobile intelligent unit that goes by the name Robert Fripp in June 1979. It began with an autograph-signing session at the Harvard Coop record store in Cambridge, progressed to a dinner and discussion at a nearby sidewalk cafe, continued for two hours of Frippertronics, his hypnotic tape-loop-and-electric-guitar gig, at the Harvard Square folk club Passim and wound up with a marathon of drinks and further discussion in the lounge of Boston's Copley Plaza Hotel. It was total Fripp immersion. Just for one day.

A guitar hero with the prog-rock band King Crimson, Fripp was in the process of shedding that skin and the grandiose gestures of the genre, for something, well, smaller, more mobile and arguably more intelligent. Fripp is a man of many ideas; his thoughts are articulated with precision and gracefulness. After King Crimson ended for the first time, in 1974, he attended the Sherbourne International Academy for Continuous Education, where he studied the teachings of psychologist and spiritualist J.G. Bennett. He aimed to communicate musically on a more intimate basis; hence the performance for 150 at Passim. The demand to get in was intense: fans jammed their faces to the windows of the basement club to get a glimpse and soak in those Frippertronics. If Fripp ever was the distant rock star, he no longer wanted any part of it.

He'd become a sideman of high regard, working with Brian Eno, playing on three of the ex-Roxy Music synthesist-theorist-madcap-lyricist-singer's solo albums. Fripp's

"There's very little exciting about me other than the famous people I know, who in turn are equally boring."

Robert Fripp

Robert Fripp of King Crimson, 1978

PHOTOGRAPH BY LISA TANNER

solo on "Baby's on Fire" remains my favorite fractured/distorted nutso rock guitar break of all time. They had also made two instrumental albums, *No Pussyfooting* and *Evening Star*, together. He played on David Bowie's "Heroes," the first three Peter Gabriel solo albums, Talking Heads' "I Zimbra" and Blondie's "Fade Away and Radiate." He collaborated on Daryl Hall's solo album *Sacred Songs,* an album that was, according to rumor, too weird for RCA to release. Hall was half of a hot commercial entity, and this was not that. (In fact, it was originally intended as an official Hall & Oates album!) "RCA heard the album and called it 'strange,'" Fripp explains. "It was finished on November 2nd, 1977. It was so ahead of its time it would have established Hall & Oates as a force around the world again." (It finally came out in 1980.)

Fripp produced and played on the Roches' debut, adding subtle electronic touches to this odd-in-their-own way folk trio. In May 1979, Fripp flew to New York from Amsterdam to back Phoebe Snow and Linda Ronstadt as they sang the Roches' "The Married Men" on *Saturday Night Live.*

"It's a very difficult song to sing," he says, "and no one but the Roches can sing it in that kind of way, but Linda and Phoebe got very close. I don't enjoy the recorded version of the song by Phoebe — she didn't allow the song to establish its character, but the TV show, from where I was sitting, sounded good. I would be inclined to say the Roches' record captures exactly the sense of the song and anything less than that perfection is obviously imperfection. But it's not very easy."

The ostensible reason for Fripp's June 1979 visit to Boston was to chat up his own solo debut, *Exposure.* We talked about it, but Fripp was in no way pushing product. Me, I was writing the story for a very good (but now long gone) Boston rock magazine called *Sweet Potato.* He was talkative, contradictory, effusive and amusing. (Some time later, when I was with the *Boston Globe* and a new version of a reanimated King Crimson was on the road, Fripp eschewed all published interviews. I swear this is true: We once did an advance phone interview for a gig with the understanding that I couldn't use any of it in print.)

For me, and I knew it at the time, this was a rare deep dive into the man's thought processes. He talks about himself in both the first and third person and while the latter can be annoying — so many star athletes (Hello, LeBron!) do it — I found it rather charming coming from him.

From his trim haircut to his bespoke suit to his erudite English accent, Fripp was every bit the proper gentleman. He proposed a toast to our "new friendship" at the hotel lounge. He eagerly tackled many subjects with intensity and depth. Yet there was a lighthearted joking side (slightly tipsy?) to Fripp as well; as he watched a woman totter toward the ladies' room for the fourth time he wondered if she might have "a small mobile intelligent bladder."

I asked if he was amazed that so many people are interested in him. "Yes, of course. It fascinates me." Then, he asked me, "Why are you interested? Are you wasting your time?"

Before I could respond, he answered himself. "I don't think this is a waste of time. This is lots of fun. We look up and we wave to people and they bring us drinks." Which they did. (Pretty sure PolyGram picked up the tab.) Later, Fripp said, "I am actually a rather boring person; there's very little exciting about me other than the famous people I know, who in turn are equally boring."

We talked about ambient and/or all-instrumental music, a field Fripp has explored with Eno and on his own via Frippertronics. "Ambience is a very important movement, and I am prepared to support it myself with my own ambient albums. Frippertronics falls into two sections. 'Applied Frippertronics' is where it's used to replace the orchestra; the examples are all over *Exposure* and *Sacred Songs*. Frippertronics music of eating at restaurants is the other, where it would be music to be listened to as one would listen to a string quartet.

"Frippertronics can be demanding — in which case it isn't, by definition, ambient. Some of it is ambient. Once in Paris, I went to this restaurant for supper and asked the manager if he would let me play there and he said yes. So, I went back the next two nights and played for supper and because people were eating I accepted the responsibility of not interfering with their digestion. It was definitely ambient music. It actually put one of the record company people to sleep. He was rather embarrassed to say to me 'I went to sleep' but, in fact, I considered it the ultimate compliment."

I don't generally dump effusive praise over rock stars when we talk, but I cannot *not* say this to him: "Your work on 'Baby's on Fire' is perhaps my favorite guitar solo ever."

Fripp pauses and smiles. "Yes, that was a good one, wasn't it?"

I later learned that the disjointed squalls and squawks were patched together — it wasn't just one crazy-ass take — which saddens me slightly but not enough to knock it from the top of my list. But there is a lesson here: never try to find out how the sausage is made. Or maybe another: It doesn't *matter* how the sausage is made. It's the result that counts.

Now: Eno. Remember, this was way before Eno was a famous record producer; he was still a hip, avant-garde self-described "non-musician."

"Now," says Fripp, "1979 is the year of the Eno. Originally, Eno acquired a credibility through working with Robert Fripp and now, ironically, Robert Fripp is acquiring a credibility for having worked with Brian Eno. This is one of those ironies of life I observe with interest and amusement. I work incredibly well with Brian because basically we're both funky English blokes. I think we're genuinely fond of each other. The fame thing, which has intruded from time to time, doesn't hurt our relationship.

"There was a time when Eno was very concerned to be successful. In 1975, when he became less interesting. Now, he's not so interested; he's more, if you like, laid back. Very happy to be what he is. Now that I'm concerned to be successful, I have lost my interest as a human being that I had three or four years ago. But in 1981, when I can abandon this particular approach, I will revert to being once again quite interesting and intriguing.

"I was working with Brian last night on the Talking Heads album which is going to be the album of 1980 — so much better than the last one. It's excellent; ideas without compromise.

"I'm very happy to drop names of famous people. I know it makes me seem to be infinitely more important than in reality I am. It makes me seem to be a lot more interesting than I am."

It's time to talk *Exposure*. The songs range between 39 seconds and 4:41, with most falling in the pop song two-to-three-minute length (not that any are pop songs). My favorite title: "You Burn Me Up I'm a Cigarette." Contributors include Eno, Hall, Gabriel, bassist (in and out of King Crimson) Tony Levin, Van der Graaf guitarist Peter Hammill, XTC keyboardist Barry Andrews, drummer Jerry Marotta, guitarist Sid McGinnis and Phil Collins (in drummer mode, not MOR-singer mode.)

"It is a series of convoluted paradoxes," Fripp says of *Exposure*. "I would accept Socrates' notion that the poet does not understand his poetry. The ideas exist on their own quite apart from Robert Fripp. Robert is an unpleasant accident the ideas had to tolerate in order to get expression on vinyl. But some people are not used to that approach — and it's more of an Eastern notion in terms of art — [so] there's a warning to those who would develop the idea that Fripp is in some way a remarkable creative force. There is the warning (spoken at the end of the record): this is a hoax. Certainly, take it seriously, but don't take it seriously. But on the other hand, you have to take it seriously, because once you have the hoax expressed, someone slams the phone down; he doesn't like the suggestion that it's a hoax. You have paradox and double paradox. The onus is thrown back on the person to suss it out for themselves. Accept nothing from someone else's convictions."

Which leads us to something Fripp has previously declared, that he's in the midst of a "drive to 1981" which will be "the year of the Fripp." How, I inquire, will this Fripp succeed in this effort, commercially, artistically or critically?

"Obviously in terms of a phrase which is absurd as '1981 is the year of the Fripp' something particular and unrealistic is involved, and I'm talking about the level of commercial success which effectively prevents me from being a human being. Some people will say, 'Ah, the time has come for the Fripp,' not 'The time has come for the strength of these ideas,' so in 1981, people will think Fripp is really a hot geezer and I've already said it's a hoax; it's not me, it's the ideas. But some people will think it's me. So, in the same way that whenever King Crimson got dangerously near to being very successful it broke up, so in 1981, in a certain kind of way, I expect Robert Fripp will break up."

But ... "In 1981, I sense that I am going to be, in market terms, very successful — a famous figure. At that point I will have to take evasive tactics. Although many parts of me are negative and pessimistic and cynical, I have this belief, if you respond to people in a fairly straightforward way without copping an attitude, there are remarkable possibilities in terms of musical performances which are not possible when you're involved in a star trip. In that context, Fripp accepts a certain kind of role, but it in no way involves me being qualitatively different from anyone else. The assumption is in some ways that the rock star is a godlike figure or a delegate from above with special credentials. I don't feel myself to be anyone particularly special. I think I'm substantially the same person that walks onstage as walks off it."

But as a recording artist and performer, he still lives in the marketplace of music and ideas. To that end ...

"To quote Victor Hugo, 'Nothing has the strength of an idea whose time has come.' In terms of all the different aspects of what I do, I personally have no difficulty in integrating them for a number of reasons. If you can have a Zen in the art of archery or motorcycle maintenance, you can have a Zen in the art of marketing and music. My compromise is not in making the record; the compromise is in selling it. The compromise is I could probably be doing more worthwhile things from a musical point of view by being in New York recording with Eno at the moment. From another point of view, how can you equate the satisfaction of playing to 150 people in Boston with recording in New York? The compromise for me is I'm spending more time blowing my own trumpet than blowing my guitar."

But, as Yeats once said and Hüsker Dü once sang, "Everything Falls Apart." "At the end of 1984," says Fripp, "you'll have a breakdown of social order as we understand it." (I confess that, with Orwell's book and Bowie's song in our heads and Jimmy Carter's declaration of American malaise, I did not find this that far-fetched.)

"There are two-and-a-half years in which a lot can be done; there are then three further years in which something can be done with difficulty and after then, it's going to be almost impossible. I have the sense, and I can't rationally explain this, but in the fall of 1981 there will be a large-scale event which will bring home to the ordinary punter in the Midwest in America that the social milieu has changed irrevocably. Something like the abolition of the motor car as a source of private transportation. Or something as severe as that, like rationing three gallons of gas a week. So suddenly in one fell swoop, the cultural life of America has changed."

Even as a solo artist, Fripp is a collaborative sort of fellow. This will not come as a shock, but he's pretty picky about who he works with. And, not surprisingly, his criteria differ from most artists'. "I don't work with people because they're good musicians, necessarily — rarely, in fact. Generally speaking, the better the musician, the more difficult he is for me. The trained musician knows what he's going to play. If he knows what he's going to play, I might as well not have him on my session. I'm interested in that point where he finds what he can't play."

There were no ground rules set for this interview. I'm not good with ground rules to begin with, but I think we were both inclined to discuss the present and future, not the past. Still, a little Crimson had to color the convo.

In King Crimson, with its innumerable lineups (dubbed "projekts"), Fripp says the other players "know what they're doing, so [my job] is 'How do I unfix them?'"

"You wouldn't believe the fights I had," Fripp says. "For example, in *Larks' Tongues in Aspic, Part One*, I wanted [drummer] Bill Bruford to play 4/4 [time] against my signature — the main theme from the guitar had no time signature whatsoever — to construct a certain perspective. Bill wouldn't, he had to play in 7/8. So, the perspective I wanted didn't exist. It was far too complicated. My approach is always direct. If something appears to be elusive, you know there's a reason for it."

Remember that "drive to 1981"? It turned out to mean the return of King Crimson. I saw them that October at Boston's Metro.

"I'm a shy guy," Fripp explained at the outset. "I'm off to the side and keep quiet." Which was mostly true but, after six songs, Fripp set off to explain what the heck he and Crimson — now with guitarist Adrian Belew on board — were doing here, you know, considering everything said above. He didn't get there. The prog crowd hooted and hollered, happy to have their reigning guitar king back in their midst.

My take, in brief, back then: "So with King Crimson, Fripp has recreated a complex bird — part soaring eagle, part wise owl, part funky chicken and part, possibly, albatross."

When I saw Crimson again, in 1984, at Boston's Orpheum, I found them "a curiously soulless vehicle. They left you dazed and dazzled, but also numb and bothered."

I've talked with bassist Tony Levin over the years. In 2021, I asked, as the longest-serving member of King Crimson not named Robert Fripp, what keeps him engaged, amused or interested after all these years?

"It's a great challenge for me, being in this band," Levin said. "This is the place where I push myself to try new techniques, to not do what I've done before, even if it's the same pieces I've played before. That's the ethic in the band, for all of us, and it's what makes it really 'progressive,' in my opinion. I can't say that I always achieve that goal of finding new valid ways to play, but it's fun moving in that direction, sometimes tossing out ideas that seemed worth trying, and all of us seeing where we're at after that."

How about King Crimson being regarded as some sort of standard bearer for prog-rock? In my head, as when someone says "punk" my first thought is Ramones, when someone says "prog," my first thought is Crimson. "My context for King Crimson," said Levin, "is just being part of the band. I'm pretty removed from what people, even the fans, are thinking about the band. It remains a great learning experience and musical challenge for me, but I don't give any thought to where we stand in the world of progressive rock or the historic element of what Crimson has accomplished. I have enough on my hands trying to play the music well."

Next experience: Seeing Robert Fripp and the League of Crafty Guitarists in 1990 at the Paradise, the League being eleven guitarists sitting in a semicircle, all equipped with acoustic-electric Ovations, playing multiple melodies, countermelodies and polyrhythms, a cross-genre blur — a symphonic slam, as it were. The League grew out of Guitar Craft Services, a music/lifestyle school Fripp opened in Charles Town, West Virginia in 1985. Fripp was not speaking to the press this time, but Crafty Guitarist Steve Ball told me, "It's for people who are intellectual and interested in a heady approach to music. But the music has real power to pull on the heartstrings. Being in the middle of it, it's hard for me to step outside and classify it, but to me it feels like rock and roll. It definitely has a sexual energy about it; the only thing that is really missing is a bass drum. We're interested in presenting something real to people. We're not interested — and Robert has never been interested — in inflating his own pretensions or kissing anyone's bright ideas about stardom."

In 1998, Fripp was back in Boston for a solo gig at Mama Kin Music Hall, the venue Aerosmith once owned. His act is an evening of instrumental soundscapes, music that could find a home on *The X-Files*: just Fripp, a guitar, a guitar-synth and foot pedals, all run through a delay and manipulated. Layers upon layers, calm juxtaposed with turbulence, ambience with a hint of dissonance, an ebb-and-flow celestial squall.

Fripp had decided to mix music and chat. He played for 73 minutes, announcing the run time after it was over by checking his watch. He noted a *USA Today* poll that fixed the average American attention span at 23 minutes, adding that "most responsible, good-hearted people will put up with 45 minutes of something they don't like." Then he took questions from the audience. One of them: How does the music *move* through Fripp?

"It works when you really know what you're doing and you abandon that. Your technique is available, but it's not controlled by the rational part. There's the assumption of innocence within the context of experience put aside."

To the uninitiated, Fripp's guitar explorations might have seemed like sonic wallpaper moving in stereo. He acknowledged as much when he joked from the stage about reluctant girlfriends being dragged to the show by nerdy, fanatical boyfriends. To the cognoscenti, Fripp's music is both a balm and a challenge, or, as one appreciative fan said from the Mama Kin floor "bizarre and difficult to digest."

As a dimly lit solo performer, swiveling on a stool, twiddling knobs and massaging the guitar strings, Fripp is an enigma. He says he may start with an idea — but then develop or abandon it. You can't lose the backbeat because there is none. Ladies and Gentlemen, We Are Floating in Space.

This is not Fripp as Capt. Speedfingers, guitar hero. It's Fripp executing a slow dazzle. It's Fripp working without a net, but capable of mesmerizing. "Every time you play," he says, "it's terrifying. Like embracing my wife [pop singer Toyah Wilcox], it becomes more and more mysterious to me, embracing the impossible. Whether I'm afraid of it or don't know, I will trust the event."

Did he enjoy the performance? a fan inquired. Fripp thought for a moment and said, "I enjoyed it enough to make me do it again tomorrow night."

After various Crimson get-togethers over the years, Fripp went on a (rather articulate) anti-Crimson tirade in *Mojo* in July 2022, quite possibly burying the band for good. On the ever-changing lineups: "It was awful all the way. Until 2013, when it became only difficult." Was it over? "I don't know." Current plans: "There are none at all." What he enjoyed most was the playing, the concerts. What he liked least: Most everything else.

I talked with Levin in March 2023. Was the Fripp-run King Crimson done, or, at the minimum, taking a long nap?

"I know better than to speak for Robert, but when I last was with him — the tour ended in Japan at the end of 2022 — we had a nice talk about the future and what might happen. His words to me were that he had no plans for King Crimson doing anything else, but he would let King Crimson speak to him if it chose to. I interpreted that to mean there are no plans and probably won't be anything else, but it's not impossible that there might be."

Levin says he knew a few months before the Crimson tour ended that Fripp was pulling the plug. "It was a pretty emotional ending for me, the tour and the band. There was no negativity, but I was very sad."

The playful and fun Fripp surfaced during the pandemic lockdown doing *Toyah & Robert's Sunday Lunch* series, a weekly wacky series of covers, uploaded to YouTube with his wife, the bouncy and buxom Wilcox. Among the choices: Metallica's "Enter Sandman," Alice Cooper's "Poison," Motörhead's "Ace of Spades," the Who's "My Generation" and "Won't Get Fooled Again," the Sex Pistols' "Pretty Vacant" and "Anarchy in the UK," Britney Spears' "Toxic," Black Sabbath's "Paranoid" and Billy Idol's "Rebel Yell." ◆

PETER GABRIEL

HALLOWEEN 1978. Anticipation is running high inside the packed Paradise as Peter Gabriel is about to take the stage, his first gig in the Boston area since leaving Genesis three years earlier.

Gabriel does not enter the venue in the usual way, with fanfare, from the wings. He comes in, unobtrusively at first, from the rear, picking his way through the 550-seat theater, winding his way through tables, chairs and people, toting a portable spotlight. He's in no hurry, lighting up faces in the crowd before ascending a few feet to the stage.

His band members do the same, emerging from different points in the club, walking through the audience, sending shards of light dancing as synthesizer wizard Larry Fast, already onstage, plays an entrancing introductory theme.

The theme is clear: He/they is/are one of us, one with us.

"I do prefer that in a way," Gabriel told me later, "because you are essentially a very regular member of the audience. You're coming out of the crowd rather than putting yourself on a higher level with a blast of trumpets and macho poses."

Seated at the piano, he opened the show not with a big bang but with "Me and My Teddy Bear," plopping his smiling stuffed friend down for a touchingly straightforward rendition of the nursery rhyme. The child within.

Another gesture supporting this premise: At one point during the show, Gabriel turned his back to the crowd and gently, gracefully lowered himself onto the out-

"I prefer essentially [being] a member of the audience. You're coming out of the crowd rather than putting yourself on a higher level."

Peter Gabriel

Peter Gabriel being held aloft by fans, 1987

PHOTOGRAPH BY TONY LEVIN

stretched hands of fans, his body passed from person to person, group to group. He was the star, certainly, but we were all part of the play. He trusted us to do our part, pass him around and not let him drop. This was the intimacy he craved after being in far bigger arenas with his prog-rock band. It was the first time I'd seen anything like that — the fourth wall broken in such a manner, the star/fan line of demarcation melted, a bond of love and trust established. Gabriel brought full-body contact to rock and roll. (This was before slam dancing, moshing and stage diving, a rather different sort of interaction — not without affection, just more bumps and bruises.) Gabriel, 28 at the time, wanted the human touch.

The song that most relates to this experience, "Lay Your Hands on Me," didn't come out until four years later, on *Security*. That was the album's North American title (Geffen Records insisted); in the rest of the world, it was *Peter Gabriel*, same as his first three solo records.

"The original idea of giving the albums the same name," he told me, "was that with, say, *Time* or *Newsweek* you remember it not by the headline but by the picture on the front. I was thinking of it like a magazine.

"Also, a lot of bands try and get each album looking totally new and different. It's like marketing soap, where the same chemicals are sold in 50 different packets, each claiming to be new and different from the others. So, I thought, particularly as I wanted a low profile, that I would adopt a fairly simple approach to the sleeves where they wouldn't be particularly exciting. They were more for sort of close second and third viewing, rather than initial shock impact." (Referencing the cover images, those first three albums are colloquially referred to by fans as "Car," "Scratch" and "Melt.")

There's something special about seeing — and then talking with — an artist who's in the process of reinvention. It is a primary pleasure of the rock critic job, I suppose, and my time with Gabriel — that first concert, one that followed in 1980, plus an interview — ranks high in my book. What made it extra special: You've liked where he's been, get where he's at now but have the feeling you're going to like where he's going even more. Genesis fit the tenor of the Yes/ELP/King Crimson/Van der Graaf Generator prog-times, but those times were a-changing. Punk and post-punk were knocking at the door. Loudly.

Genesis's accelerating popularity restricted their musical development — radical changes might rock the boat too violently — and yet Gabriel was yearning to experiment more. Additionally, and importantly, he was frustrated by the band's cerebral bent and sought to instill more passion into his music. He agrees with friend and collaborator Robert Fripp that many of the so-called prog-rock bands turned out to be artistic disappointments. "Progressive used to mean people who were exploring music, and it came to mean people who used a lot of keyboards," Gabriel says with a soft laugh.

Just as punk and post-punk hit us, it hit them as well. Some established stars who were musically sophisticated and culturally aloof scorned punk's minimalism and its low bar for professional entry. But that was not the view of Gabriel and Fripp, both of them extremely accomplished musicians. As rock's d.i.y. culture took shape, Gabriel saluted and embraced it with a song of that name, playing it at that first concert. Big was not better. Gabriel had left Genesis's vocal chores in the hands of drummer and entertainer-to-be Phil Collins.

Asked what changed in his songwriting process from Genesis, Gabriel says, "More personal, more emotional, less based on instrumental arrangement and more on songs." Short on new material at that first solo concert, he played exactly one Genesis song, "The Lamb Lies Down on Broadway" as an encore.

After leaving Genesis, he retreated from the whirlwind of the music world and did not release his solo debut for two years. The first *Peter Gabriel* is a marvelous, eclectic album. Gabriel moves easily from a full-throated rocker ("Modern Love") to a barbershop quartet ("Excuse Me") to a Randy Newman-like blues ("Waiting for the Big One") to a panoramic, orchestrated epic ("Down the Dolce Vita").

When he went out on tour, Gabriel made the decision to drop the props and elaborate costuming which had been integral to his former group. "It was important," he says, "particularly having left Genesis, because people initially knew me for that and some who hadn't particularly been into the band had seen me, perhaps, as a glorified clotheshorse. I thought I should just try and change. To get my songwriting and music taken seriously, I should start again, very simply, and try to achieve things with a minimum of extraneous devices."

By leaving the masks behind, Gabriel was able to develop his talent for projecting. Few rock and rollers thrust themselves into characters as convincingly as Gabriel does, and few rock and rollers have such a diverse array of characters — and situations — to slip in and out of.

So, there were new horizons ahead. And dice to roll. Would the Genesis fans follow him? Would he pick up new fans, perhaps those enamored of both the songs and his newly stripped-down style? (We know how that worked out, with albums going gold or platinum and Gabriel ascending back to arenas. And with Genesis holding its own, commercially anyway, with smoother songs and Collins in front.)

There's some ironic hindsight that can be employed and enjoyed. While Gabriel's albums came out on Charisma in the UK, the U.S. distribution deal for the first two albums were with Atco and Atlantic. But Atlantic rejected the third out of hand, forcing a worldwide delay in its release until he moved to Mercury Records.

"Atlantic hated it," Gabriel says bluntly, "and in their wisdom decided that the album and the artist should be given the elbow. They thought the album was too esoteric and called it 'commercial suicide.' They thought that the first one was good — 'Solsbury Hill' [the most-played song on the first album, the catchiest, most jaunty one] was a very salable product. On the second album. I seemed to be moving to left field; on the third one I seemed to disappear off the edge of the universe.

"The reaction to my album," he continues, intently, "is an example of the sort of corporate thinking where, unless an artist is going to do more than 100,000 [units], they're not even going to bother. If artists aren't encouraged and given the opportunity to experiment, then you're going to get a whole mass of conservative, non-risk music."

Irony department: Atlantic A&R guy John David Kalodner, who rejected Gabriel's third album, became the guy who signed Gabriel to Geffen for his fourth. (Sales, you know.)

Gabriel saw the future of real progressive rock in newer bands, such as Random Hold (his opening act on an early tour), XTC, Magazine, Talking Heads and Human League — groups challenging accepted conventions and taking risks.

"Risk" is a word Gabriel uses frequently when discussing music. He speaks of music in terms of "investigating and exploring." He isn't against making money, but he is disturbed by labels that think too much in terms of record sales.

"My attitude has always been to make the music that I want to make — keep that process clean — and then, when it's finished, try to sell it. Things have gone very well in Europe. If America works, great, but I'm not going to start changing the way I do things in order to encourage it to happen."

Regardless of what Atlantic Records thought, the third *Peter Gabriel* matches the high standards of the first two. The quasi-jaunty "Games Without Frontiers" is every bit as elevating as "Solsbury Hill" — maybe just a smidge more worldly. "The Intruder," the taut, slightly dissonant opening track, has Gabriel assuming the role of a burglar who creeps into a home, clips the telephone wires and leaves a "mark." (Visions of Charles Manson's gang and the Tate/LaBianca slaughters?) At first, Gabriel concedes there may be a bit of himself in the song, then backs up to say, "I think that's a little bit theatrical, but I do enjoy the menace."

The inspiration for "Family Snapshot" came from Arthur Bremer's *An Assassin's Diary*. (Bremer shot and paralyzed George Wallace, the former governor of Alabama, during his presidential campaign in May 1972.) Gabriel plays the part of the assassin, waiting along with the television camera crews for the motorcade to pass by. It is, strangely, an affecting song, both grimly horrifying and compassionate. The imminent terror lurks in the churning rhythm but, suddenly, the juggernaut-like momentum comes to an unexpected halt and we're let inside the gunman's mind: "I don't really hate you / I don't care what you do ... I want to be somebody ..."

"One of the interesting things in Bremer's book," Gabriel muses, "was his obsession with fame. He was planning the assassination — and initially, I think, he was after Nixon — to coincide with world news broadcast times, late night in Europe and early evening news in America." Gabriel was intrigued by the relationship between a killer and his victim and by the fine line that divides the sane from the insane. "In the media, criminals are portrayed as subhuman monsters and we are allowed to carry on, in the safety of our own thinking, to believe we're not like that. I think there are rapists and murderers in every psyche." He pauses, adding with a chuckle, "It's just not all are realized."

The third album's centerpiece is "Biko," Gabriel's most political song to date, in which chanting, mournful bagpipe melodies and buzzing synthesizer lines are woven into a transfixing African rhythm. "It is about the simplest thing I've ever written, just three chords. If I hadn't used a rhythm box to write the song around, I would have made it much more complicated." It may be simple, but the song is one of Gabriel's most evocative.

He began to piece "Biko" together in September 1977 after the South African anti-apartheid leader was killed in a Port Elizabeth prison. Police brutality was widely suspected, but South African police claimed Biko initiated a "scuffle" in which he was killed. An official inquest supported the police.

Biko was the twenty-first Black person in 19 months to die in police custody. "There had been so many mysterious prison deaths," says Gabriel. "When Biko was actually taken in there seemed to be enough world attention that I thought it would guarantee his safety."

The last time I saw Gabriel in concert was in 2012 at the TD Garden in Boston. It dinged that old bell of intimacy, what I'd thought back on Halloween 1978 at the small Paradise Theater.

There was music and magic, lots of it. Gabriel was onstage for more than two hours, offering a wide range of A-level stuff, from blistering art-funk to atmospheric prog-rock. Warmth, spirituality and passion — all there. More than a few times, Gabriel played the part of the masterful pied piper, leading his merry band as they skipped, trotted, twirled and strutted in concentric circles or around the perimeter of the stage.

But first there was talk. At 62, rotund and balding, with short, clipped gray hair and a white goatee, dressed in a black anorak vest over a blue shirt, black pants and black boots, Gabriel seemed professorial. He strolled out as the crowd was still settling in and the lights were still on. He explained that the concert he and his six mates were about to perform would begin with an unfinished song with the lights on — just him on piano and bassist Tony Levin — and continue in a low-amped vein, as they stripped down songs to their essentials. He noted these demo-like renditions were sometimes more interesting than the final product. Part two would be more electric — faves and rarities from his solo career — and part three would be the entirety (in sequence) of his mainstream breakthrough album, 1986's "*So.*"

And so, the journey began, although the straight talk intro and lights-on bit made the opening disarmingly low-key. In the second song, the once-menacing tone of "Shock the Monkey" was replaced by a jazzy vamp. Was this a signal that we were getting Gabriel Lite? No. As "Family Snapshot" unfolded — that song about fame and infamy written from an assassin's viewpoint — the drama kicked in. Midway through, the house went dark, and the lighting rigs — five mobile units onstage and numerous ones overhead — exploded. "I want to be somebody," sang Gabriel. "You were like that, too / And if you don't get given, you learn to take / And I will take you."

Gabriel and company packed a myriad of punches, from the rhythm-heavy "Digging in the Dirt," "Sledgehammer" and "Big Time" to the jaunty lilt of "Solsbury Hill" and the redemptive wash of "Red Rain." "In Your Eyes," a romantic song with a touch of darkness, had neat new syncopation, verging on reggae and calypso.

For years, Gabriel has embraced technology — lights, staging, video — to create a synchronous mesh with his music, whichever way it twists. It can be fierce; it can be friendly; it's often complex. This staging was starker and more minimalist than some of his tours, but it was dynamic.

The mobile lighting rigs (think *Alien*) were moved about by a crew dressed in dark jumpsuits and mesh facemasks. The lights on the tower arms loomed, swooped, hovered and probed. They could be ominous, as in "No Self Control" and "We Do What We're Told (Milgram's 37)," but almost comforting in "Mercy Street." There they seemed to cradle Gabriel. He performed the song, in part about a girl painfully missing her late father, on his back, coiling into a near-fetal position as he sang about her desire to be "in your daddy's arms again."

Video images, mostly live concert shots taken from numerous angles, including directly above the stage, some in black and white, some distorted, were projected on the side screens and behind the group. With his veteran crack band — Brookline-born Levin, guitarist David Rhodes, keyboardist David Sancious and drummer Manu Katché — Gabriel added to his legacy on this tour. He also had two female backup singers, Jenny Abrahamson (who took Kate Bush's role on the "Don't Give Up" duet) and Linnea Olsson.

The finale was "Biko," a song Gabriel's been using in this slot for decades, and it never fails to nearly bring tears. At this show, Gabriel dedicated the menacing, drum-driven hymn to the young rebels of today, some of whom have given their lives for causes they believe in. The somber tune evolved into something spiritual and uplifting when the closing "uh-uh-oh" chant was sung onstage and by the crowd as the band walked off one by one, leaving Katché pounding the beat. Emotions high. Lights out. And then a single beam of light shone down from the roof in front of the stage. ◆

GINGER BAKER

AH, GINGER BAKER, I KNEW HIM WELL. He was a jolly old soul.

No, I did not know him well — I don't think many did. And no one has ever used the word "jolly" to describe him.

In fact, this chapter is pretty much a piss-take on what I defined as my aspirations in the book's introduction: that I'd be writing about musicians whose career and music I knew and had a certain amount of insight into or intimacy with, that I made a connection and revealed some ineffable truth via music and/or conversation.

This 2014 interview with the famed Cream (and so much more) drummer was a one-off, a phone interview from his home in England. I later learned Baker was contractually obligated to do X amount of press to promote an upcoming Boston gig by Ginger Baker's Jazz Confusion. I was one of those Xs. We had a half-hour blocked out. A painful half-hour for both of us, though I think his pain was more like indifference with a soupçon of annoyance while mine was a churning pit-of-the-stomach feeling of failure to communicate. But I believe my pain is your gain. There's some humor here, much at my expense, for the reader.

Then 74, Baker was touring to promote *Why?*, his first record in 16 years (and ultimately his last). The album, which featured James Brown's saxophonist Pee Wee Ellis, was keyed around Baker's African-styled/jazz drumming in synch with percussionist Abass Dodoo and bassist Alec Dankworth. It's all-instrumental except for the title

"I make all the wrong friends and trust all the wrong people."

Ginger Baker

Ginger Baker drumming at the Boston Garden, summer 1972

song, during which there's a repeated, strangled cry (presumably Baker's) of "Why?" I'm no jazzbo, but I like it.

I knew his reputation and had just seen *Beware of Mr. Baker*, the documentary which revealed him to be a cocky, ornery cuss — combative, surly, dismissive, sometimes violent. So, I did not enter this encounter without forewarning. Still, it was the most awkward interview of my life. He evinced little interest in much of anything save reiterating that he was the world's best living drummer. I can't say I was shocked.

A few years ago, I was having dinner with former Gang of Four drummer Hugo Burnham and Baker's name came up. "The thing about Ginger," said Burnham of his fellow Brit, "is that he goes way beyond the too-familiar 'difficult' or 'cantankerous' musician, most of whom are that way because they get away with it, or because it is a game, like John Lydon does. Ginger is a miserable, miserable bastard who would be that way with or without the leeway afforded him being an iconic drummer.

"His 'greatness' is built not just on his terrific, but hardly unique, polyrhythmic abilities and mastery but on the luck and timing of who he played with and when. And that applies to any of us, really! Without those elements of his career, he'd be a muttering, shouty homeless guy."

Upside? "At least he likes Charlie Watts."

Yes, the Rolling Stones drummer was one of Baker's respected peers — they shared jazz roots — and Watts speaks fondly of Baker's skill in the film. As do many other musicians: Eric Clapton, Carlos Santana, Nick Mason of Pink Floyd, Stewart Copeland of the Police and Lars Ulrich of Metallica. I put a few of those names to Baker when I talked to him. A bunch of all-stars there, aye?

"Some of them were musicians I'm not particularly fond of," Baker said, with a gruff laugh, which may not have been intended as humor. "The drummer of — what's that silly band? — Red Hot Chili Peppers. [Chad Smith] was surprised I'd never heard him play. Well, I hadn't. I'd never heard the Red Hot Chili Peppers, either."

No surprise there. At another point, asked if there's any music he listens to or enjoys, Baker responded, "I know some people do, but I don't. I don't enjoy listening to other music much at all."

If you're getting the sense that Baker didn't enjoy interviews — even more than he didn't enjoy other people's music — you're on the right track. Still, at some level, Baker understood there was some promotional component to talking to the dreaded press.

Not a bad question, I thought, so I asked: The album is called *Why?* Why make a record? Why tour?

"To put food on the table," Baker answered. No further discussion on that point about what the music did for him, what it meant to play for audiences that still loved him (no matter what) or why jazz and not rock.

Does Baker get pleasure from drumming? "I still enjoy playing," he said, as flatly as he said everything else.

The man suffered from emphysema and degenerative arthritis of the spine as well as some hearing loss. As such, he said "Wot?" a lot, both to rehear the question and, I'd wager, to suggest the ridiculousness or impertinence of said question.

Baker cut his teeth in jazz and blues groups, but he came to fame in Cream (Rock and Roll Hall of Fame inductee, 1993), which would make him, at some point, a rock drummer. *Screech!* Baker insisted he doesn't and never had played rock. (And there's the matter of his playing Afro-pop ...)

Let's go to the tape.

I figure I'll try talking about a mutual acquaintance Baker has recorded with ...

I know John Lydon pretty well. His is one of the first and last voices in Beware of Mr. Baker. *He calls you "a man who stands for something in life that probably most of you do not, no matter how awkward this character may appear to you."*

Yeah.

You played on four tracks of PiL's 1986 album, Album. *What made you want to work with John?*

I don't know what you mean.

He, a punk rock legend, and you the same from the hippie era. What about his music did you like that you wanted to be part of?

I didn't even know he was gonna be a part of it. I just came to do some sessions.

Were you told Lydon was part of it?

I don't remember, really. It was a long time ago.

I ask because it was a collaboration I might not have expected, and it turned out very well.

[Silence]

Many music fans are being introduced, or perhaps reintroduced, to you through Beware of Mr. Baker. *Did you enjoy the movie or think it was accurate?*

Some of it was OK and some of it was not. Some of the people interviewed, I didn't know that they were going to be interviewed. People that really had nothing to do with anything.

One thing I enjoyed in the film was learning about your jazz band roots, and then your work in blues bands, into and out of Cream and Blind Faith, and then this total immersion into Afro-pop, with Fela Kuti. Can you tell me about that period? It seems one of the best of your life.

Uh, sorry, I don't know where you're coming from.

What did it feel like making that transition from a rock- (and rock star-) oriented setting to going to Nigeria, finding these new polyrhythms, kind of starting fresh?

I've never been in a rock-orientated situation.

OK, what would you call Cream and Blind Faith?

It's good music. It's people like you who put labels on things.

We critics do tend to do that.

You want to put everything in a little box and put it on the shelf.

I know that can be confining and doesn't …

In both Cream and Blind Faith, the vast majority of what we played on stage was improvised.

Well, there is rock music that's improvised, but that's not what you felt this was, right?

I don't really understand.

What about the pleasure you found playing with the other drummers in Nigeria, the discovery of that music and the joy in it. How did that feel to you?

Oh … Pass.

Asking Baker questions necessitated a fair amount of full-stops and pivots. Figuring he was living in the moment, I thought he might want to extoll the virtues of the Jazz Confusion, what they'll do Sunday. Turns out that was a stretch.

"We'll probably play most of the stuff that's on the record," he said, adding (after a prompt), "We never play the same tune the same way twice."

He doesn't play his classic Cream drum solo song "Toad" anymore. Fair enough. That was a young man's workout. But has he lost anything over the years as a drummer? "Nothing!" Baker exclaimed. "Well, stamina, yeah, but I'm still playing. I think I'm playing better than ever because of that."

Back to the past. The most emotional part of the movie, where Baker actually tears up, is about his drummer idols and friends: Art Blakey, Elvin Jones, Max Roach, Phil Seaman. Beyond family, beyond other musicians, those friendships are the most important thing to him.

This, indeed, was where Baker got the most expansive with me. "It was the guys I was listening to [growing up]. I thought they were all fucking great, and then meeting them, they accepted me on the same level as they were, which was very rewarding. They could have just laughed and said, 'Go away, you silly man' and that didn't happen. They all became very good friends of mine. Mutual respect, you know."

Now, the heroin years — 19 of them. And the Cream days while he was using ... and the Cream reunion after he kicked.

How did you get introduced to heroin?

It was a guy named Dicky Devere, another very good drummer. I was using smack before I met Phil [Seaman], and when Phil found out, he burst into tears. He was warning me don't do it, and I was already doing it. He didn't know.

I've known musicians who've been addicted, and it can be pretty debilitating in most cases. But you had a very creative period while using.

How do you mean "debilitating"?

It was not *debilitating?*

No, not at all. There are people at the top who do too much all the time and just go out and get hurt. There's people who use it with respect, so they're capable of doing what they're doing, doing their jobs. It depends, really.

So why did you quit if it seemed to work?

Well, it worked for a while. Heh-heh. I decided to get off in 1964 and it wasn't until 1980, '81 that I actually managed to do it.

In the documentary, Clapton talks about your compulsion for both drums and drugs. He says, "Ginger was pretty dismissive and anti-social, seriously anti-social." But he adds that you "had the gift, the spark, the flair, the panache. His musical abilities are full spectrum. He is a fully formed musician. He can write and compose and arrange and he is harmonic."

I am a musician, yeah. I read and write music and do all the things like that that musicians are supposed to do.

Do you have resentment that you didn't get credit for co-writing in the Cream days? Like moving "White Room" from 4/4 time to 5/4?

[pause] There was stuff I was very involved in that I never even got a thank you for, yeah.

Does it gnaw at you, or do you think, well, that was then, I have to move on?

[pause] It will never go down well with me, no.

The Cream reunion in 2005: A one-time only thing, right. Will you do it again?

I don't think so.

Why did you do it in the first place?

I didn't want to do it in the first place. Heh-heh.

What persuaded you to do it then?

Eric.

And he said ...

Um ... I don't know. He phoned me up and we had a long chat, OK.

What he said made sense?

Well, I'm glad I did it now, yeah.

You made a pile of money, $5 million I heard. Yet, the money didn't exactly stay with you. Managing money has been a problem your whole life, right?

Yeah, I make all the wrong friends and trust all the wrong people.

I'm told you're in constant pain. Your back. Does the medication alleviate that?

Wot?

I'm told you're in constant pain. Your back. Does the medication alleviate that?

Yeah. Yeah, it does. I don't move around much if I can help it. Traveling is a nightmare, even more than half an hour in a car is painful. I try to travel with as little as possible.

There is going to come a point when the end happens. People are going to be writing your obituary. What would you like the first line of your obituary to read?

I don't know. That I'm a drummer. Heh-heh.

Not the best "rock" drummer?

I wouldn't want that to be said at all.

Just drummer period?

Best drummer. Yeah, to say I was the best drummer.

Ginger Baker's Jazz Confusion took the stage at Boston's Wilbur Theatre right on time. But Baker had a habit of cutting sets short, walking offstage and ending shows prematurely.

The band wasn't more than 15 minutes into this one when Baker got up from his stool and started off, stage left. Out in the audience, jaws dropped and knowing grimaces crossed faces. Fuck me, he's gonna go! Then, he paused — forgetting something? realizing something? — turned to face us and returned to the mic at his kit. "I'm an old man, and I've got to take a piss," he explained. Truly, one of the funniest/coolest/most honest things I've ever heard on stage.

He exited, did his business and returned to lead a great concert. It was a jubilant, high percussive and polyrhythmic celebration of tribal rhythms. Ginger Baker was in his element. With musicians he respected. With an audience that paid to see him.

Four years after talking to Ginger, I interviewed his son, Kofi, who is also a drummer. He'd been playing jazz at a Los Angeles club called the Baked Potato while also playing in a trio called the Music of Cream with Jack Bruce's son Malcolm on bass and guitarist-singer Will Johns, the son of Stones/Zeppelin producer Andy Johns and a nephew of Eric Clapton and George Harrison.

I mentioned his father's aggression in the film. (At one point, Baker hits writer-director Jay Bulger over the head with his walking stick, breaking his nose.)

"I just broke my hand four days ago punching a wall. I'm realizing I'm actually my dad!" Kofi said with a laugh. "A lot younger, but I'm living as Ginger Baker at the moment, which is really stupid."

I said that when Ginger and I spoke, aside from the general disinterest and latent antagonism, he mostly said "Wot?"

"Wot?! Wot?! Wot?!" Kofi said, again laughing. "Don't ask him a question that may be even slightly ... you can't ask him *any* questions, really. If you ask him about horses and polo [Ginger's passions], he's fine.

"I'm so much like him in personality it's really stupid. My mum used to say to me, 'How are you so much like him when you weren't around him?' Because he left home when I was about six or seven. My sister's saying, 'You're fucked up, just like our dad!' And I'm, 'Oh fuck, I don't want to be like my dad.'"

I mentioned how touching it was to see father and son playing drums together in *Beware of Mr. Baker*. "That part in Colorado, when we sit down and play together, that was the best part of my life with him," said Kofi. "I could connect with him on a level that I love and he loves. I'm baffled as to why he would throw that away."

And their current relationship?

"Unfortunately, he's got to that point where it's pointless talking to him. For a start, he can't hear anything. He's been on heroin and morphine his whole life, and I think it's really taken its toll. I don't really talk to him anymore. There was this *Rolling Stone* interview where I said, 'My dad's dead to me.' It wasn't meant as 'fuck off.' It was meant like he's kind of already gone. He's past that point of no return.

"I'd love to talk to him. I'm kind of pissed off with him for not giving me a relationship through my life with him. I've had little bits here and there. I'm a drummer, my dad was a drummer. It would be such a fucking great relationship to be able to talk to my dad and sit down and play with him."

On October 6, 2019, a year after Kofi and I talked, Ginger Baker died from chronic obstructive pulmonary disease. He was 80. ◆

"As a writer, it's a danger to exaggerate your own emotions. It's probably a greater danger to conceal them."

Warren Zevon

Warren Zevon performing in Boston, 1980

PHOTOGRAPH BY MICHAEL GRECCO (GRECCO.COM/DAYSOFPUNK.COM)

WARREN ZEVON

I FIRST MET WARREN ZEVON after a show he and his band did in May of 1978 at Boston's Berklee Performance Center. I was a rock critic for the *Bangor Daily News*, down from Maine to cover two emerging talents, Zevon and Elvis Costello. (Different venues, of course.)

Costello's show was riveting and intense — bang, bang, bang, under an hour, after which he and the Attractions exited and turned up the feedback to drive us out of the theater. Zevon's was more fan-friendly, kind of fun but sloppy. Zevon was, as they used to say, in his cups. Those cups of clear liquid he'd been drinking weren't water.

Zevon was riding high behind his second album for Asylum Records, *Excitable Boy*, and its improbable novelty hit, the bloody three-chord romp "Werewolves of London." Zevon's wit carried him through some of the haphazardness. He *was* an excitable boy — a witty, intelligent, inebriated one. "Part of my guitar style is playing loud and out of tune ... but spiritedly," he quipped. I guess at that point you'd call him a functioning alcoholic.

His overall performance was messy. His songs, so charged with emotion and energy on record, were rendered tepidly. The audience became disquieted and uncomfortable. For a singer with so much to offer, he couldn't deliver the goods — and didn't seem to care. We met up briefly, post-show. It was friendly enough, but, as you might imagine, a bit awkward.

The next time we talked, it was 1980 and I was doing a phone interview for the *Boston Globe*, where I'd begun freelancing after a move south. By that point, he'd gone the 12-step AA route. I mentioned the Berklee gig. He didn't recall it, of course, but said of my assessment, "Yeah, that figures."

I asked Zevon when he knew he'd hit rock bottom. He said he'd told his then-wife Crystal about his intention and eagerness to go see Bruce Springsteen in concert. She had to inform him that he'd already done so.

"That was it," Zevon said. "It was a scary thing, but you're real lucky if the gorge rises and the self-disgust gets to a sufficient cinematic kind of thing where you *know* that you're an asshole."

That was perfect Zevon. A clever choice of words — "gorge," his disgust being "cinematic" — and the self-deprecating tone. He checked into a California facility and underwent a month-long intensive detoxification program. "They do that intervention therapy where they casually walk you into a room and there's everybody you know in the world. Each one of them has prepared a statement about all the times you were drunk, how they didn't want to tell you what an ass you made of yourself and how you imperiled everybody around you. But they're there because they believe in you. It has a pretty staggering effect."

That experience — or more likely another like it — surfaced in 1987 when Zevon released his sixth album, *Sentimental Hygiene*. With typical trenchant black humor, he sang about the routine in "Detox Mansion." There he is, merrily raking leaves with Liz and Liza, learning to be sober in the morning and golfing in the afternoon. He wrote about thinking about writing the song. I liked that he was poking a bit of fun at the celebrity aspect of rich-guy rehab, the name-dropping, but also the added pressure that comes with fame. It's hard not to fall apart, indeed.

I got to know Zevon pretty well, reviewing and interviewing him through high points and low. From the late '70s through the early '90s, when he was riding semi-high, Zevon often toured with a full band. He played full-on rocking sets with a sextet called Boulder; he called a 1991 tour with the Odds as his backing band "a cross-country existential odyssey."

In later years, Zevon toured mostly solo; he couldn't afford to bring a band on the road. His audience was at what might be termed "cult level." He'd play solo club shows, just him with a guitar and grand piano. But they weren't quiet, folkie gigs; they were pretty rollicking affairs. At one, not long after our cat had died, my girlfriend at the time, Janice, mentioned to him that Manny's meow had the same howl as Zevon's werewolf. He looked at her a bit puzzled but internalized it and, sure enough, as the inevitable encore was about to kick off said, "This one's for Manny!"

He'd play a gig at a Boston club and then schlep up to Maine to play a ski lodge. He needed to make money. Zevon's albums continued to be strong and multi-layered — the favorable reviews continued to pour in — but his audience waned and Top 40 had forgotten his name.

I asked him once if all a songwriter really needs to live comfortably is one Top 10 hit, like "Werewolves."

"Well, if you spend it wisely," he said. "Perhaps if you spend it very foolishly there's nothing to talk about three years later. It's like '00' on the roulette wheel; there is a startling overcompensation for one's labor."

In the fall of 1989, we had lunch at Musso & Frank, the hip Hollywood eatery where he was a regular. We settled in at our table, interview about to commence. The waiter came, and we ordered beverages, a beer for me, a Diet Coke for him. And then, after a beat or two, semi-alarmed, I blurted out, "Oh shit, I'm sorry. Should I not have done that?" You know, maybe it's not good form to have an alcoholic drink in front of a recovering alcoholic. Zevon paused for a few moments. Not unusual: he often took time to process before responding. It could be unnerving if you didn't know him well. He fixed me with a squinty, wry look. "Yeah, Jim," he growled. "A decade of sobriety out the window because *you're having a beer.*"

Again, perfect Zevon.

But, truth be told, Zevon's recovery wasn't exactly linear. "He had been sober for a few months, maybe six," said Crystal. "He was recording *Bad Luck Streak in Dancing School* [in 1980]. The final straw was he started drinking again. We had a house in Santa Barbara; we had a house in L.A., and the baby [Ariel]. We had this fabulous night. We went out all day picking out fabulous equipment, a stereo system, for the house in Santa Barbara. We were putting our lives together. We got in a hot tub and laughed and had a great time. And somehow in the morning, as often happens with alcoholics, if something gets too good it's more scary than dealing with the bad stuff. I went out to get the car and when I came back, he had found a bottle of cooking sherry and had drank that and found some Darvon. It was horrible. He threw his coffee cup at me when I walked in. He was saying he wasn't my father and couldn't be that guy. And that was it. I said, 'I can't stay.'

"He would get sober for brief periods but then he would go back. So, it was always difficult. But we were friends, and when he did get sober we became really close. We had a funny relationship. The 'best friends' part of our relationship survived everything else, and in a lot of ways, for me, I got the best of Warren. I didn't have to deal with the really hard stuff. We loved each other. I don't think that goes away when it's that deep and abiding."

I had Zevon's home phone number and sometimes we'd just talk. No interview involved, no tour to promote, just conversation: his observations laced with the same sort of oblique references and ironic humor you'd find in his music. We talked a lot about books and writing; he was the most well-read rocker I've ever known. His taste was eclectic and sublime — Ross MacDonald, Graham Greene, Ernest Hemingway, Stephen King, Hunter S. Thompson, Thomas Pynchon, many more.

But he had a different number in 2002, so I couldn't reach him after word of his mesothelioma, a rare cancer of the membrane around the lungs, became public. I reached out through his publicist to convey my concern and said that I'd love to speak with him if possible. We didn't connect, but I understood. He had other people, an inner circle of loved ones who were much more part of his life. I was in one of the outer circles and fine with that.

I later found out that even Jackson Browne — a longtime friend and one of the key guys responsible for getting him a record deal — couldn't get through either. "I left him a few messages," Browne told *Rolling Stone*, shortly after Zevon's death. But Browne never talked with him. "He had so many people calling — he got overwhelmed by how many people he had to talk to about this."

At that point, too, I didn't know what else he was going through. Aside from the fatal illness wracking his body, there was another relapse.

Zevon wrote a fair number of death-related songs over the years — did anyone write more? — including "I'll Sleep When I'm Dead," a semi-autobiographical one on his major-label debut. It's a rollicking, crescendo-laden rocker about proudly living the reckless life now and worrying about the consequences later. In the recorded version, after mentioning a .38 Special on the shelf, he promises to shoot himself "if I start acting stupid." In concert, after sobriety in the '80s, he changed the words to avow *not* to "use it on myself." I thought it lessened the song's impact, but I got it. I guess that character was too close to the singer and songwriter.

One of the key components of Zevon's music, as well as his personality, was his ability to intertwine the humorous and the serious — and leave it unclear which side was up. The listener (or Zevon's conversation partner) couldn't always be sure where he stood. And perhaps Zevon couldn't either. The ambiguity was a hook in and of itself.

I once asked him about "Play It All Night Long," a stomping rocker about an incestuous Southern farm family that kept playing "Sweet Home Alabama" as a comforting soundtrack. It's black-humored, touching on the plane crash that killed singer Ronnie Van Zant and two of his bandmates. Maybe that family took some small comfort or solace in the thought that Skynyrd's fate might have been worse than their own incestuous decrepitude. Was it funny?

"Well, it *is* funny, but it's also *not* funny," Zevon said. "It's not intended as a ridicule of Lynyrd Skynyrd — I don't think it's funny that rock bands get killed in plane crashes — but then the grim, crazy stuff is funny, and the overall effect is scary. It's ambivalent."

At any rate, death was often part of our conversation. In that 1989 interview, Zevon was discussing his then-current album, *Transverse City,* an oft-overlooked dark gem in his catalog. The semi-conceptual effort featured one the best post-apocalyptic songs you'd care to hear, "Run Straight Down," a dark spiral featuring David Gilmour doing some very Floydian guitar playing. You can't beat this intro, either: a mumbled "4-Aminobiphenyl, hexachlorobenzene, dimethyl sulfate, chloromethyl methyl ether, 2,3,7,8 tetrachlorodibenzo-para-dioxin, carbon disulfide." Zevon's character is one of the survivors of this environmental disaster, tired of it all and going home to watch the news at 11.

Zevon described the album as "cheerily morbid. I think we [musicians] all agreed it should be unremittingly grim. Let's take grim *all the way* — not like 'We're kind of sad, but trying to cheer you up.' If it's not funny anymore — too bad."

So, it didn't seem particularly inappropriate to ask about his future obituary. I was hardly prescient but thought there could be a chance that one day I'd be writing it. (I did.) I asked Zevon how he thought that obit would begin.

"Ow-oooh," he immediately offered, deadpan, echoing the werewolf's call. That simple, catchy rocker would be the inevitable first reference to his body of work. (It was in my story, in some way, honoring his take.) "Just three chords over and over and over," he said with a sigh, joking (or not) that "it took as long to write as it did to play it."

Just about every time Zevon played Boston, he'd change a line in that song, the one that runs "I'd like to meet his tailor!" It would mutate to "Huh, he's looking for James Taylor!" — Taylor being a local and all.

I did an e-mail interview with Taylor in August 2022 and mentioned it, quoting what Zevon sang and asked if he knew about it. He didn't. "It's the first I've heard of it," he replied, "and, being such a solid, longtime admirer of his humor and great talent, I'm delighted to learn about it."

Going back to that hit as the inevitable first reference in the obit, Zevon reasoned that there was no reason to complain. "Maybe," he mused, "you don't want to die and have it say, `This guy wrote some really sensitive, intellectual, literate songs that put everybody to sleep — this was one pretentious guy.'"

Of course, Zevon did write sensitive, intellectual, literate songs, too. Lots of them, like "Desperados Under the Eaves," "Hasten Down the Wind," "Splendid Isolation" and "Let Nothing Come Between You." But he put no one to sleep and was not in the least pretentious.

"As a writer," he told me, "It's a danger to exaggerate your own emotions. We do that, but it's probably a greater danger to hide from them or conceal them ... I realize how personal what I'm saying is, but I don't know any other way of doing it. I always took to heart Hemingway's advice: You write what you know. That's all you can write."

Zevon loved complex novelists and was acquainted with Igor Stravinsky as a teen. He could go highbrow, but liked the Ramones' "Pinhead," too. Once, he mused, "I find myself thinking 'Gabba gabba hey' and [knowing that] some pizza-eating guy thought of that phrase for some reason. That is, to me, why there is songwriting." (The phrase originated in the 1932 film *Freaks,* in the wedding party chant "Gooble, gobble, we accept her, we accept her, one of us, one of us!")

Bassist-guitarist-singer-songwriter Jorge Calderón was Zevon's frequent collaborator. They met through Zevon's then-girlfriend Crystal in 1976 and, sharing the same sense of dry humor, hit it off instantly. Well, maybe it wasn't exactly *instant*, but auspicious.

"Crystal called me one night to give her a ride to pick him up from jail, from the drunk tank," Calderón told me. "'Can you help me get my boyfriend out? He spent the night.' I said OK and went there and picked this guy up. He was sitting in the backseat and we got to the apartment they lived in. They were so frazzled that they had misplaced their house keys, so at that point I said, 'I'm Puerto Rican, I can get into anybody's house' — that was the first time he kind of like smiled at me. I went in the back of the house and found a window that was ajar, got inside the house and opened the door. From then on, we became really good friends.

"He always told me we traveled the same wavelength and had the same sensibilities. He cracked me up; I cracked him up all the time. If he would call me, we would have long, long conversations. Anytime we would hang out it was just ridiculous, which is proven in some songs we wrote together, like 'Mr. Bad Example.' It just went on and on because we laughed so hard we had to write all these verses. I kept saying, 'Let's make it really long, like one of those songs like 'Bob Dylan's Dream.' That's why the song ended up with eight verses."

Calderón sang backup on "I'll Sleep When I'm Dead," among many others, and then went on to co-write 18 songs with Zevon over the years, 15 of them recorded. Their first collaboration was "Veracruz." "That's where he finally asked me to write with him. I wrote the music and words to the Spanish part. So many songs came out of our conversations. He liked that I would say things in a special way because I would sometimes translate a thought from Spanish to English and it would come out kinda sideways and he liked that."

Calderón didn't contribute to "Werewolves of London," but he knows how the song came about. "Phil Everly gave him the idea to write a song called 'Werewolves of London.'" [Zevon played piano and served as band leader for the Everly Brothers before his solo career took off; Phil did backup vocals on *Warren Zevon*.]

"He kept that in his mind and then he got together with Waddy [Wachtel] and LeRoy [Marinell] out here in L.A. Warren said, 'I got this thing called "Werewolves of London,"' and Waddy went, 'Oh, you mean like "Aa-oooh!"' and he said, 'Yeah.'

LeRoy had this little lick that was almost, but not exactly, like 'Sweet Home Alabama,' bordering on plagiarism," says Calderón, with a laugh. "So, they all got motivated and crazy about this thing and they banged it out. They wrote it right away with the ah-oooh and everything."

The hard part about "Werewolves," says Calderón, was the rhythm. "They tried the track with different rhythm sections, and they couldn't get it right. Sometimes the easiest, dumbest groove seems to be the hardest to get, especially when you have studio guys coming in and out. I had gotten really chummy with Mick Fleetwood because I knew Stevie Nicks and Lindsey Buckingham from before. I played with them [in Buckingham-Nicks] and I stayed at their house a few times. We were friends. When they got hooked up with the English guys — with John [McVie] and Mick and Christine [McVie] — then of course we all became friends."

After a Fleetwood Mac stadium show in Miami, Calderón flew back to L.A. and went directly to the Sound Factory studio, where Zevon was doing the *Excitable Boy* album.

"I'd been working on it, doing background vocals. I'd co-written 'Veracruz' and 'Nighttime in the Switching Yard.' So, I went there to see what was going on. I saw Waddy in the back office, all bummed out. 'Why the long face?' 'Oh, man, I can't believe this — we've tried our fourth and fifth rhythm sections, and we can't fucking get this song ["Werewolves"] right. I said, 'How about Mick and John from Fleetwood Mac?' And he went 'Oh, yeah, of course!' I called and told 'em and they said, 'We'll do it.'"

Crystal Zevon's biography, *I'll Sleep When I'm Dead: The Dirty Life and Times of Warren Zevon,* hit stores in 2007. The title was truthful. There was a lot of unsavory detail, much of it relayed by friends and acquaintances. He was a sexaholic when he was on the road, and there was a combative, mean side to Zevon I did not know about. He got into verbal fights with nearly all his friends. And, actually, we *did* have one good dust-up over whether a quote he gave me and I printed was off the record or not. His pal Don Henley joined a Zevon show in Boston — which boosted ticket sales — but Henley turned it into a Walden Woods benefit. (I don't think Zevon was against charitable work, but when I asked him once — as a wave of rockers doing benefits flooded the land — he growled, "I just don't know that much about the rainforest. Unlike *Sting*.") Zevon had talked about his frustration, I printed it and he got pissed off, claiming it was off the record. We didn't communicate for a while. It was my *Globe* colleague Steve Morse who brought us back together again after a Zevon set at the Paradise.

"I did not have any altercations with him," says Calderón. "Yes, sometimes he might have gotten pissed at something I said, but it was always like two brothers that get along. But he would get into really blown-out, not-speaking-to this-asshole anymore [moods] and cut people out of his life, even Jackson [Browne], anybody he had a thing with. He was doing this song with Hunter [S. Thompson], 'Life'll Kill Ya,' and it was this humongous battle. Hunter would call and leave really insulting messages. He even argued with Bruce [Springsteen]. Even writing a song with Bruce was a hassle."

Crystal told me, "My goal was to tell his story truthfully. It wasn't easy, but I talked to him before he died and he made me promise that I would tell the whole truth, even the 'awful ugly parts,' as he put it. It was a challenge. Other people who are alive are involved in that truth.

"Warren, at his core, had a super sense of morality. I think for him it was almost like going into the confessional, in order to leave cleanly. He studied artists and read biographies and he found the process of artful creation from a philosophical standpoint something he studied all his life. Why *would* someone cut their ear off? I think he felt there might be value in [his biography]. I suppose there was an element of narcissism to it, but I think Warren knew that he had a genius IQ and had a certain talent and if that was ever recognized, he felt it was important for the person who was behind that to be recognized for who he was — the torment, the cost, I guess."

Boston record producers Sean Slade and Paul Q. Kolderie felt some of that torment when they did Zevon's 2000 album, *Life'll Kill Ya*. Zevon and I talked after the album came out and he credited the team's "Yalie deconstructionism," noting that his irony and wit went over well with his producers and that they helped sequence the songs, "from eros to thanato."

Thanato? "Death," said Zevon. "It's from the Greek god Thanatos, the personification of death, the guy who carried you to the underworld when your time was done." Death, he added, is more a reality "when you're older. You start enjoying every minute, or you remind yourself to," an early exploration of the famous "enjoy every sandwich" proclamation he made on *Letterman*. "That is what this album is for," he said. "The subjects might be darker, but the subtext might be shinier."

Zevon was years away from the hit parade. We both knew it. So, I asked if maybe he was hoping for a semi-hit. "You know me," he said. "I always say 'The job was done when I finished the songs,' but I have mood swings like a cat. I can be all puffed up like the Pillsbury doughboy [one minute], and then I'll say, 'You're so full of yourself.'"

Slade and Kolderie had different recollections of the album. "Working with Warren was really interesting," Slade told me. "After a week or so, Paul and I realized that within five minutes of him walking through the studio door you could tell whether you were going to get the good Warren or the bad Warren. The good Warren was amazing, witty, fun, the greatest guy you'd want to hang out with. The bad Warren was fiendish, hostile, argumentative and basically an asshole. And he completely admitted to that, that it was part of these weird demons that he was battling."

"It had to do with headaches," added Kolderie. "He claimed to have these blinding migraines. Whenever he was in the middle of one of those he was in a terrible mood."

Zevon wasn't drinking then, they said. Well, not alcohol. He was scarfing Diet Mountain Dew, obsessively opening a can, having a gulp and then leaving it to open another. Twenty a day. He went nuts when he found session guitarist Chuck Prophet smoking cigarettes or when Slade and Kolderie lit up a joint.

"We finished the mixes," Kolderie recalled, "and we shook hands. He said, 'We had some laughs, huh?' and I said, 'Yeah,' and that's the last I saw of him. He was personally insulting to me many times during the making of the record and it didn't really occur to me to stay friends with him. He let me know I was a punk-ass little fuckface. I was like, OK. He wanted to make a record and, as it was with Courtney [Love], you just focus on that. Tell me I'm an idiot, that's fine. I've dealt with worse than him. Producing, half of it is mood management."

Did Slade think Zevon was bipolar? "I don't think so in the strict sense of the word," he said. "He really got depressed. There was something that was hostile, and he had to suppress that or let it out. He was angry, this free-floating anger and anxiety. He wasn't comfortable in his own skin or with other people."

In the 1991 stomping polka "Mr. Bad Example," Zevon created the baddest of bad characters. His protagonist performs a life's worth of grievous misdeeds without compunction. He pilfered as an altar boy, became a swindling lawyer as an adult and went on to open an agency hiring aboriginal workers to work an opal mine while attaching their wages. For years, I thought it was a brilliant work of a fertile imagination. And it is. But while it's a comic laundry list of nefarious activity, it also calls to mind some of Zevon's own bad behavior, as does his almost pensive "Dirty Life and Times" and Crystal's book of the same title.

Miami-based satirical novelist Carl Hiaasen was a good friend and occasional collaborator of Zevon's. They co-wrote "Seminole Bingo," "Rottweiler Blues" and "Basket Case," the last also the title of a Hiaasen book.

"At the height of his popularity," Hiaasen told me in 2010, "he started misbehaving to the extent that it got in the way of concerts. Once he opened for the Grateful Dead and almost passed out on the piano keys. They said, 'Forget it, you can't open up for us,' and they're the most drugged band in the world. That's pretty severe."

On October 30, 2002, Zevon appeared on *The Late Show With David Letterman* for the last time. Zevon was Letterman's favorite musician. He'd been on the show more than a dozen times and was the fill-in bandleader when Paul Shaffer was away. In an unprecedented move, that night Zevon was Dave's only guest. He played three songs ("Mutineer," "Genius" and Letterman's favorite, "Roland the Headless Thompson Gunner") and chatted on the couch.

Zevon called it "meaningful fun" and thanked Letterman profoundly for doing so much to keep his career alive after radio had lost interest. He said pretty much the same to me during a '90s interview in New York.

Letterman asked what advice he would give others as he faced his own mortality. What did he know that we didn't? Zevon paused and said, "Enjoy every sandwich." That phrase became iconic, as ubiquitous in pop culture as the title and chorus of his 1978 song, "Lawyers, Guns and Money." I took that "enjoy every sandwich" thing literally and metaphorically. Good sandwiches *are* worth savoring, and you *should* enjoy the little things in life because it all goes away.

"He was such a gifted guy," Hiaasen told me. "Larger than life. When we would talk in his last year, he said, 'This is gonna be a lot harder on you than it is on me,' and he meant all of us who cared about him. He said, 'I went to bed so many times not knowing if I was gonna wake up. Look at it like this: I got to be Jim Morrison a lot longer than he did.'

"It was a great way of looking at it. The amount of talent was so daunting, his brain power. He was sometimes his own worst enemy, but he was in many ways a genius. When I knew him," Hiaasen continued, "he was already sober for a while. When I read Crystal's book, I don't know if I could've handled it. It was so dreadful. I didn't know that guy. He just said, when I'd mention a song that I really liked, 'I don't even remember recording it.' The separation and the difficulty, just walking away and having to reconnect, that part he regretted, not being there as a father. But all the fun, all the dope, all the booze, he just looked at me, and said, 'I had a hell of a time. I'm not sure I'd do it over any differently.'"

Zevon asked Calderón to be his primary collaborator on what was to be his final album, *The Wind.* Calderón ended up co-producing the album and writing seven of the eleven songs with Zevon. "This is before he knew he was sick," says Calderón. "He said, 'I did *My Ride's Here,* and I got so spread out with all these people I collaborated with. I got stretched out too hard. I just want it to be you and I together. There's never a problem with you — I always have fun. I don't want to argue with anybody. It's easy and we do it and I don't have to fucking think about it.'"

Many of Zevon's famous friends chipped in. Over the years, Zevon's sidemen and collaborators had included Bruce Springsteen, Bob Dylan, Neil Young, Jerry Garcia, Tom Petty, Mike Campbell, Benmont Tench, Howie Epstein, David Gilmour, Chick Corea, Jackson Browne, Mark Isham, David Lindley, Don Henley, Glenn Frey, Flea, Jack Casady, Jorma Kaukonen, Ry Cooder, Emmylou Harris, Peter Buck, Mike Mills and Bill Berry. (The three R.E.M. fellas also joined Zevon in the Hindu Love Gods, who released a self-titled album in 1990, three years after they and Michael Stipe worked on Zevon's *Sentimental Hygiene.*)

"As immodest as I am in my private moments," Zevon once told me about his collaborators, "it still kind of baffles me. Why did this guy go to all this trouble for me?"

Hiaasen recalled a phone conversation during which Zevon, whose sickness had gotten worse, said he was depressed. He'd been given liquid morphine. He'd been drinking Glenlivet.

"None of us could get to him. He hadn't finished the album, and Jorge was calling me. At one point, I was going to get on a plane and go out there. They were talking about literally taking the door off his apartment and trying to see if he was OK. He was a mess. For a long time, he wasn't reading or doing anything but sitting in that apartment. I understand it was pretty desolate and horrible. He had this loft, and everything was in gray. He'd torn out all the furniture and he'd put in all gray furniture because that was his lucky color.

"I'm glad I didn't go, because it was an ugly thing. At one point I said to Jorge and [Warren's son] Jordan, 'He's gonna end up a cliché, and he's too good to end up a cliché. He can't do this to himself; it's selfish.' 'I understand you're dying and you're bummed out, but man ...'"

"He had a major relapse," said Crystal, "and that was really difficult, especially for the children, who were trying to spend as much time as they could with him. Sometimes he wasn't available. Nobody can fault him for it. He was surrounded by a lot of people who had never known him when he was drinking and wanted one night with the Excitable Boy. So, they covered for him, brought him liquor and so on. They were pouring vodka into his Mountain Dew can. Nobody who knew him from back then — no one who knew Warren as a drunk — helped him to drink. But it was people who felt, 'I'd wanna drink if I had a death sentence.' You can't even blame them, but if enough people had said, 'You don't really want to go out like that, do you?' ... In the end, he was too sick to drink like he drank. One of our moments in the last week, he cried. He said, 'I'm sorry I drank.'"

"He bounced back, he stopped doing it, and he was perfectly good," said Hiaasen. "He told me he made up his mind; he was going to be around to see his grandchildren born and he really came out of it towards the end. We were talking again, and for [my book] *Skinny Dip*, I had sent him a manuscript while I was working on it. He said, 'I'm reading again, I can read now. I'm doing OK.' And he read all but the last three chapters. He was the one that gave me the title. Warren suggested it, the editors loved it, and he was so tickled. The last three chapters were in FedEx. He died that weekend, and they came on a Monday."

The Wind included the sweet, gorgeous ballad "Keep Me in Your Heart." It's all any of us can hope for — not eternal fame or love everlasting, just for your memory to linger for a while in someone's heart after yours has stopped beating. *The Wind* also included a cover of Dylan's "Knockin' on Heaven's Door," perhaps the most unironic song Zevon ever recorded. The resonance was obvious.

Did he believe in an afterlife?

"Warren was always seeking," Crystal told me. "He thought about it a lot. He did believe there was something. I don't know that he knew what it was, but he thought about it a lot. He was very attracted to Catholicism, coming up with a Mormon mother and a Jewish father. He did not want any kind of a Jewish service."

After Zevon's cancer was made public, Dylan started covering several of his songs in concert: "Accidentally Like a Martyr," "Boom Boom Mancini" and "Mutineer."

"He loved Dylan, and Dylan was a big fan of Warren's," said Hiaasen. "Warren was sick, and Dylan was doing a show in California. He invited Warren because he was going to do 'Mutineer' in concert." Zevon attended and met with Dylan beforehand but couldn't make it through the whole show. He was sick. Hiaasen got a voice mail afterwards: "He goes, 'Well, I just got covered by Bob Dylan. That's a sure sign of doom.'"

Which was, once again, perfect Zevon.

The last time I saw Zevon play and spent any time with him was in 2000, in the atrium of a huge space called International Place, a free-to-all midday promo gig for WBOS, an adult contemporary station in Boston that still played his music. "I just don't love daytime," Zevon said, taking the small stage, as curious passersby gathered. "This is like a puppet show in a mall." (Reference: *This Is Spinal Tap*.) He did a half-hour gig, and I met with him afterwards in his dressing room. There was genuine warmth, hugs and all.

Once, when we were talking about the rollercoaster ride of his career, Zevon said, "I get to do pretty much what I want. Sometimes, there's a gig that's not too pleasant, and there's pressure and headaches, but basically, I feel fortunate. I'm not working in the factory. I'm not breathing plastic. And people do that."

Song reference: In "Factory" (with guest harmonica by Bob Dylan) on *Sentimental Hygiene*, Zevon sings about a family whose tradition is factory work, to the detriment of their health. And the irony — oh, did the man love irony! — was that some of those factory workers were sniffing in the fumes that came from making polyvinyl chloride products — that is, LPs, his very own lifeblood.

In the jaunty title song from *Life'll Kill Ya*, Zevon sings about how, well, he said it all in the title, really. Death is the greatest humbler of all, the ultimate leveler. Some of us get diseases, some of us are knifed or shot, some of us (the lucky ones) die peacefully at home in their sleep. The Grim Reaper spares no one.

Ariel and Jordan Zevon, with their spouses, sailed out to a point in the Pacific Ocean where it was legal to scatter Zevon's ashes. And that they did. ◆

"I reduced myself to a gibbering heap of rubble ... and still I was surrounded by people who wanted to get close to me."

Pete Townshend

Pete Townshend above the Madison Square Garden stage in New York, June 1974

PHOTOGRAPH BY LINDA D. ROBBINS

PETE TOWNSHEND

"YOU'RE A POGUES FAN, THEN?"

That was pretty much the first thing Pete Townshend said to me in November 1985, as we sat down to sip tea and talk in a suite at the Berkshire Place Hotel in New York.

I was puzzled — I *am* a big Pogues fan — and wondered what the tell was. I mean, my surname is Irish, but still ... Turns out, it was simple: I'd been to London in the spring, had seen the Pogues at the Mean Fiddler and had taken their rough-and-rowdy Celtic punk ways to heart. And, as we used to wear band badges back in the day, I'd affixed a small green shamrock pin with "THE POGUES" on it — a gift from Pogues Central while I was in England — to the left lapel of my rarely worn black sports jacket. I decided to semi-dress up for the interview, my first with Pete, and pulled that jacket from the closet to go with my black Levi 501s. Unbeknownst to me, the pin was still on it from whenever I'd last worn it. Turned out to be a fantastic and fluid door-opener. He was a fan, too, so any nervousness I might have had was quelled by us talking as mutual fans of the same band.

Townshend, then 40 years of age at the time (he grew old!), was in my pantheon of rock stars — *Quadrophenia* remains one of my top albums ever — but, as much as I loved the Who, I knew there was some grim and gritty stuff we were going to get into. We soon moved past the Pogues and onto literature. Because Townshend was not there to discuss the Who — there *was* no Who at the time, they'd undertaken their *final tour* in 1982, remember? — or a solo album of his, even though one called *White City* had just come out. He was there ostensibly to chat about *Horse's Neck*, a just-published collection of 13 stories and quasi-autobiographical musings written between 1979 and 1984. Many of the stories were lacerating or self-lacerating, dealing with various destructive compulsions.

"I live in a paradox," wrote Townshend in *Horse's Neck*. "I feel comfortable with this unhappiness. I am content with misery." At another juncture: "In the public arena people are disturbed to see me consumed by nihilism, but among the truly futile I am invisible." Another: "In spurts I answer fan mail and business letters, play snooker, strum my guitar into a cassette machine, pray for forgiveness and think about what a total mess I've made of a life that had everything, and everyone, going for it."

That paradox began, he says, in 1979 after he signed two recording deals, one for the Who and one as a solo artist. He says he took on too much responsibility and began using cocaine to keep up a hectic pace. "At first, I found it a very refreshing, stimulating drug. It turned sour in about two months and, later, I started to experiment with other things. By the end of '81, I was really in the abyss.

"I reduced myself to a gibbering heap of rubble and woke up one night in some venue with a couple of bottles of brandy, [having] injected myself with whatever was available. I was literally just about breathing, covered in blood and warts and slime and phlegm and vomit and still I was surrounded by people who wanted to get close to me."

Peter Dennis Blandford Townshend came out of the abyss and wrote about it. (If you're wondering about the title, a horse's neck is a tall drink consisting of ginger ale and a liquor served over ice in a large tumbler with a spiral of lemon peel hanging inside the rim. That long, loopy twist gives the drink its name.)

How close to Townshend's real life were the characters and situations in the stories?

"There's a lot of real things, real ideas, real snatches of conversation and things," he explains. Some concern him; others came from outside. "A girl I met told me that, apart from losing her boyfriend and her baby, becoming a junkie, finding out she had cancer of the womb and being told by the doctor she had cancer because she was a whore, life was wonderful. She meant it. I burst into tears. That line struck me so deeply that I almost wanted to weave it through the whole book. I did weave traces of it through the book."

"We underrate our own resilience," Townshend says, returning to his own struggle with drugs. "I'm quite surprised. So many people tell you how ... hard it is. I didn't make any quantum leap to suddenly emerge into the space I'm in now, which is healthy and wholesome and more balanced and happier and the rest of it, but it was almost like I was walking out of a garden. The garden was very rich, abundant and lush, but it had a wall around it. And you couldn't appear to escape."

Townshend was describing the peculiar life of a rock star/drug addict, in particular the abuse of alcohol, cocaine and heroin. Alcohol and cocaine I was familiar with — who wasn't? — but heroin had not entered my veins, or my world, really. Never did enter my veins. It scared the shit out of me, but it entered my world via its use by some dear friends and rocker acquaintances, never having a positive lasting effect. I guess it worked as a temporary thing.

You might think a rock star lives in a gilded cage of sorts. Not Townshend. "I've been living in a garbage can all my life," he says, pointedly, "so I remain living in a garbage can. I know a lot of it is going to rub off on me and touch me, but it just isn't going in my mouth anymore."

Townshend smiles, pleased with both the decision and the metaphor. "I think that if you live in a garbage can, you just keep your mouth closed," he reiterates. "It's what we've got, particularly in big cities where the arts in this society thrive. It's just a fact of life that you have to live with."

Townshend credits his [then] wife Karen for the rescue. "At Christmas '81, she said to me, 'Why don't you come home?' I was living away. I said, 'I'd love to, but I have to tell you I'm using [heroin] at the moment.' She was a little bit shocked, but not particularly, 'cause I think she'd come to expect anything. I said, 'Maybe I should come home for dinner and then go away.' She said, 'No, come home and stay.' And that triggered it: She wanted me, even in that condition, when I felt that I was absolutely, completely and utterly worthless. I just decided to get myself straight."

During the interview, Townshend keeps circling back to the concept of resiliency — cheer, even — in the face of adversity. That theme also underlies *White City*, an upcoming 40-minute videotape Townshend wrote and starred in, the theme considering dead-end lives and marital conflict in a working-class section of London. The album of the same name features Townshend's best, most expansive, songwriting since 1979's *Empty Glass*.

"If there's a message, it's simply that I've recognized that in modern Western society, particularly in Britain ... futility is hope, futility is optimism. I look back through my interviews over the last 20 years and I see myself reducing everything that I've been doing to the idea that rock is a symbol of hope and optimism, and the incredible thing is, nobody has to be hopeful, nobody has to be optimistic. The potential for happiness is acutely bound up in the moment."

Townshend relates that belief to rock. "Like sex, live performance and the communion that happens in live performance is transitory. It's important that it's transitory. It sustains you, but it doesn't feed you. It doesn't provide you with what you really need, which is the ability to accept the moment. The irony is that in live performance you probably really are attending to the moment far more than you do in reality. You're *living* rock then. It's another ritual in the church of rock and roll."

Townshend launched the Who in 1964 with singer Roger Daltrey, bassist John Entwistle and drummer Keith Moon, playing revved-up R&B covers. Noted for their manic performances, surly behavior and equipment destruction, they were adopted by the mods, England's pill-popping scooter-riding youth movement of the time. But then something happened: Without turning the anger or aggression aside, Townshend evolved into one of the first songwriters to forge art out of careening rock and roll, to address real issues within the context of three-minute pop songs. "I Can See for Miles" and "The Seeker" considered the quest for personal freedom, for redemption. In 1969, he expanded his vision to the rock opera *Tommy*, about the spiritual quest of a deaf, dumb and blind pinball wizard, and made the Who superstars. In 1973, they returned to the concept format with *Quadrophenia*, examining class, alienation and generational conflict set in the mod scene.

Like the Kinks, the Who were in the second wave of mid-'60s British bands, following the Beatles and the Rolling Stones. Influenced, he says, by Ray Davies, much of Townshend's writing was — and remains — "rooted in the complexities of British society, as well as the ironies and hypocrisy involved in it."

Townshend doesn't exempt himself from accusations of hypocrisy. In 1965, at 19, he wrote "My Generation," an anthem of youthful rebellion. He conceived the famous lyric — and Daltrey sang it like he meant it, man — from the head, heart and spleen: "Hope I die before I get old!"

The Who (minus Moon, who died in 1978, but with drummer Kenney Jones) played the song on, ahem, their announced final tour in 1982.

It's not one of Townshend's proudest moments. "I played it but I didn't sing it," he says. "I wouldn't sing it. That's never coming out of my mouth again ... They're great chords. I must write new words sometime." (That proclamation, like the finality of the final tour, proved false.) With a certain bemused detachment, Townshend picks his song apart. "I did a short interview with the *Wall Street Journal* in London, and in it I ended up saying something like, 'I look back at the man I was the night I wrote "My Generation" with a sneer.' I don't sneer at work, but I definitely sneer at the sentiments. I was a ... hypocrite, really. I think over time my aim was to subvert, but at the same time infiltrate, the establishment. I think it's a great irony that the room I wrote 'My Generation' in — an indictment of the establishment and everything it represents — is smack in the middle of Belgravia, which is like Fifth Avenue, in a $400 a week apartment. Far from struggling. Hypocrisy abounds."

Now, Townshend admits, he's part of the establishment: "The establishment is not something you enter. It suddenly appears around you. You just suddenly are a member and there's nothing you can do about it. I have establishment responsibilities that I just can't walk away from."

One such responsibility is his work as an associate editor at the London publishing house Faber & Faber. "It's as much a process of providing people with an outlet, a window, a root for their own creative sources, as much as it feeds me as well."

Although he has no plans to tour, he did put a band together earlier this year to play two benefit dates in London for the Double O charity, which was formed by the Who to aid research into drug rehabilitation. Townshend says he had much more fun playing those gigs than he did during the [supposedly] final days of the Who. He played some obscure Who material, but also songs by Miles Davis and Charlie Mingus. "I wanted to demonstrate to everybody — to the band, to the audience, to the press — that I do what I want to do, I play what I want to play and I'm going to enjoy life."

At this point, his memories of 18 years in the Who are "very flat." He recalls the early days as a period of intense frustration. "They were pretty horrible. We weren't very nice people." He implies that they were pushed by negative reaction to the band. "I think if there was one major obstacle which I confronted in my life, which I had to get past sooner or later, was the physical ugliness that was thrown back in the Who's face. People used to come see us and say, 'They're ugly!' I, in some way, took that as a value judgment."

Neither does Townshend have fond recollections of the Who's intended swan song, a tour of America's stadiums. "Bitterness is a terrible, terrible thing. I started to get bitter about the fact that we seemed to be facing a fait accompli. We were a show business band. That's what we had become. We were out there to deliver. I think we forgot the essential premise of artistic entertainment, and that is that the people on the stage must genuinely be getting something from what they're doing as well. You go onstage playing things which do nothing for you, not because they're no good — I'm not saying 'Baba O'Riley,' 'Won't Get Fooled Again' and 'Behind Blue Eyes' are not good, they're great — it's the fact that they do nothing for us. They're just old hat. The audience is what you're doing it for: 'How did they cheer tonight?'"

Townshend recalls the best period as *Tommy*, post-*Tommy* and *Live at Leeds*, when "The band was playing fantastically well. I wasn't drinking very much; I certainly was never using drugs. I was just having kids; the future was a rosy place." It's doubtful Townshend would now consider the future rosy. But, clearly, he's on a steady, upward path, personally and creatively. Still consumed with work, he aims to achieve more with his life. Although he won't use the word "counsel," he does talk to heroin addicts: "If you do come out of this, you're probably going to come out of it with a whole impacted rebirth, a genesis.

"I think all art should do more than agitate," he says. "It should try to be active. That's the good thing about *Live Aid* ... the fact that in union we realize we have power to do something, and that was a really good feeling. Music can contain the promise and it can contain the hope — as much as I despise hope and optimism — but when you actually want to get down and do it, you make time and you do it."

Townshend is also making time for what he calls the "simpler" things in life. This includes spending time with his two daughters, 16 and 14, and "to be able to be faithful and to give a lot of detailed attention to the quality of the relationship with my wife, to see more of my parents, to go on holiday and really relax and not sit there twitching.

"I love to drive my kids back through London and point out the spots where I used to live. One they get very tired with is 'Let's drive past the house where I wrote "My Generation."' 'Oh no, please don't!' 'Yeah, come on, let's go down and have a look at it. There it is, up there!' And they're sitting in the back of the car, 'Boring old man ...'"

We connected again in April of 1998, this time by phone from his London studio, Eel

Pie. Townshend was about to go on a short summer solo tour. He'd been beavering away at his autobiography; Daltrey jokes that it's taking so long they're calling it *War and Pete*. (Not a bad title on several levels, actually, but it finally appeared as *Who I Am* in October of 2012, 14 years after we spoke.)

Townshend hasn't put out a new album since *Psychoderelict* in 1993. He *has* cashed a lot of *Tommy*-related checks for the Tony Award-winning Broadway show. Townshend's tour plan has something to do with wanting to atone for his behavior at *Woodstock* in 1969, when he cursed out stage-crashing provocateur Abbie Hoffman and knocked him off the stage. It has something to do with feeling those creative juices surging again. But there is no short answer with Townshend, perhaps rock and roll's reigning (and most self-critical) philosopher-king.

How self-critical?

"I think perhaps being in a band that fails ultimately, the way that the Who failed in the end [due to] circumstances out of their control, maybe, clouded the way that I looked at my career and my music."

The Who was a "failure"?

This has to do, he says, with their last two studio albums, the lukewarm *It's Hard* and *Face Dances*.

He credits his desire to perform to the autobiography in progress. "I'm still working on it very hard, and enjoying doing it, although, dear God, it's very hard work. But what writing this book is doing for me is actually releasing all kinds of musical creative juices, which it would be crazy for me to try to bury. So, to some extent, this [tour] is something that I decided to do to take time out and release some of that."

He's only booked three dates: a show in Boston, one in Woodstock, New York, and a benefit in Chicago for a children's orphanage, Maryville Academy.

"In the last couple of years, I've done a series of solo performances which have been experimental and small. I think Danny Socolof, who's involved in the Woodstock show, saw me [play a small show] in New York's Supper Club, and I think that's the kind of place that I occupy. That's the kind of performance that I'm doing. I work very much in my own private little place. But suddenly [the music] seems to be empowered, and I think empowered partly by the fact that as I write about my childhood, as I write about my years at art school, some of which involves going and talking to the people that taught me, and talking to people that I grew up with, finding that actually I was very, very smart. I'm at a different stage in my life. I'm older [53] and I'm upright in a different way, and I think I've been surprised at just how excited I've actually found the whole business of coming back to my own work and to writing.

"What I'm doing at the moment is everything that I want to do. I mean, it's the most extraordinary time in my life. I really feel like I'm in the middle of my life, and very much at the center of it."

Which brings us to the day of atonement. The *Woodstock Music and Arts Festival* is remembered as the apotheosis of the hippie era: peace, love and left-wing politics all bound together in one muddy, huggy package. Townshend, more skeptical and cynical, whacked Hoffman off the stage. *His* stage.

"I've always been extremely angry about *Woodstock.* I've been kind of quite bitchy and sneering. And I think it's time that I grew up."

Issue a mea culpa?

"Oh, yeah."

But wasn't the young rocker ticked off for pretty good reasons at the time?

"Well, that's OK [to say]," suggests Townshend, "but the years pass, and I failed to acknowledge that, because I was the dissenting voice, and there were one million people there, and one of them had a rotten time, that's been the voice that has been heard loudest. And I think where I am today, I look back and I think that I learned something vital, and I experienced something vital, and my career took a vital turn there. And the Who's career took a vital turn there. It's a good time for me to go and stand on that lawn again." [The Who's full *Woodstock* set, starting at 5 a.m. on August 17, 1969, can be streamed online. It's pretty fucking great.]

What will happen?

"There will be an Aristotelian debate which I may conduct on the stage if anybody's prepared to put up with it. I think it would be worthwhile, wouldn't it? Talking about what happened at the time. It wasn't just that I argued with Abbie Hoffman. I also argued with Mike Wadleigh, who was the director of the movie. Despite the fact that I kicked him in the head, he went on to cut a very exciting and dynamic piece of footage. I don't think I was wrong. It would be wrong for me to say I was wrong. I'm not trying to reverse what I said or take back what I said. What has happened for me is I look back and I think actually *Woodstock* was not the beginning *or* the end of a dream.

"Given enough distance, it was a moment when we all, and by this, I mean the

English performers, but mainly the American performers and the American audience, realized that it was OK to be who they were. It was OK to be Americans. It was OK to be young Americans, that there were one million of us, and we weren't even trying and there were one million of us. It was unnecessary to shout and scream and stamp our feet. We were in control.

"I wish that I had not handled it as I did. When I look back at [Hoffman's] life, I feel sorry for him. It's a strange feeling to have for such a kind of spunky, crazy, dynamic kind of guy, but you know he faded with, what's the word, with his obsolescence of that whole mood, the function of that kind of revolutionary instrument the Chicago group was supposed to represent. We had that [movement] in the UK, too. But when we realized, after *Woodstock*, all of us, that we didn't need revolution because if there was going to be any revolution, we would only overthrow ourselves. We were in our early twenties. Some of us were in our late twenties. We were already running the fucking country, or we were well on the way."

And now? "I feel immensely potent. I think it's coming from a certain sense of certainty that I have a right to be who I am. I know that sounds obvious, but for an artist this is an extraordinary thing to feel, because a necessary qualification for an artist is to have a huge ego, and absolutely no self-esteem. And I think what you actually do is inject into that mélange of confusion a sense of certainty about any attributes that you have; they become barbed and super-powerful. And I think that I've got a great trust of, not just my performing and musical ability, but my understanding of my craft."

Townshend was inspired by seeing a new pal, ex-Hüsker Dü singer-songwriter-guitarist Bob Mould, play some dynamic solo shows. "What I got from this was complete freedom," Townshend says. "The freedom to, as an artist, play wherever I like, whenever I like. And for there to be no vanity involved — in other words, I wouldn't lose money. When I went out with a tour like *Psychoderelict*, I got sponsorship and Tommy Hilfiger gave me a couple of hundred thousand dollars, but I still lost $400,000. I came back and I thought we had a lot of fun, but the price was too high. I don't want to feel like I'm paying people to come and see me play. So, I'm trying to adjust the way that I perform to the scale of the audience that I can reach these days, to the numbers of people that not only want to come and see me but that I can reach."

The old hearing-impaired gent who only played acoustic guitars onstage for a time will again shoulder an electric. "I've found a new, quite small Fender amplifier that they discontinued for a while. It's got kind of an old-fashioned mismatched sound, but that's working very well for me onstage. It's not too loud, and I play it a fair bit."

I asked how song meanings evolve over time, that what once was set in stone maybe isn't anymore.

"What I actually bring to songs now, as a performer, is exactly what I brought to them when I was younger. I wrote them to serve the audience of the day, and if there is anybody out there that still kind of relates to that piece of work on the basis of when it was first commissioned, then fine. But, as a performer, I perform it without any sense of propriety. I don't believe it's mine. I mean, as a musician I might take certain liberties with it. But now I think what's wonderful is having a few songs that have this anger, that have this edge, that have this automatic sense of don't-go-near-him-when-he's-playing-that and I can, dynamically speaking, in my performances, go very, very much in the other direction and get away with it."

Townshend, of course, is aware of how rock careers tend to flatten out creatively as the aging process takes its toll. "I see it in my peers, and, of course, I've experienced it as well," he says. [That certainly happened with the Who. No one in 2023 is clamoring to hear songs from 2006's *Endless Wire* or 2019's *Who*.]

"It's not so much just that one's creativity perhaps levels off. I think what happens is that we lose sight of the magical chemistry of serving the masses. And I think, God, how did that happen? Simply, I suppose, because of music moving to stadiums. Because the people there were denied the 'collective unconsciousness' that happens in the performance of any art.

"If the person on the stage is living in any kind of fantastical bubble, there's a problem, too. In other words, if they're surrounded with enough yes men, they end up in kind of Michael Jackson-land."

What, then, is the pop artist's role?

"They're meant to be the bunch of flowers that's on the table for today until you replace them with new ones. In pop we don't ask much, but what we do ask is that we are served, in the passing moment, we are served by the music and the artists that we hear. In the world of pop, what we want is solace and we want it now; we want cheer and we want it now; we want self-forgetfulness and we want it now."

And who, then, is Pete Townshend?

"I'm a generic celebrity. It's like I bring myself and my history to the stage. So, what's interesting now about going to *Woodstock* is that I'm grasping all that stuff head-on. And I've mismanaged it terribly in the past."

As a parting question, I ask — as I feel I must — about the fate of the Who.

"The only thing that would draw me back into the revival of the Who brand name would be that there is something musical, a dramatic platform, from which we can jump off today. [It wouldn't work if] the familiarity undermined the new ideas all the time, the familiarity of the partnership, and the sentimentality and nostalgia that accompany the reunion; it would tend to overweigh and melt down any new ideas."

As has often been the case, Daltrey has other ideas ...

"It's convenient for Roger to pretend [that not assembling the Who] is about me blocking him. That this is about me holding the reins and refusing to whip the horse, but actually it's much more about his capabilities and his choices, and his limitations as an artist. If he refuses to look at anything to do with the theater stage, in a way it's kind of nonsense. I think we, the Who, began very much in those early days as a band who approached rock and roll in a very theatrical way. We actually use the stage as a stomping-ground way of reflecting and engaging the audience, and we're unashamed about using any kinds of tricks or fables that might help that communication. To pretend that rock and roll itself is just so powerful and magical that it can work miracles is just wrong.

"We could go out and we would kill people. It would be absolutely astounding. But when it's just, when the three of us [Townshend, Daltrey, bassist John Entwistle] gather, one becomes aware of what is not, rather than what is. One becomes aware of what was rather than what will happen next."

Here's my takeaway from a 1998 Boston solo show at a venue then called Harborlights. (It was on Boston Harbor. Still is, but the naming rights have been leased numerous times, generally to banks.)

> Meet the new Pete, not quite the same as the old Pete.
>
> Then again, he never is, is he? The reinvention of Pete Townshend — the confessional, self-critical, 53-year-old guiding light, guitarist and singer of the band that was the Who — continues, and the reconfiguration of his songs (both solo and Who) progresses in concert. And this is good. I

almost hate to write this, but after absorbing Townshend's two-and-a-half-hour set at Harborlights along with a full house of 4,500, I've got to say: I understand why he does what he does and why he's not eager to put the old warhorse called the Who back together again. This rock and roll — hard-edged but warm, loose but coiled — is the kind of adult rock no one could have conceived of back in 1965, when the Who took on their elders with "My Generation."

The key point last night: Townshend is making the old new again. He gave a lot of bang for the big ($45) buck. "Anyway, Anyhow, Anywhere," the old aggro youth anthem, started in a contemplative jam-band-mode and then mutated into a power-chord bliss fest. Same with Townshend's favorite cover song, the English Beat's "Save It for Later," a snooze when he's done it solo acoustic but a heated, dynamic rocker here. [In concert, its author, Dave Wakeling of the Beat, has jokingly referred to it as a Pete Townshend song.]

The pièce de résistance was "The Kids Are Alright," where Townshend shifted the context of "the kids." It used to be him and his gang, cocky, proud. Now, it's his and his peers' kids: "Nothing wrong with my kids, nothing wrong with your kids," he said, while the band vamped. It wasn't hokey.

The implication of the Who has always been that the glory of rock and roll can shine through — at least for a moment — and transcendence might be in reach. It happened last night with this band, not the old boys' club of the Who, but very much featuring females: guitarist-singer Tracey Langran (who helped choreograph *Tommy* on Broadway) and percussionist Jody Linscott, a Boston-area native. (The group also included keyboardist-guitarist-singer Jon Carin, a former touring musician with Pink Floyd, bassist Sherman Sean and harmonica player Peter Hope-Evans.) From the stage, Townshend said, "You can see how I feel about drummers, I won't have anything to do with them anymore." Instead, he employed a drum machine. This show had a backbeat and a backbone. It also, intermittently, gave us a glimpse of Back Porch Pete, just a few geezers and gals up there a-pickin' and a-grinnin', folks who'd be sucking on straw if they could.

Keyboardist-singer John Carin was the band's anchor. Harmonica player/Jew's-harpist Peter Hope-Evans was its spice. (He handled the quivering synth part on "Won't Get Fooled Again.") Townshend clearly enjoyed playing off Langran. They dueted on "The Acid Queen," prior to which Townshend announced he and she were "both queens!" (Townshend is out about his bisexuality, among many other things.)

The show included old faves ("You Better, You Bet," "Drowned"), rarities ("A Little Is Enough," "North Country Girl") and oddball choices. Townshend opened with Canned Heat's "On the Road Again" and later played that band's other hit, "Going Up the Country." These were meant, one assumes, to conjure up the *Woodstock* festival of 1969.

Townshend had fun with his sonic reinventions, jesting to the crowd, "You go, 'Oh, what's he done to this song, ma?' I go, 'They're paying me loads of money to annoy them.' If you think I'm annoying now, think what I could do!" This followed a lounge-y reprise of "The Real Me," just prior to a mock-operatic Wagnerian/Zarathustra bit. I left to meet deadline as "Won't Get Fooled Again" began to take shape, but was told by knowledgeable sources that guitar strings were broken, Townshend left the stage, came back, had more technical trouble during an instrumental, played "Magic Bus" and then was joined by a 22-member Black choir for the "See Me, Feel Me" finale, which Townshend called "a prayer." ◆

"There's one person in the world who's
more insecure than I am,
and his name is Pete Townshend."

Ray Davies

Ray Davies performs with the Kinks at the Boston Garden, September 1981

RAY DAVIES
& THE KINKS

"IT'S LIKE DEATH IN HERE," said Ray Davies, inauspiciously welcoming me into his Minneapolis hotel room. The shades were drawn, no lights were on. Davies had been ill, running a temperature of 102 before the previous night's concert at the Metropolitan Sports Center.

The interview had been scheduled and rescheduled several times. "I'm really not trying to avoid you," he'd apologized when we met briefly the night before.

We order up hot stuff: coffee for me, hot water straight up for Davies' ailing throat. He opens the shades. Outside, the gray sky bristles with anonymous tall buildings. "That must have been one of the highest buildings in Minneapolis," Davies says laconically about the nearby Foshay Tower. "Before," he adds, "it became a megalopolis."

It's the fall of 1981, and the Kinks are on something of a roll, an arena act at last. The band's move from RCA to Arista — and Clive Davis's insistence that Ray drop his affection for concept albums and write standalone songs (hits) — has paid off. *Sleepwalker* and *Misfits* set the stage in 1977 and 1978. The current album, *Give the People What They Want*, has followed *Low Budget* into the U.S. Top 20. (*State of Confusion* would do equally well in 1983.) The Kinks are back, perhaps bigger than ever. Is Ray on top of the world? Not exactly.

"I don't think we're very popular. I'm amazed that people come to see us play." A pause, a gap-toothed smile. "Bullshit. We're the best rock and roll band in the world today."

I believe he believed both were true. I also keep this lyric in mind from "Fancy": "No one can penetrate me."

Discussing his 18 years as the lead Kink, Davies — who was 37 at the time — can't resist taking a number of self-analytical jabs at this 20th century man who don't wanna be here. Over the course of the afternoon, Davies describes himself variously as "a son of a bitch" for not giving Rasa, his first wife and "great inspiration," credit for singing on numerous Kinks songs; "a nutter" for being placed in a school for maladjusted kids at the age of 12; "a jumping jack flash" ("People kind of distrust me"); and "really insignificant" ("I'm not that much to look at").

Asked if there's a strand that runs through his songs, Davies says, "All my work has an element of weakness in it. There's a duality in what I do."

With renewed popularity comes, naturally enough for Davies, a bit of consternation. After years of smaller halls, Davies feels a bit lost in large arenas. "I once threatened someone with death if they booked us in Madison Square Garden." Yet, playing arenas is a sign of success, and Davies allows himself to savor that satisfaction. "The thing about the Kinks is we can reduce a place like that to a bar. The Kinks are now three years old. We've recreated what we started out doing. We're a dance band with good lyrics."

Davies credits the stripped-down sounds of the British pub rock and punk movements — especially Dr. Feelgood and the Sex Pistols — for renewed inspiration: "It was like seeing the Kinks in 1964. We'd lost a lot of our zing."

Mood swings. Ray has 'em. "I got really down last night," he says the day after the Kinks' concert. "I grabbed this woman [backstage before the show] and I said, 'Talk to me for five minutes.' I asked her what she did and what her home was like. I wanted to hear somebody else's problems so I could forget about mine. I wanted to prove to myself how lucky I was to be able to go and play music. I told her I was a prat. I felt like a complete git.

"I'm a very nervous person, very quiet," Davies continues in his soft north London accent. "I think it makes people even more nervous. I wish I could make people feel more comfortable with me. There's an element of weakness and an element of violence within me. Insecure? Yeah, totally. There's one person in the world who's more insecure than I am, and his name is Pete Townshend."

After Ray and I hit it off, my role evolved from fan into some mélange of fan, critic and friend. This triptych doesn't happen often, but it happens. I first saw the Kinks in December 1975, on the *Schoolboys in Disgrace* tour, at the Orpheum Theatre in Boston, the band all dressed in blue schoolboy short-pants outfits. I played 'em a lot as a college DJ in Maine; "Father Christmas" and its flip "Prince of the Punks" got a lot of airplay on WMEB. Later, as music director, I signed off my weekly playlist/missives to record labels with a demand/plea cribbed from John Mendelsohn's liner notes in *The Kink Kronikles*: "God Save the Kinks."

That 1981 interview was the door-opener to many more chats, both formal (interview) and informal (dinner, post-show hang). The last time Ray played Boston (Wilbur Theater, November 2011), we'd done an advance interview and he invited my wife and me backstage following the show. We went and found ourselves the only ones waiting by the stage door. The security guard said there was no access. I politely asked if he wouldn't mind checking again and, sure enough, mine was the only name on the list. Ray came out and we all chatted for about 15 minutes. To his credit, he was as interested in our lives as we were about his. A proper conversation.

In the mid-'70s, Davies saw rock and roll become more and more of a high-stakes business. "I wanted to leave the continent," he says. "I didn't fit in with anything. That's why I wrote 'Misfits' (a bittersweet celebration of life outside the mainstream). I hated my contemporaries — I hated the lifestyle of Paul McCartney, I didn't want to be like Elton John or Rod Stewart — most of all Rod Stewart, who I grew up with."

As a teenager, Davies lived with his older sister Rose and her husband Arthur in the middle-class Muswell Hill area of north London. Davies says he "felt like nothing," part of the post-war baby boom's disillusioned first wave. "There's a big unemployment problem in England now, and it started when I left school. I used to walk around so angry, angry about what was happening. And it was going to get worse.

"It's not all bitterness. This sounds like I'm a really bitter person and I'm not. It just gives you strength. Maybe that's the answer to 'Why have you kept going so long, Ray?'"

Davies attended Hornsey Art College, developed into "a very good art student" and found his release in soccer and music. He played guitar until the early hours of the morning with a jazz/blues/reggae group in seedy Soho clubs for the money it cost to travel to and from the gigs.

"It was the best time of my life," Davies says, drifting back. "It exposed me to a world I'd been sheltered from — I was a suburban kid. Prostitutes used to come in and put their feet up. There was this old prossy who used to hold me and dance with me. Then she used to go back out onto Wardour Street and do her job. I'll always remember her. I wish I could find her now."

Seeing the Rolling Stones in 1964 sold him on rock and roll. He found his younger "punk" brother Dave at their parents' home playing guitar; they linked up with drummer Mick Avory and bassist Pete Quaife to form the Kinks. Later that year, when they hit with "You Really Got Me," Dave emerged as rock and roll's rawest guitarist. A few years later, Ray emerged as one of rock's most perceptive lyricists.

"I read a book by Noël Coward called *Future Indefinite*," Davies says, "and I think he said, 'The greatest power I have is in my writing, and I can say the most devastating things in a joke.' I think he learnt that from Shakespeare." Hence was born "A Well Respected Man," the first of Davies' trenchant social satires. Two songs later came "Dedicated Follower of Fashion," which poked fun at those who followed fads and trends. Davies says it was drawn from real anger.

"I had a punch-out with a trendy '60s fashion designer who came to a party at my house." Affecting a snooty upper-class accent, he coos, "'Ooh, you live in a semi, do you? In Muswell Hill? Mick Jagger's got a mansion in Buckingham Palace.'" Davies told the designer what he thought about the way Jagger treated women and then hit him. Mick, Davies told me, shoved Mars bars up his girlfriend's arses. He also told me what the Kinks nicknamed Paul McCartney when they opened shows for the Beatles: Pull McCockoff.

At his artistic best, Davies teeters on fine lines, between violence and gentility and, particularly, between revering the conventions and mores of the past and sending them up. He sang plaintively about shops, china cups and virginity in "The Village Green Preservation Society," the title song of a 1969 album Davies considers one of the Kinks' best.

That duality is manifested within songs as well as stretched over dozens of albums. Though most of his songs are drawn from personal reflection, in the early '70s Davies theatrically tackled the communism/capitalism conflict — and the endemic nature of universal greed and avarice — in *Preservation Act II*. Neither of the big Cs came out looking too rosy.

"This is my street and I'm never gonna leave it," Davies sings during our interview. It's a line from "Autumn Almanac," a number sung from the point of view of a provincial gardener in the north of England. "A lot of northern people didn't like me for that," he recalls. "They thought I was sending them up; actually, I was celebrating that lifestyle."

Did it ever exist? "It existed for me," he says. Davies sang about letting the world pass by ("Sunny Afternoon") as well as running from it ("Apeman"). "I was going into my own form of escapism."

Because of a dispute with the Musician's Union and the band's management, the Kinks were banned from playing in the U.S. from 1965 to 1969. "The crucial period — the war and the flag," Davies says, launching into a vocal impression of guitarist Jimi Hendrix's "Star Spangled Banner." "The greatest and the silliest," he adds.

It became the Kinks' artistic heyday — perhaps because they weren't on the road continually, a situation that can be the death of creativity. Davies took refuge in a private world, singing melodic, decidedly English songs of complex simplicity and biting wit.

The songs were, he says, "out of step with rock and roll." Amidst psychedelia, prog rock, guitar solos, overt social protest and anti-war demonstrations, the Kinks sang clever pop songs about simpler times. Their drug of choice was alcohol, not acid. They wished for nothing more than to return to an England long past and, in doing so, became an anachronism to most rock fans. Still, the songs were among his best. *Arthur (or the Decline and Fall of the British Empire)* — a concept album based upon the World War II experiences and disillusionment felt by his uncle — remains one of rock's best anti-war statements.

But mostly the Kinks sought escape. Davies frequently returns to that period in conversation. One of those songs, "Waterloo Sunset," was called by *Village Voice* critic Robert Christgau "the most beautiful song in the English language." It's a touching, gentle, gripping rock ballad in which two lovers gain temporary solace amidst a resplendent sunset and the squalor of a train station.

"The story was originally thought of as 'Liverpool Sunset,'" says Davies, "because there was the Merseybeat scene that soon faded away ... but I thought why bother when I'm from London and here's this beautiful river. I think it's one of the most enjoyable songs I've ever written in my life. The night we finished making the record I got Rasa to drive me down — she went through hell with me, she never got any credit — to

Waterloo Bridge. I stood on the bridge, and I said, 'Yes, it's all there.' I got back in the car and said, 'You can take me home now.'"

That period also produced "Days," perhaps the second-most-beautiful song in the English language, about a lover Davies had, briefly. She was, he says, "a strong, guiding-light type of woman." When she phoned him and told him their relationship was over, Davies says he thanked her for what she had given him.

His own words took him by surprise in 1981 at a funeral for a friend. The previous year, Davies began work on a musical, *Chorus Girls*, with screenwriter Barrie Keeffe. The show, a satire about feminists kidnapping Prince Charles to save a theater from being destroyed to create Europe's largest job center, was panned by the theater establishment but sold out its five-week run.

"This was supposed to be a comedy," Davies says, "and every day Barrie would come in crying, tears streaming down his face." His 40-year-old wife Verity was dying of cancer. "I would get on the tube every morning, on the Central Line, and go into Stratford in East London. I'd turn up and wait for him for four or five hours, and all I'd get was a note saying, 'Sorry, Verity's bad today, can't work.'"

She died shortly after the show opened in April. At the funeral, actress Charlotte Cornwell read "Days." "That was," he says, pausing, still moved, "a chilling moment. Yet when I heard it recited it made me realize how proud I was of the song. I'll never be able to make records like that again."

Why not?

"A lot of it has to do with the times, where you live. I lived in a little semi. That house was magical." He doesn't elaborate.

"I have this theory," Davies says later about the present. "Commerce dictates art."

Is that meant in a cynical sense?

"Yeah, in a cynical sense — and an almost truthful belief. But my art is greater than the commerce that dictates it." In January 1979, when the Kinks' English label refused them money for tour support because they had no "product" to promote, Davies wrote "Low Budget," a song about having no money. It took him a day to come up with what became the Kinks' first gold disc with Arista. "The joke was on them in a sense," he notes.

Despite the Kinks' success, 1981 wasn't an easy year. Davies couldn't spend much time with his two daughters, aged 10 and 13. He was living out of suitcases and couldn't devote the time he wanted to the band's new album, *Give the People What They Want.*

Like a good Englishman, Davies watched the royal wedding of Charles and Diana. "As fraught as my life has been with divorce and all that," he says sincerely, "I was so proud of our royal family. The Queen is really wonderful." (Prince Charles knighted him in early 2017.) Still, he didn't approach the day with undue reverence. He watched with Graham Chapman, a friend from Monty Python, who had "conned" a local council into having a festival. Davies went, got drunk and "tried to play slide guitar with a beer bottle. Everybody was laughing at me and at the end they carried me off. One of the best days of the year."

In 2007, at an exhibit on the brain at Boston's Museum of Science, there was a list of famous manic-depressive or bipolar people. Ray's name was on it. When I told Ray about that the following year, he bristled and said, "Why did they put me there? I'm not. Like everybody, I get depressed from time to time, but I get depressed when I can't do my work. I'm a frustrative-obsessive."

The Ray and Dave Davies love/hate relationship has been well-chronicled over the years in the press. It's always fluid. There's a lot of ups and downs, legendary stories of onstage fisticuffs and offstage digs. When the Kinks were together and traveling from hotel to show, there was always one limo for Ray, one limo for Dave. (Over the years, I rode in both.)

Ray, on Dave, 1984: "I love him. But sometimes ... he's family ... and I don't really like family."

Dave, on Ray, 1993: "It's not that I really hate him, though I hate him at times. I suppose I find him more irritating and exasperating."

Since the band's 1996 breakup, one question has never gone away: will the Kinks ever reunite? It would be foolish to venture anything definitive here. They've answered positively, negatively and neutrally about it, which is to say they've been hopeful *and* dismissive.

"It does cross your mind," Ray told me sometime in the 2000s, "but it's not a good way to think. I just try to take it in stride and deal with it one day at a time."

Have they played together?

Yes. The brothers worked on a handful of songs in early 2016. "Embryonic ideas and lyrics, bits and pieces," Dave said. "We were working together and we were getting on pretty good — touch wood, touch wood. We'll have to see. Sometimes you have to let nature take its course. Maybe there will never be another Kinks album; then again me and Ray worked on the demos project [so] we might feel that need to actually do something. Who knows? If you force something, it never works."

Will it — or some songs — see the light of day? Maybe.

Will they ever tour? Unlikely. Later-era keyboardist Ian Gibbons and bassist Jim Rodford are dead; original drummer Mick Avory, best as I can tell, would rather concentrate on his golf game.

If there's no reunion, no new music, really, that's OK. What the brothers Davies — and the various other Kinks — have given us over the years is mighty strong stuff, eternal if you will. I'd argue that they made vital new music into the '90s, which gives them a leg up on the Rolling Stones and the Who. The Kinks' '60s songs are dear to my heart, but so are many of the latter-day ones. I'll take "Destroyer," "Come Dancing," "Don't Forget to Dance," "Too Hot," Dave's "Living on a Thin Line" and "Good Day" any day.

Ray and Dave have both continued on with solo projects and separate tours through the 2000s. Ray's written two memoirs and Dave has done the same. ◆

DAVE DAVIES

IF YOU'RE A KINKS FAN — or, for that matter, a Kink — you can't not appreciate the irony of this. When the Kinks play their 1966 song "I'm Not Like Everybody Else," a declaration of independence and alienation, it's always a singalong, a hall full of like-minded folks loudly proclaiming their uniqueness, whether they mean it as in they're proud fans of the fourth-ranked British Invasion band (behind the Beatles, Stones and the Who) or in their own lives, that they stick out from the madding crowd. I've always sung along with a big smile on my face.

With the Kinks either on a lengthy hiatus or gone for good, guitarist Dave Davies has taken to the road, playing with a backing band. (He did this pre-COVID lockdown and has also done so since.) At Boston's Wilbur Theatre in 2015, I saw him do "I'm Not Like Everybody Else" twice. One show. *Twice?*

I talked to him about that. It's not like Dave lacks material: his own solo stuff, songs he wrote for the Kinks and ones his brother Ray wrote that he feels closest to. Dave explained that he first did the song as a short tease; the longer version, with its gorgeous and grinding electric guitar lead-in, was the real deal.

He thought it was the quintessential Davies brothers song; when I noted the irony, Dave laughed and said it reminded him of Monty Python's *Life of Brian,* where Brian (Graham Chapman) shouts out "I am an individual!" and the assembled multitude shouts it back in unison.

"You think differently when you're lying on your back in a hospital, paralyzed. It brought a lot of clarity into me life."

Dave Davies

Dave Davies and the author

PHOTOGRAPH BY ROZA YARCHUN (SUB-ROZA)

I asked how Dave goes about structuring his sets. "I try to make it varied, but obviously I have to do songs that people know [like] 'I'm Not Like Everybody Else' and 'All Day and All of the Night.' These kinds of songs help focus me for the set. Emotionally they're very demanding, but they're songs I love to perform. I like hard-rocking songs, with people dancing and having a good time. But, as you know, rock and roll is every kind of emotion: anger and love, frustration and all kinds of things."

Dave has told the tale more than enough about how he slashed that speaker cone in his amplifier to get the raw distorted guitar sound that propelled the Kinks' "You Really Got Me" back in 1964 and got blamed/credited for inventing heavy metal (along with Dick Dale, Link Wray and others). But, as he says, there's all kinds of emotion in rock and roll — and in his guitar playing.

Five years after seeing the Kinks for the first time and a year before meeting Ray, I interviewed Dave. We were in a hotel room in Cambridge. RCA had brought him in on a promo tour to chat up his first solo album, *AFL1-3603*. That was a cheeky and prescient album title, using the record's catalog number and barcode to convey the wry implication that it was really just product. (Public Image Ltd. and Flipper would later do similar things.)

In 1967, the Kinks had a number-three British hit with "Death of a Clown," a song Dave co-wrote and sang. It was thought by some back then that he might be launching an adjunct solo career, as members of famous rock bands were wont to do. He wasn't. Although Dave recorded enough tracks for an album (with the rest of the Kinks backing him), it was never released (though some tracks dribbled out later) and Davies slipped comfortably back into his role as a Kinks co-leader/second banana and Ray's brother/friend/foe/foil. With some rippin' guitar parts to come — see "Shangri-la" and "Australia" from 1969's *Arthur (or the Decline and Fall of the British Empire)*.

"I didn't really know why I was doing that album," Davies recalls of the aborted project. "I think I felt a bit pressurized into doing it. I made a half-hearted attempt in a small eight-track studio."

"Death of a Clown" became something of a millstone for him. In his liner notes to *The Kink Kronikles* compilation, John Mendelsohn brought up a 1969 concert where Dave charged to the mike to sing his hit and, two lines in, yelled, "I can't remember the fucking words!"

"That was true," Davies admits with a sheepish laugh.

Although "Death of a Clown" was a clear example that Dave could write a great pop song — confirmed by "Mindless Child of Motherhood" and "This Man He Weeps Tonight" — he wasn't a prolific writer, and none of his songs had similar success. Ray, who did almost all of the Kinks' songwriting, wouldn't let Dave forget his one and only triumph. In the early '70s, Ray would introduce his brother with lines like, "Let's have a big hand for Dave 'Death of a Clown' Davies on guitar."

"He used to do that to really irritate me," Davies says, smiling. "He knew I hated it. Oh, the fucking names I called him. I'd scream at him, and he'd keep doing it and then I'd turn up a bit louder."

The Kinks have always been one of rock's most volatile bands, with abundant tales of intra-group fighting. Dave, who had been a Kink for more than half his 33 years when we first talked in 1980, was quick to admit, "It's silly, really, acting like overgrown children." But tension and the release of it may have been important factors in holding the band together. With the Kinks then still a going concern, Dave said he and his brother still had flare-ups, but they're less violent: "We kind of laugh about it now."

We talked again in 1999. Dave had put out a double-disc compilation, *Unfinished Business*, of Kinks songs in which he played a big role, his own solo stuff and a few outtakes. Talked turned to his brother, and I asked if it was possible to love the song but not the songwriter?

"That is a good question," he said. "There's always going to be love. I might not like his personality, but it doesn't prevent me from loving him. I don't hate his works because he can be difficult."

You either separate the two ...

"Or go crazy," Davies finishes.

I spent a fair amount of time with the Kinks during that '80s boom time, as they ascended to arena rock status in the U.S. (Some of that's recounted in the Ray Davies chapter.) Then the arena days ended. The last time was in July 1995, at the Club Casino in Hampton Beach, New Hampshire. Ray did four acoustic songs, closing with part of "Do It Again," before the band came on to finish it in grand rocked-up fashion.

Along the way, I did some of that rock star routine thing, going from hotel to concert hall in a limo. I would ride with Ray on the way to one gig, with Dave on another.

They did not ride together, and over four decades of rock talk I've never interviewed them together.

It seemed a little odd at first, their enforced separateness offstage, but then I realized they'd already spent decades together, growing up in Muswell Hill with six older sisters, in the studio, onstage, on planes.

They each had their own ideas about things, and neither minded when I had interview time slated with the other. They knew they were the key Kinks, and each had worthy takes on the band, whatever love or animosity they were showing at the moment. No disrespect to founding drummer Mick Avory or the late bassist Pete Quaife, nor many of the others who've worked under the Kinks banner.

Dave published a memoir, *Kink*, in 1997. I reviewed it for the *Boston Globe*, writing, in part, "It is often a hoot — sometimes intentionally so, sometimes not. It's also a groaner at times, as a numbing cavalcade of rock clichés rolls over you. Davies has a heart and a soul, a certain naïve sweet nature, but this is mainly an account of a debauched, if occasionally creative, life. It's a sordid, squalid run-through of semi-stimulating/semi-stultifying encounters — stories of nonstop sex (girls, boys, whomever), drugs (whaddaya got?) and rock and roll (the louder the better). Up until the alien voices come calling and a form of religion knocks on his door. It's also a story about respect and extreme sibling rivalry. [But] the dominant theme of the book is wreckage: emotional, physical, outward, inward."

He came out with another memoir, *Living on a Thin Line*, the title mirroring his best song, in 2022. Some of the sordid tales in *Kink* are retold and refurbished with a greater measure of regret. He credits meditation, yoga and "psychic energy." But mainly he writes about the stroke he suffered in 2004. He had to completely relearn how to play guitar. As the *Guardian* said in its review, "His enthusiasm for neuroplasticity — the way in which the brain lays down new pathways — is one of the book's more endearing aspects."

After the stroke, he spent a few weeks staying with Ray. About that he wrote, "My brother is very talented and gifted, and I don't want to be mean so soon, but I sometimes feel like he's like a vampire the way he draws so much energy from people. True enough, that's helped him become a great songwriter, and he knows how to channel his ability to use people in a creative way. I'm glad he has always been part of my life, but you need to be strong around him. The way he was absorbing my energy during those two weeks, eventually I thought: 'For fuck's sake! Ray, I love you, but really, I don't have much to give you."

When the possibility of a Kinks reunion comes up, as it must, I mention that we've become accustomed to seeing older bands, long broken up, getting back together.

"It's financial," Dave says. "Because you can't sell records like you used to with all these free downloads and other things. Although it's great for people to be able to access your music, writers and artists aren't going to be able to produce anything because there's not the money like there used to be. Despite people having weird and wonderful and glamorous ideas about being in rock music, it's still *work*. It's no different from any other job in that respect. You still have to make your bed and go to the bathroom. You're working with ideas and your imagination and at the end of the day you've got to put food on the table as best you can."

When Dave turned 70 in 2017, I asked him to pick and comment on five Kinks songs that have gone largely unheralded or that he feels have been underrated. He chose three of his own and two of Ray's.

"When You Were a Child" (from *Think Visual*, 1986, written by Dave)

"I've always had that part of me, my spiritual life. It seems like we grow up too quickly. Sometimes we need to revisit parts of our growing up, to go back and have a look around again and look at the trees again. How you feel at 30, at 20, at 16 and at six.

"It's important to remind ourselves of how we've viewed the world. It's important to reflect it. Not to get too sentimental, but sometimes you go back and look through younger eyes, different eyes. You can do that when you're writing. It's an opportunity to be someone else or be a different part of yourself. Life is an experiment, it's exploring. And I think if we lose our creative edge things seem [to become] bland or ordinary. We need that kind of innocence, try to remember that, or tune into it again.

"Perfect Strangers" (from *UK Jive*, 1989, written by Dave) A song that considers connections forged and connections lost.

"One of the best I've ever written, and I had to battle to get that song on the album! I thought the record company should have taken the initiative and put that out as a single. It wasn't to be. I remember Gene Harvey, the Kinks' manager at that period, saying, 'A good record company should push for that song to be the single.'

But nothing ever came of it. [I like] that constant riff that goes on in the background and those chord changes I think are hypnotic."

"Close to the Wire" (from *Phobia*, 1993, also Dave) This one falls in line with many Kinks songs, where faceless corporations wage war with the individual's heart and soul.

"In a similar way [to 'Perfect Strangers'] I had to fight to get that on the album, but I love that song. It had a similar kind of yearning, a what-to-do about these feelings and emotions. Our lives seemed to be going haywire and wrong, and the economy is bad. How do we fix these things? It's about hope as well. That kind of agrees with me. And I love good riffs. That's the basis of the work I do, really."

About the line "Whatever happens to the dreams that we shared," Dave says, "That was partly about the Kinks and partly about the condition of the times economically, people going broke. Also, the bridge harkens back to the early days of Eddie Cochran and Buddy Holly. I remembered a song I loved by Buddy Holly, 'What to Do.' It had a feeling that always stayed with me through my work and the Kinks' work." Dave sings a line from Holly's song — "What to do to keep from feeling lonely, want her only, what to do" — and says, "that song touches on a lot of emotions and memories.

"That record was really hypnotizing. It wasn't a big record, but it was an *also* record, if you understand what I mean [a song that's also on the album], and it had more impact. I found that a lot of the songs that I like personally weren't necessarily the hits, they were like B-sides. I've always kind of had that fated spot [with the Kinks]."

"Wonderboy" (a 1968 single later included on *The Kink Kronikles*, written by Ray) A breezy, bouncy pop song where Ray hopes to turn "sorrow into wonder." The refrain runs, "Everybody is looking for the sun / People strain their eyes to see / But I see you and you see me / And ain't that wonder?"

"I heard Ray play it on the piano and I thought, sometimes you get a feeling in a song that you actually want to see it through 'til the end." The song was perceived as a "failure," the first original Kinks 45 not to reach the UK Top 20. "The consequence of the song doing well or not fades into insignificance," Dave says. "The fact is that you just want to get this piece of art finished or out there so people might come across it and think, 'Oh, what's that? Cool.'

"I always had that feeling about ['Wonderboy']. It might be a bit like a Van Gogh painting where maybe no one ever looks at it and one day someone sees it and thinks,

'That's fucking brilliant! I never saw that in it before. How come I didn't notice that before?' ['Wonderboy'] has been one of those pieces of work that defies any concept of commerce or commercialism; it defies all these labels and attitudes we attach to art. Why has art got to be successful? Why does it have to be anything other than what it is? Art should teach and reflect our inner feelings, what we are and who we are and what we're doing. [To try and] answer all these timeless unanswered questions. We make up our own minds in the end. People say art is about this and that [but] maybe it's not about anything, maybe it's about everything."

I note that it is one of Ray's most hopeful, optimistic songs. "Oh sure," says Dave. "The Kinks' music is rich in those kind of hopeful emotions — where it's 'Low Budget' this month and next year flying like 'Superman.' I think all those emotions and attitudes, the fun and humor, helped galvanize us over the years."

"Scattered" (from *Phobia*, 1993, written by Ray) This buried gem spins out a complicated emotional ride in just over four minutes.

"Ray wrote it during the time that we lost our mother. I think embedded within the lyrics and the feeling is a tribute to our mother, who was really — I don't know if Ray would agree — but in my view, she was like my first guru, my spiritual mentor. I think it's very special for a lot of reasons that are probably not obvious at first. Ray likes to hide his feelings within a lot of other meanings." The accompanying video is lovely, with Ray and Dave together in the front seat of the car, Dave driving. (Ray didn't drive until later in life.) The song is nothing but upbeat in melody and rhythm, and the images of death — ashes to be scattered, a funeral service in the video — put dying in a cyclic context, the inevitable end of a life well-lived. There's sadness, yes, but as Ray sings: "To the fields we are scattered / From the day we are born / To grow wild and sleep rough / Till from the Earth we are torn / And a soul that is free / Can live on eternally."

"I loved making that video," says Dave. "It was a chance to be together but not in a flashy over-emotional way."

We talked again in 2017.

Your last studio album, Rippin' Up Time, *in 2014, was a pretty hard-rocking affair. This new one,* Open Road, *done with your son Russ, is a different animal.*

Oh, yeah. I was kind of ready for that. I felt like I needed to clarify my emotions a little differently. With *Rippin' Up Time,* it was very much a hard-edged feeling. I enjoyed working like that, but this was a very different process. Russ likes to layer vocal sounds for richness, and I took to that really well. I wanted to do something different, but not too left field, that people could latch onto and sing along with.

There's a lushness to it, some melancholic moods, a contemplative feeling. And, of course, there's the collaborative factor. I know Russ is a producer and works a lot with electronic music, so he's outside his comfort zone to an extent.

We'd been talking about it on and off for quite a while and decided to actually give it a shot. We had worked on another album, *Two Worlds,* as the Aschere Project, which was more science-fiction/fantasy, with an underlying story, a film soundtrack, really. So, we were used to working together on ideas and musical themes and characters.

How did Open Road *take shape?*

Russ landscaped some ideas that he had, and I had a listen to the musical backdrop, and I just worked with that. I'd write some verses and then I'd send them to him, and we'd talk about where we were going to go with it. We wanted to make a conscious effort to not make it a rock-pop album. That was the common direction.

What does he bring to the party that you don't and vice versa?

I'm not really sure. Russ has got a very fixed idea about where things should go. I like to experiment a lot and throw things in the pot and see if they work. Some don't work and some stick. It's really good to work with Russ because he's never short of ideas, but at the same time, he's very patient and nurturing. It took a while for us to get in gear with it, to get in harmony with it, but it's a process. Russell is a multi-instrumentalist. He's got a kind of classical background and his ambient experience helped; he's very good at shaping sound. [For] some of the songs, I'd write two lines and he'd write two, I'd write four and he'd write six. It was very much what we felt emotionally and [what] psychically worked. There was an energy that flows out of each of us. It wasn't premeditated; it was what came out. That's my favorite way to work.

What things did he impart?

He's got a very different approach to production. He'd say, "Don't play all that crap. Maybe you should think about the lyrics a bit more. What do they mean? Be authentic." He knows when a thing is genuine. Sometimes, you just need to take a breath and sing it in a different mindset.

Some songs tend to not need more kinds of guitar lines or tones or parts. I've always been about that. Whether it's "You Really Got Me" or "Path Is Long," it's a point of view you want to make work the best you can. Sometimes you don't need to put a lot of technical lines and riffs into it; some things you want to be simple and emotional. That old adage about "less is more" is very true. The trick is to find the right thing to embellish a piece of music, and Russell is really good at that. He'll suggest something very minimal that will help construct the piece of music we're working with. It's like working on a film score. You've got these characters in place and they're doing their job; it's [like] developing a movie or a soundtrack.

Is there anything different about working with your son than with another collaborator?

There was when we were putting ideas together, but once you get into the flow, it could be just two guys who are sensitive to each other's ideas. Once you push that [father-son thing] out of the way it's like any collaboration. Obviously, there's an element of trust; at times it reminded me a little bit of the very early days of when me and Ray worked together. Sometimes you just didn't know what was going to happen, but something does happen, and you work on that. It's like when you said "contemplative" — it's like a meditation. Rather than not having an idea and getting all panicky — "Fuck, what am I going to do?!" — you just sit there with a few ideas and when there's a bond between people, things happen. It's a lovely way of working.

You're considered a "classic rock" artist, the Kinks being in the Rock and Roll Hall of Fame, with this great, vast catalog of songs. But you're doing new music now, too. Is it difficult to get classic rock-oriented fans to pay attention to it?

Well, I hope not! Maybe you have a point, but I grew up with a belief that if something's good, people will like it. If it's got a genuine spark, I think people pick up on that. I like to think this album has a naturalness where people will go, "Oh, that's interesting, I like that."

You had a debilitating stroke in 2004. I've seen you a few times since in concert and you've seemed in tip-top shape. Have you fully recovered?

I hope so! I'm getting older like everybody else, but I feel good, confident. I enjoy playing and writing. When I was ill with the stroke and everything, I think it brought a lot more clarity into me life, especially metaphysically and spiritually. It allowed me a means to use this knowledge or information or a way towards meditation. Also, it reminded me we're not as in control as we like to think. You're lying on your back in a hospital, paralyzed — you think differently. Maybe we don't have any control over what happens.

When I caught Dave and his band at the Wilbur Theatre in Boston in 2015, it was a spirited show of Kinks songs and some solo material. "Living on a Thin Line" is one of the best in their catalog and a highlight of his solo gigs. Dave sings, "All the wars that were won and lost / Somehow don't seem to matter very much anymore / All the lies we were told / All the lies of the people running 'round, their castles have burned."

Post-set, the house has emptied and the roadies are doing their work. Dave and I wander back onstage. I'm in a semi-jocular manner, and after the usual answer to the usual reunion question (who knows? it's always up to Ray), I followed with, "Jesus, Dave, you know one of you will die at some point and then there *can't* be a reunion." He sort of winced, and I immediately rushed in with "I don't mean now! Not soon! I just mean ... inevitably."

Dave sighed and laughed ruefully.

And to be clear, from my perspective, whether they do or don't is both entirely up to them and not necessary for my appreciation of all they've done. I've got memories of great Kinks shows. And that's all I really need. ◆

“If you think by saving the forest
you’re going to redeem your soul, you’ve got
another thing coming.”

Leonard Cohen

Leonard Cohen performs in Geneva, Switzerland, October 2008

PHOTOGRAPH BY RAMA.

LEONARD COHEN

IF ROY ORBISON SANG ONLY FOR THE LONELY, for whom did Leonard Cohen sing? Perhaps those for whom "lonely" would be a step up from where they are — or were. There was certainly more to Cohen's music, but there's no way around the obvious: sadness, despair and longing figured rather prominently in Cohen's scheme of things, in his choice of lyrical imagery, the use of minor keys, the slow, deliberate tempos, the topics. He sang of the labyrinth of love, of lies and of burdens. He invoked Jewish and Christian symbolism, explored violence and forgiveness and employed military allegories.

Start with the dark chords of 1967's "Suzanne," Cohen's best-known tune, popularized by Judy Collins. I say "best-known," but only until "Hallelujah" went mega-viral in the pop culture world in the 21st century. And that was not Cohen's version, a semi-buried track on the album *Various Positions*, though it all came back to him. The "Hallelujah" craze started with Jeff Buckley in 2004 (his take drawn very much from a 1984 version by John Cale), followed by countless other renditions, a book and a documentary film. Most listeners latched onto the exclamation itself — "Hallelujah!" — missing the gnarlier depths and S&M allusions in the song.

You want death and pain? Listen to the musings on variety in mortality in 1974's "Who by Fire." You want grim self-reflection? Consider 1993's "Tower of Song," in which the singer rues feeling pain in places he used to use for play.

I saw Cohen and his backing octet in 1988 at Citi Club in Boston's Kenmore Square. Outside was a whirlwind of action and noise — people going to dance clubs, restaurants and bars. Busy and clamorous. But inside Citi it was dark, cool, calm and cavernous. Truly another world.

He kicked off a 25-song set with "Dance Me to the End of Love," just beginning to spin his magical web: intricate, soothing, stimulating, romantic "chamber rock," music rife with religious and historical references, tales of love gone awry, songs of a society where the deck is stacked against the good guys or, maybe, the protagonist has stacked the deck against himself. Most songs started with Cohen solemnly reciting a verse. Then, the band would ease in. Delicately. Gently. Artfully.

Talk about a decompression chamber.

Cohen's detractors would, no doubt, simply call it a depression chamber. The man knew doom, the man knew gloom. No way around it. The graceful Montreal native was a vital source of inspiration to post-punk rockers like Nick Cave and Ian McCulloch, men who've found dark empty spaces in their own lives and the lives of those they write about. But there could be a beauty in sadness — Nico told me that a long time ago, and it stuck. Cohen found it just about every time with this band's quiet storm. A narcotic with no downside.

Not everything Cohen touched was mournful. Cohen's lyrics were, of course, sharply tuned — similes such as those in "Bird on the Wire" just rolled off his tongue. Redemption, it seemed, was always lurking around the corner; Jesus's image was frequently invoked. But the overall tone of somber and serious was the antithesis of let-the-good-times-roll rock.

I first saw Cohen in 1985 at Berklee Performance Center in Boston. It was his first area appearance in a decade and formed one-third of his entire U.S. tour. Yes, three dates. I was about to enter the Church of Cohen, truly another world. Somber, sure, but it was also a place that could turn humorous when Cohen talked. He wryly noted a review comparing his deep, rumbling voice to a frog's croak.

"I've got a very, very limited voice," Cohen told me when we spoke about that later. He was, no doubt, weary of the topic by that point, but polite enough to answer the query. "I mean, I never presented myself as a singer."

I went in with all the well-worn adjectives in my head: brooding, despairing, depressive, angst-ridden. (These were by no means negatives in my musical universe.)

This was a man who sang "I did my best, it wasn't much" and "I'm sorry for smudging the air with my song."

And I came out of it emotionally and spiritually uplifted. It was not, mind you, an easy uplift like, say, Modern English's "I Melt With You," but it was palpable and profound.

A Leonard Cohen covers album called *I'm Your Fan* was released in 1991: tributes paid by Cave, Cale, McCulloch, Pixies, R.E.M., James, Lloyd Cole, That Petrol Emotion and others. *Famous Blue Raincoat*, a covers album by Jennifer Warnes, appeared five years earlier. In 1995, *Tower of Song* was added to the genre, with performances by Bono, Billy Joel, Sting, Peter Gabriel, Don Henley, Elton John and Willie Nelson, among others.

Cohen says he felt honored by the tributes. "I think there is an unbroken chain from one generation to another. I got it from somewhere, and if you're able to pass it on ... I think you have to stick to your guns. The young are very sensitive to 'the sellout,' to corruption in the artists they admire. I think they can see in my own work that — [although] I had to pay for it with a couple of decades of obscurity — there's something there: that a guy worked, that he was straight. I think it's as simple as that."

Also, I suggest, there's the fact that the guy in question never got complacent, that he kept on a quest for something intangible that might turn out to be unattainable.

"That's what one is looking for," says Cohen, "the thing that one is not sure [about]. Just to keep looking at your compass and see that you haven't gotten too far off course. You're not quite sure where you're sailing, but you know where the sun is, you know where the moon is and, somehow, there are a few landmarks and a few signs in the sky, and you can kind of steer a course. Yeah, you go off and you go under and you go around, but you have a sense of what a journey is.

"I think the only way I can describe my spiritual odyssey is to say that your memory gets better, and you realize that things don't last forever — the good ones or the bad ones ... Sometimes you feel at home in your skin, and sometimes you don't."

Cohen — the Eeyore of pop, as I once posited, half-jokingly — was very much aware of his public image. "So happy that you stayed," he intoned, before kicking off his second set alone with "Avalanche." (It was to be a long show; some *could* have had enough of the slow, dark ride and left.) He referenced the 1960s thusly: "There was a brief period of time a thousand years ago, 11 or 12 minutes called the '60s. It was a heady time. It has become a black hole and a Bermuda triangle of the cosmos. ... It was a seductive moment, but being the gloomy chap that you know I am, I was able to miss it."

Cohen's major contribution to '60s folk-pop success was, as noted, Collins' version of "Suzanne." (The woman in the song was Suzanne Verdal, the former wife of the Quebec artist Armand Vaillancourt, with whom Cohen had a platonic affair.) Yes, it's romantic, but — especially when Cohen sang it — it's dour, too.

I'd been through a tunnel and came out the other side. The last song of the night left me awestruck and humbled. It was "The Partisan," a stately World War II-era ballad about the hope for freedom. (The song was composed in 1943 by a Russian; a French Resistance leader added lyrics.) Cohen had recently sung it in Poland and dedicated it, this night, to Lech Walesa's Solidarity movement. "There are people in this world living under somewhat different conditions," he said. "It is to acknowledge their suffering and our undeserved grace that I sing this song."

I spoke with him five years after that Citi show. He was touring behind his eleventh album, *The Future,* whose title song gave the politically correct brigade a jolt. In the climactic verse, Cohen turns his darkness toward dictators and saints, the atom bomb and abortion. The future, he sings, is "murder." One might wince at the graphic imagery, turn away from the apocalyptic vision or be angered by the apparent equation of abortion and murder. That's OK. If he wrote it, he stands by it.

"What I find in writing," Cohen said, "is that at the beginning of the process you try to support your opinions — about the environment, about politics, about where you stand — and I find that even though that may make you a good citizen, it makes for a very bad songwriter. You may get positions you can applaud, but they're boring, they're alibis. If you think by saving the forest you're going to redeem your soul, you've got another thing coming. There's something else at stake.

"'The Future' is dark and funny. If I'd have nailed that to the church door like Martin Luther, it'd be a very sinister document. But it's married to a hot little dance track so, in a sense, the words melt into the music and the music melts into the words, and you're left with a kind of refreshment, a kind of oxygen."

"The lyrics are so raw, so bare ..." I started to say.

"My only regret is that they're not bare enough. I hope if they give me a few more years and a few more songs, it's going to get rawer and barer and more naked."

Cohen says that writing songs for *The Future* was, as usual, "the dismal process of trying to blacken a page or trying to find a rhyme for orange — that impossible goal. You're very much like a bear having stumbled into a honeycomb: You know there's honey around, but there's a million bees biting you and you're trying to get them out of your eyes and your ears and trying to taste the honey at the same time, and the whole thing is a disaster.

"I hasten to say that the fact that I had to break my gonads over it doesn't mean that it's good. The fact that it takes so long is no guarantee of excellence. It just happens to be the way I work. I'm not smirking about it. I don't feel reproachful toward people who have the very good luck and great genius to do it faster. Hank Williams could do it in 20 minutes and so can Bob Dylan. It just happens to take me a long time."

If Cohen has never been anyone's idea of a joyride, he does offer occasional glimmers of light, hints at redemption. The finale of Cohen's 1993 show at Berklee was, appropriately enough, "Closing Time," in which he sang about all of us being, at heart, lonely romantics. He described a summer night that was not humid but fragrant, so that we might enjoy the expectation of relief.

Cohen's backing group was tasty, ever on the mark, with the flautist Paul Ostermayer especially stirring on the swooping "Waiting for the Miracle." Violinist Bob Kurbo added bittersweet textures. There was no showboating at all — just a musicianly respect shared among the players and a debt of gratitude evinced by the man in the spotlight. A night of challenging music that was easy on the ears: one of the toughest tricks.

Cohen has long been torn between cynicism and hope. When we spoke, in 1993, he had acquired that hip cachet among young rockers. I asked where he found himself at 59.

"I think as you get older, that broad base, the range, gets very, very wide. You become more tolerant and more crotchety at the same time. More open and more critical. I think the confessional nature contracts at one end and opens at the other. You're willing to confess to yourself that you really do hate mankind, and, at another point, you're really willing to confess to yourself that you do feel a deep sense of fraternity with the whole human manifestation."

This was the kind of worldly wisdom that's not often voiced by rock and rollers. But, of course, Cohen only fit into the margins of the rock world.

It hasn't all been doom and gloom, Cohen stresses. "Thirty years [after I started], the New York press are still dredging up this gloomy stuff," he says, with a chuckle. "I've been to quite a few concerts and, really, I don't see as many laughs as I get at mine. I guess it's just the computer: They put in my name and up comes 'gloom' and 'melancholy.'"

He was not wrong about the humor. He was a droll, funny sonofabitch.

How long, I asked, could he keep pursuing his particular journey?

"The devil laughs when you make plans," Cohen answers, "but, God willing, I'd like to keep hammering away. This little resurrection I am very happily undergoing has been a great relief and very refreshing — both spiritually and financially. I'm not in a position to retire quite yet."

In October 2016, *The New Yorker* ran an exhaustive profile. Editor David Remnick reported that Cohen was battling cancer and floated the possibility that Cohen was nearing the end. "The big change is the proximity to death," Cohen told Remnick in an interview done several months earlier. "I am a tidy kind of guy. I like to tie up the strings if I can. If I can't, also, that's OK. But my natural thrust is to finish things that I've begun." He had unpublished poems and unfinished lyrics and was considering a new book. "[But] I am ready to die. I hope it's not too uncomfortable. That's about it for me."

Still, Cohen scoffed at the idea that death was imminent. It was. He died on November 7, 2016. His manager, Robert B. Kory, said he "died during his sleep following a fall in the middle of the night ... The death was sudden, unexpected and peaceful."

We all know that a famed artist's death does not necessarily mean the end of his or her creative output. There are, of course, unreleased live tracks and unfinished songs in the vault. Maybe they were always supposed to be sealed, but with the artist not around to make the call, it falls to the managers of their estate.

We thought Cohen's swan song was the wrenching *You Want It Darker*, released in October of 2016, a month before his death. As with David Bowie's *Blackstar*, Cohen was clearly contemplating the end of his run, and his ruminative, penetrating lyrics and gruff, rumbling baritone brought us deep into those bowels. There was sadness, anger and grandeur and certainly a sense of finality. (Not that death hadn't already surfaced in Cohen's work: to name but one, consider 1977's *Death of a Ladies Man*, produced, much to Cohen's discomfort, by Phil Spector.)

But it wasn't quite the finale. In 2019, we got the brief *Thanks for the Dance* (nine songs clocking in under 30 minutes), an album cobbled together from "bare musical sketches" — essentially spoken-word/barely sung poems — set to spare musical accompaniment, mostly written or co-written by his son, Adam Cohen. The elder Cohen didn't lack for admiring friends in the world of serious musicians, and many of them were enlisted for this album: Beck, Warnes, Daniel Lanois, Zac Rae (Death Cab for Cutie), Richard Reed Parry (Arcade Fire), Damien Rice and Leslie Feist. Javier Mas, Cohen's longtime bandmate, plays Spanish guitar, and that is the album's dominant instrument.

There's a stark and gorgeous video of "Happens to the Heart," directed by Daniel Askill and featuring trans actor Bobbi Salvör Menuez, who self-references as "they." Not unlike Bowie's "Lazarus," the song's power is greatly enhanced by the video. A worried Menuez, dressed like a young Cohen, walks slowly through the woods, stripping off layers of clothes before donning a monk's black robe. They find peace while meditating (and elevating) at a cliff's edge, overlooking a lake. Askill told *Rolling Stone* that he wanted to make a video that spoke about Cohen's years as a Zen monk: "a quiet, symbolic narrative that charts the letting go of ego and the trappings of fame."

It won't surprise anyone to find Cohen treading familiar territory on *Thanks for the Dance*. The tempos on the album are mostly slow and stately, the moods somber, the singer still wrestling with the labyrinthine nature of love and lust, alongside themes of loneliness, lies and loss. If some hear Cohen's music as soft rock or chamber pop, there is a sense of gravitas on *Thanks for the Dance*. There was *always* a sense of gravitas, even when he was being playful, but this project — while gorgeous, sensual and heartbreaking in places — is also underwhelming. The delicate music supports the lyrics sufficiently, but they don't often feel integrally wedded. Unlike *You Want It Darker* (and many of Cohen's earlier works), his voice is not often set among dramatic arrangements or surrounded and buoyed by female backing vocals. One welcome exception is the celestial-sounding "The Hills," where Cohen's resigned despair is countered by the uplifting voices of Erika Angell, Molly Sweeney and Lilah Larson.

Thanks for the Dance is an ideal record for the streaming age. Fans will want to hear it, but won't likely care about owning it or, if they're in a Cohen mood, it would not be one of the first albums they'd return to.

I like something the British novelist and essayist Julian Barnes wrote in *Nothing to Be Frightened Of*, a 2008 book about mortality: that he would be truly dead only when the last person ever read his words. I'd like to think that Cohen believed that, too. ◆

MARIANNE FAITHFULL

LIKE MANY OF US, I first "knew" Marianne Faithfull as the pretty, sweet-voiced singer of the Rolling Stones song "As Tears Go By." The gorgeous, well-bred, Catholic-schooled teenage chanteuse was discovered at a party by Mick Jagger and his band's manager, Andrew Loog Oldham. It was a sad song they wrote for her, a heartbreaking ballad.

Faithfull was at one time — well, variously, for four years off and on, it seems — Mick's girlfriend/muse. She reportedly had flings with Keith Richards and David Bowie, among others. She was a singer and a successful recording artist, yes, but as was sometimes the case for pretty women in a certain era, she was viewed more as a famous male rocker's consort.

Her career — her life in the public eye — goes "from 1964 to now," she told me, during one of several interviews we've done over the years. "In every era, I've had a very interesting piece of work out. It's not just luck; I know that." There were drugs, there was drink, there were parties. She made some albums. Don't think that wasn't fun. For a while. But you know how that arc so often runs. It descended, at least for Faithfull, into both addiction and oblivion. The Stones' "Sister Morphine," a co-write with Mick and Keith, was *her* song.

Then it was 1979. Years had passed, memories had faded. Faithfull seemed part of a distant past, the swinging '60s and the more damaging early '70s. Then, shockingly (at

"Making *Broken English* was the most cathartic thing in my life. Something in me changed, and I was really very happy."

Marianne Faithfull

Marianne Faithfull at the Women's World Awards 2009 in Vienna

least to us on the outside), she re-emerged as a hard-bitten, raggedy-voiced, post-punk siren, collaborating with Barry Reynolds on the vicious and visceral *Broken English* album. Dark, damaged, evocative and profane, it fit the tenor of the times.

The first time I saw Faithfull in the flesh was in 1985, on an Artist panel with Yoko Ono, John Cale and others at the New Music Seminar in New York. Having released two albums after *Broken English* — 1981's *Dangerous Acquaintances* and 1983's *A Child's Adventure* — she'd become a star of sorts again, a slightly older stateswoman of that post-punk "New Music" world.

And she was drunk off her ass, way out of control, answering questions and swapping insults in a surly, slurred voice. It was, for audience and panelists alike, a painful (if, in all honesty, entertaining up to a point) experience. There was a lot of wincing and squirming. Can't somebody help her?

Faithfull remembers that time. Well, sort of.

"I fell off my chair," she recalled, when we talked backstage at the Paradise Theater in Boston five years later. "I was hitting my bottom." (I don't think she meant the double meaning there.) "I was in treatment a month later." She had checked into Hazelden, the famous Minnesota rehab center.

But Faithfull was in top form at this 1990 show, an early gig on a 29-date U.S. tour. She had another album out, 1987's *Strange Weather*, and a live set (*Blazing Away*) was imminent. Accompanied by acoustic guitarist, harmony singer and co-songwriter Reynolds at this intimate tour de force, Faithfull wove a semi-tragic survivalist's web, a journey from the semi-innocent sadness of "As Tears Go By" and "Sister Morphine" through "Why D'Ya Do It," the nastiest song of sexual/emotional betrayal ever written, the *Fatal Attraction* of rock. Her voice was torn and ragged (yes, *that* word again), but also resonant, far-ranging and warm. Stirring and strong, Faithfull was the full-voiced chronicler of good times and (mostly) bad times. She crawled from the wreckage.

She began by singing about the pain of lost youth and quickly moved into singing about the consequences of a fall from grace. These themes came from experience and hit home. The cathartic, emotional weight of the songs was compounded by our knowledge of her past — the Stones connection, the self-abuse, the rock and roller-coaster ride.

Faithfull unveiled several new tunes, including the reflective Bono-and-Edge-penned "Conversation on a Barstool." New and old, her set kept hitting upon the tougher emotions, conflicts and tribulations: guilt, compulsion, aging. The highlight was John Lennon's "Working Class Hero," a bitter song Faithfull claimed as her own, capturing its frustration and futility. Lennon's version was more dirge, Faithfull's more a snarl. She really put the bite into "'Til you're so *fucking* crazy you can't follow their rules." She excised the final line, "If you want to be a hero, then just follow me." Given Lennon's desultory tone throughout the song, I could never tell if that was him being sarcastic or not. (While this was a far different song, Faithfull kind of did what Bryan Ferry did with Lennon's "Jealous Guy": surpassed the creator's rendition.)

Song over, she smiled. Broadly. Warmly. Faithfull sang of life's aches and pains, but she has worked, or was working, them through. Like a living Nico, this aging beauty and one-time rock star attaché had found her voice, found truth, redemption and a new life by retelling and recreating dark tales of desperate times. (Years later, she and David A. Stewart co-wrote "Song for Nico." I have to think there was a real shared spirit there.)

Faithfull calls *Broken English* her "masterpiece" (hey, it's not bragging if it's true) but also says the album led the public and her record company to expect her to deliver variations on it. Making *Broken English* "was the most cathartic thing in my life," Faithfull says. "Something in me changed, and I was really very happy. [But then] I wanted to show another side of myself, and the record company didn't want that. They just wanted more and more anger, fury, rage. And, I thought, 'Oh well, that was that: Let's move right on.' I absolutely refused to go on churning out *Broken English Mark 2*, *Mark 3* and *Mark 4*. I could have done. But I would have had to maintain a level of philosophy and rage that I would not have been able to live with."

In 1995, Faithfull was in recovery again, spending time at McLean Hospital in Belmont, outside Boston. Not surprisingly, the next time we talked, the subject of willful self-destruction, about landing foursquare at the rock and roll intersection of too much drink and too many drugs, arose. Again.

"The most delightful, the most talented, the most witty, the most everything people, they do that to themselves and we don't know why," Faithfull said. She wasn't speaking about herself at that moment — she was actually reflecting on a mutual acquaintance, former Pogues singer Shane MacGowan — but she knew of what she spoke.

After moving to New York City, she wrote *Faithfull: An Autobiography*. In it, she spun her own sex, drugs and rock and roll story. In the index, there are 21 entries under DRUGS, including *heroin (smack), MF as junkie, morphine* and, finally, *MF's recovery.*

Writing the book "changed me," Faithfull says. "Whatever it was I was so frightened of about my story ... There are some people who don't like it, some of the people in it, but some of them do." In any case, she considers it all history, and she promises a firm, polite refusal if that's where the gutter press wants to dig during interviews these days. "The salacious, dirty stories, the sex and drugs. I don't like those things. I have to learn to deal with it, but I think with the book and everything I'm not quite so touchy."

Still, "It's not good for me to be demeaned and diminished by that, 'cause I've got a lot to do, and I need my confidence and I need my hope high. That sort of chipping away isn't good. No, we don't let that happen."

In 1995, when Tom Snyder, the pompous, self-parodic *Late Late Show* host harped on the Jagger connection, Faithfull demurred, "I learnt a lot." Then, as she described her non-AA-endorsed recovery — an occasional joint, an occasional gin and tonic — Snyder erupted with, "By the way, the one you picked is a wonderful drink!"

"I have to remember to be very careful," Faithfull replied, gracefully.

Faithfull believes that a lot of rock and roll self-indulgence "is a pose, one of those things artists do. We want everything we do to be like an ambush and a surprise. So, just as people write you off and say, 'Well, that's that,' then you come up with something astounding and it makes it more amusing to you. I certainly don't do it now and I have not for a long time. And it's a pretty childish way to do things. But I do remember thinking like that, and I also know it's one of the things people are astounded by when they meet me, because I obviously am not completely physically destroyed."

Far from it. With the Chieftains in Boston in January '95, Faithfull appeared almost regal. She sang the saddest of Celtic ballads, "Love Is a Teasing," and carried it off with ragged-but-right aplomb.

In 1997, we spoke prior to a performance at the American Repertory Theatre's Loeb Drama Center in Cambridge. "It's a serious coming together of all the strands of my work," she said. "It's the most wonderful moment. I don't think the set will be the same every night. The first half will be the Weimar cabaret, which I first did at the Brooklyn Academy, and then there's an interval, 25 minutes, where you go to the bar and have a glass of wine and go outside and talk to your friends and say what you think of it so far.

That's what I would do, anyway. In that time, I will be changing into another role and come back with my band."

In 1992, she played the part of Pirate Jenny in a Dublin production of *The Threepenny Opera.* Want to hear about the nature of pure evil? Listen to the rendition of "Mack the Knife" on her *20th Century Blues* album. Irish playwright Frank McGuinness did a new translation of Bertolt Brecht's lyrics. You may know the snappy song Bobby Darin did. You may know the Broadway version and hear its whimsical bounce. "Oh, God no, no, no, no," said Faithfull of that take. "I didn't realize it for years. It takes a long time, but it suddenly hit me." In her and McGuinness' hands, the song gets extremely bloody. "Mackie with his big knife," sings a curdling Faithfull, taking Mack down to Soho, where there are "seven kids dead ... hey, there Mackie, how's she cuttin'?"

Few singers' voices lacerate as well as Faithfull's.

Mack's Ripper-like evil is eternal, she suggests. "Do you remember the Dunblane massacre?" asks Faithfull, speaking of the 16 Scottish schoolchildren killed by a gunman the previous year. "Mackie is that man. Mackie is that pedophile in Belgium. The man that did that bomb in Oklahoma. There is evil. It does exist. We are all capable of it, but we hold ourselves back. Sometimes, people don't."

Faithfull first became interested in Brecht/Weill's songs when producer Hal Willner asked her to contribute to his 1986 tribute album *Lost in the Stars.* The appeal of those songs today? "Well, they're pop songs," says Faithfull. "I know that's hard to take, but my mum — she was there, she was a young girl in Berlin, a dancer, in that period. She told me that when *The Threepenny Opera* came up, it was a huge hit, and everybody — the paperboy, the guy delivering the mail — was whistling it. It was people's music. It's the real thing."

When we spoke, Faithfull was about to begin rehearsals with pianist Paul Trueblood, with whom she will perform in a duo setting ("Faithfull and Trueblood," she quips, "good Quaker stock") and with a band featuring guitarist Reynolds, bassist Fernando Saunders and percussionist Eddie Rodriguez. Faithfull is, truthfully, a bit spacey. Her train of thought breaks down a couple of times during the interview. But it's not drugs, it's jet lag. She laughs, "I woke up at 4:30 this morning, went out to get something to eat, got the papers, went for a walk, came back and then about 8 o'clock I said, 'Better get some sleep.' It's a big drag."

After that show, *Don't Smoke in Bed*, which was pretty damn triumphant, I met up with her backstage. Faithfull and I knew each other well enough by that point. She fired up a joint and gave me a surprising full-on-the-lips kiss in greeting. (If you check the Rock Critic Handbook, it does say "You really shouldn't kiss or do drugs with musicians you're interviewing." Although there are exceptions.) Coulda seemed awkward — it certainly wasn't standard critic/artist protocol — but it didn't. She was in a good mood and had every right to be. And so was I.

The next time I saw her was in September of 2002, back at the Paradise. Wearing a black pantsuit and deep décolletage, Faithfull led a terrific Irish/Scottish quartet (keyboardist Andy May, guitarist Brian McFie, bassist Garry John Kane, drummer Johnny Boyle) through an 80-minute set before about 500 people. Occasionally donning reading glasses to check the lyrics on a music stand, Faithfull began with "I'm Into Something Good," the Gerry Goffin/Carole King by-way-of-Herman's Hermits song, a slice of '60s feel-good pop that seems about as far away from Faithfull's dark and often brooding catalog as could be expected. There was a dissonance between the song and singer. But Faithfull didn't deliver it as particularly ironic: Her voice is what it is — y'know, raspy — but she's capable of expressing simple pleasurable sentiments, too. Who'd'a thunk it?

The gnarlier stuff came later: "Broken English," "The Ballad of Lucy Jordan," "Working Class Hero," "Why D'Ya Do It."

After two decades as a damaged-but-defiant cult artist, Faithfull wears it well. Her allure comes from her rocky past and her continuing vitality. She lit a cigarette to begin "Song for Nico," saying she did so, "as I am your decadent European friend." The music had grace and danger. The sound was clear and focused, reminiscent of the best textured '80s new wave without sounding retro. She chose well from her past (including the obscure but compelling "Rich Kid Blues" and the elegiac "Wilder Shores of Love") and put songs from the new disc, *Kissin Time*, in the best light.

Those new tunes were mostly co-written by famous fans: Billy Corgan of Smashing Pumpkins (the slight "Wherever I Go"), Beck ("Like Being Born"), Damon Albarn of Blur ("Kissin Time") and Pulp leader Jarvis Cocker (the witty "Sliding Through Life on Charm," based on Faithfull's autobiography). The live renditions were far edgier and more rocking than the recorded versions.

While her latest music doesn't have the jagged quality of *Broken English*, Faithfull still feels close to those songs, "especially in performance." She says that dramatist Heathcote Williams, who wrote the lyrics for the supreme kiss-off song "Why D'Ya Do It," has finally penned a follow-up. "It's nothing like 'Why D'Ya Do It,' Faithfull says, "but it is the most ferocious, furious rant you've ever heard in your life." (It never came out; Williams died in 2017.)

"This is a very agreeable way to live," says Faithfull, of touring and playing clubs with this material. "I can become [the characters], and it's like time travel."

Faithfull made a film in 1993, *When Pigs Fly*, playing the ghost of "an Irish barmaid who is beaten savagely to death by her wicked husband." Goodness! Faithfull says her character does exact retribution from the husband. And she has a positive effect on another character, a forlorn jazz musician. "It's a revenge comedy. I am a delightful ghost."

Do not, though, call her a pop icon. "This isn't the peasant culture. We don't need icons. We need reality. Call me an icon and I'll scream. That's a copout. For anybody to be really working and to be [called] an icon, especially before you're, you know, dead, is a pain." ◆

JOHN FOGERTY

JOHN FOGERTY WAS NOT BORN ON THE BAYOU — he actually hails from northern California — but if you were a fan of Creedence Clearwater Revival from 1969 to 1972 you can be forgiven for thinking so. The quartet led by the singer-songwriter-guitarist peppered the Top 10 with nine Southern-fried hits during that era. "Proud Mary" started CCR on its way to becoming the dominant singles band of that era.

"I'd take that as a compliment," Fogerty told me in 2019 during a call from his home in southern California. "That was obviously what I was trying to do. There are, in some quarters, the so-called jam bands or album bands, people who took offense to someone having a Top 40 hit. I didn't. I was raised on that: Elvis, the Beatles and the rest of rock and roll. I was very honored to be considered a singles band."

Actually, Fogerty amends himself slightly, "The first rock and roll I was hearing was pre-Elvis. We had a great R&B station in Oakland. I really loved Fats Domino and Little Richard — that blew me away, 'Tutti Frutti' and 'Long Tall Sally' — and that might have predated [me hearing] Elvis. But I literally heard 'Blue Moon of Kentucky' by Elvis Presley on that station. I was very much taken with the persona of Elvis and the whole dangerous thing he projected."

But where did that voice come from? That voice that had legions of Top 40 fans convinced you came from deep in Louisiana?

"Rock and roll in the beginning was mostly a very Southern thing," Fogerty explains.

“I’ve had ups and downs, but I’m happy enough.”

John Fogerty

John Fogerty performs in Norway at Odderøya Live, July 2012

"I was always fascinated with the South. It just seemed really magical to me, the music and the art. There was a lilt, a wonderful difference from the life I was living, and I think I just absorbed all of that music. I've thought maybe reincarnation explains it more than anything."

When we spoke, Fogerty was just back from a European tour, resting up before an American tour with a nine-piece band that includes his son Shane on guitar and occasionally features another son, Tyler, on vocals.

"I certainly feel ready to rock," says Fogerty. A discussion he once had with pal and fellow guitarist-singer Brad Paisley illuminated one of the reasons. "It always gets to be new because [as guitarists] we can do more than just sing the song; we come up with a new solo, and that makes it fresh."

So, does that mean Fogerty sees himself more as a guitarist than singer? He doesn't exactly answer the question.

"My first attraction was guitar. Music just took me by the collar and grabbed my heart and I was interested from the get-go. Really, really young, almost before I could walk. When I was about three-and-a-half, my mother sat me down and was about to give me a present. It was a little kids' record. One side was 'Oh Susannah' and the other side was 'Camptown Races.' She explained to me these were both songs written by Stephen Foster. And I've always found that very fascinating. I'm sure at the time I thought Stephen Foster was on the record. If I remember it right, it was a group singing both songs and it was hard to pick out which one of those people is Stephen Foster, but she explained to me he was a writer, so I remember that moment very well."

Creedence Clearwater Revival broke up acrimoniously in 1972 over strife between Fogerty and the rhythm section, bassist Stu Cook and drummer Doug Clifford. (Fogerty's older brother, rhythm guitarist Tom, had exited in 1970.) John was also embroiled in an extended legal and personal battle with Saul Zaentz, whose Fantasy label Creedence recorded for and who owned Fogerty's publishing. As a result, Fogerty wouldn't play those songs in public for many years, relying instead on material from his post-CCR solo career. "I just felt like I was playing into Saul's hands if I did everything as normal and he was going to profit more from me out there performing the songs. It was a horrible career conundrum and choice because it's suicide to a career. Your fans want to come see you sing those songs; they don't want to hear you sing other songs."

The convoluted story's been told many times over the years, but I asked for the short version.

"Saul owned my music. [He] had also stolen my life savings in an offshore tax shelter. He had basically stolen our life savings and gotten away with it. The only reason that we got any money back was from our own accountant's insurance — the insurance company decided to challenge us rather than pay us pennies on the dollar and make it go away, which is all we were asking. But [Zaentz] got away with stealing those funds.

"At some point I realized I was being treated very poorly and that I wasn't being paid anywhere near a proper way. In the back of my mind, I wanted to own my songs; [they're] my children you might say. I'm talking about owning the songs themselves, the publishing, But I realized that I had been lied to by Saul and he wasn't going to allow me to own them. He had let the other members of Creedence out of their contract, but he didn't let me out of that same contract. I still owed any new material to Saul Zaentz. I found myself in the horrible position of having to give any new music, any new records to Saul Zaentz.

In January of 2023, Fogerty got a satisfactory resolution. *Variety* reported that Fogerty had made a deal with Concord Music Group to purchase a majority interest, worldwide, in the Creedence catalog. Although the U.S. rights were about to revert to him anyway under copyright law, he wanted to control the catalog globally. With the help of music biz bigwig Irving Azoff, Fogerty struck a deal that would make him the songs' primary owner while Concord retains an interest.

"Finally getting ownership of my songs now, you can see it's correcting something that has been wrong in my life for most of my life — since my early twenties," said Fogerty.

But back to the songs themselves. I have to ask: Do you love Ike and Tina's version of "Proud Mary"?

"Absolutely," Fogerty says. "I first heard it in the car. I believe it was in the wintertime, probably suppertime, and I just thought it was the coolest thing. I still do. It was a wonderful divergence from the original. Those are the wonderful things that happen [with covers]. Just recently, I heard a Willie Nelson version of 'Have You Ever Seen the Rain?' and I hadn't been aware of it, but my wife had watched the TV show *Little Big*

Lies and I thought that really sounds good. There was a wonderful, different kind of spooky vibe to the song."

In part through its use in films, Creedence's music is associated with the Vietnam War and the protest movement at home. Was that ultimately a good thing?

"I don't know that I would call it a 'good' thing," Fogerty says, but "I'm very proud of the association. It was a very unique time in American history, and my songs are still identified with that. The protesters took those songs to heart, but so did the guys who were GIs and had to go to Vietnam. That was a fact.

"Because I was in the Army, there was an insight I had that a lot of the protesters didn't have. They'd argue with my acquaintances, and I'd say, 'That guy that you're hurling epithets at, that soldier over there, he's 19 years old. He likes all the same stuff you like. It's just that there but for fortune he has to go fight because the government tells him that's what he has to do. So, he's doing it. It's just silly to be protesting your policy differences toward the soldiers. He doesn't have a choice in the matter. It's the president who has the choice. Go do your thing to him.'"

Creedence played *Woodstock* in 1969, but because they weren't on the original soundtrack or in Michael Wadleigh's movie, that fact tends to be forgotten. Shortly after we talked, Fantasy released Creedence's *Live at Woodstock* album, a complete document of their set. "I haven't listened to it," says Fogerty. "I imagine that's pretty good, 'cause I know we played really well."

Why weren't they on the original soundtrack? And why this now?

"I don't think any of us realized that our set was being recorded. Some months after the actual festival of *Woodstock*, I got a reel-to-reel tape in the mail, and it was 'Bad Moon Rising.' Creedence famously had issues because we were on so late and the audience was asleep, mostly caused by hippie dysfunction and the fact that we followed the Grateful Dead, who were obviously in character and quite dysfunctional, so it really impacted our set. Half-a-million people, or close to it, were asleep. So, the choice they sent me, 'Bad Moon Rising,' wasn't remarkable. We actually played a really hot set in spite of the fact that the audience was in such disarray in the middle of the night. But I wasn't offered 'Keep on Chooglin'' or 'The Night Time Is the Right Time' or 'Suzie Q.'

"'Bad Moon Rising' was OK, but I thought, 'I don't know, never mind.' Creedence was white-hot — we were the hottest thing on Earth at the moment. And I just thought,

'Why do I want to be in a movie showing everybody's dysfunction and the audience asleep? So, I demurred, as they say. So, we weren't on the soundtrack and we weren't in the movie. I never second-guessed that decision. Creedence did very, very well moving on past that, and it wasn't an issue.

"But time went by, and they started doing retrospectives and I think at the 25th anniversary of *Woodstock* they had a director's cut [of the film] and I said, 'Sure, fine, if you wanna put something in there, that's OK with me.' My bandmates had been making a lot of noise about my bad decision, as far as they were concerned, so I said 'OK, fine.'" ("Born on the Bayou," Screamin' Jay Hawkins' "I Put a Spell on You" and "Keep on Chooglin'" are in it.)

Fogerty readily admits he's had a rocky life — not just the lawsuits, but a divorce and alcohol abuse. He wrote a candid, somewhat self-lacerating autobiography, *Fortunate Son*, in 2015. It's named after his fiery Vietnam War-era anti-privilege song, but you can't help wondering if there might be some bittersweet irony in the title.

"No," he says. "I've had ups and downs, but I'm happy enough that I wouldn't name my own biography with sort of a fatalistic vibe. No one gets a straight going-up graph. As you know, for the man that wrote the song, me, there was much venom and spit and heated anger in that phrase, 'fortunate son.' I think my wife liked that. She even has a line of clothing and merchandise called *Fortunate Son*. So, I looked at it and said, 'You sure you wanna name a shirt that's supposed to be my shirt with that name?' But she thinks of the phrase as iconic whereas I thought of it as describing the kids of some senator who was avoiding the draft. But in the present context, it's not supposed to be ironic at all. It's just something that identifies with me."

There's also the idea that, despite all the travails, Fogerty's still out there rocking, with his kids, playing to adoring audiences. Life, as he knows it now, is good.

"I certainly look at life that way. I feel very happy about life, believe it or not. It's a wonderful trick. I've seen other people do things like this, like Nelson Mandela who was much more magnanimous than I might have been. If the right thing happens to you, and for me it was meeting Julie, my wife, it just made everything else inconsequential that was negative. [They married in 1991.] It taught me to see the beauty and the wonderful positive things. My life since I met her and with her has been absolutely wonderful. I think that's what God wants us to learn."

I wondered if Fogerty had been able to put aside the animosity with Cook and Clifford and lingering bitterness regarding his brother, who died in 1990.

"At some point, I made a point to myself of forgiving Tom," Fogerty says. "I just felt like I had to do that because he wasn't around for me to get to work it out with him. I [had] tried [but] he was so not connected to reality, dysfunctional about all of it that had happened. It was years after he had passed that I kind of kept thinking about it and working on it and thought certainly in honor of our mother I could come to a point where I'm at peace with it, which I did.

"With Doug and Stu, because they continue to — what's the word? — throw another log on the fire now and then, I kinda go 'Goodness!' but it doesn't really get my old embers flared up anymore. I just accept that that's the nature of it, that's the way that it's gonna be."

In 1997, Fogerty sued Creedence Clearwater Revisited, arguing that the band name would lead people to believe that he was part of the band. He got an injunction (they switched to Cosmo's Factory), but it was later overturned and they returned to the Revisited tag. In the spring of 2019, Clifford and Cook announced they were retiring from touring.

"Yeah, I don't know any more than anyone else knows," Fogerty says. "I can't imagine there would be any kind of trick to it or ploy, but I don't really know. Over the years, certain artists have had farewell tours and fare-farewell tours and then finally the real farewell tour."

Any talk with Fogerty must involve baseball because of his big post-CCR hit "Centerfield." It was from a 1985 album of the same name, which reached number-one in *Billboard*. I asked if the song was about anyone in particular or his own yearning to play?

"It wasn't anybody in particular," he says, "although there's a moment in the song where I say 'brown-eyed handsome man,' which is of course a quote from a Chuck Berry song. Besides the wonderful Chuck Berry song itself, I was thinking of Jackie Robinson. That's what that was always about. [Sportscaster] Dan Patrick always makes a point of telling me, 'But he's a second baseman, he's an infielder.' Dan, you don't have to be so literal here."

Who does he root for?

"My team is the Oakland A's, but I obviously have a soft spot for the Giants, too, because they came to the Bay Area first."

And, finally, because I really had no friggin' idea, I had to ask him what the hell "chooglin'" is. And why we must keep on doin' it.

"It's something I made up as a thing to kind of look like it had been around," Fogerty says. "It kinda had that boogie feeling to it as far as the music and it seemed to describe a way of being, and that is what I wanted to identify chooglin' with. You'll know it when you see it, and you'll definitely know it when you're *not* seeing it."

It happens every time he plays, Fogerty says. "Absolutely. They do it [choogle] unconsciously."

When he's working on new music now, he says, "It's my same personality, the same father who's dying to birth another new wonderful song." Fogerty laughs. "Or not. You work at it. The same guy that wrote 'Proud Mary' is hoping to dare the fates and the gods and come up with another one, but he realizes that's a pretty tough assignment." ◆

TINA TURNER

NEAR THE END OF A SHOW IN BOSTON back in 1981, Tina Turner sang, "Baby, baby, baby, you're out of time." That line from a Rolling Stones song could have been wincingly ironic. Comeback tours by older, past-their-peak rock stars can be discomfiting. And Turner had been out of the limelight for years. You approach with interest, but trepidation, too. You hope they don't turn out to be parodies of their earlier selves.

She was 42 and she'd been working, yes, but had spent the last few years on the casino and oldies circuit. But here she was at a rock club, the Bradford Hotel Ballroom (which had previously hosted shows by Buzzcocks and Mission of Burma). When she growled, "Are you ready for me? I'm ready for you," near the beginning of her set, she meant it, and we wanted it. No dusty nostalgia here. It was hot stuff all the way, undeniable evidence Turner was in no way past her peak. Sultry, sexy and commanding in a fringed silver mini-dress, Turner demanded a reaction, and, by the end of the evening, she had it. Everyone was in her clutches. As my photographer friend Susan Wilson put it, Turner's series of burning, soulful rockers was "multi-orgasmic."

Turner reportedly taught Mick Jagger how to dance; the Stones brought Ike and Tina Turner on their 1969 tour. The interplay continued. They had Tina open several of their 1981 tour dates; her Boston show included four of their songs: "Out of Time," "Honky Tonk Women," "It's Only Rock 'n' Roll" and "Jumpin' Jack Flash." She's not just repaying a debt. Backed by a muscular yet subtle five-piece band, she makes the songs fresh with sassy sensuality.

“I have become happier, and that’s something that’s very hard to accomplish in a lifetime for some people.”

Tina Turner

Tina Turner sings at Jones Beach Theater in Wantagh, NY, 1985

PHOTOGRAPH BY EBET ROBERTS

Like the marriage of genres in her version of "Proud Mary," Turner's sense of style is both rough and easy. Moreover, it's natural. The steps she did with her two female backup singers were obviously choreographed, but always free and spirited. Turner laced her songs with sly innuendo. She talked in breathy rasps; if she didn't melt hearts, she fired libidos.

Turner is a covers girl, and she's primarily a traditionalist, not a progressive. Along with the Stones, she embraces other superstar warhorses: the Beatles ("Get Back," "Help!"), Rod Stewart ("Tonight's the Night"), Bob Seger ("Hollywood Nights") and the Who ("Acid Queen"). She takes those songs and makes them her own. Her version of Sly Stone's "I Wanna Take You Higher" was incendiary, and no one else could be the seductive Acid Queen.

In the summer of 1989, I had dinner at Boston's Four Seasons with Turner and some people from her record label, Capitol. Good times. She was on one of the last stops of a whirlwind ten-city tour to promote *Foreign Affair*, an album due the following month. I had an advance copy and liked it a lot: it had both commercial, hook-laden pop-rock and more R&B-driven roots.

A few things had changed for her that decade. Success, bigger than ever before, was hers again. The multi-platinum *Private Dancer* was everywhere in 1984, "What's Love Got to Do With It" and the title song. In 1985, Turner starred as the fierce crossbow-wielding Aunty Entity *in Mad Max: Beyond Thunderdome.* Director George Miller had said he wanted "a Tina Turner type" for the role and ended up casting ... Tina Turner. (The film inspired my first hand-held crossbow purchase. My roommate Bruce Fournier and I used it to fire darts down the hallway into a corkboard with promo pictures of bands we loathed.) The theme song, "We Don't Need Another Hero (Thunderdome)," became a huge hit, earning Golden Globe and Grammy nominations. It also fit the tenor of the times. With Ronald Reagan and Boris Yeltsin spewing coded bellicosity, the specter of nuclear war was real. A future of a hard-scrabble violent life in a decimated world hit home more than I'd have liked.

Tina Turner was on top of the world. "I've got something here even I enjoy!" is how she put it, and that's why she wanted to chat it up, meet with music retailers, radio executives and some of us rock scribes. Quite obviously a woman at home with herself and her self-image, she was dressed in a stylish but demure beige pantsuit — "People expect me to walk in with leather in my funky image, but this is how I basically dress when I'm not onstage." She came across as a most personable and approachable star.

"This is the best music I've ever put out in my life. Otherwise, I wouldn't have promoted it this way." There was no concert tour in the wings at the time.

Not long after we met up, "The Best" from *Foreign Affair* became a worldwide hit. The song, an inspirational power ballad written by Mike Chapman and Holly Knight and first done by Bonnie Tyler, has stood the test of time, repurposed in sports arenas and TV commercials alike.

In addition to the new record, I wanted to ask her about the Tina Turner I'd seen in 1981. Even though she had no new album then, no new hits at the time, she says, "I had a great show, and I was pleased at that stage of my life. But I'd forgotten about the rock world. I realized that in order to be more successful — that came with touring with the Rolling Stones and Rod Stewart — I decided if you're going to be in this business this long, you need to make a mark. I decided I'd like to fill a stadium and would love to have a hit record. Then, you take actions."

Buddhism, she says, was the key. It provided her with self-confidence. "The practice promises change; you're able to manifest what you want in your life. You need a tool to help you make decisions. It's thinking from within. It's also rhythm and sound, which is connected with the universe. Saying the words — with the same tone, sound and rhythm — that is the connection to the universe; that helps you get what you want."

How so?

"I'm a changed person in the sense that I'm more calm, I'm less frustrated, I'm more in control. I have become happier, and that's something that's very hard to accomplish in a lifetime for some people. In 13 years, I've gotten my career back and am an independent woman."

Even then, though, Turner — arguably the most dynamic female rock singer of all time — was weighing retirement, at least from the stage. "If this album is not really successful," she warns, "I'm not going back out there. People think because you're dynamic, you want to stay onstage forever. Maybe some people do, maybe that's what they love. What I truly love is acting. I prefer that to the stage.

"I've been singing and dancing all my life, but I haven't been acting all my life. If I could have started out as an actress, I would have. But there were no parts for women, especially Black women. I had to develop something. I'm not saying I don't want [to play concerts], but I would like to be on my way out. This is a transition. I want to go from my work performing to acting. I want to continue to record and promote my work, but instead of traveling and touring live, I want to do my music and go on to the screen. I want to just do it from the screen."

Before *Mad Max,* Turner played the wild Acid Queen in Ken Russell's *Tommy.* "So, it's a challenge," she says. "I would like to go on to the next stage."

But *Foreign Affair* became a hit, easily hitting the "really successful" mark Turner had told me was the barometer, and she toured from April to November 1990. Though it was dubbed her "farewell tour," well, David Bowie, Elton John, Kiss and the Who could tell you all about those. Turner's *actual* final tour was her 50th anniversary affair in 2008 and 2009.

Back to 1989. Turner had been supping with music biz folk on this promo jaunt and, given the nature of these things, had been drinking champagne. And she broke out in a rash. So, this radiant, slender, 49-year-old singer and longtime sex symbol looked in a mirror and felt ... ugly.

"I started to get this rash on the lower part of my face," she says, candid as can be, tracing with her hand the path of the rash along her left cheekbone. "I became a homeopathic about 10 years ago; I cleanse my body and don't put aspirin or medicine in, so I don't really have many blemishes. That's why this little fungus was standing out. It was really awful, all white. It was really ugly, and you could really see it when I'd add powder."

She ascertained the bubbly might have been the cause of the breakout and cut it out. The rash cleared up. After taking only one small champagne sip at our dinner, Turner sighed, "The rash was gone, but so was my champagne. Oh, poo! Now, I've got to find another drink."

I did not expect that vivid an account, but talk about self-revelatory and ultra-humanizing.

"She's different every night," said Capitol Records vice president of sales Lou Mann, who accompanied her on this promo tour. "She doesn't come and do the robotic thing." Only one bad night, said Mann. An interviewer tried to pry into the past, digging for dirt on the strife-filled Ike & Tina Turner days. Tina, much more into the present and future than the past, hit the roof.

The years with mentor-collaborator-husband Ike (who died of a cocaine overdose in 2007) were well-documented in *I, Tina*, the 1986 book she co-wrote with Kurt Loder.

So were her beginnings as Anna Mae Bullock, born into poverty and misery, picking cotton in the fields around Nutbush, Tennessee. I put those potential topics in the dustbin.

When we spoke, we stayed in the present and possible future.

Turner attributes her astounding comeback — from domestic abuse, an attempted suicide, no record contract and deep debt — to the aforementioned Buddhism, a positive mental attitude and Australian manager Roger Davies, who she credits for revitalizing her career. "He was young, needing to organize his life, needing financial security and he knew more than I did. He had more contacts in terms of the business. If you split it down the table, I'm the performer-singer and Roger is the contacts. And then we come together and make decisions on the whole thing."

Davies had a keen ear for commercial pop and solicited top songwriters and producers for her. They enlisted Tony Joe White, author of the sleazy-swampy cool hit "Polk Salad Annie," for four selections that lent an R&B touch. "His connection was like a dream come true," she says. "He's really Southern, really wonderful. I think he's elated." [White died from a heart attack in 2018.]

After living in Switzerland for 20 years, Turner became a Swiss citizen in 2013. The same year she was a German *Vogue* cover girl — the oldest woman to ever grace the magazine's cover in any country. (Meryl Streep had the previous record at 62.) Turner, who speaks German, married her longtime beau, German record executive Erwin Bach, on the banks of Lake Zurich in July of that year.

Asked about performing in 2019 by the *New York Times,* Turner said that part of her life was over: "I was just tired of singing and making everybody happy. That's all I'd ever done in my life."

She did have a theatrical production she was highly involved in, the jukebox musical *Tina: The Tina Turner Musical,* which played in London's West End and on Broadway. "One fine specimen in the best showbiz tradition of the Great Big Broadway Musical," wrote Marilyn Stasio in *Variety*. It was nominated for 12 Tony Awards.

She was voted into the Rock and Roll Hall of Fame with Ike in 1991 and inducted again as a solo artist in 2021. She was named the seventeenth best rock singer of all time by *Rolling Stone* in 2010. In 2018, she published another memoir, *Tina Turner: My Love Story,* and acknowledged the new challenges she faced. She'd had a stroke and a kidney transplant, supplied by her loving husband. She was battling intestinal cancer.

The end came May 24, 2023, less than two months before this book's publication. Her death was shocking in a way but, then again, not. Shocking in the all-too-familiar blow we baby boomers on the outside receive when a favorite artist dies. It's never-ending, but we're taken aback every time. But not in that we knew she was in ill health for some time, albeit out of the public view. No particular case of death was given, just that ubiquitous "long illness" thing.

The tributes poured in over social media. From Diana Ross, Viola Davis, Mick Jagger, Magic Johnson, Debbie Harry, Dionne Warwick and many more.

Maybe Oprah Winfrey said it best on Instagram: "I started out as a fan of Tina Turner, then a full-on groupie, following her from show to show around the country, and then, eventually, we became real friends. She is our forever goddess of rock 'n' roll who contained a magnitude of inner strength that grew throughout her life. She was a role model not only for me but for the world. She encouraged a part of me I didn't know existed.

"Once she claimed her freedom from years of domestic abuse her life became a clarion call for triumph. I'm grateful for her courage, for showing us what victory looks like wearing Manolo's and a leather miniskirt. She once shared with me that when her time came to leave this earth, she would not be afraid, but excited and curious. Because she had learned how to LIVE surrounded by her beloved husband, Erwin, and friends. I am a better woman, a better human, because her life touched mine. She was indeed simply the best."◆

"I understood where [punk rockers] were coming from because what they were trying to do was wake everybody up."

Neil Young

Neil Young performing with Crazy Horse in Barcelona, Spain in 2007

NEIL YOUNG

NEIL YOUNG HAS, AS HIS FANS WELL KNOW, more musical sides than a decagon. On record or in concert, over his half-century-plus of music-making, it's anybody's guess which Neil will show up at any given time. With the exception of David Bowie, no rock star has played in as many creative fields as Young.

Here are two I have some familiarity with:

Neil Young, lover of country and acoustic music, sick and tired of playing that damned electric guitar and that wailing old rock and roll.

Neil Young, embracer of that glorious and grungy electric guitar-centered, wailing rock and roll sound.

We talked on the phone in September 1984. Two years earlier, influenced by Devo (with whom he shared a manager, Elliot Roberts) and Kraftwerk, Young went electronic with *Trans*, an album that was not well-received by fans or critics. He followed that with *Everybody's Rockin'*, a rockabilly-ish disc that was pretty meh.

In retrospect, did Young have any regrets about making those records?

"No," he says, "I think time will show that they have a place. I feel good about all of those things. At the time I'm doing it, I'm totally engrossed."

But here he was, on the phone, animated, amped up and affably cranky. He was on the move. Something in the works.

In 1970, Young went to Nashville during a break in a solo tour and recorded the song "Are You Ready for the Country?" Two years later, he included it on *Harvest*, the best-selling folk-rock album that established Young as one of the most potent singer-songwriters of the '70s.

In 1984, he was in the midst of a tour with the International Harvesters, and it looked like country music was coming our way. I asked if, all these years later, he was indeed ready.

"I'm 38 years old; I think I'm ready for it," Young said. In fact, he started and finished his Boston-area show at the New England Patriots' then-home, Sullivan Stadium, with the song. Willie Nelson, who opened the show, came out to sing with Young on "Are There Any More Real Cowboys?"

"I think I'm going to be making country records for as long as I can see into the future," Young told me. "It's much more down-home and real — almost folky — compared to the cutthroat avenues of rock and roll and the competition, which I am fed up with. I don't want to have anything to do with it. I really believe in country music. I feel like an old hound circling on a rug for the last five years and I think I finally found my spot. I believe in the country music community, the way that people support the music, the more friendly kind of approach of the deejays and the public relations side of it."

Young wasn't exactly dissing what he'd done over the past few years — full-fledged forays into hard rock, electronic, acoustic folk and rockabilly — but he was bored and looking for a new kind of kick. Which, actually, was an old kind of kick, delivered with fiddles, pedal steel, acoustic guitar and mandolin.

He'd burnt out on the "rowdy rock and roll solo," the kind of thing he'd done on *Rust Never Sleeps* and *Re•ac•tor* with his on-and-off backing band, Crazy Horse. "You've been hearing that for so long. Who cares? How many guitar solos can you play?! I've had it."

And then Young also answered the unasked but lurking question about whether he'd ever get back into rock and roll: "Play the old records!"

"Everywhere we go, people go crazy. I was very surprised they get off more on hearing fiddle than they do on hearing a rowdy rock and roll solo."

Will he miss the energy of his rocking days? "I don't miss it now. The energy of this music is much higher than trying to project or re-project what you've just described [rock and roll].

"Any group that comes along and does its thing for three or four years, unless they change, they go away, they're gone, they're finished. I'm still around because I've changed. And when people want me to do what I've already done, they only want me to do it because I'm still here. If I hadn't changed, I wouldn't still be here."

Young's band ("the best I've ever had") includes Ben Keith on pedal steel, Spooner Oldham on keyboards, Tim Drummond on bass, Karl Himmel on drums, Rufus Thibodeaux on fiddle and Anthony Crawford on vocals, guitar and mandolin. "They're all old buddies. Everybody feels like we just fell in the pocket."

Well, not everybody. Earlier this year, he took a batch of country songs he'd recorded in Nashville to Geffen, the company which put out *Trans* and *Everybody's Rockin'*. "It scared them. They didn't want to release them. They didn't know what to do with it. It wasn't mainstream pop."

Geffen was willing to allow one country song per album: Young balked. "I'm not the kind of artist that you can tell what to play and what not to play. I'm not going to be manipulated by anybody." Geffen dropped Young from its roster and sued him for making "unrepresentative" music. "I still don't understand what they sued me about."

Young called the experience "very deflating. But of course, the more everybody said, 'Don't do this,' the more I realized I must be doing the right thing. Because that's always been the case: whenever I try to do something different, everybody tells me not to do it."

Young had cut 25 country songs. Five more, he said, and he'd be ready to find a new record deal. "I'm really taking my time with this one. I really want this to be a really good record and really communicate to a lot of people. I feel good about what I'm doing. As long as I feel good about what I'm doing I know it'll be all right.

"When I get a record company, they're going to take a close look at me and I'm going to take a close look at them. We need a record company that's as good as we are ... I just hope the next company that I deal with takes a look at my track record a little more closely before they take a big chance on me."

As it turned out, things got resolved enough with Geffen so that Young recorded four more albums (*Old Ways*, *Landing on Water*, *Life* and *This Note's for You*) for the company. By 1988, however, he had returned to his old label, Reprise.

Seven years later, Crazy Horse is back in the saddle. The previous year, Young and the Horse hit a hard-rock peak with *Ragged Glory,* which is rough and raw on the surface — Crazy Horse has proudly billed itself as the world's third-best garage band — but finds Young's sense of songcraft, of melody, rarely better. The album is self-critical, poignant, imbued with the kind of emotional tussles, musical muscle and lead guitar excursions that mark Young's best work. Its title is a case of truth in advertising: no ballads, lots of feedback.

"We did the whole thing in three months, from before the songs were written until the album was mastered and turned in," says Young. "It happened kind of fast. It was like something comes along and you have to jump on and do it. You can't stop until it's done because, obviously, we knew we were onto it. And we've learned over the years that when the wave comes along, you'd better grab it. So that's what we did, and we just stayed on it until it was up on the beach. It wore me out, but in a real good way. I feel real lucky to have caught that one."

Is Neil Young Crazy Horse's main meal ticket?

"Well, we all make up Crazy Horse, and you-all are the meal ticket," says Young, laughing.

Yes, that's Young, contrary as ever, sense of humor and liberal politics intact.

Humor? This is a man who once segued his own "Alabama" — a condemnation of Southern racism — into Lynyrd Skynyrd's "Sweet Home Alabama," a condemnation of him. "I just sang 'I hope you all will remember,'" recalls Young of that night in Miami. "I thought it was a cool thing."

Young's sense of humor carries over to *Ragged Glory* via a cover of the old garage-rock classic "Farmer John." "Farmer John!" croaks Young leeringly, in the song, "I'm in love with your daughter." "It's kind of a sleazy thing for us," says Young. "There is a sleaze quotient to it that I think is important to balance the rest of the record."

And then there's the screaming rocker "F*!#in' Up" (yes, that's the way it's titled on the record jacket), whose refrain asks, again and again, why he keeps fucking up.

At a show I saw in 1996, Young closed his set with the song, but introduced it this way: "It sounds like 'Sugar Mountain,' but it's not 'Sugar Mountain.'" Instead of singing that song's opening line, Young sang the refrain of "F*!#in' Up." He paused midway through to evoke an optimist's thoughts, to figure that you've finally beaten this shoot-yourself-in-the-foot thing, only to launch back into the reality of doing it again. And he gave us a great kicker. "I just got an idea," Young said brightly at the song's close. "I wanna share this with you: It's Bill Clinton's campaign song!" And with that, Young was off the stage.

It may be a minor song in Young's vast catalog (as well as being his least, uh, "sensitive") but still: talk about a universal sentiment and self-deprecating candor. So how, and in what ways, does Young keep fucking up?

"I don't know, that's what I keep asking myself," he says. "There's too many of them to mention here. And I don't want to make one seem to be bigger than the other. You know how the press is: If I mention one, that's the only thing that bothers me unless I mention all the other ones — and there's not enough time for that."

Ah, the press. Young's been in hot water with certain elements of the press for what's been perceived as his support of Ronald Reagan. Imagine, Neil Young — the man who wrote that wonderful anti-war, anti-Nixon anthem "Ohio," a long-term environmentalist and activist — backing the right-wing president. The neo-Reaganite tag affixed to him in the mid-'80s, Young insists — quite vehemently — was taken out of context, blown out of proportion. "The Reagan-supporting era," sighs Young. "I don't think there is one president that's come down the line that hasn't done something good somewhere." Young says a "sleazeball journalist" nailed Reagan and then forced Young to his defense.

"Some people put down all presidents no matter what. Like once you get to be president, you're a fucking idiot. So, if you say anything good about any of them, they think you're supporting everything they do."

As to where Young's political passions lie now, consider this rant on the subject of the country's current censorship frenzy: "All these people who are fucking talking about morality should just take a walk downtown. They don't want to go downtown because instantly they see homeless people and they don't want to because that's not important. It doesn't fit their public stand of being a moralist. These fucking people — they're crazy."

Understand: Neil Young's America is not Ronald Reagan's.

I asked him about his switch back from country to rock, dredging up the "hound circling the rug" phrase he'd used in '84. "I got bit in the ass by a huge tick," he says, playing off the analogy with a laugh. "That's what got it going! Things just keep cycling around, I really don't know what brought me back to it. I woke up one morning and all I could hear was the loudest fucking drum I ever heard in my life in my head — so I knew that wasn't country!"

Young began his move away from country well before this year. He shifted back to rock in 1986 with *Landing on Water* and the following year's *Life*; he'd played horn-driven R&B with the Bluenotes on *This Note's for You* and temporarily reunited with Crosby, Stills & Nash for *American Dream*, contributing the record's best bits. His most successful effort was 1989's *Freedom*, a politicized record that juggled rock, folk and country and contained the anthemic "Rockin' in the Free World."

Crazy Horse rhythm guitarist Frank Sampedro, whose tenure with Young extends back to 1975, sees their association this way: "If you look at him as a tree and all the different branches on it, we look at ourselves, Crazy Horse, as the roots of that tree. He always comes back to us. There's really not a lot of fear with us that we're not going to get to play with him. It's just a matter of time. It's almost a regular thing — every three or four years we make an album. People say he's unpredictable — he's this or he's that — but it's almost like playing together is predictable."

"It's the real Neil Young, that's how I look at it," says drummer Ralph Molina.

When Young and Crazy Horse take the show out on the road, things get wild and crazy, noisy and loud. "With Crazy Horse," says Young, "it's one big, growling, smoldering sound and I'm part of it. It's like gliding, or some sort of natural surfing or something ... It's like a long ride."

Crazy Horse has collaborated with Young on some of his best albums: *Everybody Knows This Is Nowhere, Tonight's the Night, Rust Never Sleeps, Zuma*. Young's songs on *Ragged Glory*, an album which is both challenging and familiar, strike resonant chords.

"They've been around a long time," says Young, of the songs, melodies and themes on *Ragged Glory*. "In some ways, they're related to roots of other families of my music in my past and even other music in my past that I didn't make myself. I don't go through this album without hearing Hendrix, Cream and the Doors as well as my own roots."

Young ruminates on the ins and outs of long-term love, most tellingly in "Over and Over," juxtaposing comfortable bliss with nagging conformity, adding a blistering, ambivalent guitar coda. He tackles the environmental crisis again with "Mother Earth," a soft and stinging song that combines hymnlike group vocals and disorienting, albeit graceful, electric guitar trance-groove. Young dips back into the ramifications of hippie dreams in "Mansion on the Hill" and "Days That Used to Be." What he's made is an album that welcomes back old fans, those who strayed during the last decade, and calls again to those who smartly picked up on the previous year's taut *Freedom.*

Just who is Neil Young's audience?

"Some of them [still] wonder what I'm going to do to follow up on *Harvest,*" says Young with a chuckle. "Or even if I made another album since *Harvest.* There's the Rosemary Woods 18-year gap."

Young, like Bruce Springsteen, has more yahoos than you'd like to think in his audience, the drunken coyotes that show up at each and every show. I was at one where they shouted requests, telling him he was doing a good job, or, in the case of one obnoxious woman nearby, yelling, "I love you, Neil!" at every inopportune moment. Had I been closer to the yahoo and carrying either a garrote or a muzzle (damn my forgetfulness!), my only choice would have been which to employ and how I felt about the prospect of doing hard time.

Another time, my wife and I sat next to a young couple who talked incessantly through the show. I glared at 'em. Others glared at 'em. Finally, I turned to them and said, "Will you fucking shut up?" Lo and behold, five people sitting in front of us, all irritated by the same inane chatter, turned around to deliver the same message. They did fucking shut up. Peer pressure and all.

Crazy Horse did not start out with the intention of being Neil Young's band; nor, says Molina, do they consider that their only lot now. "We continue keeping our thing together," he says, "because we've never considered ourselves a backup group."

They did, however, title their last disc *Left for Dead*, a name perceived as a poke at Young for his abandonment of them. Molina says that he and Sampedro played some bits on *This Note's for You* but weren't crazy about the album's brassy R&B approach.

"Billy Talbot was saying, 'Yeah, I feel like I've been left for dead,'" says Sampedro. "Even though we usually do an album and then there's a hiatus, this one was more because it was the music. We went into the Bluenotes thing [on record] and we were part of it and it didn't work out. That's how the song 'Left for Dead' came about."

"We're survivors, that's for sure," adds bassist Talbot. "I guess so far, anyway."

How to describe Crazy Horse?

"We're all feel players, not chops players," says Molina. Which is one way of saying Crazy Horse is closer to, say, Motörhead than it is to Al DiMeola or Joe Satriani.

"With Crazy Horse," Young offers, "I'm the guitar player in the band. I play my best when I play with them. When I'm playing this kind of guitar, this is where I play it the best, because the music comes up and goes down, all the drum hits are different, there's cymbals actually playing and you can hear emotion instead of a machine."

When Young talks about his music with Crazy Horse, he'll gleefully use phrases such as "sleaze factor" and "grungy electric guitar." On tour in 1986, they played on a stage dressed as an outsized garage, complete with a giant scurrying spider. The 1991 tour is called *Smell the Horse*. Which means? "You've heard the world's greatest rock and roll bands, now smell the Horse," says Talbot. "You smell it coming and going," says Sampedro.

And now a journey into the (even deeper) past ...

Young was first recognized in Buffalo Springfield, which lasted all of two years, 1967 and 1968, but his acclaim grew in 1970 and 1971, during the 18-month existence of Crosby, Stills, Nash & Young. Then came his solo career. *Harvest* (1972), featuring "Heart of Gold," was the big hit, and it's recalled for its generally upbeat tone and pleasant folk-rock, though there are some dark songs on that record. "Alabama" and "The Needle and the Damage Done" are as harrowing as anything Lou Reed has written. But people saw what Young wrote in the liner notes of the triple-album compilation, *Decade*: "'Heart of Gold' put me in the middle of the road. Traveling there soon became a bore so I headed for the ditch. A rougher ride but I saw more interesting people there."

Young moved into the bleakest, edgiest period of his career, releasing *Time Fades Away*, *Tonight's the Night* and *On the Beach*, albums of despairing yet poignant songs. *Tonight's the Night* is one of the darkest, scariest records ever issued by a mainstream artist. It had a lot to do with the struggle to survive.

"Good musical period," says Young about those days, days when two close friends, original Crazy Horse guitarist Danny Whitten and roadie Bruce Berry, died drug-related deaths. "I'm glad I lived through it. Could have gone under a couple of times during that period. But not because I wasn't having fun. We were rolling pretty heavily. But we're still here; the act of survival is right here."

But, Young adds, "It was a pretty down period for me. I think I was disillusioned with the whole deal. When you start off you try to get where you want to get, and then you get there ... I attained a great amount of success in a reasonably short period of time, and I just felt like there were a number of people who died that were very close to me. It was kind of an empty feeling, so I reflected it in my music. I wasn't trying to hide anything."

Especially not *Tonight's the Night.* Some fans told me about an English tour where he played the title song twice, responding in his Neil-like way, to grumbling from the crowd that there wasn't enough *Harvest* in the mix.

Richard Pearson, a former presenter at Capital Radio and BBC Radio 1, has an even better story. "He might have done things differently at other gigs, but at the one I saw in the UK, he played the entire album twice," Pearson says. "I think it was 1975, right around the time I moved from Manchester to London, so it could be either city, but I think it was London, the Hammersmith Odeon. After the first set, he said something along the lines of, 'We'll be back after a short break and we're gonna play a bunch of stuff you've heard before' to much whooping and hollering." Yep, he played the whole damn thing again.

After 1978's gentle *Comes a Time,* Young entered the most hard-rocking period of his career, evidenced by the superb *Rust Never Sleeps* in 1979 and the *Live Rust* tour, double-record and movie that followed. Young calls *Rust* the culmination of his playing with Crazy Horse: "It was something to show everybody why I played with Crazy Horse. A lot of people, musicians especially, felt that Crazy Horse was not that good and didn't have much finesse. But we weren't trying to have finesse."

Young threw fans a different sort of breaking pitch with *Rust Never Sleeps.* Hard rock on one side, acoustic-based music on the other — and a surprising tribute to Johnny Rotten on both. Young was one of the few old-guard rockers to get punk. "I understood where they were coming from because what they were trying to do was ... wake everybody up, because that's what rock and roll is about. It has to have substance to it. There's an edge to real rock and roll, where it's all that matters."

Warming to the subject, he continues, "What was happening is that we started making these layered, fucking produced-sounding records, which are the foundation of schlock-rock that we have today. And we were starting to do that in the late '70s heavily.

"So, when the punk thing came along, and I heard my friends saying, 'Oh, I hate these fucking people with the fucking pins in their ears, these people are disgusting,' I said, 'Thank God, something got their attention.' These people obviously are doing something right because they're waking up these other people who are sleeping who shouldn't be sleeping."

The punks and post-punks repaid Young in 1989, when about a dozen artists — including Sonic Youth, Nick Cave and the Pixies — covered Young's songs for a tribute album called *The Bridge*. "Great songs in there," says Young. "I listen to them in my bus, and they knock me out. It's great to hear my songs done that way by those people because that's the way they feel. We don't sound like that, because we're 40 now."

In 1993, Young took another swerve into the land of oil & water or chocolate cake & orange juice. For a tour of summer sheds, he joined up with Booker T. and the MGs, the '60s-rooted, all-instrumental, groove-oriented band from Memphis, keyed around the sinuous rhythms of keyboardist Booker T. Jones, guitarist Steve Cropper, bassist Donald (Duck) Dunn and various drummers. They were the house band for the Stax/Volt roster, the musical muscle behind Otis Redding, Wilson Pickett, Sam and Dave and others. Slick, tight, disciplined.

Going into this merger, what was on Cropper's mind? "From a musical standpoint, I was skeptical," he admits on the phone from a tour stop. "I was sent some tapes to work on, bits and pieces from different live shows and albums. I'd never seen a live Neil Young concert, so I didn't know what to expect."

And when he listened? "I thought it was kind of rambling and busy and that sort of thing, which is a far cry from Booker T. and the MGs. When he first called me about this, he said, 'I'm gonna be doing something this summer and I'd like to have you guys be my band. Give it some thought, see what you think. I don't know how much of my music you know, but what I *don't* want you to do, if you decide to do this, don't run out and buy my records and learn my songs. I want you to be you. I want you to play MGs. I want you to be Steve Cropper.' And that, really, is the best compliment anybody could ever pay us."

But what about their differing styles: Do they mesh? Do they clash? "You'd have to see the shows," Cropper says. "According to the reviews I've seen, it works quite well. It feels like a great marriage, and people really get off on it. [As a guitarist] I don't take anything away from Neil; he does his own solos. I think his songs are designed around that. To me, they have that late-'60s/early-'70s thing and they venture off into certain moods."

"Neil's one of the pioneers of rock," adds Jones, in a separate interview. "The music we started playing in the '60s with Stax/Volt was the precursor to rock. When you hear it, you'll see it. It's a little louder than we played at Stax, but the music is similar. The guitars weren't as loud, but the beats were the same. I think Neil had a lot of foresight in thinking that it would work with us. It sounds very natural and not put-together." Jones says Young and the MGs scheduled four weeks of rehearsal; everything clicked after two.

Young and the MGs first met and jammed in 1991 at the Rock and Roll Hall of Fame bash; they hooked up again earlier this year at "Bobfest," when the MGs served as the house band for performers paying tribute to Dylan at Madison Square Garden. Young and the MGs clicked on "All Along the Watchtower," which became their tour's encore. Young would also sing "Sittin' on the Dock of the Bay," the Otis Redding hit Cropper co-wrote.

"I'm a rhythm guitar player at heart," says Cropper. "I don't need to get out there and flash solos all day long. I'm in my element now. I think what I do best is support other people, putting something under there that doesn't get in their way, yet edges them on and gives them a boost. But I get my chance to play. I get to pick a little bit."

All my interviews with Young were phoners. I did meet him once, in 2000, after a show at a Boston-area shed, then called the Tweeter Center, in Mansfield. I'd been talking with his wife Pegi Young and half-sister Astrid Young, both backup singers on the tour. They asked if I wanted to say hi to Neil, who had his own private dressing room. Well, sure.

I spent about 15 minutes with him in a large room, softly lit by candles, with colorful tapestries on the walls. It wasn't an interview, just a chat, but I did ask him about the rumor that he sang "Sweet Home Alabama" onstage with Ronnie Van Zant once. Nope, he said. He was going to. They'd made plans. He thought it'd be fun. And then the plane crash.

The last time I saw Young perform was in May 2010, at the Hanover Theatre in Worcester. When you hear that a famous rocker is going out on a solo tour, you immediately think, "Oh, acoustic, unplugged." But that wasn't the case with Young, who at 64 was fit, in fine voice and as determined as ever to go his own way. That included both choice of instrumentation and material. At this show, which sold out in an instant, steep ticket prices notwithstanding, Young played some hits but included a large chunk of obscure or unreleased material, too. Message implied: He's no one's human jukebox. Same as it ever was. His ideal setlist may not be yours.

The stage was often bathed in warm, amber light. Large warehouse lamps trimmed in fringe hung over an upright and a tie-dyed baby grand piano. Young started and ended the 95-minute show on acoustic guitar and harmonica. The elegiac late-'70s classic "My My, Hey Hey (Out of the Blue)" kicked it off, and "Heart of Gold" closed it. Nice acoustic '70s bookending, there.

But Young also played a lot of electric guitar, ripping through "Ohio," "Cortez the Killer," "Cinnamon Girl" and "Down by the River." When he tore into the familiar refrain, his feedback-drenched, one-note stun-guitar solo overtook the vocals, amping up the level of catharsis.

He sat at the baby grand for a romantic "I Believe in You" and at a pump organ for the environmentalist theme of "After the Gold Rush," adjusted to the 21st century. (Mother Nature will be on the run forever, or until Earth has finally had enough of us and ends it all.) He circled back to that theme in "Peaceful Valley."

Young played a new tune, "Leia," on upright piano; the gentle number about an elder looking with wonder at a newborn prompted his only real chat, explaining that it was not about his granddaughter, as he has none. (He added that he does have two grand-dogs.)

The new "Love and War," played on a semi-acoustic guitar, was wistful and dark, conjuring up a wrenching scene of a young soldier killed in war who leaves behind a young bride to explain it to their child. Thoughts of the Kinks' "Some Mother's Son" and Eric Bogle's pair, "And the Band Played Waltzing Matilda" and "The Green Fields of France (No Man's Land)," popped into my head. Other new songs included a sizzling, self-lacerating rocker ("Hitchhiker") and a droll, bluesy "You Never Call." She never calls because she's in heaven ("the ultimate vacation") and he's still working on Earth.

Young mixed gentle reflection and raucous noise. The overall tenor of the concert, though, was not of celebration, but of foreboding and nuanced mood pieces. I was all right with that. ◆

“If somebody pisses you off, you [can] get a song out of it and possibly earn money from him pissing you off.”

Richard Thompson

Richard Thompson performing at the Sanders Theatre in Cambridge, MA, November 2018

PHOTOGRAPH BY ROZA YARCHUN (SUB-ROZA)

RICHARD THOMPSON

HE'S NOT THE FIRST ONE TO SAY THIS, but I think Richard Thompson nails it for many musicians: "One of the reasons I started to play music and to write music was because I found it hard to communicate. Of course, I could communicate some things, but there were other things I couldn't. I think the reason anybody who dances or paints or does any of that stuff is because you're trying to express the inexpressible."

Music, it's been said, can convey emotions impossible words alone cannot. A female friend of mine in college was pissed off when the mixtape her boyfriend from afar sent her — this would have been around 1975 — started with the Who's "I Can't Explain." "He should talk to me," she'd say. "He can't," I'd answer. "That's why the song, the tape."

"It's like a parallel with poetry," Thompson told me in 2017. "Why write poetry? It means something that you can't express by other means. It's something that prose can't express. And I think the same way. A conversation can't express your inner life the way a song can. Often, with a song you're writing about the landscape that you carry around with you, and it's not like real life. It's parallel to life, it's a fantasy or kind of a mirror to life. And we use that mirror to describe what we see as reality."

Where do these (his or anyone's) songs come from? It's an age-old question, one songwriters and composers have been attempting to answer — or perhaps dodge — for years.

Thompson, who's written approximately 900 songs over the course of five decades, ponders the question and answers, "It varies." But he's not leaving it there. He's just pausing to collect his thoughts. He's got a few examples.

In 2015, with his then-current album *Still* on his mind, he said that the share of stories he completely made up and those cut from the fabric of his own life just about splits down the middle. "There are some songs that are completely honest and personal, and some songs are just fantasy, like 'Josephine.' I just started writing something. I have no idea what it's about. I *believe* in it, the song. And it makes a kind of sense. It's about this crazy woman, but I don't know where it came from, and I don't know why it was written.

"'Dungeons for Eyes' is something that actually happened to me. I was at this charity event. Someone said, 'You must meet so-and-so,' and I knew this so-and-so was a former terrorist, someone I know who had killed people himself and ordered people killed. He was a reformed character, a politician. I couldn't shake his hand. I couldn't do it. And that's what that song's about, a real personal experience. It was so traumatic I had to write about it. It took me a few years."

The spark of a song, Thompson suggests, can be as simple as this: "If somebody really pisses you off, as a songwriter, you get pissed off and you don't start shouting, you don't get outwardly angry. You think to yourself: 'I'm going to get you in a more effective way. I'm going to just destroy you in song.' And that's kind of the nicest revenge because (a) you get a song out of it and (b) possibly get royalties out of it as well, so you're earning money from him pissing you off."

Like many songwriters, Thompson resists defining or interpreting his own songs, arguing that by doing so you shut them down in the minds of listeners. "If you're going to talk about music, then it's nice to talk about it in an open-ended way, a nice sort of misleading way. You're dealing with an ambiguous thing, something you don't really understand yourself. That's the nature of creating something: you don't really have a hold of it. You can't pin it down. The fact is that you have to chase this bright, elusive butterfly of a ... whatever it is."

On the inside of the *Still* CD jacket, Thompson is pictured prone on the cold ground amidst a stark wintry backdrop, the neck of an electric guitar piercing his heart. "Very sad, tragic," says Thompson, with a laugh. "I suppose the idea was there's a battle between the folk-rockers and the heavy metal guys, and there's some future war in which the various strains of rock music try to kill each other, and I was an unfortunate victim."

Who killed him, the folk-rockers or the metal troops? "Well, you never know who your friends are these days," Thompson says. "Could be your own side stepping in to stab you in the heart." Going back to *Still*, I wondered if that's meant to suggest that he's still alive and well, still working or maybe still crazy after all these years?

"All of the above," Thompson says, with a laugh. "It was a working title, and it was going to be called something else. But then when you try to get rid of the working title you see people have taken it on board and it's what happened. I wouldn't place too much emphasis on the title."

Jeff Tweedy of Wilco produced the album. They had played shows together previously, and Thompson says, "Apart from sounding good — he has a really great studio and an engineer up there in his loft in Chicago — he has a really good sense of things like song structure. He'll say, 'This goes on too long' or 'Let's move the bridge' or 'That bass drum beat is going to interfere with the flow.' Sometimes, as the artist, I'm a bit too close to it. So, he was really helpful in that way, almost like a member of the band. Someone to bounce ideas off and someone who comes up with ideas. He was very useful in very many ways."

I've known Thompson since the mid-1980s and his music, of course, longer than that. The Englishman (often based in America) is a master of droll, often self-deprecating wit, be it between songs or in conversation, with quips and anecdotes worthy of John Cleese (sometimes as Cleese playing Basil Fawlty).

The root of that kind of badinage, Thompson offers, is "born of despair, mostly. It's born out of thinking 'What the hell do I do onstage?' I'm basically a shy person, so I've kind of developed this patter out of fear of silence. Sometimes I kind of attack the audience in an aggressive way, which is helpful for me just to create some sparring. It is mostly off-the-cuff. I don't plan, I don't have a script."

Thompson has to date released eighteen solo studio albums (the latest being 2018's *13 Rivers*) and three live discs. But he's also been happy to serve as a hired gun, playing on numerous avant-garde and pop and folk projects by such folks as Nick Drake, David Thomas, Henry Kaiser, Bonnie Raitt and Loudon Wainwright III.

Throughout his career, he's switched between solo acoustic and full band gigs. "It is nice to be able to do both," Thompson says. "It keeps me interested and keeps me fresh. Hopefully, it gives the audience something that isn't just the same thing every time. There's something special about the acoustic shows." In 2014, Thompson released *Acoustic Classics*, an album on which he stripped down some of his rock-oriented catalog.

An acoustic gig, Thompson avers, "is probably more reflective, because there's more emphasis on lyrics. I think of the acoustic show as a bit like church. You kind of create an atmosphere in the room and try to keep it there. And you enrich people, you kind of go heart-to-heart. I think it creates a stillness in the room, where you can get people leaning in, rather than a rock and roll show where you're kind of blowing people's hair back." While Thompson professes no preference, he does allow, "Probably I would have the band on the road more if it was economically viable. I'm not underwritten by Exxon or anybody at the moment."

If you wrestle with which version of Thompson you prefer, well, I have done a fair amount of this over the years. Having seen him in both formats numerous times I've come to firmly believe each one is the best when I'm seeing it. Like "Tear-Stained Letter" with a band and "Beeswing" on his own.

The one song he can never leave the building without playing is "1952 Vincent Black Lightning." The tragic love story between James and his motorcycle and red-haired Molly never fails to bring a tear when I hear it. (Spoiler alert: As James dies from a crash, he hands over the keys to the bike and sings, "I'll give you my Vincent to r-i-i-i-d-e.") Thompson says the song affects him, too. "There's a piece of you that you have to have in reserve, to hold back. The performer in you has to get through it. Much like an actor, you're getting into the skin of your character and you have to remember to not bump into the furniture." (Like Warren Zevon, Thompson is a contemporary writer Bob Dylan has chosen to cover. In 2013, he played the song at a concert in Clarkston, Michigan.)

"Sometimes, it's hard to get through a song. I did a thing with an 18-piece orchestra right behind me, and I did this song cycle about World War I. I was really struggling to get through it, because it had the emotional impact of the strings. Strings kind of do it to you anyway. The combination of that and the tragic subject matter. I was almost a blubbering fool onstage. It was very difficult to get through it."

Critics and fans have always rated his guitar prowess at an upper level. The *L.A. Times* once went so far as to call him "the best electric guitarist since Hendrix." Thompson generally demurs. "There's areas of life in which you excel and there's areas of life in which you kind of muddle through," he says. "I suppose as a musician I'm a more capable version of a human being than I am as a tax consultant." He jokes that in the studio he has "a built-in failure mechanism," and admits he rarely enjoys listening to his older recordings.

You think they could have been better? "Always. C'est la vie."

Thompson is a triple threat: singer-songwriter-guitarist, a master of them all. Maybe you could add one more feather to his cap: interpreter. He moves from sensitive ballads to raging rockers, from spiritual musings to caustic screamers. You'll hear some jazz, country, traditional English and Scottish folk songs, maybe even Britney Spears' "Oops, I Did It Again," played sadly, downtempo and not meant as a lark. (Surprise: it's a damn good song!)

Thompson came to a measure of prominence when he formed the great English folk-rock band Fairport Convention in 1967 with Simon Nicol. (Hendrix once joined the band onstage.) He stayed through 1971. Then, beginning in 1974 with the superb *I Want to See the Bright Lights Tonight,* he made six studio albums in collaboration with his then-wife Linda Thompson. Out of their turmoil came what is arguably the best (that is, most pained) breakup album of all time, *Shoot Out the Lights,* in 1982. (Note the usage of "Lights" again. Differently.) There's conflict strewn all across the album, but consider "Walking on a Wire," sung together, which asks where the justice is when "all the pain is on my side of the fence." Richard wrote all the songs, save for "Did She Jump or Was She Pushed," which Linda co-wrote.

For the record, Linda is at peace with her ex. She detailed some of what they went through — including their tumultuous final tour together — in a 2019 *Guardian* story. But asked if she'd forgiven him, Linda replied, "I have. It was a bad time but, Jesus Christ, it was 40 years ago. Forget it!" The two children they had together both became musicians: singer-songwriter-producer Teddy Thompson and singer-guitarist Kami Thompson, a member of the Rails. The Thompson offspring have played music with both parents.

Thompson's records are great, but his concerts are where everything takes flight. "Nothing replaces live for me," he says. "The Kate Bushes and Enyas of this world seem to get enough satisfaction from just recording, but I see recording as creating a kind of template and live as where the song gets properly expressed and communicated."

Sometimes, during a concert, you'll see a performer take requests, or more likely, hear a song shouted out that was going to be played anyway. It's possible Thompson was planning on playing the song you called for, but then again ... well, you never know.

"I tend to write a set," he says, "but I don't always keep to it. People will shout things out and I'll do requests on the spot. I go with a plan, and I think there's an overlap from night to night — the basic bones of the set — but things are gonna get changed around. I probably try to balance between stuff I want to play and stuff the audience wants to hear. Thank God that sometimes overlaps or I'd be in trouble. I think about those people who've stuck with me for 50 years — they deserve to hear something from the '60s and likewise the '70s, '80s and '90s. I like to keep a historical perspective to some extent. And also, to do some new stuff that I've never played before."

At one show, an audience member yelled the once-funny (but never-ever-now) "Free Bird!" and Thompson obliged, sort of, playing the first verse while referencing the late Lynyrd Skynyrd singer Ronnie Van Zant's diminutive stature. When someone later shouted for the Grateful Dead's "Dark Star," Thompson didn't oblige, admitting "I wouldn't know it if I heard it."

In 1991, I saw Thompson at South Easton's Blackthorne Tavern, where he rolled out a boatload of heartbreak ("When the Spell Is Broken"), tossed in some subway violence ("Killerman Gold Posse") and threw in some do-not-go-gentle-into-that-good-night rage ("Wall of Death"). Of course, there was a dollop of mayhem ("Psycho Street") and considerable melancholia ("Waltzing's for Dreamers," among others). His next-to-last song, "The End of the Rainbow," sung as a lullaby, offered a hard truth to a baby in the cradle: there's nothing there.

Heavy stuff. So, what did he choose to close the show? "Ça Plane Pour Moi," Belgian new waver Plastic Bertrand's deliriously goofy, Ramones-like novelty number from 1977. There was something magical about seeing this esteemed folkie and hybrid-style fingerpicker deluxe wailing away on an acoustic guitar, singing in French.

There was a full-band sit-down gig in October 1996 at the Somerville Theatre. Early on, Thompson admonished the crowd to get up and dance, warning that, "Security will smash your brains out, but we don't care — not our problem." The band included multi-instrumentalist Pete Zorn, double-bassist Danny Thompson (no relation) and former Fairport drummer Dave Mattacks.

Their extended rendition of "Shoot Out the Lights" was the most ferocious and chilling I'd yet heard, with Zorn playing the rockingest mandolin on the planet.

"I like the idea of contrasting moods during the show," says Thompson. "For instance, if you have a kind of dark song and then you kind of joke around with the audience it kind of throws them off or you go from something light into something heavy. I really like doing that. I also like doing that in the space of a song where the song starts out with a kind of an amusing surface to it, but then at a certain point you get a verse in and think, 'Oh, shit, this is really a lot darker than I thought. When I invested in this song in the beginning I thought it was going to be light and fluffy and it's too late to pull out. As a listener, I'm already committed to it.' That's kind of a device to get people to listen to your song."

Thompson is now at a point where some of his peers have stopped creating new music and releasing albums. Some of that may be due to songwriting burnout, but it also surely has to do with the decrease in CD sales due to downloads and poorly compensated streaming.

Thompson agrees that this newish paradigm is one reason why ticket prices are so high and so many older artists are on tour. That's where the money is. But, he says, "I like making albums. I'll keep making albums and if I have to make them in my home studio for no money, I'll still do them. But it's all about 'live' now and it has been for some time."

It is a popular misconception (one that also attached to Lou Reed and Leonard Cohen) that Thompson lives the life of the tortured artist. He *did* write a particularly dark body of work for *Shoot Out the Lights*. And even on 1994's *Mirror Blue*, when he was then happily remarried (to Nancy Covey), Thompson still sang from the dark side of street. (Thompson's marriage to Covey ended in divorce in 2018. He is currently with singer-playwright Zara Phillips. She's charming. I met her while talking with Thompson following his solo show in Lowell in the summer of 2021.)

I asked if he considered the album dark and mordant, as I did. "Dark and mordant? Aargh. Um, I can't remember what's on it, it's been so long. Hmmm. Dark and mordant? No, I see it as a varied mixture of moods, reflections on the human condition."

But when I asked if some of the story-songs on *Mirror Blue* are true, he answered straight away: "Completely true! Yeah, all those murders ..." More seriously, he added, "I'm trying to write fiction. I'm trying to write stories. I'm trying to use my imagination, which shouldn't seem all that unusual."

However, as songwriters are not always granted the same artistic license as filmmakers and novelists — hence the violence-in-rap-or-metal controversies that pop up now and again — Thompson realizes that art and reality might get mixed up in listeners' minds. "If you write a novel, you, as the author, stand at the back and pull strings. But [in my case], the 'myth of reality' is reinforced by the fact that (a) I'm the songwriter and (b) I'm the performer. As a songwriter, I have to make the story convincing, and as a performer I have to reinforce that with a convincing performance. Otherwise, there's no point in doing any of it."

Thompson laughs. "So, in a sense, that is what I want people to believe, but I hope that people are intelligent enough to realize that it is a kind of theatrical thing. The emotion might be true, but the facts are changed. That's what fiction is, and, in some cases, it can make reality more interesting or more entertaining."

During the pandemic lockdown Thompson did some for-pay Internet gigs. And he wrote a lot. "I've written two EPs, the whole next band album, and 50 percent of a musical play," he e-mailed me. "The online stuff has been a lifeline of sorts — something to keep us all connected until we can breathe the same molecules in a club or theater again. The experience is weird. One can take satisfaction from a performance well-executed and read through the comments and feel that the music got across to an audience spread around the world.

"Doing it from home is a bit lonely, and I'm glad my fellow isolator Zara can sing on a few songs with me and we can play off each other. I listened back to a couple of streams I had done from a studio, with full professional sound and video, and was amazed how good the performance was, considering how disconnected I felt. This is when you really have to focus solely on the music, get inside the music, live the music, or feel very unsatisfied.

"What do we learn from all this? The preciousness of a live concert, how every member of the audience plays a part in the process, and how wonderful it will be to get back to that! I'll never again complain about playing to a half-full house on a rainy Sunday in Ipswich! (Unfair to Ipswich).

"Financially it has been tough [and] ruinous for many. An enforced premature retirement which we hope is not permanent. Most musicians I know of my age are taking their pensions and living off that — online revenue is fairly slim. Many are selling their publishing to get through this."

Thompson's memoir, *Beeswing: Losing My Way and Finding My Voice 1967–1975,* co-written with the late Scott Timberg, was published in 2021. He resumed touring as soon as authorities deemed the coast was clear(ish) that same year.

"Richard is now in an interesting phase of his career, the legend phase," Linda Thompson told me in a January 2023 e-mail. "That's as it should be. He has turned out great work for almost 60 years. I think he's having fun."

A postscript, if you will. Like a lot of people, I discovered Nick Drake posthumously. It was 1975, a year after his death. I was in college, and I fell in love with his music, the strings, the melancholy, yes, but also, on occasion, the buoyancy. The contrasting starkness and the sweeping sound. The internal struggle made external. The obvious depression he felt, some which *I* felt. Bits of self-deprecating humor. Thompson, who has covered Drake's "Time Has Told Me" in concert, knew and played with Drake. After a Cambridge concert at Sanders Theatre in 2017, as I was backstage with him indulging in the usual post-show debauchery — a friend had brought in the most delicious cookies ever made and we munched — I asked about Drake.

"I always thought he was special. Everyone else has now arrived at the point where they agree. It took 45 years or something for them to catch up, but eventually, slowly, cream rises to the surface. Despite all his problems, Nick really would have liked to be successful and had his music appreciated as it really was not. In his lifetime, he probably sold 5,000 records total.

"He was extraordinary. As time goes on, he's even more extraordinary, a great singer and guitar player and a really great songwriter. It was a real joy to work with him. In 1968, or whenever it was, he and I were both extremely shy and monosyllabic so the conversation between Nick Drake and myself would have been not a particularly interesting phenomenon. We would nod to each other when we saw each other around town, give each other a knowing nod.

"A lot's been written about Nick, about how tortured he was in many ways. He really was unique. He didn't sound like anybody else except possibly his mother. His mother, it turns out, was a closet singer who wrote these songs on her home tape recorder, but she had no ambition to be a performer. She probably was Nick's biggest influence."

I asked, "I don't know if you'd know any more than anyone else about his death, but do you think it was suicide or accidental?"

"I'd say accidental, an accidental overdose or something or an accidental mixture of whatever he's taking," said Thompson. "I think his third album [*Pink Moon*], to me, is very, very painful; there's a lot of pain in that record. Yet, I think mentally he had kind of turned the corner. I think he maybe did some harm to himself at some other time, but I really don't know." ◆

DARLENE LOVE

CHRISTMAS HAS BEEN VERY GOOD to Darlene Love. Phil Spector chose her to sing five of the 13 songs on his 1963 compilation, *A Christmas Gift for You*, which has been called one of the greatest seasonal pop albums of all time. One of them, "Christmas (Baby Please Come Home)," has become a signature number for Love, who sang it around the holidays for 28 consecutive years on *The Late Show With David Letterman*, a streak that only ended with Letterman's retirement in 2015.

"When it started out [I thought], 'This is nice.' The next year they called, and the next year they called, and finally they said, 'You know what? We're gonna have you on every year about Christmastime.' Then they started giving me a whole month's notice. I could actually work my schedule around it. It's amazing how it started off as a little thing." That gig proved to be a major career boost for the singer. Now she's usually on tour around that time of year, not just singing holiday songs, but '60s hits and more.

A love for Christmas and all it means is no stretch for Love, who grew up in the Pentecostal church; her father was a minister.

"Christmas was always such a big thing in our church," she told me over dinner at a restaurant south of Boston as the season was ramping up in 2017. "We did Christmas plays and Christmas programs, one with the children and one with the adults. It's that idea of family. We never all get together at one time, but we get together

“Phil Spector wanted us to go on the Top 40, which was white, so if they didn’t know we were Black, they would play us.”

Darlene Love

Darlene Love performing in Boston

PHOTOGRAPH BY ROZA YARCHUN (SUB-ROZA)

at Christmastime. It's also a special time because people feel more giving than any other time. I always say in my show, 'It'd be great if we could have this kind of spirit all year long.'"

She had two Massachusetts gigs ahead of her, but there was one engagement she was only too glad to turn down: an offer from the White House to sing at the National Christmas Tree Lighting Ceremony on November 30. This was not Barack Obama's White House; nor was it Joe Biden's White House. She didn't want anything to do with the man living there then. "I was invited to sing 'Christmas (Baby Please Come Home)' for Mr. — our president — and I told him I would be busy. I'm on my Christmas tour."

She was not lying and, truth be told, Love says she had to turn down an offer from the Obama White House for similar reasons. The difference then was, "I wanted to go! I really hated to miss his last year in office."

Love, born Darlene Wright, joined a girl group, the Blossoms, in 1959 and over the years sang background vocals for a cavalcade of stars — among them, Dionne Warwick, Tom Jones, Sam Cooke, Marvin Gaye, Elvis Presley and U2. It was Spector who gave her a new surname and made her a key part in his legendary wall-of-sound in the early-mid-'60s. She sang uncredited lead on the Crystals' "He's a Rebel" and "He's Sure the Boy I Love" and Bob B. Soxx and the Blue Jeans' "Why Do Lovers Break Each Other's Heart?" and backup on lots more.

Love reckons she's sung backup on "at least a thousand songs, but you forget the ones that weren't hits. When we first started in 1958, it was slow, but by the time two years had passed we were working almost seven days a week, ten hours a day." Despite all the work, her voice never gave up. "Probably because we were so young singing in church."

While Letterman played a key part in her renaissance and keeping her in the public eye — echoes of what he did for Warren Zevon — there was also *20 Feet From Stardom,* the surprise hit documentary in 2013 about the largely unheralded world of background singers. Love's own rollercoaster ride was one of the three main threads of the film, which won an Oscar for *Best Documentary,* a Grammy for *Best Music Film* and generated lots of buzz in the music community. It also led to the republication of her 1998 autobiography, *My Name Is Love,* later that year.

In 2015, she released *Introducing Darlene Love*, an album to which friends like Bruce Springsteen, Steve Van Zandt, Jimmy Webb, Linda Perry, Joan Jett and Elvis Costello contributed songs. Later that year, joined by Van Zandt and Costello, she sang Costello's "Forbidden Nights" on *The Late Show With Stephen Colbert.* Which made me think and say: I believe you are one of a select group of artists who has performed with both Elvi.

"Very true," says Love, with a laugh. "It's amazing, because you don't think about it when you do it. After you do it, you go, "Wow, Elvis 1968, Elvis, 2015. It's a long stretch."

The first Elvis hit on her. "After we did the 1968 [comeback TV] special we actually did a movie with him called *Change of Habit* with Mary Tyler Moore. We did a lot of shooting one day and we were all breaking for lunch and I left my sunglasses in the honey wagon — which is what they call them, our dressing rooms — and I told one of the girls, 'Go on ahead, I'll catch up with you, I'm going back to get my sunglasses.'

"So, I have my glasses on the way back, and I'm walking fast and I didn't even realize the honey wagon was right where it was and he said, 'Darlene!' and I said, 'Oh hey, Elvis, how you doing?' I was going to keep on going and he said, 'Come in,' and I went, 'OK, what's happening?' and he said, 'I don't know how to tell you this, but you know I've never had a Black woman before, but right now I'm thinking about it.'

"And I said to him, 'And you ain't gonna start with me! I love you, baby, but I'm going to lunch' and that scared the piss out of me: number one, that I turned him down and, number two, that he asked me."

So, I said, applying 21st century woke standards, you were sexually harassed by Elvis Presley. Love nearly spat out the red wine she was drinking. This is not her perception, then or now: "Hey, he's the King!" Turning down Elvis did not ruin their relationship. "Actually," she says, "it was more fun, because we would give one another the eye when we were filming. Me and him were the only ones who knew what was going on. He told me a story that I loved. He said the way he learned how to sing and move, he used to go to Black churches and listen outside the window. He didn't go in the church, but he would listen to how they were singing, and if it was a Pentecostal church where they were shouting and dancing. He watched all that for years. I went, 'Wow, no wonder.'"

In conjunction with the Presley estate, she says, "We went to Germany. They do an Elvis Presley festival there. I went there because I did the 1968 special. We did the gospel segment with him, and they always want somebody to do the show who has some kind of relationship with Elvis."

There are those who accuse Elvis of ripping off Black culture. Not Love. "I don't think that's called ripping off. We all take something from somebody. I worked for Dionne Warwick for ten years. Watching her work, so graceful and such a lady, I learned a lot from her. Some of the things I do onstage remind me of her. You do it almost unconsciously."

A Darlene Love Christmas show may have a half-dozen Christmas songs and her hits from the '60s, but not just those. "I couldn't do that," she says. It also may have five from *Introducing Darlene Love* and maybe a Marvin Gaye medley or one from another male singer. Why male?

"If I do somebody else's songs," she says, "it's usually a male song. I don't like somebody saying, 'She doesn't sing it as good as her; I like so and so's version better.' When you do a male song, they don't say it's better than him or worse than him, and I've always looked at it that way. Mostly, singers that I like are male. I used to do a whole medley of songs by Sam Cooke. I always choose a song [because] I was associated with the artist. I did background for Marvin Gaye and I also did background for Sam Cooke."

The Phil Spector years. "I give him his props," Love says. "I would not have a career if it wasn't for those songs. Those songs are what made Phil famous, and they also made me famous."

And yet ...

Either Phil Spector was color-blind or he didn't want young America to think of his young female vocal acts as Black and didn't want their faces on the jackets of the singles. I'm thinking the latter and so did Love.

"Phil Spector hid us for years. We had a 'pop' sound; we didn't have a "Black" sound — [all of us] the Ronettes, the Crystals, Darlene Love, Bob B. Soxx and the Blue Jeans. People didn't know we were Black. He did that on purpose. We were Black, so we couldn't cross over. He wanted us to go on the Top 40, which was white, so if they didn't know we were Black, they would play us."

Love says it didn't anger her back then. "People [would say] to me, 'They wouldn't give you credit when you did such and such a thing' and I [would reply], 'You know, it was the business.' That was what we did in the '60s. We all have to do things in our own way."

Any thoughts about Spector's genius, and he was certainly that, are tainted by the stories about the abuse he laid on his singers — locking them in the studio, waving guns about — but his conviction for the murder of actress Lana Clarkson upped the ante considerably. We all employ cognitive dissonance when we consider the dirty deeds done dirt cheap by our favorite artists. But murder?

"I think he did it," Love says, "but I think it was an accident. The Phil Spector I know wasn't a vicious man. He could push your buttons, but if you knew him you would laugh at him. I think that's why I got away with things: [I'd say] 'Sit down, get out of my face!' He was five foot-four; I'm five-three. But he had heels on. And I had heels on. I had four-inch heels and he only had on maybe two-inch heels. I had fun with him. We got on well. I was the only person he would take to lunch while we were recording.

"He never pulled a gun on me. I told him I'd make him eat it. I was gonna be as bad as he was gonna be. I mean he's two feet tall, I can beat him up with my hands tied behind me. He was actually afraid of me because I had a big mouth. I was a bully. I would go to his house for a rehearsal, by myself, because I wasn't afraid of him. I went by one night and I heard all this noise — the dogs were barking, and I heard all this screaming and hollering — and I knocked on the door and he opened it and I said, 'What in the world is going on, Phil?' He had his gun with him. I said, 'I'm going home. Y'all crazy. I'm not coming in no house with nobody who's got a gun on his hip.'

"He'd go, 'Come on, Doll' — he used to call me Doll — and I said, 'You put the gun away or I'm going to get in my car and go home.' Fortunately for me, he thought I was as crazy as he was. And I don't know what I would have done if I'd gotten in those positions. Whenever he was at the studio and he had his guns, I would go home. It would be time to record, and he'd say 'What happened to Doll? I know she was here.' And they said, 'She went home. She ain't coming in with you having that gun.'

"He really did respect my talent. He didn't want anybody else to be responsible for making me a star. He wanted to be that person. He gave me my last name and, everywhere I went over the years, even after I left California, he tried to block any success I was having. But, hey, I'm in the Rock and Roll Hall of Fame. Can't get no better than that."

Love saw Spector's hyper-controlling personality right away, "at first, when it was happening — 'Sonofabitch, man! OK, when does this stop?' — all the way up until the time I moved to New York and started singing 'Christmas (Baby)' on the *Letterman* show. Phil Spector called them and said, 'You're not allowed to sing that on the show. If you sing that song, I'm gonna sue you.'"

He did not follow through on the threat. "That was his way of trying to control me. People would say, 'What is about him that he keeps messing with you?' and I'd say, 'He's stupid, that's all.'"

I mention that Love's second Elvis wrote the song "Little Hitler" about somebody like that. "That's what he was," says Love. "It all ends up getting you in trouble, like it got him in trouble. There were many women in that situation with him. They didn't fight back, and I think what happened with [Clarkson] was she said, 'No, I'm gonna leave, I'm gonna go home.' The other ladies got scared and just sat there."

More people than ever learned about Spector and the lives of backing singers from the *20 Feet From Stardom* doc. "They got it right," Love says. "It started out with Gil Friesen, the producer, who called me and said, 'I have this idea to do a story about background singers, and they tell me I should start with you first.' I told him some people I thought would be great to go and interview. But we had no idea it was going to turn out to be as big as it did. When they got the stars that they did, like Bruce Springsteen, Elton John, Stevie Wonder and Chris Botti — they picked the ones who really love their background singers, and their background singers are a part of what they do. I didn't tell 'em to go and get those guys, because I didn't think they could ever get those guys. But they really care about background singers. It's a part of who they are."

The movie had a pretty profound effect on everyone who saw it, but especially Love's family. "My sister and my daughter cried when they saw the movie. Hearing about what happened during those times, people started hating Phil. I said, 'Don't hate him. If it wasn't for those songs, I wouldn't have a career today.' That's why I could never hate him."

When the movie came out, Love says, "People asked 'Why were you so prominent in the movie?' I said it was because they had more film on me than they had on anybody else and because of my story.

"It gave me more work. I didn't know that with a hit movie you had to work as hard as with records. You have to promote the movie. We went all over the country. They'd show the movie, and we'd get up and talk about the movie, and we would sing 'Lean on Me' because it was in the movie. I would sing to a track. People started saying, 'Wow, she can really sing!' So that did more for me than anything."

As recounted in the film, after Love's star had fallen, she became a cleaning lady, scrubbing rich white folks' homes. Then she heard her Christmas song on the radio. It was sad and poignant, but also a signal for Love to try and restart her career.

"It wasn't so much that I didn't *want* to have a career; it's just that I couldn't find a way to *find* a career," Love says. "I never thought about asking anyone to help me. I'd helped a lot of people along the way, especially doing background, because there were a lot of people who couldn't afford to pay background singers, so you do it for little or nothing.

"But I got it in my mind that I have to sing. I was at a friend of mine's house who had just come back from a cruise. I don't even know why I thought about this, but I said, 'Do they have entertainment on these cruises?' She said, 'Yeah, but they're bad.' [I thought] 'Hmm, I wonder if I could get a job on a cruise ship — I'm *good*.' And I got a job on a cruise line. That kind of opened the door because people would come up to me and say, 'Why are *you* on a cruise ship? Why aren't you out doing what stars do? We're finding you on a cruise ship selling bingo tickets.'"

Love wasn't just a seagoing entertainer; she was part of the cruise staff. "I did a little bit of everything. But the longer I stayed on the ship the more they didn't want me doing the cruise staff work, because they didn't want their star doing bingo work. The more people that got on the ship, the more I realized I had a lot of fans who still knew who Darlene Love was. Then I ended up getting the job at the Bottom Line because Steve Van Zandt talked me into moving to New York to do this show.

"It wasn't called *Leader of the Pack* at first, in 1983. The show [a jukebox musical celebrating the work of songwriter Ellie Greenwich] just kept going, as more people came to the Bottom Line. I had never worked as Darlene Love. I always worked as a background singer, so people never saw me as Darlene Love. People went, 'Wow there really *is* a Darlene Love!'

"The Bottom Line was really my springboard. David [Letterman] came to see the show because Paul Shaffer was playing [the role of] Phil Spector. And he said, 'We need to get that girl who sings that Christmas song on the show.' David Letterman says it will not be Christmas until you hear this song."

Love is not about predestination, but she does believe "Nothing is an accident, there's always a reason for something. Me and Jesus, God, we got this thing. We good friends.

I believe that every good and precious gift comes from God. God is not prejudiced. He gives us all a gift. But what you do with that gift is your business."

Love had another life-altering experience in July 2012: a heart attack.

"I do a show in Asbury Park [New Jersey] every year. It's my favorite place to work. So, everybody is used to me being down there working. I was sick all day long, I had a stomach ache; I couldn't keep nothing in my stomach, I was uncomfortable all day, but having a heart attack is the last thing I thought I was having. My husband's driving me, I was sitting in the back seat and then I get this pain in my chest and my husband had this thought. We passed a 7/11 so we went inside and bought the aspirins they had, he said, "Take two, chew 'em without water." I chewed it, and by the time we got to work — it was a 50-minute drive — the pain went away. I said, 'No problem.'

"I did an hour-long show, took pictures, signed autographs, went back to my room and then I said, 'That was a pain I've never had before.' So, I went to the doctor the next day and told him what happened, and he did my heart and he said, 'I want you to go next door to my heart specialist.' Went next door, he put me on a treadmill, hooked me all up and he said to me, 'Did you come by yourself?' I said, 'No, my husband brought me.' He said, 'I'll meet you at the hospital at 10, we will be operating on you at 12.' Same day.

"I had a blockage. He said, 'If you had not taken the aspirin, you would be dead.' It's a blood thinner. I never had the sweats, my left arm wasn't in pain, but then I found out it's different [signs] with women. The symptoms I was having — like the nausea — women have.

"Here I am today living a much healthier life. I don't eat Snickers anymore, I ate 'em by the boxful, M&Ms with peanuts, none of that now. He said, 'Have a steak, but don't make it a habit,' and I have one every four or five months. I don't have fried food anymore. I stopped butter, all the fatty stuff. I went to an herbalist, and he told me to stop eating sugar. I did it because I wanted to live. I didn't have a hard time doing it at all. And I was a smoker for 25 years, but then I've stopped smoking for over 25 years. I always worked out, even when I couldn't get nobody to go to the gym with me, me and Jane Fonda tapes.

"And here I am. And I have a wonderful career going." ◆

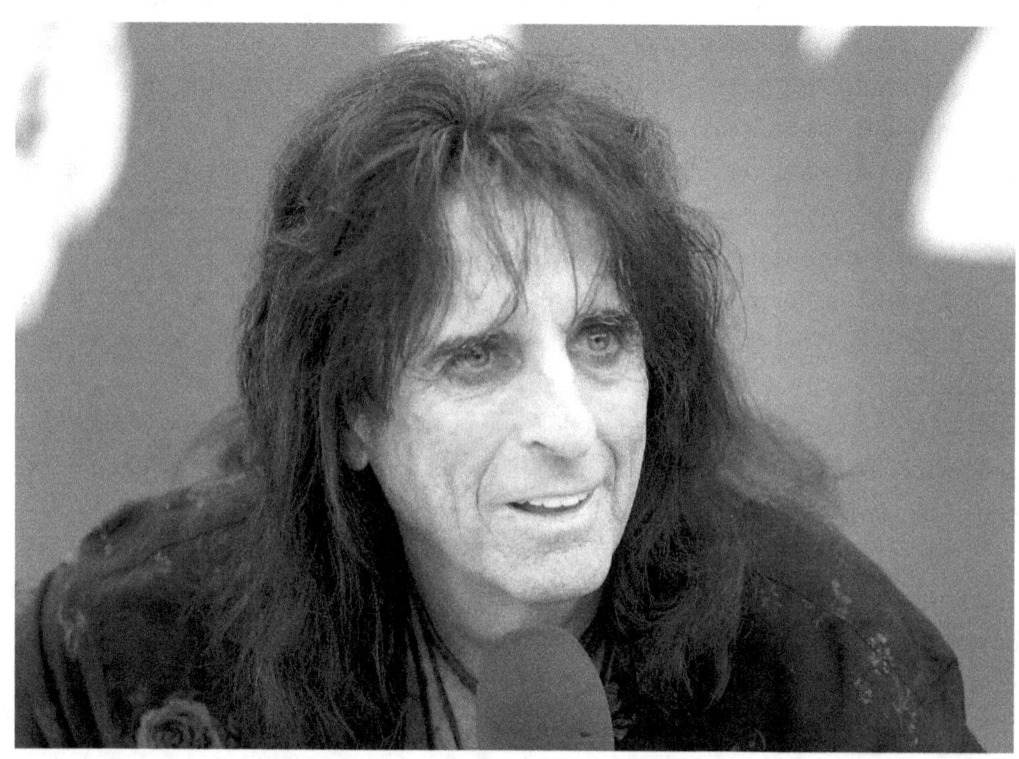

"I've been offed in every sort of capital punishment way you could be. Tens of thousands of times."

Alice Cooper

Alice Cooper speaking at Wacken Open Air in Germany, August 2017

ALICE COOPER

I'M NOT SURE WHEN IT STARTED, but I've long had both a fascination and an appalling sense of horror about executions. It probably started with Alice Cooper.

I've interviewed Alice many times over the years, and we pretty much always start with golf. He's played forever and he's very good, a four-handicap last time I checked in with him. I started at age 14 and remain, sadly, fairly mediocre, a bogey man, give or take a few strokes, capable of brilliance or utter hackery and happy to be anywhere in the 80s. But Alice is always, resolutely, encouraging: "If you played as much as I do ... I play golf every day, and I avoid stressing about anything."

The golf-every-day thing certainly applies when Alice is home in Phoenix; when he's on tour in America, his people tell me, it's every other day. Rather than do back-to-back concert dates, his schedule is concert–golf–concert. In Europe, he only gets to play twice a week. If that sounds trivial in the context of a story about a rocker, well, in Cooper's case it's not. Golf has been Cooper's salvation. "Ask anybody who's ever been addicted to anything," he says. "When they get into golf, it's the same addiction. It's like you hit a great shot and you will hit ten bad shots to hit one more good shot. It's almost like that with any drug addiction. It's very, very similar. But it's not going to kill you."

In the early '70s, before he worked out how to separate onstage Alice from offstage Alice, the singer drank heavily, one of those infamous Hollywood Vampires.

Invariably pictured with a beer in his band, Cooper started the informal club; he considered its co-founders to be Ringo Starr, Micky Dolenz, Keith Moon and Harry Nilsson. Others who came to party: John Lennon, Keith Emerson, Mal Evans, Bernie Taupin, Brian Wilson, Iggy Pop, Klaus Voormann and John Belushi. They drank at the Speakeasy and Tramps in London and the Rainbow Bar & Grill in West Hollywood.

"Lennon was one of the hardest-drinking and drugging guys that I knew," says Cooper. "He was not a lightweight. Harry Nilsson was not a lightweight. Keith Moon, of course. It's almost more remarkable that Keith Moon got to 32 years old than Keith Richards still being alive. I don't know which one is the more bizarre.

"Keith Moon was the greatest live drummer I ever saw in my life. He could play anything, but he was determined to be the world's class clown. He created his own world. It was like, Keith, 'You have made up your mind that however you go out, it will be spectacular. But there's no talking you out of jumping off that bridge into that river, is there? No? OK.' You sat there and you let him go."

Cooper, who has been sober since 1983, calls alcohol and drug addiction "the biggest challenge I've ever faced." After being hospitalized in the late '70s, he was "sober almost a year. Then I went back for a while. I did four albums where I was totally blacked out: *Flush the Fashion, Special Forces, Dada*, I forget, there's one more [*Constrictor*]. Four in a row. I don't remember writing them, recording them. I was in an absolute alcoholic state."

Vincent Furnier grew up in Detroit, a fan of (ultimately) self-destructive heroes like Jim Morrison and Jimi Hendrix — "Those guys were kind of my big brothers," he says — and he emulated what he saw when he created his character, Alice Cooper. "Alcohol was certainly part of the formula of being Alice. You want to be notorious, and it gets to the point where 'OK, I am notorious, I have proven that. Now, I want to go to the mall.'"

Cooper realized his character was getting to be more extreme than Morrison's or Hendrix's. "I was going to kill myself if I was going to try and be this all the time. There was a time where I finally got self-preservation."

When he was young, Cooper says, he considered drinking an entry-level requirement for the job. "I happened to be in that late-'60s/early-'70s time when everything went. If you weren't getting high or drinking, you probably weren't going to be in a band, because you would have been an outsider. Now, it's just the opposite. If you're getting high and you're drinking too much, you're not going to be in a band. It's one of those things where you can't have a guy in the band who's getting so high he can't perform."

Not unlike other recovering alcoholics, Cooper takes it upon himself to reach out and give back. I saw him play a Boston benefit in 2009 for a local musician-oriented recovery organization called Right Turn. And the 2015 album by his covers band, the Hollywood Vampires (using the name of his old party-hearty gang), is in large part a salute to those who've gone down the same path but not been able to get out alive.

As the frontman of the band Alice Cooper and then a solo artist by the same name (the former is in the Rock and Roll Hall of Fame, the latter is not) he's been executed at the climax of show after show. It wouldn't be an Alice Cooper concert without it. I was at the Bangor (Maine) Auditorium on the *School's Out* tour in 1972 and then saw them on the *Billion Dollar Babies* tour the following year. If I'm not mistaken, Alice was hanged the first time and guillotined the second.

Long before Marilyn Manson, GWAR and Rammstein — all acts with a bit of Alice in them — Cooper was viewed by mainstream America as the epitome of bad taste, hated in the nation.

"Oh my gosh, yeah," Cooper says. "We weren't just hated by the establishment; we were hated by rock. When we came out and we did the outrageous stage show, it was heralding to all the bands, the Grateful Dead and bands like that, that that era was over. Bands like that hated us. Until you have a hit record, you're basically an outsider. Then you have a hit record, and then two and then three, all of a sudden, you're not an outsider, you are now what's going on. And now you *have* to do a show. If you want to stay with it, you have to do a show."

In my mid-teen years, Alice Cooper *was* that show, the coolest thing going in post-hippie, pre-punk hard-rock America. And there was that boa constrictor, Katrina, pictured on the cover of *Killer* and regularly draped around Cooper's neck onstage.

For that '73 tour (64 concerts in 90 days), they hired magician and paranormal skeptic James Randi (a.k.a. the Amazing Randi) to create special effects: hacked-up baby dolls and mannequins and, as the pièce de résistance, a guillotine. As he sang

"Dead Babies," Alice did unspeakable things to the dolls. Then he sang that most necrophiliac of rock songs, "I Love the Dead."

Alice was strapped into the guillotine and his head was cut off as Mussorgsky's "Night on Bald Mountain" played on tape. Miraculously, he returned from the dead to sing the explosive/celebratory "School's Out" and, for an encore, the nasty driving-revenge-death rocker "Under My Wheels."

Capital punishment remains a divisive issue in America, but it has been very good to Cooper. I don't know whether Alice is a fan or foe — his politics lean right, so I'm guessing he's not against it — but he's made execution a big part of his life as an entertainer.

"I think I've been offed in every sort of capital punishment sort of way you could be," says the ever-affable Cooper. "Tens of thousands of times. I have been electrocuted; I have had my head cut off; I have been hung. I've been put into a coffin and had blades put through it."

Wait, what about the gas chamber?

"I haven't done the gas chamber because I couldn't figure out a way to make it exciting," he admits. "I think you could do lethal injection if the needle was about 40-feet long and came down from the ceiling."

The man may die for his sins, but he always comes back from the grave, prancing and preening. "Always with the best of taste," Cooper says.

I asked Alice to select the quintessential Alice Cooper song, and not only did it coincide with mine, he didn't hesitate: "Ballad of Dwight Fry" on *Love It to Death.* A gorgeous song that begins softly with acoustic guitar and piano, it builds into a monstrous, cathartic crescendo with Cooper — as the locked-up patient at an insane asylum — screaming "I gotta get out of here! I gotta get out of here! I gotta get out of here!"

"A classic. Probably my most psychologically disturbed song. Well-written [by Cooper and AC guitarist-keyboardist Michael Bruce], well-performed. I don't know what it is about the song people relate to, but it's about [the actor] who played Renfield in [the 1931 film] *Dracula.* He was the guy nobody ever recognized but was the scariest guy. So, we found out his name and said, 'Let's put this guy in a straitjacket,' and suddenly it was Alice: Alice was this guy.

"When we did the vocal, [producer Bob] Ezrin put me in a straitjacket and said,

'Sing your way out of this.' I said, 'Are you kidding me?' and he says, 'Nope,' and puts the straitjacket on and I'm singing in it for six or seven hours. Finally, at the end when I get to the 'I gotta get out of here!' part, I actually wasn't able to get out of the strait-jacket. Wow, talk about method acting."

It was always a concert highlight.

Alice Cooper was among the first — if not *the* first — popular rock band to incorporate such elaborate theatrics and props into its set. It was a rock and roll horror show: visceral, flashy, grotesque, seductive, gender-bending. Pretty much everyone would say these things enhanced the experience, but I wondered if there was ever a thought that it might detract.

"We spent years and years trying to say, 'OK, we are a band and we do theatrics, but we are also a really good band.' It was hard to convince people of the fact that you could actually do visuals and music at the same time because they figured one had to suffer. It's more like giving the audience more rather than taking away."

The original band ended after the lackluster *Muscle of Love* in late '73. Cooper says the band split because the musicians wanted to work on solo projects and "on top of that, weren't into the theatrics anymore. They felt we were past that. I'm going 'Guys, this is absolutely what we've been waiting for! People are now trying to look like us. Now is not the time to wear Levi's and T-shirts and try to save the world.'"

Cooper launched his solo career in 1975 with *Welcome to My Nightmare*, borrowing Lou Reed's *Rock n Roll Animal* band: guitarists Steve Hunter and Dick Wagner, bassist Prakash John and drummer Pentti Glan. The album yielded a controversially titled hit "Only Women Bleed," the single of which was retitled "Only Women" after feminist protests. The irony there is while there's an obvious menstruation double-entendre, the song, which hit number-12 in *Billboard*, is a lament about spousal abuse.

With *Nightmare* and an accompanying network TV special, Alice took a swerve toward the mainstream. Alice Cooper lite was a commercial success, but the two-year tour supporting it burned Cooper out and led to his hospitalization.

In 1997, Cooper made a pre-Halloween appearance at Spooky World, a sprawling pop-up theme park south of Boston. I spent some time hanging with him as he signed autographs, greeted fans and spoke about rock and horror movies. As an actor, Cooper has played a zombie, a monster dog and various killers.

He got Vincent Price to act in his *Welcome to My Nightmare* film. "He had the best attitude about horror. He said, 'This is *fun*!' I think there's a very fine line between humor and comedy. To me, a good horror movie is a good comedy. It's like getting on a rollercoaster. You know it's gonna scare you, but you get on anyway 'cause you know it's gonna bring you back safely. In every horror movie the premise is: Somebody's in danger and somebody's coming after them."

Midway through a phone chat we had in 2016, Cooper started singing "Set 'em up, Joe, I got a lot of stories to tell…" from Frank Sinatra's "One More for My Baby (And One More for the Road)." No, Cooper is not pulling a Bob Dylan here. Alcoholism may be no laughing matter, but Lord knows a lot of alcoholics have had a lot of laughs over the years. Some of the recovering alcoholics remember that, and that's where Cooper comes in.

The Hollywood Vampires features the Alice Cooper who dresses down a bit ("vampir*ish*," he says) singing some of rock's classics in a band with guitarists Joe Perry and Johnny Depp. As he tells it, Cooper was in the studio with Depp and a few other players when Perry walked into the room and said, "I'm in."

Perry told me, "Alice had this Hollywood Vampires idea for quite a while, and they asked me to come and sit in on the record. Then it gelled into what it is now. When they tour, it's not like a regular band with a vision of taking six months and we're all going to dedicate everything to that. It's more like a pickup band in some ways. When everybody's free, that's when it happens."

The main intent of Hollywood Vampires is to cover songs by some of the "original" HVs, the ones who are no longer with us, as well as sounding a raucous cautionary note about the lifestyle. That comes during "My Dead Drunk Friends," an original which closes the eponymous debut CD and is often played near the end of the band's shows, followed by songs like "Ace of Spades," "Sweet Emotion," "Train Kept-a Rollin'," "I'm Eighteen" and "School's Out."

In "Friends," we find Cooper alone in a bar. "All you know is he's the last guy in the bar, and he's come to the bartender and he's saying, 'OK, let's talk about what's happened to us. I'm the last one left and this place is full of ghosts, but all these ghosts are my buddies. Let's raise a toast to these guys.' It was fashioned after that type of saloon song." It devolves into a round of drinking, puking and fighting — in various combinations. Cooper says that when they got to that part, "I couldn't help from thinking of Jack Sparrow in a pirates' bar." (Doesn't hurt to have Johnny Depp in the band for that one.)

"Here we are in the studio making these records of these guys, and everybody in the studio is sober. Johnny [Depp]'s sober, Joe [Perry]'s sober, I'm sober, [producer] Bob Ezrin's sober. Everybody that comes in is drinking coffee or Diet Coke and we're making this record of these guys that wouldn't ever have a Diet Coke in their life. At the time when we were drinking with them, if you had said, 'Thirty years from now you're going to be doing a record honoring these guys and you're going to be in top shape, and you're going to be drinking Diet Coke,' I would have said, 'You're out of your mind' because none of us planned to live past 30."

So, the intent with this side project (some people are using the word "supergroup," but Cooper prefers "bar band") is to revisit a part of classic rock's past. Not *all* artists were victims of self-abuse. The Vampires do "I Got a Line on You" by Spirit, whose guitarist Randy California, Cooper notes, "passed away saving his son from drowning."

Doing that song led to what Cooper calls "one of the greatest compliments. We were in the studio and Paul McCartney was in the studio and we were playing back everything. We're doing 'I Got a Line on You' and he said, 'Who's singing that?' Johnny says, 'Alice,' and he says, 'Wow!' I got a 'Wow!' from Paul McCartney. I can live on that for 10 years." On *Hollywood Vampires*, McCartney joined on the song he wrote for Badfinger in 1969, "Come and Get It."

In 2019, I fired a few quick-hit questions Alice's way for a magazine I contribute to, www.expmag.com.

What's your proudest moment?

Careerwise, seeing my album at number-one. In my personal life, marrying Sheryl, my wife of 43 years, and fathering our three kids.

Where do you come up with your best ideas?

I get my best ideas from television, pop culture, the news. Everywhere you look there's a great headline and I can build a song from there.

If you had to choose a different profession, what would you do?

I would either be a comedy writer or a scriptwriter for films. I always seem to come up with great ideas for movies that haven't been done yet.

What is the most useful mistake you've made?

Criticizing another band without knowing them. In the early days of Creedence Clearwater, I knocked them in an interview and then ended up meeting them shortly afterwards. I had to explain myself and why I had said what I said. After that I learned a great lesson and became professional enough to live and let live.

What's the strangest experience you've had?

Working with Salvador Dali for a week.

What opportunity do you regret passing up?

I remember being approached to play the part of Pennywise in the original *It* film and I passed. I definitely regret that.

What is your most indelible childhood memory?

Seeing Elvis on the Ed Sullivan show. It might have sparked something in my brain. Also, in high school, hearing the Beatles on the radio for the first time.

While many fans enjoy Cooper now with his crack band — I last saw him live at Leader Bank Pavilion in Boston, September 2021 — the older ones still cherish those badass ACB days. Cooper did bring that back to an extent (on disc), inviting bassist Dennis Dunaway, keyboardist Michael Bruce and drummer Neal Smith to join the sessions for 2021's *Detroit Stories.* (Guitarist Glen Buxton died from pneumonia in 1997.)

"It kind of fell into place," says Cooper, talking to me before the recording actually took place. "It'll be an experiment when we get these songs in the studio to see if they sound like 1971 Alice Cooper songs. I would like it to sound like *Killer, Part Two*. I'm gonna start it out with these ideas and then see where it goes."

Is it *Killer, Part 2*? No, not quite. Those were different times for all of us. But it's a damn good hard rock record, Cooper's heaviest in years, an homage to his hometown rockers. It starts off with a cover of Lou Reed's "Rock and Roll." (No, the Velvet Underground did not hail from Detroit, but this version harkens back to the Mitch Ryder band Detroit, which covered it in 1971 and included longtime Cooper guitarist Steve Hunter.) There's also the MC5's "Sister Anne," written by the late Fred "Sonic" Smith, and a new one, "Go Man, Go," which Cooper wrote with Ezrin, guitarist Tommy Henriksen and ex-MC5-er Wayne Kramer. Plus, Bob Seger's "East Side Stories." There are 10 others, all co-writes by Cooper and Ezrin, some with additional credits.

As Cooper tells me, "I take playing Alice Cooper very seriously, I take the show seriously, I take the music seriously. I don't take myself seriously. I understand that I play the character, I understand the songs and I really make that very important." ◆

"With music, there's intoxication, an addictive aspect. Once it's in you, it's got to come out."

Peter Wolf

Peter Wolf onstage in the Netherlands, April 1979

PHOTOGRAPH BY ROB BOGAERTS / ANEFO (COURTESY OF THE DUTCH NATIONAL ARCHIVES)

PETER WOLF
& THE J. GEILS BAND

HERE'S HOW ONE FAN REMEMBERS his exposure to Boston's J. Geils Band in concert when he was a teenager, a self-described "dewy-eyed kid" from out of town: "They would start off as a three-piece and then another guy would come up onstage, and then another guy, and finally [singer] Peter Wolf would come out. They always had such showmanship and dynamics.

"Man, if you saw that band when they were in their prime, you were spoiled. You probably expected that that's how rock *is*. Well, no. They're a cut above. They were like Sly and the Family Stone. They knew how to take a whole arena and just tear it up. They set the bar for rock and roll as far as I was concerned. They could stand toe-to-toe with any band in the world."

That fan was Joe Perry of Aerosmith. He'd seen the J. Geils Band at Boston's legendary Tea Party, the same club Led Zeppelin, the Jeff Beck Group and the Who landed when they first toured. (It was the Velvet Underground's home away from home, too.) Joe has six years on me, but I felt pretty much the same from 1971 to 1974. I lived in Orono, Maine, about 10 miles outside Bangor.

The J. Geils Band, formed in Worcester in 1967, was virtually our house band when I was in high school. They played *lots*, and I don't think I missed one show. An early memory is of Wolf being a human jumping frog. I'd never seen that kind of manic energy, never felt so enlivened by rock and roll up close and in my face.

As Perry suggested, we accepted that high level of energy, the sweat, the natural showmanship as a kind of standard. I didn't miss a show, and I continued to see them after I went to college at the University of Maine. I was totally enthralled by the high energy of "First I Look at the Purse" and "Homework," only learning later that they didn't write those songs. (That'd be the Contours and Otis Rush, respectively.) The source didn't matter, of course. Originals and covers all became part of the same high-energy fabric. One song I *knew* they didn't write — and it was a highlight of their sets back then — was a long, drawn-out version of John Lee Hooker's "Serve You Right to Suffer." I'd yet to be done wrong by a woman, as Hooker and Wolf evidently had, but I yearned for that time. Oh, it would come, it would come, it would surely come.

What the J. Geils Band did in the early '70s was much like what the Rolling Stones did in the early '60s: they took obscure (or not) blues and R&B songs which they loved and pumped them up for a young rock and roll audience. They got tagged as "the American Rolling Stones" or, sometimes, "the Jewish Rolling Stones."

"They were an automatic sellout," recalls Maine's top concert promoter of the day, Andrew Govatsos. His company booked shows in the hockey barns and halls of Bangor, Lewiston, Portland and Augusta.

I had listened to J. Geils' first two studio albums at home — the eponymous debut and *The Morning After* — and, while I liked them, neither captured what I heard in concert. It wasn't until *Live Full House*, which came out late in '72, that what I heard in concert I heard on vinyl. (Seven of the eight songs were covers.)

Things got better in the studio, too, with *Bloodshot* — which had one of the first rock/reggae songs in "Give It to Me" — and *Ladies Invited*, both in '73. The band's songwriters, Wolf and keyboardist Seth Justman, were coming into their own, and the albums swung toward originals.

"Seth and Pete write virtually all the original material. It's all synthesized, filtered down through the rest of us. We all get into it," guitarist Geils told me in April 1978, following a show at the Cumberland County Civic Center. After years of seeing them live, virtually growing up with them and living vicariously through them (I remember a few weeks one summer without my parents around, living in a dorm room on the University of Maine campus, my buddies and I replicating the cover of *The Morning After*), this was my first time interviewing them.

"We don't work from charts or anything like that," Justman said. "Basically, it comes from the feelings of the individual players."

"Some of us can read music," added Geils, "but we don't let it hurt our playing."

"Our first album, we were doing a lot of stuff we were doing in the bars, lounges, and we recorded mostly live in three days and we intentionally put songs in there by other people," explained Wolf. "And we try to do that on all our albums. But I think we've developed our own thing — each song we 'Geil-ize' it. I don't think we've fallen into any traps. Voodoo or anything like that."

Wolf had his own ideas about the songwriting. "I do all of it and Seth takes parts of it and ... [a pause to reset] Matter of fact, the Beatles stole most of our stuff. Most people don't know that. We've had problems with Donny & Marie, too. A lot of people have been swiping our stuff, but we figure we've got to contribute — give something, right?"

The conversation moved elsewhere, but then Wolf zipped back to the Beatles. A thought had just dawned on him: "*Magical Mystery Tour*! That's another thing the Beatles took from us. We had a movie and everything. We had an octopus and they changed it to a walrus. We had the octopus as Danny [Klein, the Geils Band bassist]."

As we were shaking hands and wrapping up, I managed to step in the bucket. We had talked tons of music, but I couldn't help but ask... I'd heard that Wolf and his wife of four years, movie star Faye Dunaway, were on the rocks, so I asked, as innocently as possible, "How are things with Faye?" He shot me a sharp look which I interpreted as the interview had been so good up to this point and now I'd brought it into the land of celebrity gossip. I felt like a shithead for that. (The marriage lasted another year. In her autobiography, Dunaway blamed their conflicting careers. "Time, life and the world kept wearing away at our relationship," she wrote. Wolf said in an interview, "Well, we were in a romance, she worked hard and was very dedicated to her work. I worked hard and was very dedicated to my work.")

My faux pas didn't damage my relationship with the band or with Wolf. It was a blip. After I moved to Boston, I'd see him in clubs with some frequency and we'd chat, one time him telling me, scouting the ladies, "I'm here looking for the next ex-Mrs. Wolf."

The group continued to build momentum, notching hits for the title songs of *Sanctuary* in 1978 and *Love Stinks* in 1979. A change was in the wind, both for the band's sounds and its fortunes, for both good and, well, odd. Released at the end of 1981,

Freeze Frame hit the top of *Billboard*'s charts and hung there four weeks, propelled by the single "Centerfold" (six weeks at number-one). The title cut followed as the next single and went to number-four. The new video station, MTV, did for the Geils Band what it later did for ZZ Top, making video stars out of bands never before concerned with a flashy, telegenic image. Wolf was charismatic, though, a jive-talker with rapid-fire routines honed as a DJ at WBCN during the Boston rock station's formative years. Geils toured U.S. arenas with U2 as their opening act. That summer, they toured Europe opening for the Rolling Stones.

Around that time, *Rolling Stone*'s book division contacted me and asked if I'd like to write a biography of the now-hot band. Sure, I said. I had a good meeting with the group at their rehearsal space in Allston, about a mile from where I lived.

And then they broke up. Or, more to the point, Wolf decided to launch a solo career, leaving the five others to carry on, with Justman singing and shouldering all the songwriting. There was one more album, *You're Gettin' Even While I'm Gettin' Odd*. In 1985, the band ended — and so did my proposed book deal.

Why? Who's to say exactly? It wasn't a question I ever got a good answer to back then, and I've not really pressed Wolf since, though in 2016 he told the *Atlanta Journal-Constitution*, "I did not leave the band, but the majority of the band wanted to move in another direction ... They wanted to continue in a pop-techno way, [and] it wasn't my thing."

If there was bad blood, there couldn't have been that much. Or maybe time heals. Wolf carved out a solo career, but they did reunite upon occasion. I attended a private birthday party for Klein's 60th birthday in 2006: good spirits, toasts to DK all around.

But that was inside-baseball. The public reunions went very well, the ones I saw in Boston, certainly. This report comes from the summer of 2015, a show at the Blue Hills Pavilion on Boston Harbor's waterfront.

> The J. Geils Band titled their second live album *Blow Your Face Out*, and that pretty much remains their intent nearly 40 years after that album's release. If Wolf doesn't execute the jumping frog stage moves he did back in that era, forgive him. Wolf is still slender as a rail, and a whole lot more agile than folks 40 years his junior. Onstage, in concert with the J. Geils Band, he's pretty much on the go all the time. Yeah, there may be a Dorian

Gray-like picture he's got up in his attic.

The J. Geils Band are doing a brief tour without their namesake guitarist — he's stepped down — but Duke Levine and Kevin Barry are in the mix, providing that power. They whipped through a nearly two-hour hometown set.

The group — with Wolf, but minus drummer Stephen Jo Bladd — reunited for a tour in 1999 and then another a decade later. As to recording new music, that's not going to happen. What we got was this: the early-'80s hits ("Sanctuary," "Freeze Frame," "Centerfold" and "Love Stinks") packed into a nice mid-set block, but early songs from *Full House* were highlights of the set for me. Those, along with "Southside Shuffle," "Pack Fair and Square," "Night Time," "Houseparty" and "Musta Got Lost."

"Whammer Jammer," harpist Magic Dick's signature song, remains a big crowd-pleasing blow-out. "Give It to Me," the semi-reggae hit from 1973, had that frantic breakdown jam/coda after Wolf blew the whistle. This was a well-rehearsed band. No squeaky wheels evident. Serious fun.

Whatever they mean or don't mean to each other, they were a synchronous unit onstage. Maybe it's an illusion of camaraderie, or maybe it is genuine for that time onstage. If you didn't know the history, you wouldn't sense any conflict. And, yes, of course, there's a payday at the end of the night (and tour), so there are financial incentives. But the band felt like a gang, and we out there in the crowd, we felt ever so included, as always. That's one of Wolf's strong suits.

Wolf, a jive-talking ringleader, gave generous props to all, including backup singers Andricka Hall and Cheryl Freeman and very much so to Justman. When Justman soloed, Wolf — clad in black, mostly wearing shades — shook his fingers madly at him, paying tribute, miming Justman's work. Early in the set, Wolf saluted "the first song Seth and I wrote together, our first single," which was "Wait."

Wolf loves dropping the names of blues/rock legends the Geils Band shared stages with in the days of the old Boston Tea Party — Howlin' Wolf, the Jeff Beck Group, Rahsaan Roland Kirk — and by extension he's putting the Geils Band in that lineage: old-school enough to have been

> there when it was new, but with enough vim and vigor to keep it fresh for 2015. The business of rock and roll, and especially the J. Geils Band brand, is to let the good times roll, and business was good.

I've talked with Peter Wolf at least a dozen times, sometimes at his Back Bay apartment, where he served up Makers Mark, showed off his massive record collection and talked about blues and Americana, sometimes on the phone, sometimes just out and about. A solo artist since 1984, he considers himself "fortunate and privileged" to have carved out a space. The singer-songwriter has a career that's continued to build while many of his peers are retired or resting on laurels (hits). Not that he's played Geils-sized arenas, mostly large clubs and theaters, with the occasional drop-in guest bit at the tiny Lizard Lounge in Cambridge.

Wolf puts his fortune and privilege in the context of Muddy Waters and his great backing bands. His five-piece, the Midnight Travelers, is led by guitarist Duke Levine. "It's very much like a great play – everybody in the cast is important. The stronger the cast, the better the play will be. I feel the same is true with the Midnight Travelers. It's an A-team, top shelf. And, as I always say on stage, 'There might be some as good but I'm certain that there's none better.'

"It's great to have the camaraderie and the brotherhood. Because being out on a bus or being out on tour, it's that friendship and that intoxication — not just playing, but also hanging together — it's the grandest way of getting through it all.

"The great thing about the Midnight Travelers, the band of renown that I have, is they know 'em all, so [onstage] I can turn around, pick a song and we can do it. I like to have some Geils stuff, because it's part of my past and part of a body of work that I helped create, so I'd miss it if I didn't at least acknowledge some of those things."

What follows is a mash-up of some of our best yaks over the years.

Have you thought about writing a memoir? You're practically Zelig. You've have had this incredibly long and varied career and are friends with everyone from Mick Jagger to Van Morrison.

People keep mentioning [a book] to me. It's what's become in vogue. To me, what got me interested in music was that it was an opportunity to meet musicians. In the '60s, between things like *Blow Up* and the British Invasion, the Stones were pumping and Van Morrison and Them were pumping, the Beatles and Motown was pumping and Stax was pumping. It was a deliriously glorious time to be a music fan. I've somewhat started to put together a book. It would just be my admiration and stories of the people I admire and love and had the privilege to work with and get to know behind closed doors.

Nothing salacious, not a tell-all?

No, just hopefully being able to capture the character of not only why the music was great but why the artists themselves were so unique and great. I think the key is to do it without being salacious, and to make it interesting and still true and pure.

So, there'd be interest in that kind of book?

Christopher Hitchens once said in an interview, and I always keep this in mind, "Everybody has a book within them, but it doesn't mean anybody would want to read it." I don't care if there'd be interest in it. It's like making a record, I just care about making something that I would be interested in reading.

People, especially people in these parts, talk about the J. Geils Band not being in the Rock and Roll Hall of Fame. Does that matter to you? [They've been nominated five times but are still not in.]

I've attended many of the ceremonies and inducted many people there — songwriters, Jackie Wilson, the Paul Butterfield Band — and I've performed at the Hall of Fame Induction. It would be an honor, but if it happens it happens, and if it don't, you still do what you do. It's nice to receive, but it's all involved with the work.

Your seventh solo album, Midnight Souvenirs, *dropped in April [this was 2010]. You co-wrote half the songs with Will Jennings and co-produced it with Kenny White. Shelby Lynne, Neko Case and Merle Haggard all duet with you. When we spoke on the phone recently, you were ruminating about the irony of carefully crafting a CD, the sequencing, in an age where most people don't buy CDs.*

With all the technological developments, music is still being absorbed. It's just the way it's getting to people that's dramatically different. I come from the base of how important records were and how they affected my life. I feel an obligation to the tradition that I come from to continue to make the work that respects that tradition and also be aware of the new changes that are taking place and embracing that. It's an approach I'm comfortable with. Everyone has their own approach. This is mine. I don't say it's better, don't say it's worse. I think we're all rolling around in that big sea of uncertainty, trying to find our way, and *Midnight Souvenirs* is one of the things that keeps me anchored and involved. Because when the candlelight goes out it's the work that remains.

This took, what, four years to make?

A lot longer than that. I don't count. I know it's over four. The simplest answer is the last record I did [*Fearless*], which was well-received critically, people had a hard time finding it, and I didn't want that to happen. Also, there's the breakdown of the music world, the disintegration of the music industry. I think those of us who grew up in it and worked in it were in a state of shock for a very long time. It took a long time for things to settle down, and there's still an enormous amount of chaos and anarchy involved. So, I decided to put together a record in the same way people would do an independent film. Get backers to help me, and then go find a home for it that would make sense. The recording went very fast. Most of these songs were done in the first two or three takes. The songwriting took a while. It changed a lot. Kenny White and I, we'd go through the songs and see if we could find a thematic aspect that makes sense.

Are you guilty of perfectionism or over-perfectionism?

Oh, yeah. I don't think it was obsessional, but I just tried to make it as good as I could get with the things I had to work with.

Is there a sense of reemergence or reinvention for you?

It's a good question. I never took time off. The unfortunate thing in the arts sometimes is "out of sight, out of mind." I've been trying to continue, and it took me this route to come up with *Midnight Souvenirs.* I know there were times where it was painful, frustrating and filled with a lot of self-doubt, anxiety and the sense there is no light at the end of the tunnel. If that's the length of time it took me, that's what it takes. With music, there's intoxication, an addictive aspect. Once it's in you, it's got to come out.

Is this CD closer to who you are than what you wrote and sang about in the J. Geils Band?

I've gone through so much life changes; it would be silly to think I was the same I was in the J. Geils Band. Obviously, there are aspects to me that are the same, but the world's changed, life's changed. You're never in the same place. With the J. Geils Band, it took us a long time to achieve a certain kind of acceptance. It took me a long time to figure out how to be comfortable as a soloist, to feel that I'm getting somewhere.

The J. Geils Band still plays out from time to time.

To me, it's like an actor working with a certain group of people. I enjoy revisiting those songs. They're a great part of my life, so I don't see it conflicting. It's just my energies and focus is the continuum of trying to produce new work that has some kind of credibility.

There's a pensive, melancholic tone to Midnight Souvenirs, *starting with the first song with Shelby Lynne, "Tragedy."*

There are many different themes and textures to it and that's why the sequencing of it took forever. There's definitely country flavors, R&B flavors, Philly soul. As you look around my music collection there's not one type of music. It goes from blues to country, all sorts of stuff.

Will Jennings was your primary songwriting collaborator. He co-wrote "My Heart Will Go On" for Celine Dion and "Tears in Heaven" with Eric Clapton. What did he bring to your party?

Will brings a sensibility. He comes from the Johnny Mercer world of songwriting, someone who has the ability to write a specific song for a specific mood or character, not unlike the great standards that were done in Broadway plays. Will has that broad palette. Meeting with Will is like meeting with a mentor. He brings out the best and he contributes so much. Being the master he is, it's always better when his hands are on it.

When you're working with someone as talented as Will, it's like if you were working on a film with Alfred Hitchcock or a screenplay with Billy Wilder. You know there's going to be a lot offered.

And your other collaborators...

Shelby and Neko are tremendous. Merle, to me, is the last torchbearer of American country music. He has a legacy just as rich as Johnny Cash's. I can't think of a songwriter as relevant or profound in country music. I compare him, truly, to Hank Williams.

You approached him. No disrespect, but did he know who you were?

Yeah, Merle had a sense of what I was about. More important, we spent some time together on his bus, hanging out. Then, when Will and I finished "It's Too Late for Me," I thought it had such a quality to it, a tradition to it, that I thought perhaps Merle might be interested in contributing to it. He first thought it was a Lefty Frizzell song, which is a great compliment. Then his piano player told me Merle loves that song so much he's planning on recording it. I said "No, no, no, I wanna do a duet with him." Finally, we were able to get to it and do it. It's one of my prize moments. Pick several moments in my career that are important, sitting next to Merle singing was one of them.

What about performing live?

I love performing. It's been great being part of the Rock and Roll Hall of Fame [ceremonies] and sharing the stage with Iggy Pop, Ronnie Spector, Graham Nash and Bruce Springsteen and tearing it up. I love playing. That's why I like to go to clubs and see local artists I enjoy. A lot of times I'll pop up on stage. Carl Perkins and Van Morrison and I used to kid about it: it's one for the money, but it's two for the show ... It all comes down to that great moment when you're watching an artist try to create that transcendent moment or magic.

You were born in New York but have been a part of Boston's rock and roll fabric for your whole career — as a DJ, as a performer — and you've continued to live here. Many artists who come from Boston leave for New York, Nashville or L.A. What is it that inspires you about the city, that made you want to call it home way back then and keep calling it home now?

I came up here to study painting at the Museum School of Fine Arts and just grew to enjoy the town. When I started to get involved with music, there were so many colleges that hired bands for all different events, so many fraternities that hired bands for different events, and a tremendous amount of clubs, folk clubs and even in the Combat Zone back in the day, Washington Street was lined up and down with music clubs, so it gave me and the band I was with a great opportunity to play in between getting up to Maine and New Hampshire. It was easy getting on the Cape in the summer and playing. It was a healthy place to incubate to learn the craft.

Second part of the question: why stay?

For the same reasons. You sort of hang your hat up and get used to it. Coming from New York, I go to New York and stay down there but Boston, because I planted roots here and I stayed, it became home. The J. Geils Band helped break the stigma of the thing they called the Bosstown Sound, which was an invention which made people apologize if you came from Boston. So, we helped break that stigma and open up the doors for bands like Aerosmith and Boston and the Cars, etcetera, etcetera, Jonathan Richman, things like that. It seemed to be a conducive place to get music together. It had a lot of events going on. We have all the different colleges, and besides WBCN being an important station for the community and myself, there was and still is some great college radio that is unique to this town.

Your eighth solo album is A Cure for Loneliness *[it's 2016]: what's the cure for you and your audience?*

Music. It's a friend. If you're depressed, it can help you within that aspect and help you get out. Or if you feel like staying in it, it can keep you company down there too. It's a powerful — I don't want to say drug — but it's a powerful force.

You keep returning to "Tragedy." You have two different songs by that title on back-to back records! [The one on *Midnight Souvenirs* is an original, the one on *A Cure for Loneliness* was a hit for the Fleetwoods in 1961.]

Yeah, two tragedies in a row! It was a song I've always been fond of, and when I first heard I found it very haunting. There have been several versions of it: the original version was by Thomas Wayne and that was produced by Scotty Moore, who was Elvis's original guitar player. Other people have recorded it since then, but I found out a lot of people I knew didn't know of the song so I thought by rerecording it in my way, not to copy it per se but just to do an interpretation of it, might attract people to the song and the power of the song. That's why I enjoy doing covers, going back to the Geils band with "Looking for a Love" or "First I Look at the Purse." We enjoyed trying to find songs that might not be on people's radar and help them focus in on that.

When we talked around Midnight Souvenirs, *you said you viewed an album as a work unto itself and we were into the age of downloading where many people selected to buy music track by track. Now, it's the streaming era ... how does this affect you?*

Oh, boy. That's opening up a can of a lot of worms. It's been discussed and regurgitated over and over again, and I think that the answer's kind of obvious. It's not just music. Technology has affected the print media, affected radio, affected the music industry, which was the first major industry to be decimated, and then moving onto films. It's change, and that's one thing people always have to adapt to. Constant. It's a whole labyrinth of discussion, to dwell on, it's pretty obvious.

When you're making a record, are you thinking of it song-by-song rather than a whole CD?

Well, you think about it and obviously you have to be aware of the technology that's out there and what happens to things. But coming from where I come from, I feel like my job is to make a record. These days, the motivation for making a record becomes more difficult because it's harder to find places for it. People can deconstruct it, but my job is to make an album with a beginning, a middle and an end and package it and sequence it in a way that makes sense to me. It just goes out there, and you can't control what [happens]. Twenty years ago, people could take a cut and put it on a cassette player or buy the single and not buy the record. All you can do is present it how you want to and once it's out there it's sort of anything goes.

You co-wrote four songs on A Cure for Loneliness *with Will Jennings. You worked with him on* Midnight Souvenirs, *too. Are these songs from those sessions or did you write them together after that album?*

Will and I keep writing. We just keep building up a treasure trove. He's a kindred spirit and an invaluable songwriting partner. What's really unique is our personalities click and he's become a great friend and a soul brother. That's hard to find, and I'm very grateful to have someone like him in my life.

You redid "Love Stinks" as bluegrass.

We were doing an acoustic series of shows and started fooling around backstage, kidding around with some bluegrass songs. Not kidding around, I got to meet Bill Monroe and I was a big fan of Bill Monroe and the Stanley Brothers, so we were messing around with some of their songs, and I just started singing "Love Stinks." When we went out that night, I decided to call it, and we happened to be taping. Just like the "Must of Got Lost" rap, it got captured and there it was. Everybody enjoyed it, so we decided to use it.

There's humor on record, but it's reflective too. "Peace of Mind" is about being a young man once and sounds pretty personal. Is that a statement of where you are now?

I think so. It's a pretty biographical song. It's a place where a lot of people are now, especially with the strange events going on around the world. It's a time of uncertainty for a lot of issues and a lot of people — metaphysically, economically, the whole deal. That was the impetus for that song.

Guitarist J. Geils, who was born in New York City as John Warren Geils Junior, died April 11, 2017.

I spoke to Seth Justman on the phone as he was processing his thoughts about his former bandmate. "I was reading a *Creem* magazine I had kept, and [there was a story on] Duane Allman, which I had forgotten about. Jay was one of Duane's favorite players, and they were friends. When Duane died, it was horrible for everybody, but Jay took it really hard. In this article, Duane says the J. Geils Band is his favorite band. It killed me. There was a kinship with our band and them.

"Jay was a really special musician, and I think other musicians picked up on it. Duane picked up on it. Jay was an engineering student [at Worcester Polytechnic Institute] and he was fascinated by precision, but I think what really surprised people in his playing was how there wasn't just precision and mechanics. He always searched for that intangible thing. He didn't talk about it; he didn't drive anyone crazy about it. He went out of his way to figure out how to inject that extra expression into what he was playing."

Geils, who died at 71 of unspecified causes at his Groton, Massachusetts home, gave the band his name, but he was not its frontman. (More than a few people thought Peter Wolf was Geils.) Before the J. Geils Band (originally the J. Geils Blues Band) took shape, Jay, harpist Magic Dick and bassist Danny Klein were playing in a Worcester jug band. "Jay was playing acoustic guitar, and I was playing washtub bass," Klein recalled in a separate interview. "He switched to electric guitar and then, under his suggestion, I went to electric bass. He was sort of my mentor. When we got to the Tea Party, we began playing with Wolf and Stephen and then Seth." Wolf and drummer Stephen Jo Bladd came from the Hallucinations; Justman arrived after a short stint with the band Swallow.

"Our whole idea was to be a musical machine with a huge amount of humanity," said Magic Dick, also in a separate interview. "We were interested in precision performances. Jay would dig this analogy, I'm sure: It was kind of like lifting up the hood of a car while the engine was running and just digging the interplay of all the various parts. That's how this material was written and the contributions each of us made to it. It was a combination of personal input and working together."

Jay Geils was, indeed, a car nut, an avocation that became a profession after the Geils Band folded. The longtime antique car buff (particularly Ferraris) opened a shop in Carlisle called KTR Motorsports, specializing in restoring and servicing racing sports cars.

As a guitarist, Geils was skilled in rock, blues and jazz idioms. Magic Dick spent decades next to Geils, both in the studio and at stage right, in front of his amp, blowing his harp as Geils spun out sizzling guitar riffs.

"It was amazing to be part of a band like that and standing next to Jay, whose guitar was loud and powerful — though not as loud as some guys," said Dick. "So, my experience of the band live was dominated by the sound of Jay's guitar, mostly because of my proximity to him.

"Jay gave a certain drive and impetus into what we were doing. He was more interested in delivering what the song needed rather than showing off anything about the guitar virtuoso aspects of it. He felt there were so many other guitarists in that realm he would not be one of those. He saw what we were doing more as a band thing that required each person to play a particular role and be good at it. That's what Jay was all about."

"Jay and I were studio mates," added Justman. "We would stay after hours and talk about music. Jay was shy, uncomfortable in social situations sometimes. He was not all that open emotionally. He didn't tell you how he felt; he showed you how he felt. If you weren't patient with your relationship with Jay, you didn't get to those layers and didn't get to experience that, but I did and I'm better for it."

But there was friction. As no one had copyrighted the band name, Jay Geils (and partners) did so, an acrimonious move that pitted him against his former bandmates. The lawsuit was eventually settled, allowing the J. Geils Band to remain the J. Geils Band without Jay Geils.

Magic Dick said, "Underneath it all, we never forgot our early chemistry and it was genuine, despite the friction and conflicts."

Klein said, "He was my friend and roommate for many years, so [it was like] a 50-year dysfunctional relationship. What can I say? That's only because we're musicians."

Jay Geils' musical career did not end with the J. Geils Band's work stoppage. He joined some of their reunions. He last played with the band, he reckoned in an old e-mail, "at Fenway Park in 2010, and maybe one or two after that." By 2012, he considered himself out of the J. Geils Band. He had long ago reached an agreement with his former bandmates to use the name "Jay Geils" (as opposed to J. Geils) when he played out. He did so with Bluestime, the New Guitar Summit and, most recently, the Jay Geils Blues and Jazz Revue with guitarist Gerry Beaudoin.

"Of course, I'm proud of our legacy," Geils said. "I founded the band as a Chicago-style blues band, and it evolved into a bluesy rock band. I wish them well. There is no bitterness on my part. I don't know how they feel about me. I was tired of playing our brand of high-energy rock and roll."

"I think Jay wasn't as comfortable with the trappings of rock and roll life," offered Justman. "He probably felt a lot of pressure. I think for Jay it ran its course. He wanted time for other interests and maybe he was weary of some of the pressures."

The last time I saw Geils play was with the Jay Geils Blues and Jazz Revue in 2010; he played sitting down. But he was ebullient after the set, and said, "I'm also playing trumpet again — my instrument from age eight to 18 — and getting pretty good except for running out of lip!"

Jay did a reunion with the band in 1999, but by 2001 he seemed to have had it with rock. He told me then about a transition back to his early loves: swing and jazz. "My father was a big jazz fan. I got exposed very early to Charles Mingus, Miles Davis, Louis Armstrong. When I was 14, for my birthday, my dad took me to see the Miles Davis Quintet.

"That's always been my main thing. I didn't like rock and roll when it first came around. I started out being a blues player and fortunately got to play with Buddy Guy, Junior Wells, James Cotton. When the J. Geils Band formed in the late-'60s, early-'70s, the guys brought in R&B influences like Wilson Pickett, Otis Redding and James Brown, which was pretty cool. It's all a natural extension of Muddy Waters. But always, underneath all that, I was this jazz guy."

Jay Geils was married to Kris Geils for 28 years. They split in 1999, but reportedly remained on friendly terms. Tennie Komar, former lead singer of Boston new wave band Tennie Komar & the Silencers, dated Jay for five years. She was shocked by news of his death and, yet, she said, "There were numerous among us who knew this was coming. After he got picked up for his second DUI in the fall, it was bad. He couldn't get over the drinking problem. At his age, he's been smoking and drinking his whole life and it caught up with him. This is the rock and roll lifestyle issues thing."

"He had an addiction issue, but he was a very sweet man," Komar continues. "There's not much bad you could say about Jay. Everybody that met him said he was kind and down to earth. Jay didn't have an angry bone in his body toward anybody; he was a very gentle man. He was very shy, hanging back on the stage behind everybody else."

Joe Perry has also lived that rock and roll lifestyle, though it's now in the rear-view mirror. "My heart just dropped. It's not like we were buddies, but I knew him. At our age it could be anything. He could have been absolutely clean, straight and stopped smoking, and you still have to pay the piper. When I read that on my phone, it really hit home. It all flashed before me, all those years of great music. It hit hard." ◆

“It was a statement if you played guitar. It [became] an iconic image of freedom and self-expression and rebellion.”

Joe Perry

Joe Perry of Aerosmith, 2018

PHOTOGRAPH BY ROZA YARCHUN (SUB-ROZA)

JOE PERRY
& AEROSMITH

THE FIRST SUBSTANTIAL TALK I ever had with Joe Perry occurred in late 2000. We were both gawking at a massive display of electric guitars at Boston's Museum of Fine Arts during the opening party for an exhibit called *Dangerous Curves: The Art of the Guitar*. There were more than 130 on display, axes played and owned by John Lennon, Les Paul, Prince and Jimi Hendrix, among many others.

If you know nothing else about the Aerosmith guitarist and co-leader, know this: The man loves playing *and* talking about guitars.

Some may have wondered what electric guitars were doing in an institution called the Museum of Fine Arts; rock instruments sharing a roof with Rembrandt, Van Gogh and Monet. "It makes sense," Perry reasoned, "because the guitar has *become* an art form. They're like motorcycles or something — they go beyond the function they were designed for."

Perry, who donated a black Guild X-100 Bladerunner to the exhibit, told me he owned "a couple hundred guitars, but I've never considered myself a collector like Rick Nielsen. I've got guitars that are collectible but playable. I'm not going to deny myself the pleasure of their sound."

For musicians like Perry, the worth of a guitar does not necessarily correlate to its cash value. The one he most treasures is a Stratocaster "mongrel" he pieced together himself. "It's maybe worth $150, but I could never replace it. It's got my sweat all over it. I never bring it on the road without carrying it myself." Another of his stage faves: A Gibson ES 335 (a B.B. King "Lucille" model with no f-holes) with his wife Billie's face on it. Aww ...

Perry can really wax rhapsodic about electric guitars. In a talk we had years later, he noted that, "It's the only instrument that did not exist as we know it until the late '40s. Every other instrument, except the synthesizer, has been around for centuries. A couple of really brilliant guys got hold of it and moved it ahead in the '60s and it turned into something brand new. It got to the point where if you were in rock and roll you *had* to have a hot shit guitar player and it was the era of the guitar hero. It was a statement if you played guitar. If you walked down the street [with a guitar case], you couldn't get a better response from girls. The guitar was such an iconic image of freedom and self-expression and rebellion. Keith [Richards] wasn't too far off the mark when he said, "The electric guitar brought the wall down."

The namesake guitarist of the J. Geils Band died in April 2017. I'd seen the band in concert starting when I was a young teen and later got to know the members as a rock critic. I knew Geils himself pretty well and was shocked and saddened personally, but journalistically hardened enough to know I'd have to write an appreciation. I wanted to get a comment from Perry. He was recording in Los Angeles. Billie gave me his cell number and I rang him up. He hadn't heard the news.

Perry, too, was shocked, stunned and saddened. Geils was his friend and peer; they had both risen from the same Boston scene in the early '70s. He chose to salute the Geils band by using a sobriquet often applied to *his* band: the Bad Boys From Boston. That tag has been bandied about for years regarding Aerosmith, and I guess it could be interpreted a couple of ways, maybe a combination of both.

1) Bad: Owing to the hard drug habits of the self-named Toxic Twins, Perry and singer Steven Tyler, along with guitarist Brad Whitford, bassist Tom Hamilton and drummer Joey Kramer. All are in recovery.

2) Bad as in "good": Rough, ready and rockin'. Delivered the goods night after night. Worked their way up from the trenches. Take no prisoners. Badass.

The Bad Boys badge is not something Perry wants to dodge, but, he says, "The Bad Boys From Boston, that was the J. Geils Band long before they hung that one on us. I always thought it was kind of [wrong] when the press started calling us that, because as far as I was concerned J. Geils were — and still are — one of the best live bands I'd ever seen, hands down. You couldn't see more excitement than at a J. Geils show."

Perry, in fact, credits the Geils Band with jump-starting Aerosmith's career. "I think one of the things that really helped us a lot was how big they were in Detroit. People were looking for the next band from Boston because of them and they welcomed us with open arms. They helped shape what we were doing and helped us realize how playing live was everything, from the way we arrange our songs to building our set."

Aerosmith has had a lot of well-documented highs and lows — including Perry's departure from the band in 1979 (he rejoined in 1984) — but one of the best highs was that first period, getting signed and releasing that first album.

"No doubt," says Perry, in a later interview. "The summer right before it really broke [in 1973], we were an entity, but we were still having trouble making ends meet, paying the rent. But we always managed. Right around that time, every time we'd go out and play some club there'd be 30 people there and next time there'd be 60 there — that's probably one of the best times in any band's career, when you start to feel that.

"I remember being at a gig — I think it was Shrewsbury, some high school — and we had just come back from a trip through Ohio, playing clubs and colleges. It was after the first record was out. It was a 2,000-seat place, and it was packed. Last time we played in Boston, we were still calling up all our friends to say, 'Come and see us.' All of a sudden, people were standing outside waiting to get in. I remember that gig so specifically. Our manager at the time walked in and said, 'Boys, we came to play!' and he had this wad of one-dollar bills.

"We weren't in it for the money or the limos or anything like that; we just wanted to not have to worry about the rent so we could keep doing it. To this day, it's really about that. The money just gives you the freedom to do what we do. But that was it, that day it felt like something switched, something changed."

Late in 2021, Aerosmith came out with a hard-rocking, bluesy record that harkens back to those early days. And it's something of a mystery. *1971: The Road Starts Hear* was culled from a 50-year-old two-track tape recorded on Perry's Wollensak reel-to-reel. The band was barely a year old at the time. The tape's whereabouts (in fact, its very existence) was unknown for years, until it was found in a van the band once used.

"This record is a bolt out of the blue," says Tom Hamilton. "All of a sudden, it's just there! When I first heard it, it was like hearing some young new band. 'Listen to those little shits play!' I'm still racking my brain to try and remember when and how we recorded this," he continues. "Tape? Demo? Rehearsal? For me, the thing that makes it so mysterious is that the guitar, bass, drum and vocal parts are almost exactly what eventually went on the [first] album." (Most of these songs are on that LP, which was recorded the following year and released in early 1973.) "Joe seems to remember something about a two-track tape machine, but I can't figure out how we got the quality. I mean, it's funky and raw but everything's there."

"Some people thought it was at a soundcheck at a gig in Lowell," says Perry, "but I think from the way it was set up — we only had two microphones and we had to experiment where to get the best mix — it was probably recorded in the basement of the rehearsal room [we used] at a Boston University dorm. It sounded like a more controlled environment and has the vibe of the way we rehearsed there." If so, Aerosmith's roadie and right-hand man at the time, Mark Lehman, set up two mics, one for Tyler's vocals and one for the rest of the band, and pushed "record." You can hear a smattering of applause from invited friends or, perhaps, students passing by and stopping in for a listen.

At the start, Aerosmith played cover songs. That was the way of the world in the pre-punk early '70s. "To play clubs back then," says Hamilton, "you had to do Top 40 commercial crap and play five sets a night, six days a week, which would have turned Steven's throat to gristle. At first, it was all covers, but then Steven and Joe started getting together and writing. Then, we only played gigs that let us play our originals along with the covers of our choice."

Their developing sound was clearly blues-based — the band specialized in revamping old blues and R&B songs — but, Perry says, "I thought it was the kiss of death to sit around and play slow blues. If it was a blues song that rocked, that was another story."

At BU, Perry says, they made a deal with the person who ran the dormitory: Aerosmith got to use the rehearsal room if they did some free gigs for the school. "I think we got the better part of the deal. We only played two or three times. We played whenever they asked, but they didn't ask for too many and they liked the idea of having a rock band playing in the basement." After rehearsals, Aerosmith would pack up their gear and stuff it into closets: a ballet company shared the space.

It is almost astonishing how crisp and tight *1971* sounds, given the likely setting and situation. Modern production tools can punch up the sound, but Perry claims there was no extensive cleanup. "Really, not much. They have programs you can run if the vocal is too far back, to a degree they can isolate that and make it a better mix. But this [tape] is pretty much natural." He maintains the difference from the original tape to what was released is minimal: "I'd be hard pressed to tell if it were a blindfold test."

For their Columbia Records debut, Tyler brought in six of his own songs; he and Perry co-wrote one and they had a cover of Rufus Thomas's "Walkin' the Dog." On *1971*, there are four of Tyler's ("Somebody," "Mama Kin," "Major Barbara" and "Dream On") plus the Tyler-Perry co-write "Movin' Out" and their rocked-up rendition of Thomas's 1963 hit.

Rehearsals were not casual affairs. "Steven was definitely the maestro back then," recalls Hamilton. "Very demanding. Rehearsals were fun, but serious business. Every note counted. We knew what we wanted, and we rehearsed in minute detail."

One treat of *1971* is hearing the embryonic "Dream On," the ballad that broke the band, with some different lyrics. Tyler puts his all into it, hitting the ever-accelerating high notes — in a rehearsal, never intended for airing outside the band! "It's really amazing to hear how close we were playing it then to how we play it now," says Perry.

The other four guys initially weren't keen on recording Tyler's song. With its piano-based intro and slow build, "Dream On" was something of an outlier and, Perry says, they definitely envisioned themselves as a band where "rock and roll was key. But we also knew 'Dream On' had something to it. Steven had it pretty much together when he came in [to the Commonwealth Avenue apartment in Boston the band shared]. He had a piano in there. I'm not sure *how* we got a piano into that apartment. But we heard the riff over and over again and it became part of our DNA. We built it up. We also knew it was really hard to get a rock and roll song on the radio past a certain point and, with that ballad, we didn't know where it was going to go, but it worked."

Perry says, unlike some bands, there's no massive backlog of unreleased Aerosmith songs waiting to see the light of day. "It would be great if we had an album's worth of unheard material," Perry says, "but it didn't work that way for us. On the other hand, there are a lot of songs — like 'Dream On,' 'Sweet Emotion' and 'Kings and Queens' — where there's a different vocal, or guitar solo or tempo. A different vibe. I think that would probably be more interesting for fans to hear."

Perry says those outtakes have the high-quality sound they achieved with producer Jack Douglas at the Record Plant in the mid-'70s. "I'm anxious to dig into some of those and hear some of those different takes."

Following the lead of pop singers and country stars, Aerosmith booked a Las Vegas residency titled *Deuces Are Wild* at the Park MGM Hotel in 2020. Joe and I talked before the pandemic hit in March and forced a change of plans.

They were approaching the engagement strategically. "You've got to be a little more careful there because of our audience," Perry adds. "They say the population there changes every two-and-a-half days, and people are coming from all over the world. A lot are coming to see the band, but others to see a magician or Cirque du Soleil or the *Love* Beatles thing. Hopefully, we win 'em over. We'll play things [that are] a little more tried and true — we don't want anybody walking out — but people should know we have more than five albums out there.

"We're gonna start pulling a few of those things out. There are eight to ten songs that we will always put in the set, unless it's like we're gonna just play this album or that album. I think even with ten songs, that leaves you with five spaces to fill up with songs we've been dying to play live and never got to."

The residency was rescheduled, and they were about to head for rehearsals in Vegas when, in late May, a bomb dropped on the band. Friendly fire, so to speak.

"As many of you know, our beloved brother Steven has worked on his sobriety for many years," read a band statement. "After foot surgery to prepare for the stage and the necessity of pain management during the process, he has recently relapsed and voluntarily entered a treatment program to concentrate on his health and recovery. We are truly sorry to inform our fans and friends that we must cancel our first set of Las Vegas residency dates this June and July while he focuses on his well-being."

I talked to Perry after that. "It was really about his getting his surgery," Perry says. "His feet were a mess over the years because of his motorcycle accident [in 1981], and it just got worse and worse and worse. I couldn't believe he was out there doing what he does [performing]. He had to go in and get the surgery and he just didn't leave enough time. The calendar was working against us, between the COVID thing and all that. He was ready to go, the doctor said, 'You can't go out' and that was it.

I asked Joe what his thoughts were about Steven's continuing use of opiates, which scuttled plans for the band, crew and fans. Anger, compassion, empathy, disappointment?

"Yeah, well, disappointment for a minute," Perry said. "It's a huge bummer, but then it's like this: Life throws shit at us all the time and you've got to either be angry and do damage to yourself with the stress of it or accept it for what it is. There's that saying

— change the things you can and accept the things you can't. Boy, is that true. That's one thing you can count on. In life, if you've learned one thing, stuff is always going to change.

"It wasn't anger. It was more about realizing that we're all human and we're all vulnerable and stuff happens. I hope he's going to be OK; I *know* he's going to be OK, because he wants to be out there singing as bad as anybody. We learned a long time ago, especially after the band got back together — and this applies to everybody — [you think] 'If I could only get them to do this.' And there comes a point where you realize nothing you do is going to change them and you have to accept them for who they are. I'm not [just] talking about Steven, I'm talking about everybody in the band. I'm sure people have said shit about me a ton of times."

Asked how Tyler was doing, Perry said, "Great. I talk to him almost every day."

Perry scrambled and reassembled the Joe Perry Project, his side band, for a couple of summertime blues festival dates in Brazil, a gig at Hampton Beach Casino in New Hampshire and opening for old pals ZZ Top in Boston at Leader Bank Pavilion.

Aerosmith got back in the saddle in September, playing outdoor concerts in Bangor and Boston. When they played Fenway Park, the show was big and bold. Tyler was in fine form, singing "Dream On" and playing piano from the top of the Green Monster before they reassembled onstage for "Walk This Way," "Sweet Emotion" and Muddy Waters' "Mannish Boy" (complete with Fenway fireworks). It was also, by virtue of playing to 40,000 people in a ballpark, the kind of show most people had to watch on the giant video screens. The band looked good under those stage lights on the big screens and the shots were synced perfectly.

Joey Kramer was, once again, on the sidelines; his drum tech John Douglas was at the kit. "It beats the shit out of you, playing drums," Perry said. "It's really tough [and there's] a lot of personal stuff, but the bottom line is Joey — and every drummer I know of who plays hard rock — has joint problems. Physically, it's one of the hardest gigs out there, and you have to be in really good shape. He's paid the price and had problems with every joint. That's why we had to have John sit in. He's really stepped up to the plate. It was amazing. The show is pretty much there. He's played 32 shows."

The Vegas run resumed after Boston, but then hit the skids near the end. The band scrapped some shows, saying Tyler was feeling "unwell." Aerosmith said in a statement. "Stay healthy and we'll see you in the new year!" ◆

"Without humor, you're dead.
I always knew I was funny."

Lemmy

Lemmy leads Motörhead at the Eurockéennes de Belfort in France, July 2011

LEMMY
& MOTÖRHEAD

AS I WRITE THIS, I FEEL LIKE I should be gobbling a handful of amphetamines and quaffing a fifth of whiskey to get in the spirit. When Motörhead's main man Lemmy still rocked among us, I did down a few shots of Jack Daniel's with the man over the years. (No speed or blow, though. One must have rules.)

Lemmy meant a lot of things to fans of both metal and punk, neither of which he was quite part of, though intimately connected to both. I'll get to the music part, but first I need to note that, over my years of chatting with him, he was a witty and worldly conversationalist.

Not everyone knew that. There was the public image. In 1982, Mark Cooper called Motörhead "greasy snipers" in *Record Mirror.*

The one time I raised the Motörhead image cliché, an old jape that they were essentially gorillas in leather jackets, the bassist, bandleader and singer-songwriter responded, "We're not gorillas. I think we're, let's see, monitor lizards in leather jackets? ... English poets in leather jackets? ... knights in shining armor." And "the old contemptibles." Said with pride.

Talking to Lemmy back in 1991, I suggested that he was the father, or maybe the grandfather, of modern metal. "Not me," he said. "I'm not a grandfather yet. I'm respected, which is nice. But I'm a fucking idiot, the way I do things."

Every Motörhead concert I can recall — and I must have seen more than a dozen over the years (headlining clubs, opening for Alice Cooper, on a festival bill) — began with these words from Lemmy: "We are Motörhead, and we play rock and roll." So simple, so succinct, yet so ... obvious?

Yet, I think this is what he was trying to say to fans of metal, to fans of punk, to critics like me who divined that Motörhead had adroitly bridged the two genres: this was, pure and simple, his version of rock and roll, a tradition he picked up from Little Richard, Chuck Berry and the Beatles.

Motörhead swung and swayed as it bludgeoned. Crude as it may have seemed to the untrained (or squashed) ear — "Jesus Christ! What an onslaught! Is it 130 dB yet?!" — there was a certain finesse, even dignity, about what the band did. They weren't a cartoon or a cliché. They may have inspired many a wanna-be-dangerous tattooed rocker and countless speed metal bands, and they sure played fast, but that's not exactly where they came from. And I don't think I knew any rock fan — no matter what their preferred genre — who didn't dig Motörhead in some way.

Lemmy wrote songs about sex (in favor of it) and war (against it), but there was no idiotic, quasi-Satanic posing. This was heavy, working man's music. Motörhead was about anti-authoritarianism ("Eat the Rich," indeed), melody plus crunch, all tangled up in Lemmy's gruff bark, as if (figuratively) he was gargling whiskey and glass.

Lemmy didn't equivocate about his enjoyment of speed and coke. My friend and former Boston-based rock critic/colleague Ernie Welch recalls this from 1983: "I covered Motörhead at the Paradise, the *Another Perfect Day* tour with Thin Lizzy alumnus Brian Robertson on guitar. I was chasing down the set list prior to the band bombing the stage, and before the road manager split to get one copied, he asked if I'd like to meet Lemmy. I did. Lemmy was sitting alone in a cramped room at a small table with a large bowl of cocaine and a quart of Smirnoff blue label (the 100-proof variety), both of which he was consuming at a breakneck pace. We chatted about his band and music in general for a few minutes when Lemmy asked if I'd care for a spoonful and swig or two.

'No thank you, Lemmy. I'm reviewing the concert tonight and have to maintain objectivity.'

'A man with integrity,' said Lemmy. 'I like that, Ernie.'"

Lemmy was, however, virulently anti-heroin, writing a powerful and persuasive piece in *RIP* magazine in the '90s. "Your life becomes a search for heroin; the only way you can get up is if you have some," he told me. "Otherwise, you lie in bed shivering and cramped up. Doesn't sound like much fun to me."

Ian Fraser Kilmister was born in Stoke-on-Trent on Christmas Eve 1945, just months after World War II ended. On December 28, 2015, Lemmy was, as his song goes, killed by death, as will we all be. (Cancer, to be specific.) I'm sure he was well aware of the Spinal Tap-esque humorous redundancy of that song title; hell, "Killed by Death" may have even been a tribute to the Tap. Lemmy had a wicked sense of humor about what he did and the world at large.

As a youth, Lemmy roadied for Jimi Hendrix. He joined Hawkwind in 1971 and sang lead on their great single "Silver Machine." He got booted out after being busted for drugs crossing the Canadian/U.S. border. (As many, including Lemmy, have said, it was not drugs per se but the wrong kind of drugs — speed, not acid.)

For years, I thought Lemmy must have written "Kings of Speed," but nope, that was Dave Brock and Michael Moorcock (channeling Lemmy?). The last song he wrote for Hawkwind was "Motorhead," the B-side of the (even faster) "Kings of Speed" single.

Motörhead was born after his exit from Hawkwind. The trio made its vinyl debut with an original titled "White Line Fever" on the 1977 compilation *A Bunch of Stiffs* on Stiff Records, a thunderous blast in the midst of Stiff's leaner pub-rock and pure pop stable. (Motörhead later released "Motörhead" as a single. It appeared on a couple of albums, too.)

That early version of Motörhead included former Pink Fairies guitarist Larry Wallis, who happened to be playing Dingwalls one night in 1985 when I was in London. I went alone, fell right into the club's down 'n' dirty vibe, drank, bought my bartender drinks, mixed with the punters. Between sets, I was at a pinball machine, batting the silver ball around when I was chatted up by a leather-clad, mutton-chopped fella with a couple of prominent moles. He wanted to play, too, but was skint (apparently) and barked, "You got 10 pence?"

Of course I did, offering a pocketful of coins I couldn't readily identify. I couldn't help but also think of how he allegedly got his nickname – him saying "Lend me a fiver!" – but that was a tale Lemmy disputed. I knew Lemmy from various rock writer/musician encounters in Boston, but I'm sure he had no idea who I was specifically, me showing up at his local in London. So, I reintroduced myself and we hung out together, drinking, laughing, pinballing and listening to Wallis and company tear it up. One of the great nights of my life.

So, who was Motörhead?

My favorite description came from a *Creem* writer who said Motörhead essentially was Lemmy and two or three other guys who were not Lemmy. (Aficionados, Ernie Welch among them, can of course pinpoint differences among the various bands and champion one or the other.) Nine other musicians served alongside Lem over the past four decades, including four who have left life's stage: drummer Phil "Philthy Animal" Taylor (d. 2015, at 61, liver failure) and guitarists Wurzel (né Michael Burston, d. 2011 at 61, ventricular fibrillation triggered by cardiomyopathy), "Fast" Eddie Clarke (d. 2018 at 67, pneumonia) and Wallis (d. 2019, brain tumor).

In 1991, Motörhead was Lemmy, Taylor and Wurzel and Phil "Wizzo" Campbell on guitars. Lemmy maintained at the time this was the best yet, even with the friction: "We're all maniacs. A band is like a family – 'Go to your room! Upstairs without any supper! You can't borrow the car tonight!' It's my life, man. There's always a few hiccups, but I know how to handle it, more or less."

By 1995, Wurzel and Taylor were gone and Mikkey Dee was on drums. That year, I told Lemmy I'd just seen the movie *Outbreak*, a runaway hit about a virus run amok. (Imagine that!) Jimbo, the young, chimp-snatching shady trader, is one of the film's early villains. How did they costume him? Why, they put him in a black Motörhead T-shirt, which, even though partially covered, can be glimpsed by the discerning eye.

"A Motörhead shirt?!" exclaimed Lemmy. "Excellent. Can't get any better publicity than that. It's like, before we were a disease; now we're a virus! People just have to breathe us in."

Wizzo, Dee and Lemmy comprised the band's longest-running lineup. The day after Lemmy's death Dee told loudwire.com, "Motörhead is over, of course. Lemmy was Motörhead. We won't be doing any more tours or anything. And there won't be any more records. But the brand survives, and Lemmy lives on in the hearts of everyone."

Some years back, I posited that Lemmy was the Jerry Lee Lewis of heavy metal. (OK, he'd argue the terminology, but stay with me.) Consider: They were both icons of their genres. They were both surprisingly enduring and often confrontational. They both liked their booze, pills and women and could get a little messed-up at times, but both had a dead-solid perfect rock and roll aesthetic. They were heroes and villains, avatars and reprobates. Cocky and defiant, they played the game by their own rules, and lived this credo for ages.

But, of course, time waits for no one. This was posted on Motörhead's Facebook page:

> There is no easy way to say this ... our mighty, noble friend Lemmy passed away today after a short battle with an extremely aggressive cancer. He had learnt of the disease on December 26th, and was at home, sitting in front of his favorite video game from the Rainbow [a fave haunt in his adopted city, L.A.] with his family.
>
> We cannot begin to express our shock and sadness, there aren't words.
>
> We will say more in the coming days, but for now, please ... play Motörhead loud, play Hawkwind loud, play Lemmy's music LOUD. Have a drink or few. Share stories. Celebrate the LIFE this lovely, wonderful man celebrated so vibrantly himself. HE WOULD WANT EXACTLY THAT.

Lemmy had a long stretch of victories — small ones maybe, by Black Sabbath or Metallica standards — but victories nonetheless. Was Motörhead a cult band? Sure. But a cult band that made 22 studio albums, sold 15 million of them and had an impact well beyond those sales figures. (And a band that continues to churn out live albums from those endless deep vaults every veteran band seems to have now.)

In "Thunder and Lightning," Lemmy proclaims, "I always wanted the dangerous life" and sagely observes, "You'll get more pussy if you're in a band." (Every time he opened his mouth, the truth poured out.) At the very end, Motörhead tackled the Stones' "Sympathy for the Devil." *Kerrang!* again: "*Bad Magic* is proof that Motörhead remains the greatest rock and roll band on God's scorched Earth."

Unlike, say, Warren Zevon's *The Wind, Bad Magic* does not sound like the work of a man anticipating or contemplating impending death, even though death is strewn throughout the 13 songs. That, for Lemmy, was just business as usual.

Consider how it plays out in Motörhead's best-known song, "Ace of Spades," living the life while facing the inevitable: "I don't wanna live forever." Or in "Them Not Me," a fast rip through a world of traffic fatalities. Lemmy tapped into that forbidden thought that passes through our brains sometimes when we hear about highway carnage. I felt guilty feeling any relief that I've been spared by fate, and others weren't, but Lemmy shouted it out loud.

When Lemmy died, former Gang of Four drummer Hugo Burnham, reacting on Facebook, wrote: "Live fast, die old. (Is 70 old? In rock years, probably, yes.) The joke about what-kind-of-world-will-we-leave-for-Keith-Richards-and-Lemmy now loses one of its characters."

Motörhead's motto — again a bit of Spinal Tap in there — was "Everything louder than everything else." (That also became the title of a live album.) It was funny, but not a joke. Of the many solar-plexus rattling, steamroller-on-speed times I saw Motörhead, I once listened to the second half of a gig I was reviewing from a corridor at the Paradise, off the main room, band out of site. There was another, in 2011, where I had to leave the main room during a House of Blues gig. It was just ... too ... punishing. Usually, the pleasure and pain aspects shook hands and made a deal; this time, pain took the upper hand, although my eardrums still took a beating.

Lemmy told me that too many people, especially Americans, didn't get his dry sense of humor. "Without humor, you're dead," he said. "I see these thrash-metal bands now that have got no sense of humor at all and that's fatal. They're all so terribly intense, beavering away at it, they just don't know that they're funny. I always knew I was funny."

How's this for juxtaposition? In 1997, I saw an early-evening show at the now-gone rock club Axis, across from Fenway Park. The gig coincided with game time. The The looks incoming Red Sox fans gave the incoming leather-clad, studded, tattooed Motörhead fans? Priceless. (I was both a rock critic and a Red Sox season ticket holder.) I did a review for the *Boston Globe*:

> Motörhead has long been the standard bearer of bone-crushing, eardrum-pummeling, body-pulverizing hard rock — a juggernaut of speed, a nonstop attack of rebellion and feel-good bad attitude. ... The trio played a new song that sounded a lot like the old songs: a big, thick, grinding slab of nasty, exhilarating rock and roll. Lyrics? Song title? Sorry, folks.

> I'm not that sharp. Even Motörhead's soundman didn't have a clue, when asked later. [When Lemmy talks between songs what] he spews is largely unintelligible, if somehow authentic. He did rip through the recognizable classic "Ace of Spades" as an encore.

His sort of music (loud, fast) being mostly a young man's game, did Lemmy ever see himself stepping back from the stage? You know, retiring? I suspected I knew the answer to this, so it was mostly a set-up, but Lemmy was appropriately incredulous and up for it.

"You just don't consider giving up. I mean, what else am I gonna do? A fucking talk show?! If I quit Motörhead, I'd have to do something, right? So, I might as well keep on with the one that's known." (Frankly, I'd have loved a Lemmy talk show, but that's beside the point.)

"It's a great thing for keeping you young, this business," he said. "Suddenly, you look around and think, 'This is weird. I'm sure I'm only 21. Something's wrong here. Go back and check the figures.'"

Onstage, Lemmy had his vocal mic set impossibly high on the stand, faced down, so he had to strain to sing upwards into it. The sight always made me think of a hanged man, all stretched out.

He was much more than the anchor of a power trio; the bassist called himself "a deep guitarist. I was a guitar player first, so I'm used to playing chords," Lemmy told www.bassplayer.com in what was likely his final interview. He played a Rickenbacker through a modified Marshall stack.

"It's just like playing the guitar without the top two strings. I just made chords out of what strings I had left. It's unorthodox, but it works for us. I hate it when I see a band and they're thumping along, the riff is great, and then the solo comes in and the riff dies because the guitar player has to play the solo. So, I always said to myself, I'll back it up — put some extra bits in, like two-note chords or something like that."

With Motörhead, there was always more wit and humor than met the ear on first listen; he was a Monty Python fan and quick with a riposte. Despite a fascination with the machinery of war, he was appalled by its true horror. He knew history. He collected Nazi memorabilia, not because he was pro-Nazi (far from it), but because he thought the gear looked cool. "I only collect the stuff, I didn't collect the ideas," he told *Rolling Stone* in 2009. "I've always liked a good uniform, and throughout history, it's always been the bad guy who dressed the best," he told *The Independent*. "Napoleon, the Confederates, the Nazis. If we had a good uniform, I'd collect ours as well, but what does the British Army have? Khaki."

Lemmy was diagnosed with hypertension and diabetes in the '90s, prompting him to curb some of his excesses. (He swapped Jack Daniel's for vodka, cut down a bit on cigs, don't know what he did about the speed or coke.) Lemmy had a dangerous arrhythmia and, in 2013, got a defibrillator in his chest. He reportedly said he'd been close to death during surgery and called his adjusted lifestyle "dogged insolence in the face of mounting opposition to the contrary."

In September 2015, Motörhead had to pull the plug after playing three songs at an Austin, Texas gig. Lemmy walked off saying, "I just can't do it." They had cut a gig short in Utah the previous week. A lung infection was blamed. But Lemmy recovered, and Motörhead finished up a 12-date November-December European tour December 11th in Berlin. They closed the set with "Overkill" and Rammstein's "Pussy." Less than three weeks later, Lemmy all but died with his boots on. Maybe not as close as the Yardbirds' singer Keith Relf (electrocution onstage), but pretty close.

"I never expected it to last this long, obviously," Lemmy told me 27 years ago, as the band's lineup had shifted again. What kept him/them going, Lemmy said, was this: "We aren't appreciated. We're still hungry." They had a new album out: *Sacrifice* was one of their best and the recipient of a five-star review in *Kerrang!*, but it was available in the United States only as an import. Motörhead was once again searching for a U.S. deal.

"We're always the underdog," said Lemmy. "You can always be angry for us. We only got famous for about two years, '80 and '81, and then we went down again. Nowadays, nobody's interested in the music. They don't understand anything that isn't obvious. But if you betray your own music, what else is there left? You go to your grave ashamed."

Lemmy once told *Classic Rock*, "Death is an inevitability, isn't it? You become more aware of that when you get to my age. I don't worry about it. I'm ready for it. When I go, I want to go doing what I do best. If I died tomorrow, I couldn't complain. It's been good."

Like most Motörhead fans, I was in it for the thrill, the fist-pummeling pleasure of that helter-skelter ride. In 1991, I was caught up listening to the *1916* album, digging the fast and familiar, crunching, witty trips through high-spirited low-life celebrations and Lemmy's minute-and-a-half tribute to his pals and rock brethren the Ramones. That was the lickety-split spelling contest of a song that was "R.A.M.O.N.E.S."

I was taken aback, in the most pleasant way possible, as the album wound down, getting to the title track. "1916," is something else — a mournful elegy by Lemmy and cellist James Hoskins detailing the anguish of battle from a grunt's-eye view. The war is World War I, the battle is Sommes, but the song was released when the Gulf War started. I put it up there with the Kinks' "Some Mother's Son" and two written by Eric Bogle: "And the Band Played 'Waltzing Matilda,'' best done by the Pogues, and "The Green Fields of France (No Man's Land)," best done by The Men They Couldn't Hang.

Lemmy told me about the genesis of "1916." "I was watching a documentary and there's all these old guys taken back to the scene of the crime. They're about 90 years old and they're describing it, and this one guy described his friend dying in his arms and he was crying — 70 years later. It's affected him all his life. He says he never has a day go by without dreaming of it. You could say I'm taking advantage of that hardship, or that I'm paying respect to it. I saw it as respect.

"There's something in us that is really stupid and wants to march up and down all day going, 'Yes, sir!' We have it in us to kill on orders. Believe me, I see this generation doing it. There's a war song on all of our albums, about the futility of it."

In the song, Lemmy takes on the voice of a 16-year-old Brit, off to fight the Germans in World War I. Like Neil Young's "Powderfinger," it's sung with great knowledge and yearning, from beyond the grave. Lemmy sang about the fighting life — the brawling and the whoring — a gang of mates all bound together. But, ultimately, what were they bound for? Not glory. They were cannon fodder, the role of the foot soldier.

The ballad, Lemmy explained, was written 18 months before the first Gulf War, adding that the other three guys in the band (Wurzel, Wizzo and Taylor) didn't want it on the album. They didn't play on it and saw it as a radical, very un-Motörhead-like departure. Which it was. Sorta like the Beatles' "Yesterday."

Lemmy's vote prevailed.

"It's an extremely benevolent dictatorship," Lemmy says of the band's dynamics. "Usually, I put it to a vote. Unless I'm so fucking uptight that I want it badly."

I'm glad he was so fucking uptight about that one. This may be heresy to the headbanging faithful, but it's my favorite Motörhead song. ◆

GEORGE CLINTON

AS GEORGE CLINTON AND HIS P-FUNK ALL-STARS prepared to go onstage at the Channel rock club in Boston, I went to order a last pre-show drink. It was April 1984. The line at the bar, not far from the restrooms, was five deep, and people were pushing past to get to the loo. Someone hurried by, knocking me slightly forward into the guy in front of me. Who was Black.

No big deal, right?

And it wasn't, but the guy I bumped turned to face me, and both of us — keenly aware of the potential for a racial blowup — tensed. Maybe he thought I had jostled him on purpose, so I let loose with a string of mea culpas; simultaneously, he did the same thing, thinking somehow maybe *he* was at fault, falling back into me. Then we paused our apologies, realizing how ultra-sensitive and ultra-polite we were both trying to be, so careful not to touch off any conflict between us, or heaven forbid, to spark something larger scale between others. And then we had the biggest laugh and high five. One nation, y'all.

There was some context. On a previous tour, Clinton and company played a hockey arena north of Boston. My *Boston Globe* colleague Steve Morse was there and recalled, "The show was way oversold. I was mugged on the floor by some Black kids who held me down and ripped my wallet right out of my pants. Also, a local resident who was upset with people parking on his property up the street came into the lobby

"People in this country get along pretty good, but a small amount of people have the power to manipulate."

George Clinton

George Clinton onstage at the Capitol City Carnival in Centreville, Virginia, September 2007

brandishing a gun, but he fortunately left. It all ended up being a front-page story." As I recall from the reports, there was some running amok and vandalizing in the neighborhood. And, yeah, it was Black kids doing the damage in white neighborhoods, which of course pissed off the white folks no end. Boston has this history you may have heard about. The busing crisis of the '70s and the ever-unfolding fallout ...

The Channel was technically located in South Boston. On the fringe of it, but still. Of all the white, potentially racist, exclusionary neighborhoods in Boston at the time, Southie was number-one. But on this night, all was copacetic and cool. Any body contact that was made on the dance floor, and there was quite a bit of it, was *welcome* body contact. The crowd was split 50/50 Black and white, truly the most integrated club show I'd ever been to.

Clinton, the ageless funkateer, had that in him, to create an almost mythical melting pot of humanity. The groove was all that mattered to this nation-for-a-night, and we all barked along happily as Clinton went "Bow wow wow yippie yo yippie yeah."

"That is the reason we do what we do," he once told me. "To make it one nation under a groove."

Clinton and I spoke in October 1999, on the verge of the new millennium, when the computers were going to crash and the world would come to either a standstill or an apocalyptic end. (Those were pretty much the only two choices, right? We laugh in hindsight, but the fears then were real.)

So, what did Clinton plan on doing?

Not fretting. In fact, he was going to do what he does best. The Rock and Roll Hall of Famer, the Atomic Dog himself, was planning to be in Fiji, dressed in some outlandish, colorful garb, cavorting about a stage, leading his 19-piece band in a celebratory set of "Give Up the Funk," "Maggot Brain" and "Free Your Mind ... and Your Ass Will Follow." At the time, he'd been working as a professional musician for parts of six decades. We can add two more now. That makes eight.

On the cover of his second solo album, 1983's *You Shouldn't-nuf Bit Fish*, Clinton was pictured wide-eyed and open-mouthed; the text asked, "Inspired madman or complete jackass?" I loved that he could pose the question, entertain both sides and ask us to think about it. Pretty sure he was probably OK with whatever side we came down on.

Basically, Clinton sees dark clouds *and* silver linings. In previous interviews, he'd raised the "planned obsolescence theory of pop," and he did it again when he spoke in 1999. "It's hard to get a record on the radio once you've been around this long. I don't care how good the record is. They have this planned obsolescence concept, and they don't like to break that. But we've always been one to buck the concept and say, 'Let's go out on the road.'"

What was the key to maintaining energy and interest over such a long stretch of time?

"Liking what you're doing," he said, simply. "The energy becomes its own replenisher. If I ever get to the point [of thinking I can't do this anymore] I try to think of the alternative, and the alternative is real hard to think about. What am I gonna do 9-to-5? I go, 'Hell, yeah, I can do this some more.' I love it, it's my job. I get to go to work for play. I feel lucky."

Despite a massive trail of LPs in various guises, and thousands of gigs behind him, Clinton hardly felt too old to rock and roll or, if you will, to funk. "I think it's the other way around. I think this makes you feel younger. Old is relative to how you think and feel. Even other guys in the group who've gotten older, I keep telling them all you have to do is *think* about playing four hours a show and you start losing weight."

At the height of boring white jam-band mania, I wrote something to the effect that P-Funk was the only jam band that mattered, cheekily echoing Epic Records' boast about the Clash. But I meant it. These were deep psych-funk jams worth getting lost in, seeing where the myriad of musicians might take it. I won't say there wasn't downtime, but there were more than enough fireworks to stay the course.

I asked Clinton if his world was getting crazier or saner. "I guess it's probably getting more sane," he said. I believe I detected a whiff of sadness. But then he brightened. "I gotta come up with a new craziness 'cause everybody's catching up [with me]. I'm gonna move it into the sixth dimension!" You believe him. Keep in mind that sanity, especially his version of it, is relative.

Clinton is both a solo artist and the brains behind Parliament, Funkadelic and the P-Funk All-Stars. Parliament began in the mid-'50s as a doo-wop harmony group; Funkadelic was a funk-rock machine that kicked up in the late '60s. They've also performed as Parliament-Funkadelic: think of them as an African-American Clark Kent/ Superman act.

Clinton has been touring for years with the P-Funk All-Stars, comprised of Parliament-Funkadelic players. His record company bio credited Clinton with lead vocals, band referee, galaxy traffic cop. In concert, his band would generally play three to four hours. Part of that time, Clinton is the visible ringleader. Other times, he says, "I go out in the audience and check it out for myself. Then, I go 'Damn, it's fun being up there,' and I go back onstage."

He also goes offstage to rest or watch, whatever. At one show in a big Boston club, I had backstage access, so I watched some of the gig side-stage. There was, as always, lots of action and hijinks out in front, but I couldn't spot Clinton. Not that it mattered. His bandmates were getting down and acting up. Turns out Clinton was standing behind me. He came up and we talked a bit, leaving the merry mayhem to others for a little longer before he rejoined the fray.

Clinton's music has been a favorite source of sampling by hip-hoppers; his funk style is the blueprint for virtually anyone out there playing in that field. While Clinton has always enjoyed being borderline naughty — judging from his music, two of Clinton's primary interests are sex and laughter, ideally combined — he's nowhere near as nasty as some of the rappers who've used his tracks. And though he feels spiritually close to the hip-hop generation ("They're the clones I was talking about [on *The Clones of Dr. Funkenstein* album]; basically, they're using the same music, remixed and turned around and made a brand-new, legitimate thing out of it"), Clinton doesn't express any of their anger or violence.

Clinton appreciates the artists who've sampled his music, a long list that includes De La Soul, Digital Underground, A Tribe Called Quest, Ice Cube, Redman, Dr. Dre, Bobby Brown, Public Enemy, Yo-Yo, Trey Lewd, Eric B and Rakim, Eazy-E and N.W.A. "I love the fact that they do that. They help keep us alive. Otherwise, we wouldn't be around."

What concerns him is that hip-hop [in that era was] "a male-dominated thing. It's a party thing, but it's not as universal without the girls and everything. It's like the girls get left out. The other thing that's lacking in the hip-hop world is the musicians type of vibe. Mainly, hip-hop, to me, is like a newspaper, almost like warfare, trying to get the news out."

One thing he shares with many rappers is frustration about American life. In 1993, he promised to air some of his grievances on *Hey Man ... Smell My Finger,* a solo album then in the works. I remarked that the title sounds a tad rude.

"Rude?!" says Clinton, with a laugh. "That's pretty mild from me. It's basically reflective of some of the things going on in the news today. Clinton. The New World Order. I call it the New World Odor: Something stinks. Right now, the vibe is somebody trying to turn everybody against everybody else."

There was another Clinton in the White House at the time, so I asked if he had any attendant hope for the new president who shares his surname, especially after 12 years of Reagan-Bush.

"I'm optimistic with him trying to do right, but I'm really afraid somebody's gonna try to help him do wrong," says the funkier Clinton. "I've got a feeling, like the *Mission: Impossible*-type trips. It happened with Carter — big-time business laying off a lot of people, making whoever's in there look like shit. This time, instead of laying them off, there's gonna be all this terrorist stuff that's been happening around the rest of the world.

"To me, we got the most devious terrorists in the world with the CIA. All of a sudden, this country is going crazy. We have to really watch out we're not forced into gay-and-straight riots, anti- and pro-abortion riots, Black-and-white riots. People themselves get along pretty good, but I think we have a lot of help when it comes to the media, particularly a small amount of people who have the power to manipulate. All you do is press one or two buttons and you have a race riot. I'm suspicious anyway, but somebody tries to blow up the World Trade Center, and you get all these things going ... it's like somebody's trying to spike the punch."

But for all that, Clinton says, "I never liked to write a song that didn't come out positive. I know bad shit exists, but I'm always trying to make 'em end positive. It's the easiest thing in the world to write a sad song, but to me that's like tippin' the concept. It works good, but there's enough blues singers."

His songs can be silly; they can be profound; they can be a mix of the two. Stuff like "Do Fries Go With That Shake," "Mothership Connection," "Atomic Dog," "(Not Just) Knee Deep," "Bop Gun," "Flash Light," "Maggot Brain," "One Nation Under a Groove," "Cosmic Slop" and, perhaps, that theme song, "Free Your Mind ... and Your Ass Will Follow."

I particularly love the "Fries" song. Clinton and company treat that fast-food flirt like it's the most important query in the world. "It has to be funny," Clinton says. "If it was not funny, you would go crazy for real and you would end up as fucked up as the people you're singing about. You would be so pissed off you would end up as bad as they are."

A P-Funk set, according to Clinton, is "Whatever we can get to 'til they unplug us." As the chant goes, "Ain't no party like a P-Funk party / 'Cos a P-Funk party don't stop!" And the party does go on. Value for money. "I figure one and a half hours is pretty much what anybody else would give you, we give you the basic stuff, stuff you know. That is for the people. Then we play another two hours, like George Clinton bonus tracks, and we are going to do whatever we want here. That is for us. We sing anything we feel like singing. If you make it to the last hour, you really want to be there. And it's really good."

Clinton knows in some ways he's asking a lot of his band and his audience. "Our attention span is not geared for three hours. People have to get up, go to work. We have to trick 'em into staying for a good time." (I did leave one P-Funk show before it ended. I felt bad for doing so, but I was exhausted at the three-hour mark.)

We got to talking about *Dope Dogs*, a 1995 album that has a lot of nefarious characters; most of the songs use dogs both as central characters and metaphors for the human condition. Why dogs? "Because we basically are animals ourselves. We tend to think that [being human] separates us from that. Dogs are supposed to be our best friends, but we also use them as the epitome of what you wanna do to somebody when you don't like 'em: you dog 'em out. It's a weird relationship we have with dogs. Some people love 'em to death, spend a fortune on 'em to keep 'em alive and bury them richly. Some people eat 'em, a weird thing to do with man's best friend. When I saw people use them as drug dogs, after they're done using them ... they're so strung out from their habits. They have dogs in laboratories where they test chemicals."

For all the nasty situations woven into the songs, Clinton leaves you feeling uplifted. "To me, everything will be all right by Thursday. That's what I always tell myself."

The next time we connected, in March 2003, he was calling from Atlanta. The band was headed to the Palladium in Worcester, Massachusetts.

How many P-Funkateers are with you this time? He doesn't know. Yells to an assistant. He's told 24, which is on the upper end of this collective bunch of lunatics, where the minimum number is 18. It sounds exhausting — the logistics, the transportation and all that — and Clinton concedes it is taxing. But once everyone's onstage all that goes away.

No thoughts of retirement? "Retire from what? I don't know what that means. I'm gonna do this 'til I can't do it no more. I love fishing, but I don't want to fish that much."

Long before hip-hop crossed over to a white audience, Clinton and company crossed that bridge, and did it without alienating their core constituency. One nation under a groove, as the song goes. "We very seldom have incidents," he says. "There can be all kinds of combinations of age, race, height, gender. And we're open to the very last second figuring out what people want us to play. Like we were playing in Aspen to all these white inheritance kids who heard we're funky and nasty, and they were ten times nastier than us. They use us as an excuse to have a good time. I enjoy it myself. I go out there, I start dancing, get soaking wet."

Under Clinton's command, funk, rock, soul and psychedelia collide gloriously. There's comedy, there's intensity, there's absurdity, there's politics. And there's the wild man with the multi-colored hair (or hair extensions) at the center of it all, prompting me to ask what colors he was sporting these days. Again, he's gotta ask somebody because, he says, "I'm colorblind." He gets his answer: "Blue, red and black. And gray!"

P-Funk and its various offshoots and spinoffs have given us glorious slabs of funk, from "Maggot Brain" to "(Not Just) Knee Deep." There have been barbed political jabs, like in *America Eats Its Young* (1972) and *The Electric Spanking of War Babies* (1981). In 2003, George W. Bush had decided to follow bad advice (or be willingly misled) and attacked Iraq, believing it was developing nukes.

"We keep telling ourselves we're going to help the world," Clinton says, "and then we go fuck 'em."

So, what is P-Funk's role in this crazy-ass world?

"To make you think. You don't have to be a reactionary. I don't preach, but I'm thinking about something I hope comes out [in the show]. At the same time, we're dancing."

Clinton had spent four years trying to put together an album he was calling *The C Conspiracy*. The theme? "Going overboard with conspiracy. People have made 'liberal' sound like a bad word. I'm trying to make it a *real bad* word — that is, a word to be proud of." (That album actually never came out; several tracks made it onto disc elsewhere.)

In 1993, Clinton and the P-Funk All-Stars performed with Red Hot Chili Peppers on the *Grammy Awards* before a worldwide audience of a billion. It was hard not to think that the inmates had taken over the asylum. The world saw Clinton sporting blue-and-yellow dreadlocks and an amazing technicolor dreamcoat, P-Funk vocalist Garry Shider in an oversized diaper with balloons attached to his backside, Peppers singer Anthony Kiedis in a mutated geisha gown and an Indian headdress, other Peppers in faux-sackcloth and one P-Funk guy all gussied up for a white wedding.

The world heard the Peppers' pop-funk hit "Give It Away" segued into Clinton's 1978 anthem "One Nation Under a Groove." (Clinton produced the Chili Peppers' second album, *Freaky Styley*, in 1985.) It was hilarious, but it was also transcendent. It looked like lunacy, but it made a musical-cum-racial statement — and it was a whole lot funkier than "We Are the World" or "Ebony & Ivory."

"One nation is a reality," says Clinton, of the song and the concept. "To be able to do 'One Nation Under a Groove' after the rhetoric of 'Give It Away' — that's a lot of good-time vibe, letting everybody realize that no matter how chaotic it looked, it's tight; we're close. Anthony was the one who suggested we do 'One Nation.' To me, the fact that we were out there doing it together represented something. It choked people up. The vibe was so thorough, the music was so hard, everybody froze in their chairs until it was over, but then everybody went crazy. When it was over, [I went] 'Damn, that was neat!'"◆

"All instruments, including synths, are not more or less than crutches for an artist to express himself."

Edgar Froese

Edgar Froese and Linda Spa of Tangerine Dream

PHOTOGRAPH BY ROZA YARCHUN (SUB-ROZA)

EDGAR FROESE
& TANGERINE DREAM

THE GUYS IN TANGERINE DREAM — that would be leader Edgar Froese, plus more than 20 others over the decades — always gave us the silent treatment in concert. Never spoke much (if at all), and not a word when I saw them. No hellos, no goodbyes. No band or song introductions, no humorous chit-chat. Certainly no "We're happy to be in [your city here]! [Your city again] fans are the best!"

Was it a purposeful statement of remoteness or distance? Were they, like their countrymen and techno peers in Kraftwerk, trying to present themselves as more machine than man? Or a melding of the two?

I asked Froese about it back in 2012, which would, sadly, turn out to be the last time I saw Tangerine Dream in concert. (He died three years later from a pulmonary embolism.)

No distancing intention at all, Froese said. "We are fan-friendly and that's why we don't talk during the sets. What would be necessary to say? In my view, a spoken language is always a kind of a lower octave against the music. Also, people who start talking about music try to explain the unexplainable. The best way of communicating is the freedom for everyone to step in and out of your own score of life."

Simply put, music sometimes best expresses the inexpressible. Or gives you a time-out from feeling you have to articulate something. Just float along and let that score take over. Dream on.

As stoic and taciturn as he was onstage, Froese was not at all averse to talking offstage. In fact, I got the feeling he relished a good exchange of ideas, about music and other things. His English, like many Germans, was excellent. I interviewed him by phone several times from the '80s into the 21st century and met him in person once, after that 2012 show at Boston's House of Blues. It was one of the most transfixing gigs I've ever been to. I'll even go to that overused rock-crit word "mesmerizing." Tangerine Dream took you to another (better) world, at least in your head.

Here's how Froese put it when we talked: "Tangerine Dream is just there to tickle the ears of those who can imagine changing their consciousness. Saving the world and dancing the bad vibes away for just one night we would leave to Bruce Springsteen and others from the straight rock league."

It was about the synths and sequencers; but it wasn't all about those synths and sequencers. "Even in the old analog days," said Froese, "the machine didn't do anything. But people didn't know it. There was a preconception to machinery, to computers, and the preconception said quite clearly, 'You just have to look at it and the work gets done.' That's ridiculous. All instruments, including synths, are not more or less than crutches for an artist to express himself. Defining those instruments in categories like 'robots' and 'human' just shows how little the common music consumer has understood about what sounds really are."

The band did a *Phaedra Farewell* tour in the spring and summer of 2014 and captured it on a three-CD set. Their website promised it was not goodbye forever, more a move away from concert tours, that they would still do one-offs. There have been two albums since Froese's death: *Quantum Gate* in 2017 and *Raum* in 2022. Froese's son Jerome was but is no longer in the group; Edgar's widow, the painter Bianca Froese-Acquaye, manages Tangerine Dream, which consists of Thorsten Quaeschning and Paul Frick (both manning synths, etc.) and string player (violin, viola, cello) and synthesist Hoshiko Yamane.

Founded in 1967, Tangerine Dream has been thought to be in the forefront (or well up in the mix) of — you name it — krautrock, prog, electronic, techno, trance, ambient, new age. Though the music has a pulse (or pulses), TD was never a dance band and had negligible effect on EDM. When I saw them in 2012, I wished the EDM kids could experience the rushing melodic waves and crisscrossing rhythms, but of course they didn't, Edgar being "old" (what could they possibly gain?) and the crowd being both smallish and over 40.

I once asked Froese about the EDM kids. "I listen to a lot of electro youngsters," he said. "Some are on a very creative level and others maybe should work on something else. But here we are talking about subjective opinions. Every musician, every artist, is learning from other artists. My master was J.S. Bach, even if that's not that obvious in all of the TD sequences, but it's true. I am not proud; I am just filtering what runs as an inspiration through my system. That exactly is what the young musicians do by listening to the old or newer TD stuff. That is more than correct. I am just proud that life has given me the chance to be part of such a great, creative family of musicians."

Tangerine Dream released more than 300 albums. Froese thought that included 64 soundtracks, the best-known among them being *Sorcerer, Thief* and *Risky Business.* I have long thought my real life — anyone's real life — would be better if accompanied by a TD soundtrack. In addition, he made more than 20 solo albums. Truly, he was the Stephen King of electronic music. (Tangerine Dream scored the first film made from King's *Firestarter.*) What differentiates an Edgar Froese disc from a TD one?

"Ten fingers against 40 fingers," Froese said. "The truth is that you never can satisfy every member within a band with your concept, composition and, later, performance ideas. Working with others on a fair basis means democracy instead of dictatorship. Even with your best ideas you have to listen to what your colleagues may have to say — so, finally, your composition has to convince others as well as it has to reflect your own musical identity. On a level of pure solo work, you are only responsible to yourself. It sounds easier but it's sometimes even harder."

Soundtracking, which became big business, entered their world in 1977. "When we first came to Hollywood and started scoring, we didn't know anything about the business," said Froese. "[*Sorcerer* director] Bill Friedkin gave us the fantastic chance to support our career in a way we had never dreamed of. Scoring is hard and professional teamwork. You have to understand the logic and logistics of how sound and a picture is combined in order to reach a certain effect. Often the people in the theater just subconsciously realize that there is a score which has a great influence on the ongoing movie sequence. It's a great learning process working for pictures and understanding the philosophy of directors, producers and forecasting musically the reaction of the audience."

I thought Tangerine Dream's *Sorcerer* music (1982), particularly the closing "Betrayal (Sorcerer's Theme)," brought an intense B-movie up to an even more intense A-level.

Tangerine Dream's sound evolved over time. Froese looked at it this way: "As a kid, life is a complete mystery to you on each and every level. Your perspectives on the world are endless. There is a horizon, the final line far away, but it's not there for you; it's only there for others. Your drive and energy to look behind every hidden curtain is nearly endless. Later, when the disharmonious stupidity of the business forces you to make compromises, it definitely changes quite a few of such unlimited perspectives. Also, you are getting older, becoming an adult in knowledge and experience. That changes your consciousness and therefore life philosophy. So, each phase in musical life has its highs and lows — it just matters if the confidence you have in what you originally wanted to do is strong enough in order to keep your basic identity. I'm pretty convinced that I worked hard enough to let this originality shine through to all of TD's work.

"What was a musical revolution 30 years ago is a classic today. That's what is so adventurous about arts — to be able to express yourself in the given moment."

Steve Wilson of Porcupine Tree has called Tangerine Dream's 1972 album *Zeit* his favorite disc ever. The British band Kasabian named them as "spiritual influences." The late English DJ John Peel said, "They have made the music the star of the show, not the musicians and not the means of the music. A new creative energy."

Many players and guests have passed through the TD portals over the years. Drummer Klaus Schulze was there in the early days. Other key players included Christopher Franke, Peter Baumann and Johannes Schmoelling. Tangerine Dream might have seemed to be, at least to an outsider, Froese plus whomever else he brought on board.

I asked Froese his thoughts on the group's fluid lineup. "As a man who never looks back, I think of my comrades on this long way with respect and often good memories. Not all of them have been masters of a funny entertainment league, but all of them have left their colors to the band. But it would have been impossible to go with the same people for more than 45 years and keep on talking about the good old days at the war, front-firing sound missiles into the nowhere. Silly. Each new idea needs a form to transport it — that's why I love to work with professional newbies."

Tangerine Dream first made it to vinyl in 1970 with *Electronic Meditation*. Early efforts were experimental, jarring and avant-garde, much like the side-long suites Pink Floyd was creating at the time. The band didn't ensnare me until the live album *Ricochet* and its third studio release, *Stratosfear*, both in 1976. It was, at times, scary music. Brooding, Foreboding. All was not well out there.

Here's how Froese viewed the creative process and journey. "Think about leaving a safe road where everything is signposted and all communication works and is approved by authorities and finally by law. You just make a U-turn and drive straight into a jungle in which you never have been before. Everything can happen within a few minutes. You just follow the law of causality: If your next turn is false or stupid because of the inexperienced situation in general, you can't blame anyone except yourself. Also, because it's your idea, you will get all the shit [from] your colleagues who had a different opinion. That's often horrifying."

In 2011, Froese talked to the *Washington Post* about the band's early, stormy work. "It was wild," he said. "An experiment against everything. Maybe it had the same root that punk came from. You stand up and you're against everything — the establishment, some social movements, tastes in music, the mainstream. And you say, 'Okay, let's turn everything upside down and start again.'"

I asked if, in 2012, that spirit still coursed through him.

"We have maybe been the first electric punks in history in 1970," Froese said. "But besides the wilderness and fight against the old-fashioned ideals of the establishment myself had by founding the band in 1967, the basic idea to go with a great number of colleagues all the way from the absolute chaos to the highest level of perfection in studio work and life performances — that was the great idea behind TD."

In the '90s, though, Tangerine Dream was in a more mellifluous place. When I reviewed them in 1992 for the *Boston Globe*, things had shifted. I wrote this:

> The music throbs, pulses and percolates, but there's not much implicit terror in this year's model, which played an oft-mesmerizing, nearly three-hour show at Berklee Performance Center. Tangerine Dream is a lot warmer now. It's a sensual sonic bath. You could shut your eyes and dream your own dream or watch the band ply its trade in the chemical smoke and follow the precise laser-lighting. None of it — the music or the lighting — was particularly jarring, at least, not in the old-style sense. Though

> they've recorded 50-some-odd albums, Tangerine Dream is not a band to look back; nine of the songs were unrecorded and unreleased. The bulk of the others came from *Rockoon* and *Canyon Dreams.*
>
> The rich, layered, synth-based rhythms and melodies generated by Linda Spa and the Froeses, Edgar and his son Jerome, flowed purposefully, pleasantly, like a series of stones being tossed in a pond and observing the overlapping ripple effect. To this band, songs are journeys, simultaneously bumpy and restful. Neat things enter along the way, many of which, like the percussion and distant chant-like sounds, are programmed into the synths. In songs like "Homeless" and "Rockoon" — which closed the first and second sets last night — there was much more grandeur than tension.

I am glad I didn't use the term "new age." (Tangerine Dream notched five consecutive Grammy nominations in that category during the '90s.) Years later, when I asked Froese about that spurious category — good for Enya maybe, not so much for TD — he said, cryptically, "There are so many new ages blown into the atmosphere by false prophets that it's like an inflation for the good spirits. But where is the new aspect — especially in music? Where are the knob nerds who promised to have the electric key to paradise?"

The latter-day Froese used the term "arrogant" to describe the early days of Tangerine Dream. "We thought we were far ahead of our time. We were using instruments most people didn't even know about." At that point, too, Froese expressed a certain disdain for musicians who burrowed deeply into the dissonant end of the avant-garde. "It's so easy to do," he said. "A computer offers you so many possibilities, so you drift away and say, 'OK, I'm going to live in my little tower and know I'm a genius and the rest of the world is very idiotic and stupid, so I live on my own and I make a record and nail it on the wall and look at it.' That's bullshit!"

We discussed music, perseverance and mortality. He was 68 when we last spoke. "If you are always concerned that you will beat Methuselah — aiming at 120! — 68 is just half-way through. A calendar is set up by those folks staring the whole day and watching their skin shrinking. So, seriously, if you are working on an art form which is timeless you will participate even through body and mind.

"It always depends from looking forward or backwards. Most humans after they have reached a certain age are just looking backwards. But that's the cow's business, always masticating the same grass and hay a hundred times — and I am not a cow."

What then is the key to keeping the spirit alive?

"As a child," Froese said, "I always felt strange, born into a jailhouse with no key available. I needed 68 years to work my way through the brick wall — now in the next 60 years I will be sending sound files not heard before. You will be experiencing how music sounds outside the jail."

And then I posed this: They called James Brown the godfather of funk and Elvis the king of rock and roll. Was there any particular title he'd like in terms of synth-rock?

"When I am gone, they should search for the mystery of the dark candle in the big white room."

On January 20, 2015 that search began. Jerome Froese posted, "The Captain has left the ship. I'm very sorry to inform you that my father Edgar Froese passed away. And as you already know: Life plays no encores. Rest in peace, Edgar. You will be sadly missed."

And on the Tangerine Dream website: "Edgar once said, 'There is no death, there is just a change of our cosmic address.' Edgar, this is a little comfort to us." ◆

"I no longer have a problem with how many Bob Dylan songs I sing in a set. I'll sing all I want."

Joan Baez

Joan Baez with the author, Boston, 2018

PHOTOGRAPH BY ROZA YARCHUN (SUB-ROZA)

JOAN BAEZ

THE FIRST TIME I SAW Joan Baez she was part of Bob Dylan's Rolling Thunder Revue, November 27, 1975 at the Bangor Auditorium in Maine. I was a sophomore in college and me and my friends slept out on a frosty night in front of the venue to buy 15th row tickets. One of my better decisions — despite the frozen kidneys. Seriously. That concert remains in my Top 10.

The last time was in Boston at the Boch Wang Theatre: September 15, 2018. It was a lovely show, part of her *Fare Thee Well* tour. I laughed when she talked about how anal she used to be about anybody making noise in her Cambridge coffeehouse days and was making up for that by saying "stupid shit" onstage now.

When I interviewed her by phone a few weeks earlier, she said to come backstage after the show for a hello. So, we met up, and the first thing I do is to deadpan compliment her slowed-down and heartfelt cover of Judas Priest's "Diamonds and Rust." There might have been a flicker of "This guy's an idiot" in her eyes, but I think she got the joke pretty quick. Onstage, after playing it, she had said, "If you're gonna write one hit in your lifetime it might as well be that one."

"I listened to [the Judas Priest version] the other day 'cause it popped up," she told me. "I love it. I *love* it. Of course, I don't write 'cover' kind of songs so having that covered was a big thrill for me."

I suggested that, aside from bringing her song to an audience that may never have heard of her, the English metal dudes may have earned her a bit of cash. "I haven't thought about it," she said. "I'll have to check."

The audiences that come to see Baez, naturally enough, love what they're getting — that voice, those songs and more than a soupçon of liberal politics. If it can be said that liberal performers sing to liberal audiences, making it an echo chamber, there is also, I think, to some extent, the validation and sense of community.

"Exactly," Baez says. "So, you're singing to the choir? You bet I'm singing to the choir; those are the ones who start to march."

As to the *Fare Thee Well Tour*, make no mistake: it isn't that Baez doesn't love what she does. Although she's had to make alterations in her singing and admits she can't hit some of the notes she used to, it's not because her voice has failed her. No, the reason Baez undertook a farewell tour in the fall of 2018 had everything to do with the grind of touring at 77.

Asked about hanging up her guitar, Baez laughs and says, "It's more me hanging up the bus. It's more the extended get-up-in-the-morning, get-on-the-bus and go-to-the-show. Sometimes you get very tired. I love the new album [*Whistle Down the Wind*] and I love the concerts — but it's taxing."

Whistle Down the Wind — the title track is a Tom Waits song — is her first album in a decade and has charted higher than anything she's done since 1975's *Diamonds & Rust*.

Before we talked on the phone, I thought, by way of introduction, to tell her that we had met very briefly backstage at the *Newport Folk Festival* in 1995.

"I didn't do anything untoward?" she asked. No, I said, but honestly, I don't recall you being in the best of moods. A bit curt, abrupt.

"Oh, I'm horrible when I'm not in a good mood. Not anymore, but I was. It's like 'Don't interrupt the queen,' right?"

Baez has been on the folk scene — sometimes crossing over into the pop world — since playing *Newport* in 1959 ("at the beginning of time, before they made guitars," she once joked). Baez recorded her eponymous debut album the following year and became one of the '60s musical icons of activism alongside her one-time boyfriend Bob Dylan. While she does write songs, she's best known as an interpreter, bringing others' music to higher public awareness. In 1971, she scored her only Top 10 hit single with the Band's "The Night They Drove Old Dixie Down."

Dylan still plays a part in Baez's life — his music, not him personally — and liberal activism remains very much at her core. She's a painter as well and, in 2017, showed portraits of Martin Luther King Junior, her ex-husband David Harris (who died in 2023), Congressman John Lewis, Harry Belafonte, Václav Havel, herself and, yes, Dylan at an exhibit called *Mischief Makers* in San Francisco.

When Baez was inducted into the Rock and Roll Hall of Fame in 2017, there were some who said, "Joan Baez? Rock and roll? Isn't she a folksinger?" Baez gets that and says her reaction to the induction "was either 'What am *I* doing here?' or 'Why the fuck did they wait so long?' Somewhere in between those."

Critics and fans have called Baez's voice "angelic." Asked if she concurred, Baez says, "When I was younger, I can honestly say yes. I certainly don't anymore." She has been upfront about her voice, the changes it has gone through, the work she's had to do. "The vocal cords are just difficult," Baez explains. "If you first saw me at *Newport* [in the '60s] I didn't know what a vocal coach was from a hole in the ground. Then, I always had this image of myself as this Miss Natural Talent so I'm sure I waited to get help until way too long, and that hasn't helped the decline of the muscle. But I'm happy with what I have."

When she was 35, "someone finally convinced me to get down off my high horse and go see a vocal coach because things weren't happening the way I wanted them to happen. I've done it ever since. The first one was classically trained and just wonderful and opened up a whole other toolbox for me. Then he passed on and I did see several other people. About six years ago I was thinking, 'Oh boy, this is the end, I can't pull this together' and [I saw] an ear-nose-and-throat guy. [I thought] maybe there's something interfering with whatever — warts on my chin or something. He said, 'No, everything is fine.' And I said, 'So, this is it for 71?' and he said, 'This is perfect for 71.' I said, 'I'm going to shoot myself,' and he said, 'Would you like to see my vocal therapist?' I said, 'Sure.' This woman was young and she's amazing and I see her once every three or four months. The first three sessions she gave me this amazing amount of tools that I didn't know about, that I didn't have, and [my voice] was recognizably different by the time I was on the road later. I'm comfortable and happy. I'm not trying to reach notes that I can't reach anymore and I'm not grieving about it. I'm working on what I have, and I like it a lot."

On tour, Baez is backed by multi-instrumentalist Dirk Powell, percussionist Gabriel Harris (her son) and singer Grace Stumberg, who started as Baez's personal assistant in 2011 but soon graduated to backup singer. "Grace is young. brilliant and fun," Baez says. "I had to give up certain songs I hated giving up and one of them was 'Forever Young.' My soundman said, 'Why don't you let her take the high note?' So, we made this beautiful duet out of it. No one's going to care who's taking that high note. It came out brilliantly."

Baez has been including about half-a-dozen Dylan songs in her concerts. Since she brought up "Forever Young," I risk her "Time Rag" wrath by asking about Bob. (She had written "Time Rag" after a *Time* reporter who interviewed made the piece all about Dylan.) "I don't have that anymore," she says with a laugh. Playing Dylan's songs is "just the easiest, the most fun. In a way, it's the closest thing we have to a movement when you sing [one of Dylan's anthems]. There's such a response from the public and such a response from me. It comes from down in my gut somewhere. After all the BS over the years between me and Bob — I never knew how he felt."

Frankly, Baez breathes life into these songs which people haven't heard sung live this way in some time. The ones Dylan hasn't retired still don't come close to versions people recognize. Baez brings them back home.

"That's true," she says, recalling that a young student from Parkland [Florida site of a 2018 school massacre] sang "The Times They Are A-Changin'" at a kids' march. I thought 'Was that the only thing they could find?' Because the youth at this point does not have an anthem that really competes with that in any way shape or form. That tells us a lot about those songs ... Since I love doing those songs and no longer have a problem with how many Bob Dylan songs I sing in a set, I'll sing all I want."

Painting two Dylan portraits recently led her to a better place about the man she once ruefully called a ghost. "By the second portrait, I put on all his music randomly and I just cried. I thought 'Good lord, what am I carping about? I got to *know* this guy. I got to *sing* with this guy." Any stuff that was still left vanished. Anything that was resentful or stupid just went. What a treat was that."

One of the best tracks on *Whistle Down the Wind* is her version of Antony [now Anohni] and the Johnsons' "Another World," whose lyrics mourn the decline and death of nature, the world as we know it. "It's so moving, and the darkness is, unfortunately, something that I relate to with every fiber in my body," says Baez. "Do I think we have long on this Earth? Not really. Do I think my granddaughter's going to have a future? Not really. And it's because of the level of politics, which is unimaginable and is taking us down. [Although] I think we're going to be taken down faster than that by global warming."

Yet, Baez tries to find some sort of equilibrium between that sense of darkness and the idealism which fans ascribe to her. "You have to, or I wouldn't bother getting up — and some mornings I don't. But I think the trick right now is the we-shall-overcome-this has to be sort of like the Parkland kids. They know what it is they want to overcome. Now, that's a possibility. And I think they get our support. And with the people who are doing work with refugees all over the world. You pick your level of success and [try to] live up to it. You have to overcome that much, just to think in the broad sense and in the long sense."

Music and politics remain intertwined in Baez's life and music. Her take on the state of politics in 2018? "I think as long as we maintain a high bar of deniability and have practically no expectations, they are a part of all of our lives in a way they never have been before," Baez says.

Meaning?

"A deniability of the state of politics, starting in this country and the people who've picked it up around the world. We're sort of the leadership of bullies — that's the mildest thing to say. I don't know what will happen in the states now, I'm going to hopefully put voting [registration] booths/tables in the lobbies. Mind you, it's not my normal instinct to say, 'Everybody go vote,' but at the moment" — she laughs slightly — "I would suggest people go and vote for a turnip before they go and vote for what would continue this death parade we're on."

I first became aware of Baez's music and public image in the late 1960s, and one of the things I remember is seeing her — well, a caricature of her — in the funny pages. Right-wing cartoonist Al Capp had a character in his *L'il Abner* strip called Joanie Phoanie.

Capp actually lived not far from where Baez performed in Cambridge. In her early days, she played the tiny Harvard Square folk club Passim with her sister Mimi and Mimi's husband Richard Fariña.

Baez's recollection of Joanie Phoanie might make for a laugh now, but then? Did it hurt? "No," Baez says. "I had two things. One, was the people around me saying, 'You can't let him get away with that.' In my head, a voice was saying, 'Why not?' I didn't really care. But the influence from the outside was really stronger, and I got myself all irate about it, but it was not a big deal for me. I felt that my manager had been more insulted than I had: they depicted him as a money-grubbing Jew."

Well, when the other side goes after you …

"You've done something right." ◆

K.D. LANG

K.D. LANG IS CURLED UP ON A COUCH, barefoot and dressed in baggy black athletic garb. We're in a New York hotel suite in the autumn of 1995, and she's pondering the nature of the sensual, romantic songs she and longtime collaborator Ben Mink have penned for her upcoming album, *All You Can Eat.* There's a whole lotta love going on here. Warm love. Steamy love.

Are listeners meant to assume that the first-person voice lang uses is her? That they're not "character" songs?

"Oh, no," she says firmly. "The 'I' is totally me. They're all autobiographical. They're all from my experiences, and they're all my feelings."

Then might we infer that lang is in love?

"No, I'm not in love," she says. "And it wasn't written for any person in particular. I can't offer you some great love story or some terrible love story."

So, she is ... available?

"Yeah, I'm available."

Perhaps, I say, a nation of lesbian hearts may be set aflutter as that news breaks.

"OK," she amends with a laugh, clarifying a bit. "I'm single, but I'm not available at the moment. I'm taking a break."

Four years ago, lang stole everyone's heart. The Canadian singer-songwriter had just burst out of the hip "new country" clique and into the pop mainstream with her

"I didn't want to be Reba McEntire or Randy Travis.
I wanted to be a rebel."

k.d. lang

---

k.d. lang sings at the Cambridge (UK) Folk Festival, August 2008

album *Ingenue* and the hit single "Constant Craving." She shed country music for a more languid, lush pop style: more torch, less twang. If Patsy Cline had been her early model, Edith Piaf, Julie London and Peggy Lee had joined her.

Lang also came out of the closet and into prominence as a singer, stylist and star who happened to be a lesbian — shocking no one — but, more shockingly, also a Lawrence Welk fan. She teased her audience with that in concert, by teetering up to the L-word. "There's something pent-up deep inside of me," she said at Boston's Wang Center, bringing a hush to the crowd. "I'm gonna tell you. I ... am ... a ... Lawrence Welk fan."

Whoosh! Soap bubbles rose up from the drum riser, stars lit up the black backing scrim and lang swirled gracefully as she crooned "Miss Chatelaine" against the rich tapestry woven by her 10-piece band. The audience smiled and swooned.

These transitions seemed pretty painless for the Canadian. The country music establishment was never too comfortable with her, as a prominent vegetarian, activist for People for the Ethical Treatment of Animals and country singer with an un-country-like edge.

"In reality, I never wanted acceptance there, because that would have meant I was a part of the mainstream of what I hated about country. Because I always loved the people that were more on the outskirts, anyway. I mean, I have great respect for Patsy [Cline] and Tammy [Wynette] and George [Jones] and Lefty [Frizzell], but really, I didn't want to be Reba McEntire or Randy Travis because that would have meant I was doing something too accessible. I wanted to be a rebel."

She came out in an interview with the *Advocate*, the national gay and lesbian magazine, after tiring of the nod-and-a-wink "androgynous" references and various code words. As with the Indigo Girls and Melissa Etheridge, who came out later, her "secret" wasn't exactly a surprise to anyone who'd seen her. And it had no adverse effect. Her straight fans didn't give a hoot; gay and lesbian fans supported her honesty and courage.

Lang hasn't been completely out of the loop since 1992. She recorded songs for the soundtrack of the long-delayed movie *Even Cowgirls Get the Blues*. The film, released last year, stiffed; the album, though it went gold, was not considered a huge success.

"It was almost a selfish project. I think the failure was fantastic for me. Because I think you start to believe the hype. You start to believe anything you do is going to be a hit: 'I'm so great any piece of music I put out is going to be revered.' But in the back of my mind, no matter what I do, [I know] I'm going to be criticized because I've had success."

She acted in the independent film *Salmonberries*, shedding her clothes for the role. "Naked is naked," she says of the experience. "I don't think anyone is completely comfortable [doing that], but I manage to soothe myself in thinking it's a refreshing thing to see someone zaftig naked on film. I finally had myself at this point of understanding that it was probably very, very good for my body image to do it. To step through that boundary and just go, 'This is my body, the body I've had for 30 years.'"

She also spent some time in Los Angeles and in the limelight. Life in the fast lane?

"Living in Hollywood ... going to premieres ... getting into the designer thing. I was faced, somehow, after *Ingenue*, with standing in front of this smorgasbord, and I had all these options and temptations and all of these people going, 'Oh, you're great! Wear my clothes! Come to this opening! Go out with me because I'm beautiful!' And you have all this stuff laid right out in front of you and, I have to admit, I went into it, I think, because you have to. I had to. I had to experience it to know that I really don't belong there.

"I'm not judging it," lang continues, "and I'm not saying it's not great, because it's art and everybody's just doing their thing. I'm just saying I don't feel that it enhanced me as an artist and that it actually detracted from my focus of why I'm a singer. [Fame] is a byproduct of what is really happening. And what's happening is I have to create."

So, L.A. was a phase? "It was an experience. I think it was something I had to go through, and I'm not saying I'm not going to do it again. It's like a drug, when you go, 'You know, I've always kind of wondered what heroin was like,' and you try it, and sometimes you get out and sometimes you do it again."

Her Los Angeles experience is where the *All You Can Eat* album title came from — out of the artist-as-celebrity syndrome. "Some people can eat all the fried food and some people can eat all the doughnuts and some people can eat all the pasta. But it's really up to you, because no one is going to tell you what's right and wrong. That it's a gray, fucking mess now. There's nowhere to turn for truth and for direction. There are no role models. There is no truth. There is no religion. There is no justice system. It's all internal."

lang came back down to earth at her farm in Vancouver, British Columbia, reconnecting with old friends. "They knew me before I was famous," she says, "and it's not like I was coming back across the track, but I was. It's clichéd, but it's true. I mean, they treated me how they treated me before, so the foundation of the relationship wasn't that I was famous, or wasn't that I was rich, or wasn't that I had anything to offer them."

How, in lang's position, can you meet new people and trust them?

"I have to say, right now, that I don't. Which is a direct conflict of my basic nature. I grew up in Nowhereville, Canada, and my parents dragged me to Sunday school every week, so I really have a foundation of basic values. And I really, really believed in people. And I've had some people burn me. So now I'm developing this sort of misanthropy and it's sort of ... sad, but realistic."

That cynicism doesn't enter her music. "No, because music comes from a much purer place. I am ultimately, and forever will be, optimistic. I'm more jaded than I used to be, but I will never [have] a cold stone heart."

While in Vancouver, lang began writing and recording the songs for *All You Can Eat* with Mink. The sound and pace of the album follow gracefully from *Ingenue.* On that album, she said in 1992, she was searching for "vulnerable, honest" romantic music. She'd fallen in love, and her music, she said, reflected that: "Feeling pain, love, emotion at a more intense level. As an artist, vulnerability and innocence is something I strive for because I think that taps into the higher consciousness of art itself."

About *All You Can Eat,* she says, "I think there are obvious similarities, because Ben and I are involved [artistically] and there are background vocals and strings. The drums are dry, everything is dry except my vocals. Although the arrangements are quite elaborate, it's direct.

"In terms of writing style, I hoped that the lyrics would be more direct, more cut and dried, more honest, less metaphorical and less romantic. I guess I write to soothe or affirm my own feelings. I don't know so much if I write for anyone at all. One of my biggest aspirations as a writer is to be able to dig and dig and dig, to have your emotions be accessible. As I was writing this record I was kind of taking self-inventory."

Her earlier albums had a tongue-in-cheek quality. "Definitely. It was a bit of a guard, a mask, and I don't think I was aware of it at the time. The older you get, the more you realize, 'I'm a lot more sensitive than I ever thought I was.'" She credits Roy Orbison, her late pal and collaborator on "Cryin'," as a major influence.

How important is control to lang? Is she a control freak?

"Freak? No. I'm opinionated and I have definite visions. I think the more confidence I gain, and the more maturity I gain, the less control I need."

A song doesn't pass muster, she says, until she and Mink are both comfortable with it. The two have worked together for a decade. A completely cool relationship, she says, adding, "I wish I could have one with a woman that way."

Why hasn't she?

"Well, I haven't had 10 years to spare."

Does lang have any fear that *All You Can Eat* won't replicate the success of *Ingenue*?

"You never know. Honestly, I stopped predicting because the music industry is so unpredictable. On a certain level, I'm completely afraid. But on another, I've pleased myself [in that] I've done my very best. If it sells, great! I would love if people accepted it because it's my blood and guts. If they don't, I'd be disappointed, but I also know I gave it my best."

Lang has no butterflies about performing. "Piece of cake," she says. She describes her offstage life as lifting weights, doing yoga, mountain-biking, hanging with friends, cooking, painting, going to movies and riding her Harley-Davidson.

With all of her emotional life laid bare now, what might be her closet secret?

She wishes she could, you know, *rock*. "I don't understand rock and roll. But I do love bands like the Pretenders, Chrissie Hynde. And I love, love, love Björk. And I'm jealous as hell I can't be more 'alternative' sometimes. My voice is my voice, and I think that's why I've settled in as a songwriter, because there is not music for me as a vocalist other than what I carve out. My voice has a certain texture and a certain richness and a certain vibrato that really dictates the music I write. I don't sound that good singing rock and roll. Sometimes I'm really jealous of their style. Sometimes I go, 'I wish my voice could sound rough.' But it doesn't. Hopefully, what I'm doing is essential in a contemporary context."

I caught up with her again in early 2018 to talk about *Ingenue* and *Ingenue Redux*, the latter the name lang has given her tour, as she celebrates the 25th anniversary of her career breakthrough best-seller. (k.d. was the name *she* took long ago, the letters standing for Kathryn Dawn, then upper-cased.)

lang was a boundary breaker and a genre stretcher. In concert, her mix of older country-stoked music and the new emotional chamber-pop gave fans both a sophisticated hoedown and a languid celebration of romance. "There was antics, there was props, there was costumes," lang says, on the phone from her Calgary home, of her 1992-'93 tour. "There were ways that I incorporated show business in my performances. I would say that's useful exploration."

Ingenue is not a sassy album. It doesn't have a hard kick or a cutting edge. What it does have are seductive melodies and a palpable sense of vulnerability. lang offers a caress and a cruise, a lush, full-bodied, dramatic take on the labyrinth of love. To celebrate its quarter-century, her label issued a remastered version with some previously unreleased live cuts.

She's taking a seven-piece band on the road, playing the album in its entirety. There won't be bubbles or props. "No, my extravagance this time is the musicianship," says lang. "I feel very confident with the musicians and the arrangements that we're going to be laying on people. I mean, it's a nice stage set. It's beautiful, it's comfortable, the lights are incredible, but, really, it's about the music. I deliberated a long time about how to approach the music and how to present it again and it came down to not superimposing my experiences and my relationships and history with the record, as much as just letting people really have their moment with this music."

What's the difference between her approach then and now?

"Maybe," she says, "that I've honed in on this a little bit with age: that truth, honesty, vulnerability and presence are the ingredients of performing live. I think I have the capacity, the experience and the wisdom now to maintain the kind of focus and confidence to sell an internalized record. *Ingenue* is a very insular record. It's quite dark, or it can be viewed as dark. It's very moderate-to-slow paced, tempo-wise, and when I was younger, I don't think I could have pulled it off.

"I think my audience is skewing a bit older, so they're a little bit more settled, and the throwing of bras and panties has kind of waned." She adds, with a laugh, "I think Tom Jones probably still gets them."

lang toured Australia and Canada last year — the album's actual 25th anniversary — but was hesitant about mounting a U.S. tour. "I didn't really want to tour the States, [but] my conscience said, 'You have to, it's what you do.' This is exactly what I feel my job is. It's propelling me to want to go on the road. There is nothing more suitable to me or honest for me than singing live. To me, singing live is everything. It's who I am, it's what I am."

The soaring mezzo-soprano was nominated for five Grammys in 1993 and won for *Best Female Vocalist.* She has three other Grammys, including one in 1990 for *Best*

Female Country Vocal Performance on her debut album, *Absolute Torch and Twang. Ingenue* spawned the hits "Constant Craving" and "Miss Chatelaine" and sold more than three-million copies worldwide, but it was "pivotal" in other ways too, lang says: "It carried a social marker as well with the LGBT community, with me coming out and having an impact on society that way."

lang was, as the *London Sunday Times* put it in 2008, "the poster girl for lesbian chic." She won multiple awards from GLAAD (Gay & Lesbian Alliance Against Defamation). She became publicly cause-oriented. She's no less political now, but not, this time, in concert. "I am not going to make political statements from the stage, which I generally do. I'm going to let the music be an ointment and a salve. I think people know where I stand, and I think people just need a break. I need to sing."

Her 12 studio albums include a duet disc with Tony Bennett and last year's collaboration with Neko Case and Laura Viers, *case/lang/viers.* Her last solo effort, *Watershed,* came out a decade ago. Asked if she has new material ready to go, lang says, "No, I am not clicking in on a vision. I have songs and I have an idea of where I want to go, but I haven't got all the ingredients together. I'm not feeling inspired in one particular direction enough to really gravitate towards. There's music that I love but I haven't figured out how I fit with it and how I move forward with it, so until that happens, I'm not going to do it. I'm in a position now where I don't *have* to make music unless I'm feeling it. And I kind of love that. I like to not feel pressured or rushed. I think I have made music that's honest, but I feel like sometimes my motivation was, maybe, influenced by pressure or success or outer influences. And I'm not going to make another record 'til I know exactly what it is.

"I am so far removed from the music business right now," she says. "I'm almost 60 as well. The combination of being out of Los Angeles and getting older and the fact that the music business is changing so much so fast, but I think the music business has always changed so fast."

She was disappointed with the response to 2011's *Sing It Loud.* "We toured that a lot. The shows did well, but the record didn't do well. Also, I'm middle-aged. You're at a point where it's kind of a no-man's land. You're not young, you're not old, you're not a 'legend' yet, so you're just floating around in this middle period thinking 'No one really gives a fuck what I think.' And I don't even know what I'm saying at this point."

A move from Los Angeles to Portland, Oregon in 2012 wasn't exactly due to career burnout, she says, but close to it. "I think that helped facilitate my move, but I know who I am and I know what I am. I am a singer, but I don't feel like I have to produce [an album]. I think it's quality, not quantity."

She fell in love in Portland and now lives with her partner in Calgary. For lang, who holds dual citizenship, there was another motivation to return to her homeland: Her mother. "My mom is still alive, thank goodness, and I'm spending more time with her. She's not ill, but I mean she's 94, so she has stuff."

She admits that the move "is also kind of why my business has lagged a little bit." So be it. Her attitude: "I'm going to embrace it and be with my mom and have my family and live my life."

The awards in the '90s were nice, lang says, but now, "I never watch the *Grammys.* They don't represent what's happening to me. They don't come close to mining all the amazing music that's out there right now. I think maybe that the *Grammys* is a bad example of what's out there because there is so much great music right now." ◆

"If you have faith, your whole life is put in a new perspective. You get to work, but enjoy the work at the same time."

Roy Orbison

Roy Orbison in a vintage publicity photo

PHOTOGRAPH BY BILL FORSHEE, FROM THE DAVID BIEBER ARCHIVES

ROY ORBISON

THIS IS NOT A BOAST. This is a coincidental sad reality.

I did the last interview with Roy Orbison and reviewed his next-to-last concert. We spoke by phone about ten days before his death; he was in France at the time. A week later, he played a Boston club, the Channel, the second of two shows he did that weekend.

I first saw Orbison in 1984 at a summertime venue called the Club Casino, just off the Hampton Beach boardwalk in New Hampshire. I'm not sure what I expected going in, but I'd become a fan after years of not paying attention because, well, you know, he was of that "older" era. Punk and post-punk music was my first choice. When I wanted to make history fresh again, I went back to the favorites I grew up with, the British Invasion bands and the hard rock and glam rock of early-mid-'70s. Orbison meant pre-Beatles, pre-British Invasion. I mean, who does the Ooby Dooby dance? I had this notion that Roy — who was all of 48 at the time — and his music were dated.

Boy, was I wrong. Stupid wrong. And never was I so happy to be so stupid wrong. At the Club Casino, I was in the midst of a swooning, Roy-loving full house, and I felt every bit at one with them. Kinda like I did with the crowd when the Clash first came to Cambridge in early 1979. Different crowd, different venue, different kind of emotion, but a similar feeling of bonding and togetherness. I fell right into it with ease. When I wrote the review for the *Boston Globe*, I raved.

It was an eleven-song set. Rarely had I heard a singer invest so much of himself in song. Orbison had a rich, three-octave range with what was once termed a "glass-shattering falsetto." His voice soared over the swelling chords, those songs of abject despair and loneliness bringing a chill to the spine and a lump in the throat. That pretty woman who always kept walking by! The lonely man: "There goes my baby / There goes my heart / They're gone forever / So far apart."

The fact that he wrote these songs meant something, too. He was not just a great interpreter; these were his thoughts, his vision. That tiny O he made with his mouth when he sang, the majestic, operatic sound that came out. Elvis Presley said he had the "most perfect voice" and called him the "greatest singer in the world."

I met Orbison after the show. He was all modesty and warmth. I asked why he thought he was still so popular. "We always show up on time — well, most of the time," Orbison said, playfully understating it in his soft Texas drawl. "And we do a fair job on the show."

I spoke with two women, Reni Grilli and Sharon Allison, both about 12 years Roy's junior. "I've cried, I've done it," Grilli told me, about hearing Roy. "His voice is like a pure instrument."

I, too, was verklempt. Thing is, Grilli and Allison weren't just fans; they were his backing vocalists. Singing the old songs with Roy, they both agreed, never got old.

Three years later, Roy and I were back at the same venue. "I can usually feel something in the air," he said, post-show, when I asked for his take on what had just gone down. "But I didn't this time until it overwhelmed me. It's like people are saying, 'We loved what you did, we still do, and we're gonna show you.' This year was a blessing, the Rock and Roll Hall of Fame [induction] was a gift. It's like they found out something big. I don't know, [but] if enough people say you're wonderful, maybe there's something to it."

When we parted, there were hugs. This was back when guys didn't routinely hug each other upon greeting and departure. But we did and it felt just right, genuine. I can feel the warmth of his embrace now, writing about it so many years down the road. Mercy!

I asked Orbison how deep the emotions ran for him, in the studio and onstage. He confessed that, when he first started to record, he broke down and cried during a session. The emotion cut that deep. And after all those years on the concert trail, "If I think too much or go too far, then I start crying and get all stuffy."

Success first came to the Texas native with "Ooby Dooby," which became a hit on Sam Phillips' Sun Records, the Memphis stable of Elvis Presley, Jerry Lee Lewis, Carl Perkins and Johnny Cash, in 1956. Until 1964, he was a regular presence in the *Billboard* Top 10 and a huge star in the UK. Listen to Orbison and you hear the swirling string arrangements, the multiple crescendos and, mostly, at the center of the song, that dramatic bel canto tenor, often expressing a dreamy kind of heartbreak or loneliness: "Only the Lonely," "Running Scared," "Crying," "It's Over," all of them intimate expressions magnified, looming large.

Times change. And the journey certainly had its low points. Orbison's career plummeted after the mid-'60s; although he remained a steady concert draw, he lost his hit-making mojo. Personal tragedy also struck: his first wife, Claudette, died in a motorcycle accident in 1966; two of their sons died when his house caught fire in 1968.

In 1988, some 24 years after Orbison's last Top 10 hit — several lifetimes in pop-music terms — Orbison was back, this time on the album chart. He wasn't performing alone, though. He was one of the Traveling Wilburys — the others being Bob Dylan, Tom Petty, George Harrison and Jeff Lynne — and their album, *Volume One*, was number-nine in *Billboard.* The first single, the modest, melodic "Handle With Care," was climbing.

Orbison was on a roll. There was his election to the Rock and Roll Hall of Fame, the prominent (and eerie) use of his song "In Dreams" in *Blue Velvet*, an HBO concert special with Bruce Springsteen, Elvis Costello and other famous friends called *Black & White Night.* That November, we were on the telephone, Roy in Paris, me in Boston.

As the Wilburys were fresh, I thought I'd start there, venturing that even if you'd never heard of the band, when Orbison enters "Handle With Care," there was no mistaking the voice and the sentiment: "I'm so tired of being lonely / I've still got some love to give." If there was ever a line for him to sing ...

"... that's gotta be it," Orbison said, with a laugh, finishing the thought. "I felt it was pretty typical of what I should be singing."

But is that the real Roy Orbison? Is he really the lonely guy's Lonely Guy? That certainly is the public image.

"It's just the kind of guy that comes out sometimes when I write," Orbison said. "Probably, it's one side of my personality coming through. I read a lot into what I write, and it's mostly feelings. There's some happy ones, too. On the new album, there are a couple of occasions where I'm in good shape. It's still matters of the heart. There's some up things, but there's still a little frustration there," he chuckled.

That album, *Mystery Girl,* was due to come out in January 1989, his first new album in a decade. Virgin Records had sent me an advance cassette, and I'd been living with it and loving it for a few weeks. Bono, T-Bone Burnett and Jeff Lynne were among the guests. I wondered, when he played town, if he'd draw anything from it.

He said his band had not fully rehearsed the new songs and it would be improper to foist too much unknown material on audiences. He thought he might play a couple of new songs and, on his next tour, maybe more. (He didn't and, as we know, there was no next tour.)

Orbison was poised for a transition. He was looking to let, at least temporarily, some of his past go. "This is the first time in a long time that I feel the old phasing into the new," Orbison said. "I never felt like the older songs were in the past; they were always very current to me. I feel like the new material needs to be done. I think everybody's going to like this album; it's got a lot of heart and soul."

Still, he spoke of his older material — his classics — this way: "They are still very, very close to me. I couldn't hardly cheat myself and not do the best I could do."

Rock stars from Bono to Bruce had sung his praises. He was newly hip. He hated the term "comeback trail" so I didn't use it, but I did ask if he was excited for what lay ahead. He said he was, in a manner of speaking. Restrained excitement, maybe.

"It's very pleasing, as you might well understand," Orbison said, modestly. "It's a nice thing that people say good things about you. I think it means more to me that they are in the business. A few of the people I've met said, 'I got in the business because of you' or 'You inspired me.' That makes me feel really good ... it also tells you where you are. If you ever wondered if you're reaching anyone or touching anyone."

What about that voice? What techniques did he employ to maintain it? "I don't do anything particular to look after it," he said. "I think that if I had been wondering whether it was still going to be, it might not have been. But I always went right ahead ... I'll never forget my father singing for me when I was a teenager. His voice still sounded very, very young. That's what struck me. He must've been 40, which I considered to be very old. I was blessed with his voice to some degree."

At 52, Roy Orbison was a happy, humble man. "My voice is a gift," he said. "My talent is a gift; the life process is a gift; the opportunity for the journey is a gift."

Orbison named two key turning points for him, one deeply personal, the other professional. The personal one, which occurred in 1985, was a born-again Christian experience.

"I've been developing a personal relationship with myself and with Jesus Christ and it just kind of smooths everything," he said. "If you have faith, then your whole life is put in a new perspective. You get to work but enjoy the work at the same time. If you grow spiritually, you do what's in front of you and let the results speak for themselves.

"You set out to whip the world," he continued, "and then you get beat up a little bit. In my case, you say, 'Father, I'm gonna let you have it. I've done what I can do.' You turn your will over to God."

Barbara Orbison, his wife and manager (she died in 2011), had urged him to back off from expressing those born-again sentiments in interviews. Orbison, quoting her to me, said, "'You're being pretty specific here.'" And then his response: "I kind of have to be."

The professional revelation came a year earlier. He was playing a date in Canada. As he approached the venue, he took a look at the marquee. It read: "Roy Orbison — Sold Out." A lightning bolt struck.

"What I realized, all of a sudden, was most people came to hear me. They knew I was gonna sing, and they appreciated me before I even walked on. I think everyone needs to grow a little bit and work on themselves, and that was one of the things. You don't need to be so insecure that it's going to affect your performance. It just dawned on me that there was a little bit of love there to start with. So, I just relaxed and everything started turning around."

Surely, he'd seen similar marquees over the years, so why he'd realize that at such a late date is a mystery. But it did. Maybe it just struck the chord that said: "You still matter."

Throughout the years, Orbison was one of the best bets in live performance. His voice was remarkably untarnished by time. His songs don't seem like relics of another age; rather, they express timeless, deep emotions. "To be a songwriter-singer," he told me, "means the songs come from deep within. You treat them as an artist, with that much respect."

I reviewed the second of two shows he did at the Channel, December 3, 1988. This is what I wrote at the time:

The rumors of a guest shot by Keith Richards or Robert Palmer, both around town, didn't pan out. But it didn't matter. Orbison, a black-dressed rockabilly survivor, his black-dyed hair appended with a late-'80s ponytail (!), didn't need them. The man can sing. He's the premier pop balladeer, and his voice retains all the technical qualities (he sings in the same keys and has the same range) and emotional nuances as it did a quarter-century ago. Which is, frankly, astonishing. That is, if Orbison hadn't been proving this year after year, on the club and theater circuit, through good years and bad.

The only downside of Saturday's set — a near-sellout, as was the previous night — was that Orbison did no Wilburys music or any upcoming solo stuff. This concert was, as were many before it, an interim gig, something to placate the faithful until that new LP is released.

If anybody deserves this long of a freeze-frame, it's Orbison. His shy/sincere emotional investment in "Only the Lonely," "In Dreams," "Cryin'," "Blue Bayou," "It's Over" and "Running Scared" (among others) remains unquestioned. These heartbreaks and occasional triumphs matter still. Most prominently, the vocal crescendos are unmatched, especially during the mountain-climbing ballads, situations that induced awestruck smiles amongst the crowd. Orbison is that rare pop singer where you yearn for the ballads and tolerate the rockers. But his tough, taut backing band put a solid kick into "Mean Woman Blues," "Ooby Dooby," "Down the Line" and "Oh, Pretty Woman," and Orbison actually seemed more at home with these rockers than ever.

Orbison is a legend who refuses the easy Chuck Berry-walk-through, an artist for whom the present matters as much as the past — i.e., his unswerving commitment to his classics. What we all want is a glimpse into the future, and Orbison did not provide that Saturday night. Next time, he assuredly will. For now, we can revel in Orbison's history without being bound by it — there is absolutely no way to leave a Roy Orbison show without sporting a wide grin. Whatever pain he's gone through in song is cathartic: The fact that he can still bring that out and bring shivers to the spine is awe-inspiring.

Three days later, Orbison suffered a heart attack at his mother's home in Hendersonville, Tennessee and died.

In 1992, I was in a New York hotel room talking with k.d. lang. Orbison had been a huge influence and, later, a friend and collaborator. They'd recorded the heart-wrenching duet "Crying" in 1987 and won a Grammy for it: Orbison's fifth. A Lifetime Achievement Award was bestowed upon him in 1998.

"He was so beyond the surface and the frivolous part of human nature," lang said. "People always thought he was so lonely and sad and everything, but, *au contraire*, he was very strong and very peaceful. He was a legend, and yet he was really humble." ◆

www.ingramcontent.com/pod-product-compliance
Lightning Source LLC
LaVergne TN
LVHW061218100826
845148LV00004B/795
* 9 7 9 8 9 8 5 6 5 8 9 8 9 *